The Germ of Justice

The Germ of Justice

Essays in General Jurisprudence

LESLIE GREEN

Great Clarendon Street, Oxford, OX2 6DP,
United Kingdom

Oxford University Press is a department of the University of Oxford.
It furthers the University's objective of excellence in research, scholarship,
and education by publishing worldwide. Oxford is a registered trade mark of
Oxford University Press in the UK and in certain other countries

© Leslie Green 2023

The moral rights of the author have been asserted

First Edition published in 2023

All rights reserved. No part of this publication may be reproduced, stored in
a retrieval system, or transmitted, in any form or by any means, without the
prior permission in writing of Oxford University Press, or as expressly permitted
by law, by licence or under terms agreed with the appropriate reprographics
rights organization. Enquiries concerning reproduction outside the scope of the
above should be sent to the Rights Department, Oxford University Press, at the
address above

You must not circulate this work in any other form
and you must impose this same condition on any acquirer

Public sector information reproduced under Open Government Licence v3.0
(http://www.nationalarchives.gov.uk/doc/open-government-licence/open-government-licence.htm)

Published in the United States of America by Oxford University Press
198 Madison Avenue, New York, NY 10016, United States of America

British Library Cataloguing in Publication Data

Data available

Library of Congress Control Number: 2023935120

ISBN 978–0–19–288694–1

DOI: 10.1093/oso/9780192886941.001.0001

Links to third party websites are provided by Oxford in good faith and
for information only. Oxford disclaims any responsibility for the materials
contained in any third party website referenced in this work.

To Denise Réaume

Preface

This is a selection of my essays in general jurisprudence—the theory of law 'as such', or law 'in general'. I have chosen papers that, I hope, make some progress on the problems they address, or at least clarify what needs to be done before progress is likely. The Introduction that follows says more about jurisprudence as I see it, and more about progress.

The influence of H. L. A. Hart, Joseph Raz, and, more remotely, Hans Kelsen will be evident on almost every page. I have sometimes rejected their conclusions about law, but I usually look to them for leads about how to start thinking about a problem. Sometimes I found that I had to start over, but starting over can be influenced by how one started.

In selecting these papers, I took advice from John Gardner, with whose early death I lost a co-teacher of twelve years, a model colleague, and a beloved friend, and from Brian Leiter, another great friend and a generous interlocutor for more than two decades. Alex Flach of Oxford University Press tried to cajole me into publishing such a collection long before I got around to it. Other projects intervened (including other projects that Alex cajoled me to undertake) but I was eventually worn down. My thanks also to Jordan Burke, who saw the project through to completion.

I have tried to acknowledge the help of those who invited, replied to, criticized, reviewed, or influenced these papers in the final footnote to each chapter. But here I want to single out for special thanks the following people in whose company I had the privilege of many enjoyable and illuminating hours talking about jurisprudence: Tom Adams, Farrah Ahmed, Matthias Brinkmann, Luís Duarte-d'Almeida, James Grant, Kate Greasley, Asif Hameed, Chris Hinchcliffe, Sam Kukathas, Maximilian Kiener, Hafsteinn Kristjánsson, Patrick O'Brien, Adam Perry, Basil Salman, Robert Simpson, Harrison Tait, Leah Trueblood, Charles Tyler, and Matt Watson, among others. I learned more from them than any of them learned from me.

This book was completed in the face of a grave threat to my life. Without the support of the ALS Clinic at Sunnybrook Hospital, Toronto, of Dr Peter

DeRoche of Mount Sinai Hospital, and of kind friends, I could not have finished it.

Once again, Denise Réaume got more than she bargained for. She has made it not only possible but worthwhile for me to keep going.

Leslie Green
Oxford
27 November 2022

Acknowledgements

The following chapters draw on papers originally published as indicated below. I thank the editors and publishers for permission to reuse that material here, usually with some changes. Parts of Chapter 1 also find their way into the Introduction to the third edition of H. L. A. *The Concept of Law* (Oxford University Press 2012), but that Introduction also contains other material, and it reflects some changes in my views since Chapter 1 was written.

1. 'The Concept of Law Revisited' (1996) 94 *Michigan Law Review* 1687.
2. 'Law as a Means', in P. Cane ed., *Hart-Fuller: 50 Years On* (Hart Publishing, 2009) 169–88.
4. 'Positivism, Realism, and the Sources of Law', in P. Mindus and T. Spaak eds, *The Cambridge Companion to Legal Positivism* (Cambridge University Press, 2021) 39–60.
5. 'Gender and the Analytical Jurisprudential Mind' (2020) 83 *Modern Law Review* 893.
7. 'Positivism and the Inseparability of Law and Morals' (2008) 83 *New York University Law Review* 1035.
8. 'The Morality in Law', in L. Duarte d'Almeida, J. Edwards, and A. Dolcetti eds, *Reading HLA Hart's 'The Concept of Law'* (Hart Publishing, 2013) 177–207.
9. 'Law and the Role of a Judge', in K. Ferzan and S. Morris eds, *Legal, Moral, and Metaphysical Truths* (Oxford University Press, 2016) 322–41.
10. 'Should Law Improve Morality?' (2013) 7 *Criminal Law and Philosophy* 473.
11. 'Hume on Authority and Opinion', in D. Butt, S. Fine, and Z. Stemplowska eds, *Political Philosophy, Here and Now: Essays in Honour of David Miller* (Oxford University Press, 2021).
12. 'Associative Obligations and the State', in L. Green and A. Hutchinson eds, *Law and the Community* (Carswell, 1989) 93–118.
13. 'The Forces of Law: Duty, Coercion, and Power' (2016) 29 *Ratio Juris* 164.
14. 'The Duty to Govern' (2007) 13 *Legal Theory*.

Contents

Introduction: A Philosophy of Legal Philosophy*   1

I. LAW, AS SUCH

1. *The Concept of Law* Revisited   31
2. Law as a Means   57
3. Custom and Convention at the Foundations of Law*   80
4. Realism and the Sources of Law   105
5. Gender and Jurisprudence   126

II. LAW AND MORALITY

6. The Germ of Justice*   153
7. The Inseparability of Law and Morals   175
8. The Morality in Law   198
9. The Role of a Judge   225
10. Should Law Improve Morality?   250

III. THE DEMANDS OF LAW

11. Hume on Allegiance   283
12. Associative Obligations and the State   305
13. The Forces of Law   333
14. The Duty to Govern   356

Name Index   379
Subject Index   383

*first published in this collection

Introduction
A Philosophy of Legal Philosophy

1. This Book

These essays in legal philosophy treat problems of general jurisprudence, that is, the theory of law as such: questions relevant to Canadian law as much as Czech Law, to canon law as much as customary law. I hope they make progress on the issues they discuss. But I have also chosen them in the hope that they will be within the reach of students of law, philosophy, or politics who are theoretically inquisitive but may have no prior grounding in the subject. I therefore tried to ensure that most are free-standing and avoid unnecessary technicalities, so that others may not only to only eavesdrop on, but join in, these conversations in legal theory.

The title essay (Chapter 6) was intended to be my inaugural lecture as the Professor of the Philosophy of Law at Oxford, in 2007. It examines the relationship between applying law and achieving justice. The lecture was never given. It was postponed, first owing to family tragedy and then by other pressing priorities. Time passed until giving it as an 'inaugural' would have been incongruous. So, years after the paper was written, I revised it for first publication here. In compensation I let it have the limelight, if only titular.

Some of these essays have descriptive and conceptual concerns: the nature of law, the role of coercion in law, gender in law and jurisprudence, the relations between law and morality. Others focus on values: how should law be applied, how should judges do their jobs, what is law's contribution to morality, what entitles some to rule or obligates others to obey? Though wide ranging, the essays do not cover the subject. Nor do they add up to *a jurisprudence*, if that means a compact set of ideas from which may be derived answers to the main problems of legal theory. I do not believe there can be such a jurisprudence. Repeated attempts to distil a theory of law from a few diaphanous propositions about freedom and equality, or sovereignty and sanctions, or meaning and metaphysics, have always failed, and the time has come to stop doing the same thing over again while expecting a different result. We must work in a modular way. If we can deepen our understanding of questions about law in general, ensuring our answers are consistent with each other and with what we already know, that is enough. At any rate, it has been my approach.

These pieces do nonetheless belong to a tradition of understanding law developed and elaborated by Hume, Bentham, Austin, Kelsen, Hart, Raz, and many contemporaries who hold, as I do, that all law is positive law. Legal positivism, in this sense, is the idea that the basis of law is entirely social. All law is the creation, whether intentional or accidental, planned or chaotic, of ordinary, dateable, human thought and action. Nothing is law merely because it would be reasonable, fair, efficient, or even logical for it to be law; everything that is law is law because it was made in a way that is recognized as making law. I believe the 'sources thesis', as Joseph Raz dubbed it, is part of any adequate theory of law.[1] I do not demonstrate that thesis. (Few interesting ideas in legal philosophy admit of demonstration.) Happily, jurisprudence makes progress—in ways I will explain—and I am relieved that others have done about as much as we can, for now, to make the sources thesis plausible. If these essays contribute to our confidence in legal positivism, they do so by clarifying what that approach commits us to, detaching it from certain common errors, and showing how key problems in legal philosophy have solutions that conform to it.

Chapter 2 comes closest to a résumé of my own view. It begins with Hans Kelsen's idea that 'law is a means, a specific social means, not an end'. It takes work to unpack that slogan. What is Kelsen denying? No one holds that law itself could literally be 'an end'. Whose end? On the other hand, all law that is deliberately created is made with some end in view, if only to repeal or consolidate legislation. I think we can go further. Law is constitutively oriented to certain ends. We cannot distinguish a system of legal rules from the rules of a game without attending to who and what the rules aim to regulate, and why. I return to this issue in Chapter 7 in studying some connections between law and morality and then single it out for focused attention in Chapter 8, where I criticize H. L. A. Hart's claim that the necessary content of law is fixed by what it takes for a society to survive or for law to enjoy voluntary compliance. I argue instead that positive law has features that make it *apt for* supporting morality, and that is how law must be used by people like us, in

---

[1] Joseph Raz, *The Authority of Law* (Oxford University Press, 1979) chap. 3.

our circumstances, with our needs. That is just one of several 'necessary connections' between law and morality, in one sense of 'necessary'.

How do I square the idea that law has constitutive ends with my vote in favour of Kelsen's proposal that law is a means? Nothing is a legal system unless it aims at regulating violence, but other things also have that aim, and even have it constitutively. (The World Peace Association, for example.) So we cannot identify law by reference to its aims, even though there are aims law must have. We cannot identify law without considering how it *goes about* its constitutive aims, and that is the sense in which law is a 'specific social means' and not 'a [set of] ends'.

Law's means have a special institutional complexity, however, which Kelsen oversimplifies. He says law is essentially and entirely a system of coercive norms, an idea shared by legal philosophers from Jeremy Bentham to Ronald Dworkin. It is also a view that resonates with common-sense ideas about law. I air doubts about it in various places and bring them together when considering Frederick Schauer's claim that law is *in fact mostly* coercive and there is no point in debating whether coercion is an 'essential' feature of law or not (Chapter 13). Like some other contemporary legal theorists (including those discussed in Chapters 4 and 5), Schauer distrusts 'conceptual analysis' and wants more attention paid to empirical evidence. I think jurisprudence is already attentive, for it is the facts that show that law is a site of coercive force and also that some laws coerce no one. In principle, there could be legal systems in which all laws were like that. Only the final ('in principle') point depends on something more than coercion-counting. I hold that it is a necessary feature of legal systems that they can *provide for* coercion (when necessary) but not that they always do provide it. Law has other means at its disposal, including the creation of duties and duty-related norms and the ability to harness extra-legal, social power to its ends. These facts are perfectly familiar. Then why expend philosophical energy nit-picking about what is necessary to law, or about the precise differences between coercion, duty, and power? It promises a deeper understanding of familiar facts about law. That is the aim of general jurisprudence, and deepening our understanding is, I will suggest, one of the marks of progress in the subject.

2. Other Books

Not all law is found in books, and neither is all jurisprudence. But much of it is, and any approach to jurisprudence involves the study of books. A course in jurisprudence sends students to a library—be it analogue or digital—rather than to a courtroom, laboratory, or kitchen.[2] If they are lucky, they will read Aristotle, Aquinas, Bentham, Austin, Kelsen, Hart, Dworkin, Raz, and other giants of the subject. In this book, I spend a lot of time in the company of other books, but not as authorities or as objects of intellectual history. I am looking for clues about how to approach some problems of general jurisprudence.

In the Anglosphere, no book of legal theory has proved more clue-filled than H. L. A. Hart's *The Concept of Law*, first published in 1961. I introduce leading ideas from that book in Chapter 1, so that might be a point of entry to these essays. Hart found his own clues to legal theory in the works of Bentham, Austin, and Kelsen, but he was diffident about this. *The Concept of Law* is lax in its scholarly apparatus, and it buries important elaborations and qualifications in notes at the end, which, Hart says, the reader may consider or ignore at will.[3] Here is his justification for that set-up:

> I hope that this arrangement may discourage the belief that a book on legal theory is primarily a book from which one learns what other books contain. So long as this belief is held by those who write, little progress will be made in the subject; and so long as it is held by those who read, the educational value of the subject must remain very small.'[4]

In this Introduction I want to explore three injunctions implicit in that passage:

- legal theory should be more than 'books about books';
- legal theory should aim to make progress; and
- legal theory should be of educational value.

These points do not amount to a jurisprudential methodology, but in the popular sense of 'philosophy'—a general attitude or approach to work and life—they do express a philosophy of the philosophy of law. Before we can

---

[2] On the supposed relevance of diet to jurisprudence, see Jerome Frank, *Law and the Modern Mind* (Tudor, 1936) 137. Frank does not, however, provide the reader with any recipes that might make for healthier judicial decisions.

[3] These are Hart's discursive notes that appear between 277 and 308 in the third edition (H. L. A. Hart, *The Concept of Law* (3rd edn, Penelope A. Bulloch and Joseph Raz, eds; Leslie Green, intro, Oxford University Press, 2012)). The scholarly and bibliographic notes between 309 and 325 were written by me with the help of Tom Adams.

[4] Hart, *The Concept of Law*, vii.

examine that, however, we need to consider a more basic presupposition on which those injunctions rest: that there is something to learn about law 'in general', that general jurisprudence can succeed or fail at understanding the nature of law as such.

3. Choices

Problems in general jurisprudence often begin with, or take us back to, fundamental questions about the nature, or 'definition', of law. But some scholars hold that law in general is a thing *without* a nature (or, perhaps, that it is a thing whose nature is to have an indeterminate nature). The set of things we intelligibly call 'law' is a purely nominal kind, and no analysis can pin down all the things to which it applies in a way that we might think of as plausible or correct. If there is nothing to get right in general jurisprudence, there is also nothing to get wrong. And if that is so there is no focus for the subject, nor any serious prospect of making progress in it, or finding value in it.

Ideas like this often turn up in debates about the relations between law and morality (for example, in the arguments in Chapter 9). Some writers hold that if no empirical considerations settle such questions, there is nothing else to go on and we might as well stipulate a 'definition' of law to suit some extrinsic purpose: a definition that is uplifting, or profitable, or intellectually stimulating. In thus 'choosing a concept of law' we might, for example, think of seriously unjust laws as non-laws, or as valid laws that are seriously unjust, or as marginal or defective law-specimens, or as punishments for original sin. There is no fact of the matter, empirical or conceptual: the decision falls within our inalienable freedom to choose concepts.

Theorists of starkly different outlooks have been friendly to such ideas.[5] It is not so clear what they have in mind. There is no doubt that vague concepts can be sharpened in various ways or that some socially prevalent concepts, such as race, should not be used and that others, such as gender, should be reformed. If this is 'choosing concepts', then fair enough. But all such

---

[5] Among the philosophers considered here, Brian Leiter and Frederick Schauer propose choosing a concept of law with an eye to predictive, empirical concerns. Others, including Ronald Dworkin, John Finnis, Michael Moore, Liam Murphy, and Jeremy Waldron prefer that we guide conceptual choices by moral or political considerations. See Philip Soper, 'Choosing a Legal Theory on Moral Grounds' (1986) 4 *Social Philosophy and Policy* 31. (Contrary to rumour, this is *not* the point of Hart's remarks about the 'broad' concept of law: see Chapter 1, section 5, this volume.)

interventions presuppose that there is a concept of some shape on which to operate. If there isn't, the idea of choice is inapposite. We only choose when, for some (adequate if not exigent) reason, we select an option from a choice-set. If there were no constraints, how could we know what options are in that set? Moreover, if legal theory is a matter of 'choosing concepts' why should it fall to jurisprudence to do it? Why not turn the definition of law over to the anthropologists or poets to decide and then just work with whatever they hand us?[6]

Perhaps concept-choosers see themselves as legislators. It is certainly one of *law's* functions to provide authoritative guidance by drawing lines where we need them. Suppose a constitution says that human rights are subject only to such reasonable limitations as are 'prescribed by law'. That legal system had better tell us whether, for constitutional purposes, 'law' includes only statute, or whether rights may also be limited by common law or administrative regulation. Different constitutions with similar provisions may define 'law' in different ways, depending on the list of rights they include, the constitution's structure, and local presuppositions about legitimacy. But these legally important chores have little philosophical importance. If Canadian law were to hold that Indigenous law is not really law, it would be of no more jurisprudential interest than if Canadian law were to hold that American law is not really law. The theoretical question 'What is law?' is not a legal question and its answer cannot be found in statute or case law.

Some find the source of their conceptual powers not in legislation but in science. According to 'naturalism', philosophy should adopt the methods of the empirical sciences which, some say, learn nothing from 'conceptual analysis'. Into that vacuum rushes whatever definition of law proves useful to the 'successful' sciences of society.[7] If 'law' turns out to have no scientific use, it should go the way of phlogiston. It all depends, then, on our criteria for scientific success. If it is a black-box power to predict and control behaviour, law will be one thing; if it is to provide an explanatory account of social reality, law will be another. Maybe we get to choose the criteria for success, too. But

---

[6] 'Yet law-abiding scholars write:/ Law is neither wrong nor right, / Law is only crimes/ Punished by places and by times.' W. H. Auden, 'Law, say the gardeners is the sun' in his *Collected Shorter Poems, 1927–1957* (Faber and Faber, 1969) 154–6.
[7] How far the neighbourhood extends, and what its resident sciences are, has never been agreed. We are not going to be able to develop jurisprudence based solely on physics or chemistry. We allow the social sciences in the door. Then everything from functionalist anthropology, behavioural psychology, neo-classical economics, cognitive science, to social surveys gets touted as the key to a science of jurisprudence. On this basis, 'ordinary language' philosophy should qualify. It was exquisitely, minutely, empiricist, and less encumbered by theoretical apriorisms than most subjects on that list.

then why not choose criteria that give the best understanding of the concept of law, taking law as we find it, without regard to whether that concept has predictive utility? The natural sciences do constrain humanistic inquiry. We cannot have philosophy revising Planck's constant. The question is whether this constraint permits other forms of inquiry and, if it does, whether it contributes anything beyond marking the no-go zones. Lawyers sometimes associate an empirical, fact-driven, approach to law with American legal realists and their heirs in what used to be called 'sociological jurisprudence'. If the realists were empiricists, they must have been very timid ones, for they rarely left the laboratory of the law reports. Their atoms were the facts *as reported* and their molecules were patterns among such facts in so far as they indicate general attitudes *of judges*. It would be a poor sociology of law that worked within those constraints.

Others with empiricist sympathies took a broader view, including David Hume (Chapter 11), who thought history and even common sense might help us understand the nature of law. In our day, Brian Leiter (Chapter 4) and Frederick Schauer (Chapter 13) suggest that the concept of law is determined by whatever proves most useful to a predictive social science of law. On this view, neither the lawyer's professional idea of 'law' nor our common concept of law, is of interest unless it happens to pick out something causally efficacious in the social world.

There is no denying the relevance of reliable evidence to general jurisprudence. A legal system does not exist unless it is generally effective in a society, and understanding effectiveness requires attention to empirical questions in sociology and psychology. Or again: general jurisprudence attends to the complex causal relations between law and the social (accepted, effective) morality of a society. The law typically bears the imprint of our social morality, but in Chapter 10 I suggest that the connection can also run the other way round, for what is unlawful can affect what people regard as immoral (moreover, what people regard as immoral can sometimes affect what is actually immoral). Here too, jurisprudence needs empirical evidence, and I offer a little second-hand evidence of law's capacity to do good by making good. But these empirical conjectures presuppose that we have already done some conceptual work in pinning down the nature of law, and also the nature of morality. That work cannot be deferred or displaced by something else.

We cannot know what sort of evidence could be relevant to predictive projects in jurisprudence until we have an adequate understanding of the concept of law. For example, the American realists' leading conjecture, that outcomes in appellate courts are underdetermined *by law*, obviously presupposes some idea about the boundaries of law. To know that common commercial practice or a court's sense of fairness lie outwith the law, we need to know where the law starts and stops. As most of us do most of the time, the realists simply use the concept without explaining it. But nothing in their work shows that the concept of law lies beyond explanation, or that it takes whatever shape proves handy to advocacy or social psychology.

It is not worth inquiring whether law is social, or its means coercive, or what its relations are with morality, until we understand *what it would be* for law to be social or coercive or moral. Whatever philosophic banner we fly, this requires conceptual analysis. We could ask around to see what most people think—that might be suggestive—but some people we ask will have a poor grasp of the concepts that interest us, and others may just get annoyed and refuse to discriminate ways that would be useful. No one likes a pedant. ('Would you say the tax advantages to marriage *coerced* you into marrying, *gave you an incentive* to marry, or were a *welcome support* to your free decision? Explain.') Some jurisprudence that passes as empirical, or 'experimental', is therefore merely passing-off. Surveying people on whether they would call their marriage coerced is 'experimental philosophy' only in the sense that surveying them on whether they would call the Treaty of Versailles 'the cause' of Nazism would be 'experimental history'.

Political theorists have generally done better with such issues, for example in characterizing institutions like states, markets, or political parties. They recognize the difficult cases in distinguishing a political party from a state organ or from a pressure group, or in distinguishing authoritative allocations from distribution by a monopolized market. But they do not seem tempted to say that gives license to 'choose concepts'. (Nor has anyone ever suggested that a good theory of political parties is a theory of a good political parties.) In the study of politics, 'operationalization' is understood to aim at operationalizing *something*, and research can flop owing to poor operationalization just as it can flop owing to a spreadsheet error or a mistake in proving the existence of an equilibrium.

Law, as part of the political system, is a mind-dependent feature of the world. We can learn about law by learning about the concept of law (and related and contrasting concepts). The concept of law is what it is. It is shaped, not by philosophizing—let alone by stipulating—but by living. Common classifications, inferences, presuppositions, and social interactions are what make concepts in and of law. Some concepts are sharper, and some are vaguer or show other kinds of complexity, so legal philosophy aims to make things explicit and more precise. But it is possible to do that crudely, hastily, poorly, etc.—which shows that there is, after all, a *there* there. Such work does involve 'analysis', but only in the sense that most contemporary Anglophone philosophy does. It disciplines judgements by demands for clarity and rigour rather than inspiration or consolation; it is willing to test conjectures against hypothetical as well as real cases; it sets out looking for necessary and sufficient conditions (but it is not embarrassed if it fails to find them); and it learns from ordinary and professional language and from the institutions and practices that such language structures. It is not trying to revive the methods of a Russell or Carnap.

Conceptual analysis in this modest sense is unavoidable in jurisprudence. We cannot count instances or make generalizations until we know what counts as what. Is mediation more efficient than adjudication? We had better know what adjudication is. Is the rule of law always desirable? We need to start with the rule of law. If our answers to such questions only ever take the form, 'for present purposes "the rule of law" shall mean . . .' we are either legislating or writing a term paper. That is why the best jurisprudents do *so much* conceptual analysis—even when they deny it or do it *malgré eux*. They know that law is not whatever we can squeeze out of a factor analysis of judicial decisions, and they know that coercion is not whatever incentivizes people to conform to law. It doesn't matter that they publicly foreswear analysis. Philosophers are not always reliable witnesses to their own work. Observe what they do, not what they say. That is a good empirical rule of thumb.

That is as much 'methodology' as there is in these essays. Apart from occasional side-ways glances, the work is substantive and tackles problems familiar to legal theorists. I spend time in the company of books by philosophers from Hume to our contemporaries, but I focus most often on leads (and dead ends) proposed by Hans Kelsen, H. L. A. Hart, and their critics. Even when they are not in the foreground, they are in the background. Some of my results offer concurring judgements: I affirm some well-known theses about law, but on less-than-familiar grounds. In other cases, I dissent, for some influential claims in modern jurisprudence prove untenable. And, inevitably, all of this involves some janitorial work along the way—clearing up detritus from other efforts including, in one case, my own.[8] Jurisprudence is rarely as tidy as philosophers want it to be, but that is no excuse for leaving the workplace in a mess.

---

[8] Chapter 3 revises some points in Leslie Green, 'Positivism and Conventionalism' (1999) 12 *Canadian Journal of Law and Jurisprudence* 32. The main arguments and conclusions of that paper still seem correct to me, and I draw on them here, but it over-emphasizes some less important issues at the expense of more important ones. I have now tried to rebalance the discussion.

4. Theories and Theses

Assuming, then, that there is a subject that could repay study, I return to our three injunctions: legal theory should be more than 'books about books'; it should aim to make progress; it should have educational value. Let us start with books.

4.1 Complexity

Jurisprudence consists in theses, arguments, and proposals about how to understand law in general. Too often, however, 'books about books' in jurisprudence describe legal theories as if they were orchestras playing in harmony—imperativists, positivists, realists, etc. Yet with one exception no important perspective even claims a conductor.[9] It is worth asking whether law has a necessary moral aim, maybe even a *telos*, but it is of little interest whether an affirmative answer qualifies one as a 'natural lawyer'. Theoretical perspectives at that level of generality are more like traditions of political argument—the liberal tradition, or the socialist tradition—than they are like theories in physics or psychology. They are loose approaches to law within which we find dispute and disagreement, including disputes about what is central to a tradition and what is peripheral or even alien to it.

Jurisprudence is thus not so much community as it is complexity. So it is, for example, with legal positivism—the view that all law is positive law. That idea is susceptible to competing interpretations. Two influential ones, the idea that law is a matter of *social convention* and the idea that there are *no necessary connections* between law and morality, prove to be mistaken and distracting. Understanding why helps clarify the nature of law.

In Chapter 3 I tackle conventionalism in jurisprudence. David Hume shows that there is an arbitrary element in much law, and that some moral obligations we consider 'natural'—including respect for private property— are in the following sense conventional: they only exist because of, and are valuable in virtue of, the benefits of a common practice that could have

---

[9] The exception: '[I]n virtue of her mission received from God, the Church . . . contributes to the ensuring of peace everywhere on earth and to the placing of the fraternal exchange between men on solid ground by imparting knowledge of the divine and natural law.' Pope Paul VI, *Gaudiem et Spes* (1965) s 89 <https://www.vatican.va/archive/hist_councils/ii_vatican_council/documents/vat-ii_const_19651207_gaudium-et-spes_en.html>.

been otherwise. (Hume's views on the authority of law are considered in Chapter 11.) If 'conventional' means a 'matter of common practice' then some laws are undoubtedly conventional, since they rest on customs, which rest on common practice. Nothing is a source of law unless it is constitutively recognized as such by basic political institutions, especially the judiciary, in accordance with their customary practices. Only such practices explain why, in Scotland, Erskine is a source of law whereas, in England, Blackstone is not. But contemporary theorists suggest law rests on convention in a more focused sense. Hart and Dworkin hold that this sense is a distinctive feature of positivism (though for Dworkin it is a distinctive error). Both are wrong. There is no affinity between conventionalism and positivism and, as I show in Chapter 3, the most fundamental legal rules are customs that are *not* conventions.

A second definition we find in textbooks says positivists are those who hold that, 'there are no necessary connections between law and morality'. Hart is to blame for that formulation, and many followed him in this error. The word 'necessary' threatens exercises in metaphysics or modal logic. In Chapter 7 I avoid the technology and treat the problem as legal theorists typically did, allowing 'necessary' its full range: things that *in some sense* must hold. I show that positivists can, and did, acknowledge several necessary connections between law and morality, throughout the range of 'necessary'. More important, some of these are connections to moral *vices*, not virtues. Lon Fuller and his followers cherish 'the morality that makes law possible', the 'internal' virtues of legality.[10] But what about law's internal vices, the immoralities that law makes possible (and those it tends to aggravate)? Some jurisprudents spend so much energy prospecting for, and then burnishing, a nugget of necessary goodness that they neglect the possibility that it is also in law's nature to bring special forms of evil into the world.

Those are two (illuminating) errors that are often made about, or absorbed into, legal positivism. But we could run into similar hazards in epitomizing any other general perspective in legal theory. Must natural lawyers deny that unjust laws are laws? Did adherents of 'critical legal studies' hold that *no* legal questions have determinate answers? The slightest acquaintance with the literature reveals contrasting answers. When 'books about books' march us, chapter by wearying chapter, through the grand 'isms'—natural law, positivism, realism, 'critical legal studies', 'interpretivism', feminist jurisprudence,

---

[10] Lon L. Fuller, *The Morality of Law* (2nd edn, Yale University Press, 1969) 33–94.

'queer theory', post-colonial jurisprudence, transnational jurisprudence—setting out crisp definitions of what such theories hold, we can be misled into seeing these as a series of unified opponents rather than as internally complex traditions addressing diverse problems. Anyone who starts out in jurisprudence with the dominant aim of *being a natural lawyer* or *following a realistic approach* is going to be without resources to do the hard work of assessing individual jurisprudential theses. Fruitful disagreement in jurisprudence begins at this granular level, not in deciding between 'theoretical perspectives' on law.

4.2 Perceptions

In *On Liberty*, J. S. Mill reminds us that 'when the conflicting doctrines, instead of being one true and the other false, share the truth between them . . . nonconforming opinion is needed to supply the remainder of the truth'.[11] There is no doubt that 'nonconforming opinion' is entitled to bandwidth, and that any case for free inquiry includes the possibility that a 'nonconforming' doctrine may have part of the truth. But why and how far is nonconformity a matter of theoretical disagreement?

Above, I warned against thinking of different jurisprudential perspectives as offering unified answers to common problems. What then about disagreements between individual theorists? Rarely can one side be said to be grossly abusing language, making errors of logic, or denying obvious facts. Such missteps happen, but they get corrected. Sometimes theorists do unwittingly 'talk past each other'. But more common are differences in *perception*: an inability to notice something because one has little interest in it or because one's attention is focused elsewhere. I think this explains a lot of the conflict between legal realists and legal positivists, for example. They mostly agree that law is a matter of social fact, that judicial decisions may be underdetermined by law, and that judicial outlook has great influence in the appellate courts. What is there left to disagree about? Mention of the higher courts contains the clue, and I track it down its significance in Chapter 4, where I argue that realists tend to treat as merely *permissive* even the legal sources that positivists treat as *binding*. Many self-styled positivists do not notice the role of

---

[11] J. S. Mill, *On Liberty and Other Writings* (S. Collini, ed., Cambridge University Press, 1989 [1857]) chap 2.

permissive sources of law, many self-styled realists exaggerate it. Here, each supplies 'the remainder of the truth'.

Differing perceptions can produce even wider differences. The string of 'perspectives' listed at the end of 4.1 includes differences in outlook that cannot be understood as philosophical disagreements of any kind. A task that one theory of law treats as central another may regard as marginal or even irrelevant. Failing to see this is one of the most damaging errors in jurisprudence.[12] In Chapter 5, I show how one perspective—here, a sort of feminist legal theory—can go off the rails by imagining theoretical conflicts where none could exist, then inventing implausible explanations for the nonexistent. There are feminist theories of justice and equality, but no feminist theories of the existence conditions for momentary legal systems or of the concept of law. This is not because general jurisprudence has a blind spot about women or because feminist jurisprudence is not trying hard enough. These approaches differ because they are trying to solve different problems, not all of which are even problems in jurisprudence. It is a fault not to see a theoretical problem that needs an answer; but it is another fault to suppose that every perspective offers an answer to every interesting question about law.

4.3 Appreciation

Approaching jurisprudence via the 'isms' also risks leading one to suppose that the most significant facts about law are the those that most clearly distinguish *a particular theory* from the others. That is a fallacy. A sharp division between theories may turn on a point that is jurisprudentially modest. By 'significance' I mean, not what we perceive, but what we think matters *about* what we perceive. It is one thing not to see any difference between the existence of a duty and the absence of a power—either of which might mean one cannot enter a contract—it is another to see it but not appreciate why it matters. This holds at the general level too. Some people see no difference between 'inclusive' and 'exclusive' legal positivism, or between legal realism and legal sociology. Others see it, but do not see anything in it.

---

[12] It is also damaging in legal education, particularly in 'theoretical perspectives' courses that mislead students by their very structure into thinking they will have to choose between, say, natural law and post-colonial jurisprudence. (What would that even mean?) Those courses are often responsible for the pointless, inert, 'theoretical introductions' stranded at the front of otherwise excellent doctrinal, comparative, or historical dissertations.

Divergent appreciation is familiar in life, so it is surprising that many legal theorists miss its influence when they are at work. Everyone knows that some people lack any appreciation of music, art, football, or friendship. They may never have cultivated it; it may not be 'their thing'. Most humanistic fields include an appreciative element that needs to be cultivated by exposing oneself to works or performances, reflecting on them, trying out various approaches and interpretations—often without knowing whether they will ever pan out. The remark, 'this looks like a child could have done it', often betrays a lack of artistic appreciation. The remark, 'this is just a matter of semantics', often betrays a lack of philosophical appreciation. Without a capacity to appreciate significance, every logically possible distinction in jurisprudence looks like a theory-defining difference, every short-of-conceptual necessity a 'mere contingency', and so on. It is even possible not to appreciate the significance of whole fields of inquiry. Some distinguished legal theorists are unresponsive to *all* of general jurisprudence: they are in a life-long love affair with the common law, or with private law, and believe these are law's most perfect specimens. You can't disprove a romance.

4.4 A 'Canon'?

A final possible worry about 'books about books' would not have occurred to a philosopher writing, as they used to say, at 'mid-century'. Subject surveys risk presuming, or creating, a 'canon'. What must be read? What is negligible? What if jurisprudence were to end up with 'closure of the canon', in the way fourth-century Christians decided no further writings could ever be Holy Scripture? Would we be limited to turning Bentham's critique of Blackstone over and over, in hope of some new insight, or to expounding once again true meaning of the Hart–Dworkin debate?

If this is the source of anxiety about 'books about books' it is exaggerated. Whatever the status of other fields, the jurisprudential 'canon' remains unstable and open. Reading lists and encyclopaedia entries have changed vastly over my own career. When I began teaching, there was no expectation that students would read anything published before 1961; many of their professors did not. Now, the dark ages do not start to lift until around 1986. What sort of canon is it that keeps forgetting its sacred texts, letting them slip from the status of scripture to apocrypha, and finally into oblivion?

It is true that some readers feel 'excluded' when first encountering the debates of modern jurisprudence. But we do not need a hypothesis of canonical

THEORIES AND THESES 15

discipline to explain that. Every academic subject tends to become 'scholarly': to speak in shorthand, to argue finer and smaller points, and to require an increasing upfront investment on the part of a new reader. That is as true of law itself as it is of jurisprudence.

In addition, some students feel alienated from jurisprudence for the reason others feel excluded from corporate and commercial law: the fields revolve around concerns that are not theirs or presuppose values they do not share. So it is with remedial projects such as 'queer theory' or 'post-colonial theory' in law. Though often maligned as 'identity politics', the ambition to encourage focused bodies of inquiry and literature can be beneficial, at least as a division of labour. It can also be damaging. It may encourage people to believe such projects are needed, not to respond to issues others omit, but to correct philosophical errors they commit. Then it is a short, fallacious, step to suppose that errors must *cause* the omissions, because no theory of type F could ever have the resources to understand concerns of type G. In a way, that is charitable. It assumes that if a work does not address certain problems, it is not because the *theorist* takes little interest in them, but because the *theory* cannot integrate them. That is a mistake all the same. A tendency to think that all philosophical errors and omissions are forced—that they are unavoidable results of a given approach—should be added to the list of known biases in human decision-making.

It is true that in jurisprudence as in every other subject, every discipline, there are methods of inquiry and expectations of training, literacy, and even style that are loosely shared and somewhat distinctive. These can produce, for a time, more homogeneity than is helpful. But they have not yet, in jurisprudence anyway, added up to anything worth calling a 'canon'. Even in the West, essential reading in one legal culture is often regarded as marginal or unhelpful in another. It may be entirely unknown.[13] Law is a jurisdictionally limited subject, and those limits can unwittingly restrict general jurisprudence, the purely local being mistaken for the universal. On the other hand,

---

[13] There is a problem of linguistic isolation. In politics, repentant colonizers are willing to contemplate anything in recompense—short of actually returning the land to its original occupants. In the humanities, repentant 'canonizers' are willing to do anything short of actually preparing to study 'excluded' works. Most Anglophones are no longer willing to read even German or Latin— let's face it, a humiliating state of affairs for law or jurisprudence—so they are not likely to learn Arabic or Pali in order to tackle philosophical writings on *Sharia* or *Vinaya Piṭaka*. Anglophones who declare their ambition to decolonize the 'canon' of jurisprudence often cling to that most recusant of imperial presumptions: 'What can be said at all can be said in English, and what we cannot read in English we will pass over in silence.'

this fact is itself well known, and such knowledge tends to limit the sort of authority people impute to philosophical reflections of any one legal culture.

5. Progress

Jurisprudence should aim to make progress. Hart said books that primarily discuss other books make little. Let's assume he means theoretical progress. (As opposed to, say, moral progress.)

The alleged obstacle to progress cannot be literary engagement; a lot of *The Concept of Law* launches from an examination of doctrines in other books. The objection must be to the sort of jurisprudence book that is non-judgemental, for instance, one that reports that 'Austin held X but Hart held Y', or 'Hart and Dworkin disagree on three matters . . .' without telling us who is right, and why. Such books may offer a description of jurisprudence, but they do not add up to descriptive jurisprudence. However long they labour in the library, at some point every theorist of law needs to take a stand on which of the contrasting views are more plausible.

Perhaps 'books about books' might nonetheless exhibit jurisprudential progress till now, and in that way invite readers to consider the trajectory ahead. They would not offer a 'key to all jurisprudences' since there is no unified explanation of their aims. Nor could they be a 'sum of all jurisprudences' since some theories of law made no progress at all and some do contradict each other. (Progress may evolve from dialectic, though not by asserting both contradictories.) But a book about jurisprudence books could nonetheless record partial or interim progress, just as a book about the sciences might record the progress made by Newtonian mechanics or Darwinian evolution. Exhibiting the fruits of progressive research programmes might help us understand how they emerged and give us ideas about how to move forward.

Of course, we can only record progress if we can recognize it, and it is controversial what counts as progress in any of the humanities. Some think the progressive parts of jurisprudence can only be the *non*-humanistic parts that involve empirical or formal inquiry, perhaps in psychology or deontic logic. In the natural sciences, progress includes greater power to predict and control our environment. Jurisprudence is not optimized for predictions. But that is no accident. Among other things, we want to know how judges ought to decide cases according to law (and what 'ought' means in this context), but we are not trying to predict how judges *actually will* decide cases. Any judge or court may predictably misapply, or deliberately break, the law. As for the formal sciences, their potential contribution to progress seems slight for a different reason. There is a problem of carry-over. Unless we are confident that formal models are *models of* something of jurisprudential significance, we are no further ahead. General equilibrium theory made a little mathematical progress, but it was inertial as far as political economy was concerned. So far, the prospects of formalisms in legal theory seem no better placed. Possibly jurisprudence cannot progress without certain results in deontic logic, but it does not progress much with them either.

The awkward truth is that we need a notion of progress fit for jurisprudence but find nothing ready-to-wear. I therefore propose the following *marks of* progress in legal philosophy, without trying to knit them into a prescriptive theory.[14]

5.1 Shrinkage

Philosophy can progress by shrinking, by which I mean spinning off other fields that were once part of philosophy. Ancient philosophers speculated on the movement of animals, human physiology, and the elements; Newton's *Principia* is entitled *Philosophiæ Naturalis*. We no longer count biology or physics as philosophy. The boundary between the special sciences and philosophy is never sharp: cosmological questions blur into epistemological and metaphysical ones. There are clear enough cases, however. Acoustics is not aesthetics. When sound waves meet a boundary, musicology cannot help us work out whether to expect transmission, reflection, refraction, or diffraction. But neither can physics explain the lyricism of the first movement of Schubert's Eighth Symphony or make sense of the question whether the work would have been better had it been completed. In the nineteenth century, jurisprudence sold its stocks in speculative history à la Ferguson or Hegel; in the twentieth century, the ruminations of a Duguit or Pound were bought out by legal sociology. The scope of jurisprudence changed, but within its new range it became more productive. It is progress to stop trying to do what you cannot do.

---

[14] Why not prescriptive? Because we cannot be sure that aiming to produce a theory with the three marks of progress is the best way to make progress. We may need an indirect strategy.

5.2 Convergence

A second mark of progress is convergence on particular theses (rather than on general theories). Is there any? Some influential writers, including John Rawls and Jeremy Waldron, think legal philosophy is characterized by disagreements so deep that we will never concur.[15] But they have in mind evaluative disagreements, or a subset of them: moral disputes (except those about 'the right') or political disputes (except those about procedures).[16] If general jurisprudence were a branch of, or were dependent on, moral philosophy, then it would inherit those disagreements. Why are *they* intractable? Because moral disagreements include disagreements in attitude as well as belief, and attitudes can be intransigent in the face of evidence or argument. That is the simplest explanation.

Others are tempted by a more elaborate explanation, drawing on W. B. Gallie's claim that some concepts are '*essentially* contested'.[17] Gallie said a concept is essentially contested if and only if it is an evaluative cluster-concept whose extension is fixed by relations to an historical 'exemplar', disputes about which cannot be settled empirically, and where the disputes have the following interesting property: if we were to converge on 'a right answer' to what the concept covers, we would have better reason to think we had *lost* that concept than that we had found the answer. These are not merely concepts the essence of which is contested; they are concepts contests about which is *part of* their essence. Underlying that idea is a sort of pluralism, according to which it would be a matter of regret if we were to pin down a disputed notion. Best to keep our disputes going, so that no angles or interpretations ever get left out.

I am not confident that any concepts meet all of Gallie's conditions. Gallie said that law does not. (One example he proposed was art.) Legal theorists

---

[15] John Rawls, *Political Liberalism* (Columbia University Press, 1993); Jeremy Waldron, *Law and Disagreement* (Oxford University Press, 1999).
[16] If there were ineliminable disagreement 'all the way down' there would be nothing (else) to write about.
[17] W. B. Gallie, 'Essentially Contested Concepts' (1956) 56 *Proceedings of the Aristotelian Society* 167. For discussion in the jurisprudential context, see Leslie Green, 'The Political Content of Legal Theory' (1987) 17 *Philosophy of the Social Sciences* 1. In 'General Jurisprudence: a 25th Anniversary Essay' ((2005) 25 *Oxford Journal of Legal Studies* 565, 578), I said that although 'law' is not an 'essentially contested concept', the concept of 'the rule of law' probably is, on the ground that the latter is an endemically disputed evaluative concept. For reasons given below, I now doubt that the term usefully applies to either.

who adopt his explanation for conceptual disagreement therefore often drop the requirement for an historical exemplar and the requirement that permanent contestation be valuable. That abandons everything distinctive in the view. It leaves us with evaluative cluster-concepts, where enough typical but non-essential attributes will bring something under the relevant concept. Those are familiar and worth keeping in mind. But they do not point to any special kind of 'essential' controversy. It is variations in attitude and interests that leads us to emphasize some elements in a cluster over others. This is a special case of the sort of divergence in perception or appreciation that I mentioned above.

Despite such value disagreements, convergence in jurisprudence has proved possible. There is now quite wide agreement on following theses:

- All law was created by someone or emerged from the activities of some group.
- Some laws command nothing.
- There are intelligible legal questions that lack a uniquely correct legal answer.
- There is a duty to avoid legal wrongs, not merely a duty to suffer penalties or damages if so ordered.
- Some people have no moral duty, not even prima facie, to obey every law.
- The rule of law is a good thing, but only with qualification and only in some circumstances.

I picked these, you will doubtless have guessed, because although there is indeed a *very broad* consensus on them, for each there is at least one famous writer who denies it. Should we be worried? Nowhere else in the humanities does convergence require near-unanimity. Moreover, theoretical disagreement about law may be motivated, not just because philosophers and lawyers are professionally disputatious, but because there can be rewards for defending startling, even nonsensical, ideas. Originality has allure. How boring to read—one more time—that law regulates its own creation, or that international law is only partially systematized. How exciting to hear that law is a self-referential 'autopoietic' system, or that international law has 'liquid authority'! The most plausible explanation for such doctrines is that they were conjured in order to be (or sound) original. Convergence on jurisprudential theses is not only consistent with, but is sometimes a cause of, noisy disputations (and pseudo-disputations) at the margins of the subject.

5.3 Understanding

A final mark of progress is a deeper understanding of jurisprudential problems. We make progress on existing problems when we find options, connections, and solutions that we had not recognized. We progress when we go from knowing that there are legal rules to noticing that some are strict and some are loose ('standards', 'principles'). We progress when we find that these rules come in different normative types (obligations, powers, permissions), and yet again when we see that they can fulfil different social functions—and not necessarily one per type. It is progress to understand how rules can be offered and taken as reasons for action, not merely as indicators of other reasons. It is progress to understand that rules have existence conditions of various sorts: some exist because they are authenticated by other rules; some exist only because they are practised. Such insights may arrive in any order, and there are surely more to come. But all of this is progress over the simplistic idea that 'laws are rules' as well as over the crazy idea that 'there are no rules'.

There is also progress in finding new problems or seeing new aspects of old ones. We can understand why Tocqueville doubted that an informal constitution (like that of the United Kingdom) properly counts as a constitution. It consists of uncodified, ordinary laws and conventions; the hierarchy among them is weak; and even 'constitutional' statutes can be changed at will by ordinary legislation. However, further reflection reveals that the code agreed in Philadelphia in 1787, with its asserted supremacy and entrenchment, *is* the American constitution only because it too rests on uncodified customs and practices (especially, on the courts' practice of recognizing and applying it as higher law). But then every constitution—however formal, however rigid—rests on practices this informal and fluid. It turns out that the problem is not to explain how there could be an 'unwritten' constitution; it is to explain how there could be a *written* one.[18] Discovering a problem most failed to appreciate, lurking amidst propositions on which they agreed, is another kind of progress.

Jurisprudence can progress in at least those three ways. Of course, progress is not our sole aim. We also need to preserve what we learned. In addition to scholarship and 'research' (if that is what jurisprudence does) we need to *curate* what we know. Maybe that is another role for 'books about

---

[18] We owe the clearest identification of the problem to John Gardner, *Law as a Leap of Faith* (Oxford University Press, 2012) chap. 4.

books': not in canonizing legal philosophies, but in explaining them, placing them in a new context, or displaying them from a new angle, or in the company of fresh ideas, so as to make them intelligible and perhaps useful to those who follow us. A curator protects what we know and value against becoming incomprehensible when social or philosophical contexts change, or when distractions lead us to forget what we once all knew. We do not need a 'Flame Deluge' for jurisprudence to turn into cryptic memorabilia.[19] The flame throwers of social media are doing enough to abet our culture of forgetfulness. Jurisprudence could be part of a firebreak.

6. Payoffs

Let us assume, then, that we approach jurisprudence as something more than the study of books about jurisprudence books and do so in a way that allows for progress and helps preserve it. But we also want it to have educational value, to contribute to someone's intellectual formation. We cannot just assume that every (potentially) progressive inquiry does that. Exploring a cave can produce progressively better maps of the cave, something of great practical use, but the educational value comes from speleology or archaeology or some other discipline.

6.1 Jurisprudence and Law

Might the educational value of jurisprudence lie in its contribution to the study of law? Unfortunately, for most of its history law itself had little educational value. Nor did lawyers pretend otherwise. Preparation for legal practice was a matter of training, not education. The training was local: a brilliant English lawyer could be utterly lost in a Spanish court. There is rarely much of universal interest in any kind of training, whether in weightlifting, knitting, plumbing, or lawyering, and that is why its natural home is outside universities.

Not until the revolutionary work of the legal humanists in the sixteenth century did the study of law transform into something that might contribute to intellectual life. The humanists brought new approaches to the texts of

---

[19] Walter M. Miller, Jr, *A Canticle for Liebowitz* (Lippincott, 1960).

Roman law that were retrieved in the Renaissance, and they put scholarly order into legal-historical inquiry. Their revolution was, alas, limited and short-lived. In most places, and for a few more centuries, training-for-practice and a pietistic recitation of Roman rules remained the sum total of legal 'education'. Even today, many students study law only because they want to practice law. Many of their professors teach it because they do not. But teachers have the customers to think of and usually want to deliver the goods. That is why, compared with departments of history, mathematics, or philosophy, law schools often struggle to sustain a scholarly ethos, and why some law teachers value citation by a court more than critical notice by a colleague.

The most prominent legal philosopher to tie the value of jurisprudence to the practice of law was Ronald Dworkin, who said that jurisprudence is but 'the general part of adjudication, silent prologue to any decision at law'.[20] A thinker of astonishing range and brio, Dworkin nonetheless viewed law through the lens of litigation, actual or possible. His idea was that jurisprudence is 'silent' in the way physics is silent in engineering: not always used but always present. The theories give the fundamental explanations of why a claimant deserves to prevail in a lawsuit, or why a bridge is sure to stand, but we need not appeal to the fundamentals in daily work, where we rely on authorities, handbooks, tables, rules of thumb, and close enough measurements. In reality, however, theory and practice are one, so education in the (correct) theory makes for better practice.

Dworkin's reasons for seeing legal philosophy this way developed gradually over time, ending up with the claim that there is no fundamental difference between law and morality.[21] There is just one big system of interpretation that requires good moralists, qualified by the study of jurisprudence for employment throughout the boundaryless territory of value. I cannot assess that idea here (I discuss another aspect of Dworkin's philosophy in Chapter 12); but I do want to notice one point. Although he was, in some sense, a 'moral realist', Dworkin never held that moral propositions are susceptible to verification or refutation. It was pivotal to his case that this should be irrelevant to their possible truth. So my analogy of physics:engineering = jurisprudence:law was

---

[20] Ronald Dworkin, *Law's Empire* (Harvard University Press, 1986) 90.
[21] The *early* view: Ronald Dworkin, *Taking Rights Seriously* (Harvard University Press, 1979) chaps 1, 2. *Middle view*: Dworkin, *Law's Empire*, chaps 1–3; Ronald Dworkin, 'Hart's Postscript and the Character of Political Philosophy' (2004) 24 *Oxford Journal of Legal Studies* 1; *Late view*: Ronald Dworkin, *Justice for Hedgehogs* (Harvard University Press, 2013). Over time, the arguments get bolder, more intricate, and much longer.

wrong. Even if some truths of physics outrun the evidence, not all do, and there are expert physicists on whose authority we may rely. Litigation is different. There are expert witnesses, but there are no 'expert counsel' for judges to qualify, who then authoritatively explain moral truths to the court. The 'uniquely right moral answers' that judges are supposed to seek exist only 'in principle', that is, their being truth-apt is not excluded by the unavailability of any proof procedure.

Perhaps it is not surprising, then, that judges are not notably interested in how moral philosophers think they should decide cases. Judges worry about proof. And the trouble runs deeper. Philosophers help themselves to any conclusions that follow from true premises by means of truth-preserving rules of inference, such as *modus ponens*. Lawyers have less freedom. We cannot 'deduce' what the law actually is from true legal propositions together with truth-preserving inference rules. We cannot take all valid norms in the US Constitution and, by inference, derive the rest of US law. We need to discover what norms Congress and the courts created under the auspices of, or using the powers granted by, norms of the Constitution. These new norms can include special standards for legal inference, and these may for legal purposes even displace rules of logic (including deontic logics).

It is not only inference that is an unsafe guide to legal conclusions. The same is true of moral justification, including the best justifications for the settled law we have. If P is the extant law, and J is the best justification for P, it does not follow that J is already the law. The relation *J-justifies-P* is atemporal. Law is historical. The best justification for P (given the rest of the law) may be something no judge or legislator has ever heard of and, were it drawn to their attention, might be repudiated or voted down. On the other hand, *accepted*, *endorsed*, or *proclaimed* 'justifications' for P could well be law; but that is because accepting, endorsing, proclaiming, etc. are ordinary, positive acts, and in most legal systems are sources of law. In common law systems, for example, in addition to what lawyers used to call 'black letter' law, there is law derived from the purposes that are taken to justify or 'underlie' black letter law. Does this not show that law needs jurisprudence, or at least the part of it that offers justifications? Just the contrary. The legal importance of accepted justifications shows how deep the positivity of law runs. A particular legal system can be more or less friendly to such 'purposive' interpretation, but that is a parochial matter of local colour. Legal training would be a failure if it did not teach students the parish lore, but legal philosophy cannot help with that.

6.2 Jurisprudence and Moral Thought

A different proposal is that good jurisprudence contributes to good moral hygiene. Hart says jurisprudence has value in promoting clear thinking about law, and that helps us avoid moral mistakes. For example, he believes there are fundamental moral conflicts where, whatever we do, we will cause harm or do wrong. Some theories of law paper this over, for they maintain—via widening cycles and epicycles—that if it would be seriously wrong for a judge to order something, then the law does not (not finally, not in its paradigm case, not properly interpreted . . .) require it. But jurisprudence teaches us that there are laws so evil that we should refuse to apply or obey them, and if that means a price must be paid in violating the rule of law, or an oath, or an institutional duty, so be it. Only a jurisprudence with a broad concept of law, one that acknowledges unjust, unfair, or unreasonable laws as authentic laws, leaves adequate room for this judgement.[22] We study legal theory to learn that.

Hart's argument is unconvincing. All one needs to leave room for final moral assessment is a distinction between our obligations other-things-being-equal and our obligations all-things-considered. Even if it there were a prima facie duty to obey or apply the law, it would not take us from 'this is the law' directly to 'this merits obedience'. What is more, we will not be led to near sheep-like obedience unless *there is* a universal duty to obey the law. Above, I listed denial of that thesis as one point of broad convergence in modern legal theory. Hart's approach did not stop him from making a mistake about it.

Historically, most discussions of law's authority focused on the question of what might justify lawmakers' right to govern and the subjects' correlative duty to obey. (See Chapters 11 and 12.) But there are other important issues here, one of which is helpfully isolated by John Finnis: who, if anyone, has a *duty* to govern? He argues that this is justified by the effective capacity of certain people to perform tasks essential to the public good. In the concluding essay (Chapter 14) I push back (a little) in the interests of consent theory—as I also do in discussing Hume (Chapter 11)—but I am most interested in how we characterize the tasks and how we determine which ones can properly be delegated to others. The questions are complex. To the extent that they turn on moral judgement, however, clarity about the concept of law makes a very limited contribution.

---

[22] Hart, *The Concept of Law*, 206–11.

The fundamental problem here is a general one. What could precision or clarity of thought—intellectual virtues—have to do with the practical virtues of morality? The debate is ancient, but I would not bet on a close correlation. Possibly, what a person needs to excel at the logic-chopping clarity of analytical jurisprudence is in tension with cultivating the generosity and empathy needed for wise decision-making in morality. Those may be more a matter of right-feeling than right-thinking, or they may depend on thinking of a different sort than is promoted by any brand of jurisprudence.

6.3 Jurisprudence and 'The Capacity to Think'

A last-ditch apology for the educational value of jurisprudence holds out for the non-specific benefits of the subject. Students are told that in studying the philosophy of law they will gain transferrable skills that carry over to subjects like contract, constitutional law, or conflicts. What skills? The *capacity to think*: to reason systematically, to parse complex arguments, to notice subtle distinctions. The objection is glaring: if they haven't been able to develop these skills in working with legal arguments, how will they ever master them in working with philosophical arguments?

In their requisite 'skill sets', law and jurisprudence are close cousins. They differ mainly in the fact that in law finding a relevant authority strengthens an argument, while in philosophy the 'appeal to authority' is the name of a fallacy. It would be strange if students found that law comes easily, while jurisprudence is arduous because *there* one needs to learn to think and appraise arguments. More often, they are thrown off balance by the fact that in legal philosophy there are no practical authorities of any kind—no one before whom you must kneel (unless you sign up to a dogmatic religious jurisprudence), and our theoretical authorities are limited to the more technical and historical areas of the subject. It is a feature of legal philosophy that you need to do it on your own, though in the process you can have the pleasure of doing it in dialogue with some of the most penetrating thinkers, past and present.

David Foster Wallace said that the value of the liberal arts lies not in teaching the 'capacity to think', but in encouraging you in 'being conscious and aware enough to *choose* what you pay attention to'. The liberal arts show 'How to keep from going through your comfortable, prosperous, respectable adult life dead, unconscious, a slave to your head and to your natural default-setting of being uniquely, completely, imperially alone, day in and day out.'[23] This applies to lawyers in spades. Academic lawyers have ways of being imperially alone *together*. Mention 'sovereignty' in England and most lawyers think in unison of, and with, Albert Venn Dicey. In US law schools, every 'theory' of free speech struggles to break the shackles of the First Amendment and its labyrinthine doctrine. What could be more dead, unconscious, and lonely than that? Sovereignty and free speech matter. Why suppose that everything worth knowing or valuing about them begins (and usually ends) at home?

As part of the liberal arts, legal philosophy reminds us that we are not slaves to our own (legal) heads, that there is an escape from the 'default setting' of one's own little legal system, however profitable and powerful it may be. This points us towards a final point—for now—about the educational value of jurisprudence.

7. Entrée

If we want a case for the value of jurisprudence, its contributions to law, morality, or 'how to think' are the wrong places to look. The best case is hiding in plain view. Jurisprudence contributes *to philosophy* and through philosophy to the humanities in general. Some legal theorists treat their subject as an import business. They scour philosophy or linguistics or economics for an idea or technique that might apply somewhere in something to do with law. The results often feel narrow or opportunistic, but it is a fair defence that jurisprudence should take what help it can find. Still, that underestimates the extent to which jurisprudence is in the import–export business. Jurisprudence has things to teach fields like moral and political philosophy, the study of practical reason, and the theory of action, as well as problems about rules, rights, obligations, intention, responsibility, causation, and more. It is not the only subject with valuable exports on offer, but it is a central one and is often under-employed.

I doubt we can say more in defence of legal philosophy as part of a liberal education than we can say in defence of history, mathematics, or music. Nor need we. Philosophy has intrinsic value and contributes to the humanities, and they contribute to and partly constitute our humanity. Explanations must end somewhere. We can explain and, in these essays, I try to illustrate, the

---

[23] David Foster Wallace, *This is Water: Some Thoughts, Delivered on a Significant Occasion, about Living a Compassionate Life* (Little Brown, 2009), 60.

role of jurisprudence in helping us understand our institutions and, through them, our cultures. What is law that people take pride in its rule? How and to whom do legal institutions distribute power? Can law help achieve justice? What might we gain, or lose, by limiting the reach of law? What entitles law to rule; what do we owe it when it does? Anyone who wants answers to questions like those will want the help of a general theory of law. There are features law has in every society in which law exists, just as there are features of markets and features of political parties that turn up wherever those institutions are found. This idea—that there is something that law in general *is*—needs to be re-interpreted and re-explained as the rest of our knowledge and attitudes change. It would be irresponsible for jurisprudence to proceed as if we had learned nothing not known to Aquinas or Bentham. But that is no cause for pessimism. It means there is always work for jurisprudence to do.[24]

---

[24] I thank Tom Adams, Kate Greasley, Brian Leiter, Grégoire Webber, Wil Waluchow, and participants in the Oxford conference on this chapter and some of my other work, held online during the Covid pandemic of March 2021.

I
LAW, AS SUCH

1
The Concept of Law Revisited

1. A Précis and a Puzzle

Law is a social construction. It is a historically contingent feature of certain societies, one whose emergence is signalled by the rise of a systematic form of social control and elite domination. In one way it supersedes custom, in another it rests on it, for law is a system of primary rules that direct and appraise behaviour, together with secondary rules that identify, change, and enforce the primary rules. The most fundamental secondary rules are customs of key political actors. Law may be beneficial, but only in some contexts and always at a price, at the risk of grave injustice; our appropriate attitude to it is therefore one of caution rather than celebration. Law pretends, also, to an objectivity that it does not have, for whatever judges may say they in fact wield serious political power to create new laws. Not only is law therefore political, so is legal theory—there can be no pure theory of law: concepts drawn from the law itself are inadequate to understand its nature. Legal theory is thus neither the sole preserve, nor even the natural habitat, of lawyers or law professors; it is just one part of a general social and political theory. We need such a theory, not to help decide cases or defend clients, but to understand ourselves, our culture, and our institutions, and to support serious moral assessment of those institutions, an assessment that must take into account the conflicting values in life.

Those are the most important theses of H. L. A. Hart's *The Concept of Law*, first published in 1961.[1] Like other great works of philosophy, however, Hart's book is known as much by rumour as by reading, so it would be unsurprising if, to some, my précis does not sound like Hart at all. For what circulates as his views—including in law schools—is often starkly different. Isn't Hart the dreary positivist who holds that law is a matter of rules that rest on a happy social consensus? Doesn't he think that law is objective, a matter

---

[1] References in this chapter are given in parentheses in the text, using the pagination in H. L. A. Hart, *The Concept of Law* (3rd edn, Penelope. A. Bulloch and Joseph Raz eds; Leslie Green, intro, Oxford University Press, 2012).

of fact? Doesn't Hart celebrate the rule of law and take its rise as an achievement, a mark of progress from 'primitive' to modem society? Doesn't Hart think that liberty and justice are possible only through the certainty that clear law provides? And isn't his whole theoretical approach straightjacketed by a disproved, or outmoded, distinction between fact and value? Isn't Hart concerned more with semantics than politics?

Between those conflicting readings of—maybe I should say 'attitudes toward'—Hart's book, there is also consensus about the way *The Concept of Law* changed the direction of Anglo-American legal theory. It brought it into conversation with contemporary philosophy. It clarified questions that remain on the agenda for jurisprudence: Is law always coercive? What are legal rules? What is a legal system? Do judges have discretion? What are the relations between law and morality? How could international law be binding? The book, together with some of Hart's preliminary essays, also offers ideas and distinctions that still help us think through solutions to those questions: 'the internal point of view', 'primary and secondary rules', 'the rule of recognition', 'core and penumbra', 'content-independent reasons', 'social and critical morality'.

How then can there be such a wide divergence, not only about whether such an influential theory is correct, but simply about what it holds? It is impossible to put it down to style. Hart is a clear and honest writer: every technical term is purchased in the coin of necessity; the occasional obscurity of language is never a cover for shallowness of thought; humour and irony he uses to lighten, not conceal. In part, the *Zeitgeist* moved on. *The Concept of Law* was no more able to escape time and context than any other book. Its language, tone, and examples are rooted in an England, and its philosophical style in Oxford, of the 1950s. But it contains ideas and insights that transcend those origins. Much legal philosophy still takes *The Concept of Law* as a foundation or foil, so it is worth trying to explain its leading ideas in a way that, while mindful of context, is not obsessed or distracted by it. I will approach that not only, as in the opening précis, by 'translating' Hart's concerns into recent idiom but also by re-examining the book in light of its later Postscript. I want to consider what stayed the same, what changed, and what difference any of that made to the cogency of the theory.[2] My aims here are mainly expository and interpretive, but I also want to introduce some lines of inquiry

---

[2] Some literary history: *The Concept of Law* was first published in 1961, based on a series of Oxford lectures Hart gave over the preceding years. In 1992, a second edition of the text (repaginated) was published, together with part of a reply to critics that Hart left unfinished at the time of his death. The editors, Penelope Bulloch and Joseph Raz, prepared that for publication. Hart had projected two parts. The first was mainly a reply to Ronald Dworkin. The second, which never got beyond sketchy notes, was to address other critics—Raz among them—who,

and criticism developed later in this book. I am especially interested in Hart's last ideas about rules, coercion, law and morality, and about method in jurisprudence. Here we find some of Hart's second thoughts and hints at new directions. That will give us a better understanding of the ambitions, achievements, and failures of the theory.

2. Law as a Social Construction

2.1 Constructivism, positivism, and normativity

Constructivism used to be wildly popular in the social studies, where the term was applied to almost any anti-realist, anti-essentialist, or anti-determinist thesis about social life. A lot of that was decorative and challenged no descriptive or normative thesis. For instance, if 'everything is a social construction', as some said, then nothing follows from claiming that something is a social construction. Race is a social construction; and so are prisons, police, and pistols. It sounds like a bold theory, but it is barren. It is like being told that God does not exist, only to find out that the interlocutor does not believe in the existence of dogs either. Once we lose our terms of contrast and everything is on an ontological par, constructivist talk is pointless.

Sometimes, however, constructivism was the more serious thesis that certain familiar objects not only have a social history but were created in the course of that history. We must here distinguish the banal claim that *discourse about* an object has a history from the substantive, possibly controversial, claim that the *object itself* does. (That the word 'electron' was invented in 1890 does not show that electrons were.) The interest in constructivism about an object of inquiry depends on how likely anyone is to deny it. It is pointless to speak of the social construction of fashion or money, as it is obvious to pretty much everyone that fashion and money are constituted by human conduct and attitudes. It is more interesting to learn that races are socially constructed, because some people do believe, falsely, that the classification of

---

Hart acknowledged, found points of 'incoherence and contradiction' in the work (239). Hart chose to add a Postscript rather than revise the book, because, as Bulloch and Raz write, he 'did not wish to tinker with the text whose influence has been so great'. In 2012 a third edition, with a new introduction by me, was published. It preserves the text and Postscript (and the new pagination) but with the help of Tom Adams I rewrote Hart's scholarly and bibliographic notes, which were long superseded. Hart's own discursive footnotes were left unchanged. For insight into the conception of the book, see Nicola Lacey, *The Nightmare and the Noble Dream: A Life of H.L.A. Hart* (Oxford University Press, 2006).

people into races is a 'natural' one of deep biological significance. The most potent forms of constructivism are those that surprise us with the news that an object of scientific attention owes its very existence to social history.[3] It really is astonishing to learn that some serious mental illnesses arose, proliferated, fell out of fashion, then disappeared. Yet when they were in vogue, they caused immense suffering.

Is it at all surprising to hear that law is a social construction? The claim that law is a phenomenon with a social history, that it did not always exist, that it took shape gradually, and that it could one day disappear, might come as a surprise to those who associate law with reason out of time, with what P. F. Strawson once called the core of human thought that has no history.[4] For instance, it might surprise a Stoic:

> [T]rue law is right reason in agreement with Nature; it is of universal application, unchanging and everlasting ... We cannot be free from its obligations by senate or people, and we need not look outside ourselves for an expounder or interpreter of it. And there will not be different laws at Rome and at Athens, or different laws now and in the future, but one eternal and unchangeable law will be valid for all nations and all times.[5]

However we fill out the idea of a 'social construction', this passage shows that Cicero does not think 'true law' to be one. Of course, he knows there is also sublunary, so-called, 'law' (so-called, incidentally, *by everyone*) and he knows that it does indeed differ at Rome and Athens, that it is always in flux, and it has only local validity. But it would surprise Cicero, as it still surprises contemporary adherents of related views, to hear that *all* law is like this, *including* all 'true law'. That is what Hart holds.

Hart's theory places law in history. Not just Icelandic law, which had to await Iceland, or canon law, which needed churches, but all law, everywhere and as such. The same even applies to 'true law', the paradigm specimens of

---

[3] 'I respect someone who can argue that quarks are socially constructed: this is a daring and provocative thesis that makes us think. I feel a certain guarded admiration when a fact whose discovery was rewarded with a Nobel Prize for medicine is described as the social construction of a scientific fact; anyone who shares my respect and admiration for fundamental science has to sit up take notice. I do not find it similarly thrilling to read about the social construction of events that could occur only historically, only in the context of a society.' Ian Hacking, *Rewriting the Soul: Multiple Personality and Sciences of Memory* (Princeton University Press, 1995) 67 (footnotes omitted).
[4] P. F. Strawson, *Individuals* (Methuen, 1959) 10.
[5] Cicero, *De Re Republica* (T. E. Page et al., eds, C. W. Keyes, trs, Loeb, 1928) III: xxii, 33.

law that live up to the ideals appropriate to law-hood—and even to those ideals themselves. These are all creatures of history. The fact there is law (at all) is an interesting contingency in the development of some human societies. The law of every jurisdiction is wholly a consequence of the contingent activities of people. The 'normativity' of law—its character as a system of action-guiding and action-appraising norms—is another social construction, and in the same sense. It is a function of people's actions and intentions. Nothing is a norm unless someone or other uses it to guide or assess someone's action, belief, or emotion.[6] Anything else is a would-be norm, or someone's idea for a norm.

But isn't all this constitutive of legal positivism—the view that all law is positive law? It is not: Hans Kelsen, for one, repudiates the constructivist thesis. He agrees that general jurisprudence should restrict its attention to positive law (the only law there is), and he agrees that law is a system of norms, but he denies that norms are historical. Activities such as ordering, deciding, legislating, ruling, or directing amount to law only within a system of other norms that *make* them law, and norms, he asserts, exist only if they are valid. What places Kelsen on the far side of constructivism is his assertion that validity 'means' (just is, can only be understood as) the fact that people ought to behave as the norms require. This 'ought' is not susceptible to further explanation, save what follows from the constraint that 'ought' cannot be derived from 'is'. Kelsen therefore concludes that, although the sources of law are all constructed, their character as laws is not. Everything constructed is an 'is'; laws are 'oughts'. How then could all law be positive?

Kelsen struggles to unfankle this. He says that the historically ultimate norms in any legal system (the 'first Constitution' if there is one, the legally fundamental customs if there is not) must be validated by a norm that is *not* historical. (Remember: If they are not valid, they do not exist.) Kelsen first thought of this unhistorical norm in a Kantian way, as a 'transcendental-logical presupposition', and he called it the *Grundnorm* (the 'basic norm').[7]

---

[6] To use a norm to guide is to use it to bring about action by rational causation, not merely by changing the situation so that its subject is bound to act in some way. To be guided by N in V-ing, a norm-subject must know that N exists, know what counts as conformity to N, and see the existence of N as a reason for V-ing. Some things are therefore ill-suited to be used as norms, and some things are impossible to use as norms. See Chapter 3, this volume.
[7] Hans Kelsen, *Pure Theory of Law* (2nd edn, Max Knight trs, University of California Press, 1967) 193–205. The doctrine is not orthodox Kantianism, as the transcendentally 'necessary' presupposition is only necessary *if one wants* to interpret laws as norms. One could interpret them as non-normative social power. Unlike supposedly basic categories of thought, 'law' is dispensable.

This is not a positive norm, but rather a (putatively) necessary condition for interpreting any actions or events as creating or constituting norms. Sometimes Kelsen calls it a fiction rather than a presupposition, but by that he does not mean a myth, story, or ideology. Those are also social constructions, made and transmitted by people. The sort of fiction Kelsen had in mind is one 'posited' only by theory, and while a theory can state or describe norms, it cannot create them.[8] Thus, positivists need not be social constructivists about law.[9]

This shows that Hart's constructivism is far from obvious. It is surprising indeed to be told that *all of law*, from a mundane statute to the ultimate, constitutive, norms of a legal system are social constructions. Actually, they are social constructions of social constructions.[10] Their building blocks are not brute facts but institutional facts, including rules that exist only when practiced. But isn't that a 'category mistake?'[11] How could rules—abstract objects—be practices, which are historical events? It sounds like confusing numbers and numerals. There is no mistake: (i) Rules are not constituted by practices; Hart says a social rule does not prevail amongst a group unless people in that group practice it. (ii) Practices are not events. Practices are series or sequences of events, and series and sequences are abstract objects. People can see a sequence then use it as a norm—as a rule—just as one might see a branch lying the forest floor as an arrow then use it to point a direction. Neither an action-attitude sequence nor a piece of wood is 'inherently' normative. They are so only if used to guide conduct, belief, or emotion. How could something that is actual, a mere incident of use, be normative? The same way a right-angled piece of wood could be a carpenter's square—by

---

[8] After his encounter with the Marburg neo-Kantians (especially Hermann Cohen) Kelsen came under more eclectic, less 'transcendental' influences, including the work of Hans Vaihinger. Compare Hermann Cohen, *Logik der reinen Erkenntnis* (Bruno Cassirer, 1922); Hans Vaihinger, *Die Philosophie Des Als Ob* (F. Meiner, 1918). For a contemporary discussion of fictionalism, see R. M. Sainsbury, *Fiction and Fictionalism* (Routledge, 2009). Kelsen shed his Kantianism in stages. It is fading in *General Theory of Law and State* (Harvard University Press, 1945), and in the second edition of *Pure Theory of Law* (M. Knight trs, University of California Press, 1960/1967). In his final, incomplete, work, *General Theory of Norms* (M. Hartney trs, Oxford University Press, 1991)it is abandoned, leaving instability in the theory as its residue.

[9] We can add social constructivism to the list of stereotypes of positivism discussed in the Introduction to this volume. It is only one possible version.

[10] On the nesting of social facts, see John Searle, *The Construction of Social Reality* (Free Press, 1995) 79–126.

[11] Scott Shapiro, *Legality* (Harvard University Press, 2001) 189: 'it is a mistake to identify rules with practices. Rules are abstract entities, whereas practices are concrete events that reside within space and time.'

being used to try right angles.[12] In fact, it is hard to see how anything could serve as a norm if it were *not* someone's representation of what someone ought to do. We could leave a trail of breadcrumbs to guide our way home from the forest, but not a trail of abstract 'oughts'.

2.2 Constructivism and Anti-essentialism

Hart's theory is constructivist in a second way. It is anti-essentialist about law. There are paradigm cases of legal systems, and necessary features of those cases, but there are also borderline and analogical cases where we quite properly speak of law. Is international law *law*? It is not very systematized and has patchy effectiveness. (When he wrote, Hart thought it was not systematized *at all*. That was probably wrong.) Does that mean international law is 'not really' law? Hart simply refuses that sort of question. Once we explain the ways international law is like domestic law and the ways it differs, there is no more work for jurisprudence to do. We are not called on to render an accounting, and report that international law has, say, 54 per cent the nature of law, as if it were like a whisky's alcohol by volume.

There is no essence shared by all phenomena properly called 'law'. At that level of generality, we are imposing a nominal order on items that are connected by criss-crossing relations of partial analogy, sharing enough features for it to be useful to bring them under a common term, but little more than that. How then can law have a nature for us to study—how could there even be a 'concept of law'—if there is nothing that law (essentially) is? The answer is that when we study law in general we do *not* study all phenomena properly called 'law'. We study *legal systems* (English law, Roman law, canon law, etc.) And we do not study them because legal systems are the essence of law, any more than political scientists study political parties because they are the essence of politics. We study them because they are institutions that provide a window on our cultures and have great social and moral importance. There may be necessary and sufficient conditions for something to be (a paradigm case of) a legal system, and for a legal system to exist, even it is pointless to seek anything so definite to cover all law 'properly so called'.

---

[12] The English and German 'norm' is a borrowing from classical Latin '*norma*', a carpenter's square. In English, *norma* is first attested as a synonym for 'rule' in the writings of the English judge Sir Matthew Hale (1677); the word 'norm' makes its English debut only in 1821. (*OED*, 3rd edn, 2003, *sub* 'norm, *n 1*')

2.3 Constructions of Rules

One hesitation about social constructivism and its suggestion of building reality is that it sounds too deliberate. Gender is a social construction yet there are no named people who made it up. Gender norms vary among societies, but at a given time and place they can be resilient, resisting even strenuous attempts to change them. That makes some people suppose, wrongly, that gender is 'natural'. There is a point, then, to social constructionism about gender. It reminds us how gender differs from sex, and helps us reflect on how something that is the upshot of uncoordinated agency can be resistant to deliberate change.

Putting agency in its place is one of the main critical achievements of *The Concept of Law*. Laws, say Thomas Hobbes, Jeremy Bentham, and John Austin, are expressions of someone's will: they are general commands of a sovereign, backed by threats of force.[13] But, as Hart shows, that model cannot explain the variety of forms of law, how sovereigns can be bound by their own rules, or how law survives the death of the commander. Above all, it cannot explain the normative character of law, the fact that law not only forces us to do things, but imposes obligations, or duties, on us to do them. (82–91) A person's say-so has that power only when that person is authorized to make norms. Sovereign bodies are legally authorized to make law, but we need to explain the laws authorizing them as much as any other laws. Are we now tumbling back down towards the *Grundnorm*? No. There is an exit with a soft landing among practiced, customary norms. People use customary practices as norms, and such norms—not imperatives—are the ultimate basis of law.[14]

Law, Hart argues, is a union of rules: primary rules that guide behaviour by imposing duties on people and secondary rules that provide for the identification, change, and enforcement of the primary rules. Among the secondary rules, the 'rule of recognition' has special importance. It exists only if there is customary practice among those whose role it is to identify and apply

---

[13] Thomas Hobbes, *Leviathan* (C. B. Macpherson, ed., Penguin, 1968) 311–35; Jeremy Bentham, *Of Laws in General* (H. L. A. Hart ed., Athlone Press, 1970); John Austin, *The Province of Jurisprudence Determined* (W. E. Rumble ed., Cambridge University Press, 1995).

[14] Customary norms could have their origins in imperatives. Leader can order, 'Everyone follow me!' and that may give rise to a custom of following Leader in such circumstances. But not solely because Leader ordered it. If everyone replies, 'Get lost!'; no norm of follow-the-Leader is likely to emerge. On the other hand, Leader can say, 'I'm going this way, but don't mind me. Just do your own thing.' Everyone may nonetheless follow Leader, and then start to use follow-the-Leader as a norm, without so much as a by-your-leave.

primary rules, a practice of using the rule of recognition as the ultimate criterion of legal validity. That rule of recognition is neither valid nor invalid; it either exists as a matter of social fact or it does not. When people do use it as a standard for appraising conduct, the language of 'validity' and 'invalidity' comes to life, and a legal system is (gradually) born.

According to what is often called the 'practice theory', a social rule exists in group G, whenever there is a regularity R in the behaviour of people in G such that: (1) many people in G conform to R; (2) lapses from conformity are usually criticized by the G-ites; (3) the criticism referred to in (2) is in turn regarded as justified; and (4) R is accepted as a standard for the behaviour of people in G. 'Acceptance' in (4) is a technical term. It does *not* mean consent or approval. People who conform to R accept R whenever they suppose they have some reason to use R for guidance. One can be paid to accept a rule or forced to accept it. One can be forced to accept R because otherwise one won't get paid.[15] Rules are thus to be identified and understood from the 'internal point of view' of those who use the rules as a standard—for whatever reason—even if, from an 'external point of view', they appear as behavioural regularities only (88–91).

Whether we judge this theory satisfactory depends on what we hope for. Is it even a '*theory* of rules'? That depends on what you think such a theory must offer. Hart's ambitions are limited. He wants to explain the difference between a rule and a non-normative habit or a prediction about behaviour. He wants to work out existence conditions for social rules. He wants to identify the occasions on which rules are offered and cited as reasons for acting. And he wants to know about different types of rules and what they contribute to a theory of law. That is all. There are many philosophically interesting questions about rules that Hart's account does not address. The 'practice theory' does not define or analyse 'a rule'.[16] It does not address the 'rule-following paradox'. It does not offer moral or practical justifications for having or following rules. It does not tell us how rules may be learned or taught. Hart does not treat these problems because the problems that he is trying to solve do not depend on their answers.

---

[15] Note, however, 'forced to accept' is not the same as 'forced to do what the rule in fact requires'. The forcing has to result in the forced seeing some reason to use the rule as a guide. If force simply closes all other options, it need not work through anyone's rational capacities. Normally, then, force can only produce acceptance indirectly.

[16] For the suggestion that Hart practically treats 'rule' as a primitive, see Thomas Adams, 'Practice and Theory in *The Concept of Law*', in John Gardner, Leslie Green, and Brian Leiter eds, *Oxford Studies in the Philosophy of Law*, vol. 4 (Oxford University Press, 2021) 1–31.

Hart's success with the problems that he does treat varies. His main targets are two sorts of reductionists: imperativists like Bentham and predictive behaviourists like the Scandinavian 'realists'. Against these, Hart's arguments are decisive. What about the positive claims of 'practice theory' on its own terms? It matters whether it is able accurately to detect the use of social rules. That need not tell us everything else about rules, any more than a litmus test that detects the presence of an acid will tell us much about the nature of acids. Possibly, to design a test for acids one first needs to know a lot about acids. Hart assumes we know enough about rules to get started.

Nonetheless, there are difficulties with his account.[17] There are rules that exist outside social practices (e.g. an individual's rules); there are social practices that are not rules (e.g. widely approved openings in chess that are not among the rules of chess); and citing a valid rule is often meant as a justification for one's behaviour, not merely a sign that there is some other justification for it.

The third point is the most telling. Judges and lawyers commonly cite rules *as* reasons for deciding or advising something, not merely as periphrastic summaries of (other) reasons. Here, Hart does not go beyond noting that this is the case and showing how it refutes predictive-style forms of realism. He does not explain how it could be intelligible to cite a rule as one's reason. Why are we not always required to give the reasons for the rule, in default of which mentioning the rule is not merely incomplete but senseless? In the moral philosophy and in decision-theory of the era, this was a lively question, and Hart knows about its bearing on rule-utilitarianism, so it is odd that he does not try to answer it. Joseph Raz later made a solution to it the centrepiece of his own account of rules as 'exclusionary reasons', one of his major departures from Hart's theory.[18] Had Hart considered this issue, he would probably have thought that it belongs with justificatory questions outside the province of general, 'conceptual', jurisprudence. We do in fact cite rules as reasons, and for jurisprudence that is enough. What Hart does not see, or at least not clearly, is that it is unlikely that we *would* cite rules as reasons if that were rationally unintelligible. It may be unjustified to cite a rule as a reason, but someone concerned to understand law from the internal point of view will want an account of how rule-citers see things. In any event, Hart does not

---

[17] On the points to follow, see Ronald Dworkin, *Taking Rights Seriously* (Harvard University Press, 1979) 48–58; Joseph Raz, *Practical Reason and Norms* (2nd edn, Oxford University Press, 1999) 50–8; and Leslie Green, *The Authority of the State* (Oxford University Press, 1990) 44–9.
[18] Raz, *Practical Reason and Norms*, 37–45, 181 ff.

address such problems, and nothing in his writing about rules and practices should be interpreted as if it does.

Hart has the greatest difficulty, by his own lights, in handling obligation-imposing rules. Whether a rule that imposes a legal or moral obligation is justified in doing so is a question of morality. But jurisprudence does need an account of *what it is* for a rule to be obligatory: not all legal rules create obligations for their subjects. On this front, Hart's proposal is that a rule is obligation-imposing if and only if (a) the rule is believed to be socially necessary, (b) it is reinforced by serious social pressure, and (c) it is categorical in the sense that compliance is not conditioned on its subjects' wishes and may conflict with their immediate self-interest (86–8). If we are thinking of legal, as opposed to moral, obligations, these conditions need not apply directly. A rule of recognition could say that all legal norms enacted on Tuesdays are to be interpreted as imposing obligations. What makes these norms obligatory is that they are Tuesday-norms, not that they are thought socially necessary, enforced by serious social pressure, and are categorical. But those conditions must apply directly to the ultimate recognition rules. Judges and others have a duty, not just a permission or power, to apply the law as identified by those rules, and there is no 'higher' law to authorize that.

Hart was never satisfied with this account, no doubt because he saw that it does not fully exfoliate the view that one has an obligation only if one is subject to some kind of pressure. He campaigned against that idea in his criticisms of the coercion-based theories of Bentham, Austin, and Kelsen only for it to seep back, in, dilute form, into his own theory. Moreover, the asserted rule-dependence of obligations opens Hart to criticisms put by Ronald Dworkin and many others. There can be obligations in the absence of social rules. One can coherently believe one has an obligation to save a drowning person without there being a shared rule that one is to do so, and without believing there is, or even should be, such a rule. (Maybe the occasions of obligation are too finely sensitive to particular facts to be regulated by any rule.)

Dworkin distinguishes rules that are a matter of 'concurrent' practice, when people converge for common reasons independent of their agreement, and rules that are a matter of 'conventional' practice, when their reasons are agreement dependent. It is a conventional practice in the United States that people drive on the right because it is a sufficient reason for conformity that each expects everyone else to do the same. It is a concurrent practice that they care for their own children; each does it without conditioning their action on the expected conduct of others. Dworkin holds that Hart's theory is suited only to conventional rules then argues that endemic controversy about the scope of all conventions shows that duties must have another, moral, foundation.[19] Channelling, as he so often does, his inner Kelsen, Dworkin avers that *no* practiced, conventional rules are themselves normatively binding.[20] Conventional practices are obligation-relevant only to the extent that they express attitudes or gives rise to expectations that could figure as minor factual premises in moral arguments for following those rules. Even the 'keep right rule' is a norm, thinks Dworkin, only if its existence triggers a moral reason of fairness or utility for people to drive on the right when enough others do.

As I explained above, this wrongly interprets Hart as offering answers to justificatory questions.[21] In the Postscript, Hart does not see how badly he had been misread and proposes a compromise. Acknowledging that there are (justified) obligations that are not rule- or practice-dependent, he now confines his theory to conventional rules where, 'general conformity of a group to them is part of the reasons which its individual members have for acceptance . . .' (255). The ultimate rule of recognition is, he thinks, such a convention: '[S]urely an English judge's reason for treating Parliament's legislation (or an American judge's reason for treating the Constitution) as a source of law having supremacy over other sources includes the fact that his judicial colleagues concur in this as their predecessors have done'. Law rests on 'a mere conventional rule of recognition accepted by the judges and lawyers' (267).

In Chapter 3 I will examine a conventionalist theory in detail. Here, I want to anticipate a couple of points. First, we should delete the word 'mere' in Hart's second formulation. It is not plausible that the *only* reason officials ever conform to a rule of recognition (or other fundamental rules) is that others do so. In the United Kingdom the supremacy of parliamentary statutes as a source of law rests, not only on a common practice of treating them as supreme, but also on a belief that this practice is democratic and is central to

---

[19] Dworkin believes this distinguishes conventional rules from concurrent rules based on morality or, as he sometimes says, 'normative facts'. Though endemically controversial *in practice*, moral rules may *in principle* be fully determinate, he thinks.

[20] Dworkin agrees with Kelsen that: judicial decisions are the primary subjects of legal guidance, that no practiced rule can itself be normative, that law is essentially coercive, and that there are no 'gaps' in the law. I am not aware of a satisfactory explanation of why Dworkin follows Kelsen so closely, and so silently.

[21] Theorists who, following Dworkin, wrongly think Hart is offering a kind of justification for rule-following or rule-citing are legion. Kevin Toh and Brian Leiter have made me see how pervasive this error is. For discussion of the problem Hart was *not* trying to solve, see David Enoch, 'Reason-Giving and the Law', in Leslie Green and Brian Leiter eds, *Oxford Studies in Philosophy of Law: Volume 1* (Oxford University Press, 2011) chap. 1.

our culture. In the United States, the supremacy of the Constitution seems to rest, not only on common practice, but also on a belief that it set up a just form of government or was ordained by wise men with whom it is important to keep faith. Such beliefs do not have to be correct, and they do not have to be universally shared, but they are normally present along with reasons based on common practice. What is needed for a rule of recognition to be conventional in Hart's sense is simply that, whatever (other) reasons officials have for applying it, they would not do so unless there were also a common practice to that effect.

A second point about Hart's conventionalism:[22] The rule of recognition is an obligation-imposing rule. It not only identifies the sources of law, but it also directs judges and others to apply the law as identified. Recall Hart's account of obligation-imposing rules: they regulate matters considered important, they are enforced by serious social pressure, and their requirements are categorical. Are these conditions met? A US district court that ignored all rulings of the Supreme Court or started to apply Sharia as law would probably get everyone in a lather. But is that true generally? Is it true of a Supreme Court that ignores its own precedents? That is not so clear. Nor is it clear that, when there is a settled convention, there is 'the standing possibility of conflict between obligation or duty and interest' that Hart says is a mark of a categorical requirement (87). Judges may have preferences among recognition rules, preferences that reflect their views about power, legitimacy, and so forth. But if the predominant attitude of each were the desire to conform to convention, the push and pull we find with obligations would be unusual. On this point, Hart came nearer the truth the first time round: breaking ranks can be tempting, even for judges, but it is an occasion for criticism and pressure to conform. Alas, that also holds where there is no rule at all, but only a reason of general application. Debate about the characterization of social rules continues, and there are other options that fit a broadly Hartian theory of law.[23] But neither the simple practice theory, nor Hart's conventionalist revision of it, will work.

---

[22] For other doubts about Hart's argument see Julie Dickson, 'Is the Rule of Recognition Really a Conventional Rule?' (2007) 27 *Oxford Journal of Legal Studies* 373.
[23] Including Raz, *Practical Reason and Norms*; Frederick F. Schauer, *Playing by the Rules: A Philosophical Examination of Rule-based Decision-making in Law and in Life* (Oxford University Press, 1993); Andrei Marmor, *Social Conventions: From Language to Law* (Princeton University Press, 2009); and Scott J. Shapiro, *Legality* (Harvard University Press, 2011).

3. Law and Power

So far we have this: law is a construction of social rules which exist only when there is a certain consensus of action and attitude. That may sound like a rather complacent view of an institution that is, in the end, an instrument of social control. What about conflict, coercion, and power?

3.1 The Division of Labour in Law

Hart argues against Austin's top-down, pyramidal view of law as orders of a sovereign backed by threats. It is acknowledged that that view was crude, but some feel that it was salutary and that Hart, in making legal positivism more subtle, loses its punch. Law is not just about consensus and agreement; it is also about conflict and disagreement. A lot of activity in appellate courts is highly politicized and consists not of applying settled law but settling arguable cases. That easily fits with Hart's theory: high courts exercise a lot of discretion. Hart does, however, require consensus at other points if things are to get off the ground: at least the rule of recognition needs significant agreement about which activities make law. Whose agreement? Here is Dworkin's rendition of Hart's theory:

> The true grounds of law lie in the acceptance by the community as a whole of a fundamental master rule (he calls this a 'rule of recognition') . . . For Austin the proposition that the speed limit in California is 55 is true just because the legislators who enacted that rule happen to be in control there; for Hart it is true because the people of California have accepted, and continue to accept, the scheme of authority in the state and national constitutions.[24]

What is wrong with that as an account of the 'grounds' of law is obvious. Many people in California have no idea what the 'scheme of authority in the state and national constitutions' amounts to; some are not even aware that there *is* a state constitution. There is also something wrong with it as an interpretation of Hart's theory. In a pre-legal society, social norms can exist only with broad support. 'In the simpler structure [before the emergence of law], since there are no officials, the rules must be widely accepted as setting critical standards for the behaviour of the group. If, there, the internal point of

[24] Ronald Dworkin, *Law's Empire* (Harvard University Press 1986) 34.

LAW AND POWER 45

view is not widely disseminated there could not logically be any rules (117).' Customary rules require general buy-in. However,

> ... where there is a union of primary and secondary rules ... the acceptance of rules as common standards for the group may be split off from the relatively passive matter of the ordinary individual acquiescing in the rules by obeying them for his part alone. In an extreme case the internal point of view with its characteristic normative use of language ('This is a valid rule') might be confined to the official world. In this more complex system, only officials might accept and use the system's criteria of validity. The society in which this was so might be deplorably sheeplike; the sheep might end in the slaughter-house. But there is little reason for thinking that it could not exist or for denying it the title of a legal system (117).

I quote this passage at length because the point it makes is important to understanding the nature of law and to understanding the political significance of the fact that law has that nature. Custom and social morality are immune to deliberate change; they evolve gradually. For a small and stable community, they are fairly good ways of running things—throughout much of private life that is how we normally run things. But large and complex societies also need deliberate mechanisms of social control that enable customs and other norms to be publicly ascertained and to be changeable forthwith, by the say-so of the rulers, by majority vote, or whatever. This is made possible by institutionalization: the emergence of specialized organs with power to identify, alter, and enforce the rules. The resulting division of normative labour is a mixed blessing, bringing both gains and costs: 'The gains are those of adaptability to change, certainty, and efficiency; the cost is the risk that the centrally organized power may well be used for the oppression of numbers with whose support it can dispense, in a way that the simpler regime of primary rules could not' (202). So, law is *not* universally good or good without qualification. Its institutional character makes gains possible, but it also makes costs possible, costs that a society without law is less likely to bear. Even short of the limiting case where *only* the officials accept the law, a typical society under law depends less on a broad social consensus than it does on a narrow elite consensus.[25] What the existence of law requires of the general

---

[25] This skates over the question of which officials matter, and of how the role of 'official' should be characterized. Generally speaking, Hart means to include at least judges and legislators, and 'official' takes a socio-political rather than legal definition.

population is little more than acquiescence with respect to the mandatory norms of the system.

There is nothing cozy or communal about the consensus on which law rests. It does not presuppose an agreement on values; it does not exclude significant dissent in the operation of law. This shows why the romantic belief that every legal system expresses the values of its community is incorrect. Even a just and valuable legal system can end up arcane, technical, and remote from the lives of those it governs. Owing to the division of normative labour, law runs a standing risk of becoming, in a word, legalistic. Every legal theorist acknowledges that law is morally fallible. Hart's contribution is in showing that some of the ways law can fail are intimately connected to its nature as a social institution.

3.2 Coercion and Power

The idea that law is essentially a coercive apparatus resonates with the layperson's view and has been popular in jurisprudence. Hart thinks it mistaken. Every legal system contains some norms that are not coercively enforced, and it is conceivable that a legal system might be composed entirely of such norms (199–200). What would be the point of sanction-free law? The same as the point of law backed by sanctions: to direct people how to behave. Sanctions are the law's Plan B. Plan A is that its subjects should conform to it without further supervision. Where a need for direction exists without a need for reinforcing motivation it is not uncommon to find laws without sanctions.[26]

One important class of these is power-conferring norms, legal rules that create the capacity to change legal norms and statuses, for example rules that empower people to legislate, incorporate, contract, or marry. Where the powers in question are voluntary (as these examples generally are), people are free to exercise them or not at their option. Someone who does not follow the law's recipe for legislating, incorporating, contracting, or marrying fails to do so, and the resulting 'marriage', for example, would be null and void. But no one is punished for failing. Or should we say that nullity is itself the

---

[26] The United States Code, for example, contains norms telling people how to show respect for the flag. ('The flag should never be used as a receptacle for receiving, holding, carrying, or delivering anything.' 4 U.S.C. § 8 (h). It provides no penalties for breach of these norms. Their function is only to guide.

punishment and that these are, after all, coercive laws? Hart explains why we should not: we do not have two distinct things here, an order to do something and a sanction for disobedience. There is no order, and the 'sanction' is nothing other than the power-conferring rule itself. Kelsen proposed a work-around to save the coercion theory. He said power-conferring rules are only fragments of laws, so it is not surprising that no sanction can be found in them: the sanctions are tucked away elsewhere in the legal system. There are sanction-bearing rules requiring one to support one's spouse; what the power-conferring rules of marriage do is tell us whether someone has a spouse and, if so, who it is. One way or another, a law is linked back to coercion. Hart's reply to this move is revealing. He does not say that Kelsen's reconstruction is impossible or illogical. He says that it is unmotivated and at variance with the following methodological constraint on jurisprudence:

> The principal functions of the law as a means of social control are not to be seen in private litigation or prosecutions, which represent vital but still ancillary provisions for the failures of the system. It is to be seen in the diverse ways in which the law is used to control, to guide, and to plan life out of court (40).

There is no essentialist, 'metaphysical', answer to the question of how to divide up legal material among individual laws; the best approach is one that lets us understand law as it is for those who actually use it, most of whom live outside courtrooms. Power-conferring rules are thought of, spoken of, and used in social life differently from rules that impose duties, and they are valued for different reasons. 'What other tests for difference in character could there be?' (41). This epitomizes Hart's method. To Holmes's 'bad man', law is all about costs to be avoided; to the lawyer it is all about possible and actual court cases (and fees to be earned). Theories of law have been spun out of these cyclopic viewpoints. They treat what is real but marginal as if it were central. Whole dimensions of legal importance are left out of their flat and reductive pictures.

All that is correct as far as it goes. However, if we want to attend to *all* the 'principal functions of the law as a means of social control' we must go further than Hart does here. It is indeed a mistake to try to reduce power-conferring rules to duty-imposing rules, or to represent nullity as a kind of sanction. But it is not a mistake to notice the ways that power-conferring rules are bound up with social power. Why care about coercion in the first place? One answer is connected to responsibility: people who are forced by threat to do things are generally not held responsible for having done them; their will is overborne. Many legal penalties are not that severe, however (short of persistent refusal to pay them). Nonetheless, they do affect people's incentives, and that is true of power-conferring rules as well. Coercion is the hard edge of law's power; the incentivizing and expressive character of legal norms belongs to its soft edge.

Laws rendering invalid marriage between people of the same sex or of different races were not like criminal punishments for homosexual conduct or like fugitive slave laws. Still, it was *no accident* or unintended by-product of the relevant power-conferring rules (or the combination of power-conferring rules and interpretation rules) that rendered these marriages void. That was their purpose. Without resorting to anything as crude as orders and sanctions these laws attempted to shape both individuals' lives and the common culture. They had some success. We need to bear this in mind when we think about the functions of rules that Hart benignly refers to as providing 'facilities'. Not all laws are coercive, but non-coercive laws do something that coercive laws also do: they express and channel social power. They can do it through their content and through more structural features. Voluntary powers, for example, parcel out legal control to those who can exercise their will (so, not to infants or the demented); individual powers parcel it out to individuals (so, not to social classes or nations). That may not force anyone to do anything, but it does shape the social world in ways that are not only predictable but often intended by those who create and apply such laws.

4. Law and Morality

A central problem of jurisprudence involves the pluriform relations between law and morality—both customary, or 'social' morality and ideal, or 'critical', morality. Hart is famous for insisting on a disjunction here—people who know nothing else about his theory know that he holds, as he put it in his landmark Holmes lecture, that 'there is no necessary connection between law and morals'.[27] We have already seen above (Section 3.1) why law need not reflect the moral values actually endorsed by the population it governs. But what about the moral values that *should* govern them? Does Hart mean to say that there is no necessary connection here either? In *The Concept of Law*, he

---

[27] H. L. A. Hart, 'Positivism and the Separation of Law and Morals' (1957) 71 *Harvard Law Review* 593, at 601 n. 25.

sometimes formulates the thought differently. At one point he describes the core positivist thesis as holding that, 'it is in no sense a necessary truth that laws reproduce or satisfy certain demands of morality' (185–6). That seems narrower: it is possible that there are necessary relations between law and morality that do not require that all laws 'reproduce or satisfy' sound moral standards. Hart's first, broader, formulation found little favour, not even among those who share his view that law is a social construction.[28]

4.1 Law's Aim

Law is not just a system of rules; it is a system that serves various purposes. Thomas Aquinas thought law also has an *overall* purpose for it is, he claimed, 'an ordinance of reason made for the common good'.[29] Modern suggestions along these lines include the idea that law is made for doing justice, coordinating activity, or justifying coercion.[30] These claims are intended, not as suggestions about possible ideals for law, but about *constitutive aims* of law. A system of social control that did not have these aims would not be a legal system, just as an institution that did not aim at the pursuit of knowledge would not be a university. Having constitutive aims does not itself establish any connection with morality. That depends on what the aims are. No appliance is a dishwasher unless it is for washing dishes, and its capacity to wash dishes is one of the main criteria for judging whether a dishwasher is good. But washing dishes is not normally a morally significant activity, so a good dishwasher is not a morally good dishwasher. The usual suggestions for a constitutive aim of law vary from the morally charged to the morally neutral. Doing justice is morally good; coordinating conduct is morally neutral; and licensing coercion is morally ambiguous.[31]

The sort of connection to morality also depends on how far the constitutive aim succeeds. Hart's argument presupposes that human survival is

---

[28] I explain why not in Chapters 6 and 7 of this volume.
[29] *Summa Theologica* II-I, q. 90 a. 4.
[30] Guiding conduct: Lon L. Fuller, *The Morality of Law* (rev. edn, Yale University Press, 1969); coordinating activity: John Finnis, *Natural Law and Natural Rights* (2nd edn, Oxford University Press, 2011); doing justice: Michael Moore, 'Law as a Functional Kind', in R. P. George ed., *Natural Law Theory: Contemporary Essays* (Oxford University Press, 1992) 221; licensing coercion: Dworkin, *Law's Empire*, 93.
[31] Does licensing coercion mean 'providing a justification for such coercion as is going on'; or 'ensuring that no coercion goes on that is not justified' or 'coercing people whenever it would be justified to do so'? Dworkin never tells us. Perhaps his criterion of 'fit' entails that it is in part the first, and in part at least one of the other two.

morally good, and that a normative system that did not aim at it would not be a legal system. It also holds that, for a legal system to exist, it must deliver the goods, if not to everyone all the time, then to some people much of the time. A thing with a constitutive aim normally gets quite a lot of latitude before we disqualify it as a member of the relevant kind. A dishwasher that is defective or broken is still a dishwasher, provided that if repaired or modified it would have some capacity to wash dishes. The same holds for legal systems. Unified sets of laws that are very defective at doing what laws are supposed to may nonetheless count as paradigm legal systems. This follows from the fact that to *aim* at something does not require *succeeding* at it.

In his last reflections on this problem, Hart seems no longer to think that law need even aim at survival. He now joins Max Weber and Hans Kelsen, who deny that law has a constitutive aim of any kind. (As I explain in Chapter 2, Kelsen says 'law is a means, a specific social means, not an end'.[32]) Hart writes, 'I think it quite vain to seek any more specific purpose which law as such serves beyond providing guides to human conduct and standards of criticism of such conduct' (249). No mention of survival here. Perhaps Hart is not withdrawing his earlier claim, however. Perhaps he is denying that law can be *identified* by any such aims—there is no purpose that is both universal among and unique to legal systems. Law may have the aim of promoting survival; it may do so by making and supervising rules. Neither distinguish law from things like custom, religion, and morality; on the contrary, they are shared features.

4.2 Legal Validity and Moral Principles

The third point of contact between law and morality is different. Hart allows that while moral principles are not necessarily a source of law, they could be, provided they were so authorized by things that *are* a source of law. Thus, Hart thinks that, while the rule of recognition is necessarily a social construction, the criteria it deploys need not be. He does not think that moral principles are law because they are valuable principles or because they justify existing law. But he thinks they can become law if, one way or another, someone puts them into the law.

---

[32] Hans Kelsen, *General Theory of Law and State* (A. Wedberg trs., Harvard University Press, 1949) 20.

Here Hart takes a stand on one of two ways of interpreting the constructivist thesis, in favour of what is often called 'inclusive' legal positivism which maintains that the sources of law *can include* principles of ideal morality, and against 'exclusive' legal positivism, according to which they cannot.[33] His route to this conclusion is hard to retrace, no doubt because, when he wrote the main text, these alternatives were not yet distinguished. Nonetheless, his unambiguous view in the Postscript is that legal validity need not be purely a matter of a norm's 'pedigree', that is, features 'concerned only with the manner in which laws are adopted or created by legal institutions and not with their content . . .' (246)[34] Instead, legal validity *could* turn on moral propriety—if positive law requires that.

The point is much debated, and we need not decide the issue here.[35] But it is worth clearing up one confusion Hart adds to the debate. The question whether the criteria in the rule of recognition can include moral principles is not the same as the question whether these criteria are matters of 'pedigree'. There are two possible contrasts with pedigree. There is one contrast with *content* and a different contrast with *morality*. If a federal law is invalid because it trenches on an exclusive provincial jurisdiction in education, that is a non-pedigree matter of content ('education'). If it is invalid because it is unjust, that is a non-pedigree matter of morality.[36] But we also need to ask the dynamic question of how it came to be that legal validity got conditioned on respecting a substantive domain or conforming to certain values in the first

---

[33] Hart calls his position 'soft' positivism, but 'inclusive' positivism is more common and perspicuous since the theory holds that law *includes* anything to which law refers. The term is due to Wil Waluchow: W. J. Waluchow, *Inclusive Legal Positivism* (Oxford University Press, 1994).

[34] The pedigree metaphor was introduced by Dworkin, *Taking Rights Seriously*, 17. It appears nowhere in *The Concept of Law* except in Hart's reply to Dworkin, where Hart rejects the characterization.

[35] The theory is defended by W. J. Waluchow, *Inclusive Legal Positivism* (Oxford University Press, 1994), and by Jules Coleman, *The Practice of Principle: In Defence of a Pragmatist Approach to Legal Theory* (Oxford University Press, 2001). It is criticized by Joseph Raz, *Ethics in the Public Domain: Essays in the Morality of Law and Politics* (Oxford University Press, 1994), chaps 9 and 10; Scott Shapiro, 'On Hart's Way Out' (1998) 4 *Legal Theory* 469; and Leslie Green and Thomas Adams, 'Legal Positivism', in Edward N. Zalta ed., *The Stanford Encyclopedia of Philosophy* (Winter 2019 edn) <https://plato.stanford.edu/archives/win2019/entries/legal-positivism/>. For scrutiny of the literature, see Kenneth Eimar Himma, 'Inclusive Legal Positivism', in J. L. Coleman et al. eds, *The Oxford Handbook of Jurisprudence and Philosophy of Law* (Oxford University Press, 2012) chap. 4.

[36] We need to be cautious. In law there are technical homonyms of many moral terms, including 'justice', 'equality', and 'discrimination'. These gradually get even more technical through judicial interpretation, so that even an express reference to justice in a constitution may refer only to justice-as-the-law-sees-it, defined by some multi-pronged test. That is source-based.

place. Positivists hold that *that* is a matter of history. Inclusive positivists hold that morality bears on law because history *made* morality bear on it.

That seems to suggest that morality could properly find a role in legal argument and decision only if it were invited in. Hart raises the possibility of an invitation via the ultimate criteria of validity.[37] But is any invitation needed?[38] No one thinks judges can rely on grammar or arithmetic only if the law specially invites those principles in. Perhaps no invitation is needed for morality either and, like many other standards, it is operative in court unless ousted by the law. If so, Hart is proposing a solution to a problem that does not exist.

The closest Hart comes to an argument on this point is the following. He considers a hypothetical constitution that makes complete moral propriety a test for law. Nothing is to count as law if it is *in any way* wrong, inhumane, unjust, unfair, etc. He says there would be nothing illogical about this. '[T]he objection to this extraordinary arrangement would not be 'logic' but the gross indeterminacy of such criteria of legal validity. Constitutions do not invite trouble by taking this form.'[39] If 'logic' includes conceptual argument, however, there may be such an objection. Joseph Raz argues that this would not merely be inviting trouble, it would be incompatible with law being capable of having the authority it claims.[40] Hart could not consider an argument that did not exist when he wrote the book. But by the time he wrote the Postscript, elements of it were known. Perhaps the reason he never completed the second part of the Postscript is that he did not know how to handle them.[41]

5. Choosing Theories

The final topic I want to explore is methodological. I will say no more about the idea for which Hart is most famous, namely, that law (and other social institutions) must be described in a way that incorporates, or explains, the

---

[37] Tony Honoré thinks the invitation comes through the moral claims that law makes. See his 'The Necessary Connection between Law and Morality' (2002) 22 *Oxford Journal of Legal Studies* 489. This suggests that an institution that made no moral claims would not have to answer to moral argument. Many institutions would welcome that defence: markets, robber gangs, etc.
[38] See Joseph Raz, *Between Authority and Interpretation: On the Theory of Law and Practical Reason* (Oxford University Press, 2009) chap. 7.
[39] H. L. A. Hart, *Essays in Jurisprudence and Philosophy* (Oxford University Press, 1982) 361.
[40] Joseph Raz, *The Morality of Freedom* (Oxford University Press, 1986) chap. 2; Raz, *Ethics in the Public Domain*, chap. 10; and Raz, Between Authority and Interpretation, chap. 5.
[41] But see Hart's remarks on Raz in *Essays on Bentham* (Oxford University Press, 1982) chap. 6.

'internal point of view' of those who live and work with the law. That idea goes back to Weber, Dilthey, and even Vico, and it has found wide favour. More controversial is a different lesson some draw from Hart: that we should choose a theory of law, maybe even 'our concept' of law, on moral grounds. I set out general doubts about the notion of 'choosing concepts' of law in the Introduction to this book. Does Hartian jurisprudence depend on such a choice?

In the Postscript, Hart tries to revise (or clarify) his views about law and morality in answer to Dworkin's charge of pedigree-ism. But he reasserts his view that general jurisprudence can be, and should be, 'descriptive'. This does not deny that descriptions presuppose views about what is important, significant, or worth mentioning about their objects.[42] It presumes that it is possible to explain law without, in that explanation, making any moral assessment of any features of legal systems. Why stand firm here? Why not at least concede that, even if the criteria for identifying law are themselves factual, our best reasons for adopting *that theory* are moral, a view sometimes called 'normative positivism'.[43] Contrary to the imagining of many writers, Hart never affirms that.

He does, in a few pages, assert some advantages for moral decision-making of what he calls the 'broad' concept of law, one that acknowledges unjust, unreasonable, or pointless laws as fully fledged laws. Some theorists take this as a proposal that we should create or endorse a legal theory on the grounds of its moral value. That could be interpreted various ways: the moral value of vaunting the theory in scholarly work, or promoting it in public, or trying to get the legislature or courts to create or interpret laws in line with it. In all such pragmatic arguments we are hamstrung by a lack of reliable knowledge of the facts, most importantly, knowledge of how people will react to our endorsing our legal theory on moral grounds. Are we to adopt a noble lie, telling people it is *true* that law is a matter of social fact, irrespective of the moral value of asserting *that*? But then we will need to consider the moral value, and risks, in that sort of lie. And so on. None of this has ever been

---

[42] Julie Dickson, *Evaluation and Legal Theory* (Hart Publishing, 2001).
[43] For a sample of the sort of doctrines I have in mind, drawing in varying degrees on Hart's own arguments, see Neil MacCormick, 'A Moralistic Case for A-Moralistic Law' (1985) 20 *Valparaiso Law Review* 1; Thomas Campbell, *The Legal Theory of Ethical Positivism* (Dartmouth, 1996); Jeremy Waldron, 'Normative (or Ethical) Positivism', in Jules L. Coleman ed., *Hart's Postscript: Essays on the Postscript to the Concept of Law* (Oxford University Press, 2001); and Liam Murphy, 'The Political Question about the Concept of Law' in ibid.

specified with enough precision, or backed by enough evidence, to warrant confidence.

How did this idea get associated with Hart's theory? If it represents his view, why does he never appeal to it in his own defence in the Postscript's discussion of evaluation in legal theory? In passing he repeats his claim that theoretical clarity is a necessary preliminary to moral deliberation, but that says nothing about what clarity is or how it is achieved. Legal theory may need to describe values and the fact that some people endorse them, but 'Description may still be description, even when what is described is an evaluation'.[44] No 'normative positivism' here.

The only proof-text for this doctrine is one sentence in Chapter IX of *The Concept of Law* which, in honour of how often it gets cited, I shall call *The Sentence*. Its context is this: Hart is trying to tackle the claims of Gustav Radbruch and others who think that legal positivism, whatever its merits, is politically dangerous. Having lived through Nazism, Radbruch came to think its rise was caused by a reverse *trahison des clercs*, and that had German legal theory only been *more* moralistic and *less* dispassionate the Germans would have been better immunized against fascism. On this view, a 'narrow' concept of law, one that excludes evil laws from the category of full-blooded laws, is supposedly safer than the positivists' 'broad' concept, which puts good laws and evil laws in the same column conceptually (though not, of course, morally). After exposition and clarification, we get *The Sentence*: 'If we are to make a reasoned choice between these concepts, it must be because one is superior to the other in the way in which it will assist our theoretical inquiries, or advance and clarify our moral deliberations, or both' (209). Hart's answer is 'both': the broad concept of law is theoretically correct and, contrary to the supposition of Radbruchites, morally benign.

Let us begin with an elementary point. Hart never says the moral hygiene argument is needed to complete his case that something is law if and only if it satisfies the sort of social tests he identifies. Indeed, in his roughly contemporaneous Harry Camp lectures (1962), he frames the issue without even mentioning the possibility that moral considerations could play a role in the analysis of law:

[T]oo little has been said about the criteria for judging the adequacy of a definition of law. Should such a definition state what, if anything, the plain

---

[44] Hart, *Essays in Jurisprudence and Philosophy*, 241.

man intends to convey when he uses the expressions 'law' or 'legal system'? Or should it rather aim to provide, by marking off certain social phenomena from others, a classification useful or illuminating for theoretical purposes?[45]

These are the only options that are mooted. The question of adequacy does not involve any choice between theories that show law as it is versus theories that improve moral deliberation. It is a choice between 'definitions' based in *ordinary language* and those based in *theoretical utility*. Hart favours the latter, and so insists in *The Concept of Law*: 'we cannot grapple adequately with this issue if we see it as one concerning the proprieties of linguistic usage' (209). Apart from requiring attention to the 'internal point of view', that is the only explicit methodological advice Hart has for us: linguistic analysis can bear 'only on a relatively small and unimportant part of the most famous and controversial theories of law'.[46] For jurisprudence to leave everything as it is, and merely remind us of 'the existing conventions governing the use of the words "law" and "legal system" is . . . useless'.[47] *The Sentence* thus reiterates Hart's trademark view that substantive problems of jurisprudence cannot be resolved by lexicography or even by stand-alone techniques drawn from 'ordinary language' philosophy.

Hart says Radbruch began as a muddled legal positivist then, convinced of the dangers of his own view, revised his theory of law and recommended others do the same. So, *The Sentence* is a *reply* to a particular case for conceptual reform. It is not a free-standing argument for a concept of law. Compare proposals to reform the concept of 'sex'. It is sometimes alleged that 'sex' inspires false binary thinking; it effaces and oppresses non-binary and trans people; it entrenches the power of men over women—so we need a more supple, more social, classification of human bodies, or maybe none at all. To such pleas for reform two sorts of response are possible. Type (A) concedes that if sex were malign, we should reform it but denies its malignity: 'Reform is not necessary: the concept of "sex" does not bring those hazards. "Gender" does; but let's not confuse sex and gender.' Type (B) denies that the malign connotations of 'sex' in ordinary language are sufficient reason to reform the concept: 'Sex is a real distinction with scientific value and, in humans,

---

[45] H. L. A. Hart, *Law, Liberty and Morality* (Stanford University Press, 1963) 2–3.
[46] Ibid., 4.
[47] Ibid., 5. How *The Concept of Law* got its reputation as one of the bravura performances of Oxford linguistic philosophy is, in light of these passages and the whole structure of the book, a mystery. Perhaps it was the title.

one that picks out morally salient capacities. We need it as it is.' In reply to Radbruch, Hart offers both an (A)-type and a (B)-type argument. The (A)-type argument even gilds the lily: Hart says not only is the Radbruchite wrong to think legal positivism is malignant, it is also morally *superior*! Hart's (B)-type case is that legal positivism is correct and theoretically useful even if it deviates from ordinary usage. He does think a correct understanding of law is a better foundation for moral deliberation than a confused one. He does not think it correct *because* it is morally useful. The point of the (A)-type argument is to deflect a conceptual reformist's confused plea, but when such a plea is not at issue, as it is not in the Harry Camp lectures, (A) drops out of sight and the action is about (B).[48]

This whole discussion is but one of Hart's many attempts to find a kernel of good sense in a case that he judges to be flawed. That sort of charity pervades *The Concept of Law* and it is a virtue all the more conspicuous now that so much legal theory is laden with shouty put-downs and empty boasts. Hart's reading of Radbruch as misguided reformer is the best he can do for Radbruch. Maybe he should have tried harder. Still, it is ironic that Hart's effort at a charitable interpretation of someone *else's* theory should be held up as evidence that he did not really endorse his *own* theory.

In the end, Hart is sceptical of the power of *any* argument in jurisprudence as a prophylactic against evil: 'So long as human beings can gain sufficient co-operation from some to enable them to dominate others, they will use the forms of law as one of their instruments' (210). No theory of law is going to stop them using law if they can. Law is a dangerous instrument and, although jurisprudence can help us understand why it is, jurisprudence cannot make law any safer. Whether that is bleak or merely realistic, it is not the view of someone who thinks legal philosophers can improve the world by improving the concept of law. I am sure Hart is right about that.

---

[48] If I am correct and (A) is only a response to a misguided proposal for conceptual reform, then why does (B) take just sixteen lines of text (209–10) whereas (A) runs on for eighty lines (210–12)? Doesn't this prove that Hart thinks the moral hygiene argument is a key part of his positive case? It does not. The demonstration that law has the structure and content he defends does *not* take place on page 209. *It takes place over the preceding 208 pages.* By the end of Chapter IX, the case for legal positivism is complete, apart from two residual issues—explaining law's relations to morality, then, in Chapter X, testing how far the theory helps us understand international law. Moreover, the brief discussion at 209 involves just one restricted context, what Hart refers to as a 'pathology' of a legal system when, 'after revolution or major upheavals', the connection to the old rule of recognition is broken (208). It does not apply to non-pathological cases of law.

2
Law as a Means

1. An Instrumentalist Thesis

No one doubts that individual laws often serve as means to promote or secure certain ends. The rule against perpetuities is a means of setting temporal limitations on the grant of an estate. Bundles of laws working through statutes or fields of doctrine are also means to ends, including ends that are, under other descriptions, means to further ends. Enacting the Fewer School Boards Act,[1] for example, was intended as a means to the end of reducing the number of Ontario's school boards, which was in turn intended as a means of uncoupling education from property tax, which was intended as a means of asserting financial discipline (and other sorts of discipline) over local schools, which the government of the day considered a desirable end. Examples like that make the instrumentality of laws sound like a top-down affair. Just as often it is bottom-up. It is not only legislatures and courts but also individuals who use laws as means to their ends. Leona Helmsley wanted her dog to be adequately provided for after her own death. So she left it US$12 million in trust, through the helpful instrumentality of the laws of New York State. And every day lots of sensible people make wills, contracts, and powers of attorney; they marry, sue, and incorporate, all using the special means that laws provide. None of this is remotely controversial.

The same cannot be said of the following thesis: '[L]aw is a means, a specific social means, not an end.'[2] In fact, few propositions in general jurisprudence are as controversial as that one. For Kelsen is not just saying that particular laws are instruments for securing collective or individual ends. He is saying that this is true of law itself: it is part of its specific nature, of how we identify law. And he goes further: law can only be identified as a means of a

---

[1] Fewer School Boards Act, SO 1997, c. 3.
[2] Hans Kelsen, *General Theory of Law and State* (A. Wedberg trs, Harvard University Press, 1949) 20.

The Germ of Justice. Leslie Green, Oxford University Press. © Leslie Green 2023.
DOI: 10.1093/oso/9780192886941.003.0003

special sort, and not as an end of any sort. I am going to call that the instrumentalist thesis about law, and I am going to defend a qualified version of it here.

Lon Fuller considered some such thesis to lie at the core of his disputes with H. L. A. Hart (and others) over the nature of law. Fuller writes, 'A statute is obviously a purposive thing, serving some end or congeries of related ends. What is objected to [by Hart] is not the assignment of purposes to particular laws, but to law as a whole.'[3] And if law does have a purpose 'as a whole', then why not organize our theories of law around that purpose, instead of focusing so much on the means, procedures, and structures characteristic of legal systems? Is the instrumentalist not putting the cart before the horse?

Hart, on the other hand, agrees with Kelsen: we cannot assign significant ends or purposes to law 'as a whole'.[4] Undeniably, there are things that law necessarily does. For example, law provides institutions that authenticate and apply norms. But that sort of thing is not law's end in Fuller's sense—it is the means by which law goes about its (various) ends. Hart thought law's means fell into two broad classes: those that are 'means of social control', and those that provide individuals with 'facilities for the realization of wishes and choices'.[5] Law does both through the creation, recognition, and application of rules. Other social institutions pursue law's ends by other means, for example by creating economic incentives to which people are likely to respond, by altering the physical environment to change their feasible options, or by assassinating them before they can interfere with the government's plans. Law is distinguished from these institutions less by what it does than by how it does it: law is less a functional kind than it is a modal kind.[6]

This is not the only idea about law that has ever been called 'instrumentalist'. Brian Tamanaha has a laundry list of others, covering most of the

---

[3] Lon L. Fuller, *The Morality of Law* (rev. edn, Yale University Press, 1969) 146.
[4] H. L. A. Hart, *The Concept of Law* (3rd edn, Penelope A. Bulloch and Joseph Raz, eds; Leslie Green, intro, Oxford University Press, 2012) 248–50; see also the review essay, Lon L. Fuller, 'The Morality of Law', in H. L. A. Hart, *Essays in Jurisprudence and Philosophy* (Oxford University Press, 1983) 343–64.
[5] H. L. A. Hart, 'Positivism and the Separation of Law and Morals' (1958) 71 *Harvard Law Review* 600, 604.
[6] I am not claiming an exclusive distinction here. If L is distinguished by the fact that it φ-s by χ-ing, then it is a mixed kind. I am claiming an explanatory priority for the modalities in identifying legal systems: law and other social institutions all φ, but among the φ-ers, law is the institution that φ-s *by χ-ing*.

alleged sins of the American legal system.[7] He complains that, in the United States, law is widely practiced with indifference to the social good, judges reason from the bottom line up, lawyers care more for wealth and power than for humanity or justice, 'cause lawyering' corrupts legality, and so on. What links this miscellany is the alleged fact that in the United States, 'law is widely viewed as an empty vessel to be filled as desired, and to be manipulated, invoked, and utilized in the furtherance of ends'.[8] That view is obviously not the thesis advanced by instrumentalists like Kelsen or Hart. And what makes it repugnant has little to do with the idea that law is a means to an end, and much to do with the alleged popularity of the view that law may be 'filled as desired', and the chilling hint that any sort of manipulation in service of such desires would be just fine. Those attitudes do not reflect any thesis in general jurisprudence; they betoken a vice, one that in plain speech is usually called selfishness.

Other attitudes, not relevant here but sometimes called 'instrumentalist', involve a view, not about law, but about jurisprudence. This view holds that a theory of law should be oriented, not to the truth about law, but to the promotion of socially useful ends. In Chapter 1 I explained why that view cannot be attributed to Hart. But there are strains of that idea in Fuller, who thinks that jurisprudence should above all provide 'direction posts for the application of human energies'.[9] If that is the game, instrumentalism begins with a handicap. As publicity material, 'Law is a means!' would flop. It would not inspire lawyers or judges; it would not awaken the student who already finds law boring enough without leaden interventions by legal philosophers. However, it is not the job of general jurisprudence to inspire; its job is to produce a correct (philosophical) explanation of the nature of law.

In this part of that task, I approach the work as follows. First, I argue that the instrumentalist thesis, though controversial, is a rendering of a view of law that is *not* so controversial. That gets instrumentalism on the table as a candidate interpretation of that view. Then, I try to clear the leading falsehoods and fallacies standing in the way of accepting the instrumentalist interpretation. Naturally, this approach cannot amount to demonstrative proof. But it may make a view that many intuitively accept more perspicuous, more plausible, and more secure.

---

[7] Brian Z Tamanaha, *Law as a Means to an End: Threat to the Rule of Law* (Cambridge University Press, 2006) 1.
[8] Ibid.
[9] Ibid., 632.

2. The Instrumentalist View

Law is not a surd feature of the universe, like the speed of light. Law belongs to the meaningful world of ends and means. By 'meaningful' I refer to the fact that we can make sense of a lot of human action by understanding it as adopting means to achieve certain ends in light of the situation as the agents see it. The view of law as primarily a matter of means to ends is the foundation of Jeremy Bentham's entire legal philosophy. It is elaborated, crudely and at length, in Rudolf von Ihering's late works.[10] It structures Max Weber's analysis of the state and law, and in a different way, Karl Marx's theory of law. It is implicit in H. L. A. Hart's idea that law is an institutionalized system of social rules aimed at securing some basic social goods, for at least some people. And it is explicit in Joseph Raz's observation that, 'The law is not just a fact of life. It is a form of social organization which should be used properly and for the proper ends', an expression of what he calls 'an instrumental conception of law'.[11]

Now, those names might lead you to suspect that only positivists and fellow travellers adopt an instrumental conception of law. Nothing could be further from the truth. There is no other way to understand Aquinas, who says, 'A law, properly speaking, regards first and foremost the order to the common good'.[12] Law is oriented to that good. Law also has other species-typical features: it is a general kind of order, issued by an authoritative source, and promulgated to its subjects. But for Aquinas, these features are all explained by the fact that law is a means in the service of an overarching end:

> Whenever a thing is for an end, its form must be determined proportionately to that end; as the form of a saw is such as to be suitable for cutting. Again, everything that is ruled and measured must have a form proportionate to its rule and measure. Now both these conditions are verified of human law: since it is both something ordained to an end; and is a rule or measure ruled or measured by a higher measure.[13]

---

[10] Rudolf von Ihering, *Law as a Means to an End* (I. Husik trs, Macmillan, 1921; [1st edn, 1877–83, 2 vols]).
[11] Joseph Raz, *The Authority of Law* (Oxford University Press, 1979) 226; and Joseph Raz, *Between Authority and Interpretation* (Oxford University Press, 2009) 102–6.
[12] Thomas Aquinas, *Suma Theologica* (Fathers of the English Dominican Province trs, Benziger Brothers, 1947) vol 1, Pt I-II, Q 90, art. 3, 9.
[13] Ibid., Pt I-II, Q 95, art. 3, 1015.

Aquinas thus parts company with the instrumental *thesis* set out in Section 1, which denies that law is 'for an end'; but he just as obviously embraces an instrumental *conception* of law. One cannot have teleology without *teloi*, and in law the relevant ends are brought about through means to which Aquinas paid careful attention. The false association between an instrumental conception of law and legal positivism—the thesis that all law is positive law, all law is an artefact—flows from the mistaken assumption that nothing can be an instrument unless it is created as an artefact. Not so. An instrument may be an *objet trouvé*, a naturally chipped piece of flint, made by no one, but picked up and put to some use. (Customary law is a bit like that.) And even if an artefactual rule may be measured by a 'higher measure' that is not itself an artefact, the artefactual rule nonetheless remains a means of directing and assessing conduct.

Teleological instrumentalism of Aquinas' sort lives on in some contemporary theories of law. It is adopted by Fuller, who, while agreeing with Hart that law is 'the enterprise of subjecting human conduct to the governance of rules',[14] thinks Hart misses the upshot that law must therefore be a 'purposeful enterprise'.[15] Now, 'purposes' and 'enterprises' may have nuances absent from 'ends' and 'means', and Fuller often prefers the former terms in order to emphasize the special features of his own brand of legal instrumentalism. But at other times he is just as happy to speak plainly. Of his famous desiderata of legality—the 'inner morality' of law—Fuller simply says, 'All of them are means toward a single end'.[16] Law, on Fuller's account, is an institution on a mission. It is a set of means to a particular end.

All these writers share what I am calling an instrumental conception of law. What divides them is (inter alia) the instrumental thesis about law, that is, the claim that law can only be identified by focusing on its species-typical means. But what are law's means, and how do they relate to anyone's ends? We are going to need some abstract, but necessary, preliminaries about instruments and values.

3. Means, Ends, and Instruments

Kelsen says that law is a means, not an end. The hard part is the second, negative, proposition: law is not an end. We cannot decide whether that is false

---

[14] Fuller, *The Morality of Law*, 74.
[15] Ibid., 145.
[16] Ibid., 104.

unless we have some grasp of how it could be true. But the affirmative claim is no less puzzling: What would it take for law itself to be 'an end'? Whose end?

The creation of particular laws is among the ends of law, in both legislation and adjudication. So laws can be ends. One might also make it one's end to establish legal systems where there are none, or to improve or protect them where they already exist. But that does not show that law is an end; it shows that law-establishing and law-protecting can be ends, which hardly seems controversial. Could Kelsen be suggesting that we can understand law without reference to any ends? Surely not. He repeatedly affirms that law is a means; but in the context 'means' is a relational term, and the relevant relata are means and ends (which is why we speak of a 'means-ends relation'). If law is a means at all, there must be some ends to which it is, or is taken to be, or could become, a means.

A more promising interpretation is this: law's means are more important in identifying law among other social institutions than are law's ends. Law has various ends and law should serve good ends. Perhaps law should serve good ends as part of the nature of law. But what makes law special are the means by which it serves those ends. Law's ends are not distinctive: there are no ends universal among or unique to all legal systems, no ends that unify and explain all features of its means. This helps interpret Kelsen's cryptic remark that 'legal norms may have any kind of content'.[17] Kelsen does not mean that a law could be a rock or a slug. Indeed, he asserts that every law has special features that might naturally be called the 'content' of law (e.g. delicts and sanctions). His point is this: the same means that gave us the Fewer School Boards Act could also have given us a More School Boards Act, or a School Boards (Restoration) Act, and all of these Acts would have been law, and they would have been law in virtue of the means by which they were produced, rather than the character of the ends at which they were aimed. But isn't that legal positivism after all? No. To get positivism we need to add at least the proposition that the ultimate law-producing means are all artefacts. We have not added that.

What, then, of 'means'? To the extent that there is any difference between means and instruments, the instrumentalist thesis interprets law as an instrument. It would be intelligible, if unidiomatic, to say, 'Drawing an equilateral triangle is a means of drawing an equiangular triangle'. After all, to do the second, you need only do the first, and having done the first, you have an

---

[17] Kelsen, *General Theory of Law and State*, 113. Could this be the thought that gets garbled in Tamanaha's remark about seeing law as an 'empty vessel'?

MEANS, ENDS, AND INSTRUMENTS   63

iron-clad guarantee that you have achieved the second. I do not think that is a means in the instrumentalists' sense. The instruments with which one might draw an equiangular triangle include things like protractors and pencils, not equilateral triangles. This has nothing to do with the concreteness of the former. Many instruments are abstract objects, including mnemonic devices, truth-tables, and, of special interest to jurisprudence, norms and systems of norms. What is important is that these instruments are distinct from the ends to which they are put, are capable of being brought under intentional control, and can be assessed as being more or less well adapted to produce their ends.

This explains why there is often a close relationship between L being instrumental to E and L being causally efficacious in helping to bring about E. The role of causal efficacy tempted some, including Weber, to suppose that instrumental reasoning, in law or elsewhere, is somehow more objective or scientific than is any reasoning about value. That could at best be true of the causal premises in instrumental reasoning. It is not true of all the other premises or of the conclusions. We reason: (1) L most effectively produces E, and we enthymematically conclude, (3) someone ought to adopt L. But there is a suppressed premise (2): E is worth producing. Neither (2) nor (3) are 'objective' or 'scientific' in any way that would have impressed Weber. That is evident with respect to (2), since it is about what values merit pursuit; but it is also true of (3), since that is a deontic statement expressing what someone ought to do.

This is worth mentioning because it highlights a central issue about instrumental value. Some find it tempting to say that if L* is better able to produce E than is L', then L* has greater instrumental value than L', on the ground that it gives more E-bang for one's L-buck. But nothing has instrumental value that lacks value. Something inherits its instrumental value from the end to which it is a means. If that end is worthless, then it has no value to pass on to L. So L* may be more effective than L' in producing E and yet be utterly valueless. This sounds odd only because it can be useful to speak of L* *as if* it had instrumental value, prescinding from any assessment of its ends. That is how we often talk about people's reasoning when we are uncommitted to, or uncertain about, the value of the ends they pursue. It is how the bureaucrat or economist or democrat might speak when considering how to attain an end taken as 'given' by the government, the client, or the people.

Kelsen is aware of this issue, but mistakenly thinks it shows that all effective means have 'relative' value: if L efficiently produces E, then L has some positive value, relative to E.[18] Now, relative values certainly exist. American dollars have relative value, for their value as a medium of exchange or store of value varies in relation to the demand for other currencies. But the fact that L stands in a means-end relationship to some E does not show anything about L's value. What gives dollars their value is their use as a medium of exchange or store of value, which media and stores are themselves valuable, and therefore worth pursuing as (intermediate) ends. In contrast, if E is worthless (e.g. the satisfaction of a desire for a saucer of mud, for no further reason),[19] then L does not get relative value from being a means to E, for E has no value to contribute. The most efficient pump draws no water from an empty well.

Not all ends are instrumental. On plausible assumptions about value, chains of instrumental reasoning must ultimately bottom in ends that are not of value only as means to further ends. I shall follow traditional usage and say that non-instrumental ends are intrinsically valuable. Unfortunately, this term is also in use to pick out ends that are absolutely, unconditionally, or inexplicably valuable. I want to leave open the possibility that intrinsic values may be relative to time and place and, in that sense, not absolute, and also the possibility that even intrinsic values are liable to further philosophical explanation. It is also useful to note one more distinction within the realm of intrinsic value. I am going to call it the difference between dependent and free-standing values.[20] An intrinsic value is dependent if the explanation for why it is of value necessarily includes reference to the fact that it is of value to or for someone (or something) capable of appreciating the value that it has. A beautiful sunset is of intrinsic value because it is of value to people (or animals) that have the capacity to take sensual pleasure in its colours or to respond to it under the aspect of beauty. Doesn't that turn sunsets into instrumental values? No. The way in which sunsets are of value to their responders is not as something that can be brought under intentional control so as to produce more or less of the value in question. Sunsets are not instruments. We value them for what they contribute to our lives, not for what we can do or attain by 'using' them.

---

[18] Hans Kelsen, *Introduction to the Problems of Legal Theory: A Translation of the first edition of the Reine Rechstlehre or Pure Theory of Law* (B. L. Paulson and S. L. Paulson trs, Oxford University Press, 1992 [1st edn 1934]) 16. And compare Kelsen, *General Theory of Law and State*, 436.
[19] I adapt Elizabeth Anscombe's famous example, in *Intention* (2nd edn, Blackwell, 1966; 1st edn 1963) 70–1. (But note that *pleasure* derived from satisfaction of this desire could be a further reason.)
[20] For a similar division, though using a different terminology and to a different purpose, see Joseph Raz, *Value, Respect, and Attachment* (Oxford University Press, 2001), which influenced my thinking here.

Any things whose intrinsic value is not explained in that sort of way (i.e. by the fact that they are of value to or for an appreciating subject) I shall call 'free-standing'. As such, they would be of value, not as means to some end, like income, and not of value to or for someone or other, like sunsets. They would be of value for their own sake, in themselves. This last idea is very difficult to elucidate, though many, including Kant, think it easy to exemplify: persons have that sort of value. Someone who is not only of no use to anyone or for anything, and who is not loved, admired, or even considered by anyone, even they have value in themselves. Kant called such things 'ends in themselves'.

Into these murky waters I wade no further. I do not think that law is or could be an 'end in itself', nor am I aware of any opponent of the instrumentalist thesis who advances the contrary view. My focus will therefore be on law's instrumental or dependent-intrinsic value, and on how law's means stand in relation to such values.

4. Five Fallacies about Instrumentalism

As I said, the instrumentalist thesis is one interpretation of a commonplace conception of law, a view shared by philosophers as different as Aquinas and Bentham. But it is an interpretation that has become so encrusted with errors and fallacies that it can be difficult to see the thesis for what it is. It can help to remove them.

Kelsen is responsible for some of these. In the first edition of the *Pure Theory of Law* he elaborated the instrumentalist thesis in this way: 'The law is a coercive apparatus having in and of itself no political or ethical value, a coercive apparatus whose value depends, rather, on ends that transcend the law qua means.'[21] The elaboration spins out two further claims. The first is that law is not only a means, but a *coercive* means. The second is that, because law is a means, it can have no moral or political value 'in and of itself'.

Both elaborations are errors. It is not necessary here to review the arguments establishing that the use of coercive force is neither essential nor unique to law. Much of that work has been done for us, and I will do some

---

[21] Kelsen, *Introduction to the Problems of Legal Theory*, 31.

more in Chapter 13.[22] But Kelsen's second elaboration, that law has 'in and of itself no political or ethical value' has rarely come under scrutiny.

Assume law is (or can be) a means to valuable ends, so law has (or can have) instrumental value. Why does that commit us to denying that law can have non-instrumental value? Consider the general claim:

(F1) If law is an instrument, then it is a mere instrument and can have no non-instrumental value.

As it stands, (F1) is a plain non-sequitur; yet it turns up fairly often in legal and political philosophy. John McTaggart criticized the idea that the state might have non-instrumental value, and there is no reason to think he would have spared (or distinguished) its legal system. In a warning to his fellow idealists who, he feared, were stumbling down the path to state-worship, McTaggart wrote:

[W]hatever activity it is desirable for the State to have, it will only be desirable as a means . . . Compared with worship of the State, zoolatry is rational and dignified. A bull or crocodile may not have much intrinsic value, but it has some, for it is a conscious being. The State has none. It would be as reasonable to worship a sewage pipe, which also possesses considerable value as a means.[23]

Fine mockery; and in its day possibly therapeutic. But the argument does not accomplish much without the implied assumption that only conscious beings can have intrinsic value. Possibly McTaggart is concerned to show that the state does not merit worship. Worship, however, is a very special way of engaging with things of intrinsic value. Many things that are not worship-worthy are nonetheless of immense intrinsic value: Ben Nevis, the great redwoods, the Goldberg Variations, Guernica.[24]

Mountains, forests, and works of art are not instruments, so although they help us understand intrinsic value they do not test (F1). But other things are and do. The Victoria and Albert Museum has an eighteenth-century flute

---

[22] See Hart, *Concept of Law*, 26–42; Fuller, *The Morality of Law*, 106–11; Joseph Raz, *Practical Reason and Norms* (Oxford University Press, 1999) 154–62; John Finnis, *Natural Law and Natural Rights* (Oxford University Press, 1980) 266–70, 325–32.

[23] J. M. E. McTaggart, 'The Individualism of Value' in his *Philosophical Studies* (SV Keeling, ed, Edward Arnold, London, 1934) 109.

[24] Or if their value merits some kind of worship, it is not the kind that worries McTaggart.

made by Peter Bressan.[25] New, it was a superb instrument, of such good acoustical design that copies are still made and played today. Yet none of that explains why Bressan's flute is under glass in the museum. That has to do with a different aspect of its value. The Bressan flute is a splendid example of the woodturner's craft. Its ebony is sectioned by elegantly proportioned silver bands, and into the wood the maker insinuated, in tiny hand-cut channels, strands of silver wire, achieving the effect of a delicate engraving on the wood's surface. The Bressan flute is certainly an instrument; that was (and remains) its primary role in human culture. But it is no mere instrument; for it has further value that cannot be explained by the fact that it can be played easily and in tune.

Could (F1) be false in general yet true of law? I doubt that law has aesthetic value, though I have heard proud draftspersons speak as if their work does, and some civilians and code-enthusiasts revere the orderly arrangement of legal materials as if it shares the spare beauty of Wittgenstein's *Tractatus*. Those attitudes seem misplaced, but perhaps that betrays my own insensitivities: if a proof can be elegant, why can't a legal system, abstractly considered, be beautiful? In any event, there are more interesting possibilities to consider.[26]

The first is genealogical. The law now in force did not spring into existence a moment ago. It developed and evolved over long periods, subject to many influences, bearing the imprint of crucial struggles in our history. Drawing-board constitutions and legal systems imagined by philosophers or law professors tend to remain on the drawing boards—when we are lucky. If they take life without causing catastrophe, it is usually because they have adapted to their societies in ways unanticipated, and perhaps unwelcomed, by their authors. Law's adaptability contributes to instrumental value, but the path-dependent adaptations can become constituent aspects of the society law regulates. When people are aware of these, they may become attached to them, and these attachments can have intrinsic value. That a legal system developed particular techniques, honoured particular values, vested authority in certain institutions—these are all culture- and path-dependent features of law that can give law value independent of its success at serving the ends it is meant to serve. Law's legacies, ceremonies, and formalities can be valued in themselves and can even merit honour. When things go well, the legal system

---

[25] Victoria and Albert Museum no. 452-1898.
[26] I do not contend that these are the only sorts of intrinsic value law may have.

itself will deserve respect, even when it includes rules that are sub-optimal and rulings that are off mark.

To forestall misunderstanding, I am only arguing, against (F1), that this much is possible, not that it is necessary. And I am not suggesting that intrinsic value in a legal system's history is its dominant value, or that it should always be honoured, efficiency be damned. That would be silly. But exaggerating genealogical value is not the only foolishness around. Holmes complains, 'It is revolting to have no better reason for a rule of law than that so it was laid down in the time of Henry IV'.[27] Does anyone really argue that a complete reason for applying an old rule lies in the fact that it is old? Most who emphasize the value of old rules have in mind two things: first, the fact that a rule is old may be a reason for thinking it serves us well—it has stood the test of time; secondly, to preserve it lends stability to law, and people rely on law being stable. Others go beyond any instrumental considerations. They are attached to their law and take pride in the fact that a still-existing rule was laid down in the time of Henry IV. This would have struck Holmes as repugnant if not nonsensical, for it recognizes values that are invisible given his self-imposed blinkers. In the continuation of that famous passage, the blinkers let in little light:

> for our purposes our only interest in the past is for the light it throws upon the present. I look forward to a time when the part played by history in the explanation of dogma shall be very small, and instead of ingenious research we shall spend our energy on a study of the ends sought to be attained and the reasons for desiring them.[28]

If one responds to history only 'for the light it throws upon the present', and if the only aspect of the present one cares about is the 'explanation of [legal] dogma', then a lot of good, and evil, in one's history is bound to go unnoticed. But there are reasons for caring about the history of law that are not (now) reasons for adopting that law, and there are reasons for concern about our law's history that have nothing to do with how we should write a treatise or advise a client. We have become attached to it and its ways; it has become part of our collective life. We can also value old books, old languages, and old houses, in part because of their antiquity. There are societies (not, regrettably,

---

[27] Oliver Wendell Holmes, Jr, 'The Path of the Law' (1897) 10 *Harvard Law Review* 469.
[28] Ibid., 474.

our own) that venerate old people. No one thinks this is best explained in terms of their use value.

The second sort of intrinsic value in law is a time-slice of the first. Law may have organic value as an aspect and expression of the society it serves.[29] Our legal system can be of value to our society because it is our law. It is easy to lose sight of this amid the flurry of cosmopolitan enthusiasms. And in open, mobile, pluralist societies, the word 'our' sounds unpleasantly nativist, essentialist, and exclusionary. Yet it need be none of those things. The law of an open and tolerant society is still its law,[30] and the involvement of such a society in creating and administering its law is something that is of value even when (instrumentally) better results might have been produced by different means, for example by rule of an imperial master. The extent to which law has organic value varies, as do the aspects of the legal system that express it. The English used to hold the common law in this sort of regard; in the United States it has mostly been reserved for the Constitution, in Québec for the Civil Code, and in Scotland for most aspects of the legal system that are not English.

Genealogical and organic values are not present in all legal systems (never mind all possible legal systems). They are contingent on aspects of political culture and on the content of the law. Nor, when present, are they the most important values those systems have—that would be to confuse intrinsic value with great value. But acknowledging law's non-instrumental value does require adjusting the instrumentalist thesis somewhat. We need to drop Kelsen's idea that law can have no value in and of itself. At the same time, however, it is improbable that law would have intrinsic value if it did not *also* have instrumental value—if it were an 'idle ceremonial'.[31] Law's (potential for) great instrumental value makes it a central political institution, and that centrality sustains its (dependent) intrinsic value for the society whose law it is. Needless to say, for the same reasons law has the potential for dependent, intrinsic dis-value. We can be ashamed of our law, humiliated by its place in our culture, or deeply alienated from it—attitudes that we may not have with respect to an equally bad legal system that is not our own.

---

[29] Cf. Raz, *The Authority of Law*, 258–60.
[30] And thus the openness of a legal system to foreign or international law does not show that it has ceased to be 'our law'.
[31] I borrow the phrase from David Hume, who uses it to describe what would become of justice when respect for its rules no longer served human ends: *An Enquiry Concerning the Principles of Morals* (C. W. Hendel ed., Liberal Arts Press, 1957) 15.

(F2) If law is an instrument, then law always has some instrumental value.

I turn now to an objection that comes from the other direction. We laid the ground for it above. Off-hand, (F2) seems out of place. Isn't the message of the instrumentalist thesis that whether law has any value, and what value it has, depends on the ends that law serves, and on how well it serves them? What instrumentalist would even moot a proposition like (F2)?

Kelsen comes close. He begins on the footing that a law exists only when it is valid: an invalid law is not a law that has the property of invalidity; it is no law at all: '[b]y the word "validity" we designate the specific existence of a norm'.[32] Then Kelsen asserts that a valid norm is not only one that belongs to the legal system, but also one that is binding (i.e. is such that its subjects ought to do as it requires) in virtue of its membership in the system. Clearly, he needs an escape route, not only because some actually existing laws are awful and ought to be disobeyed, but also because the *question whether* any law ought to be obeyed is a moral question, and on his account should therefore be excluded from a pure theory of law.

Here is Kelsen's (F2)-style escape. Whenever we use a norm (however stupid, inhumane, or unjust) to assess conduct as being in or out of conformity with that norm, we assess it from the point of view of one kind of value, namely, relative value. Hence, since law regulates its own creation, a valid law always has value relative to the higher norms that authorize, permit, or require its creation. This does not give law the absolute value that Kelsen thought natural lawyers impute to valid law: 'no absolute value is claimed for law. It is taken to have entirely hypothetical-relative validity.'[33] All the same, relative value is a kind of value, and Kelsen invokes it again when he explains the lawyer's notion of justice: 'judging something to be just is simply to express the relative value of conformity to a norm'.[34]

Hart is also guilty of this error, if only in the second degree. He never follows Kelsen in denying non-relative values, or in denying that moral values may conflict with law's demands and prevail over them. Still, a residue of (F2) infects his controversy with Fuller. When Fuller says the desiderata of legality

---

[32] Hans Kelsen, *Pure Theory of Law* (M. Knight ed., University of California Press, 1967) 10. This does not deny that some invalid laws and legal transactions are used *as if they were* valid. (For example, courts sometimes give people the benefits of a void marriage *as if it were valid*, on equitable or other grounds.)
[33] Kelsen, *General Theory of Law and State*, 436.
[34] Kelsen, *Introduction to the Problems of Legal Theory*, 16.

add up to an internal morality of law, Hart bridles. His first line of defence is concessive: Fuller's desiderata require rules, and when rules are steadfastly applied we may not have substantive justice, but we do have like cases being treated alike, and thus 'one essential element of the concept of justice'. 'So there is, in the very notion of law consisting of general rules, something which prevents us from treating it as if it is utterly neutral, without any necessary contact with moral principles.'[35] Some legal positivists grumble about that concession, since it does not sound like something a positivist should concede. But that is trivial compared to the fact that the concession is wrong. If the rules are bad enough, no justice of any kind, administrative, formal, or otherwise, results from their steadfast application. When an evil rule is not applied to someone covered by its terms, there is no one to whom an injustice is done, no one entitled to demand that the evil be perpetuated.[36] There is no injustice 'in the air'.

Hart's second line of defence is offence. He says Fuller moves illicitly from what 'ought' to be done relative to some standard or other, to what 'ought' to be done morally speaking: 'We say to our neighbour, "you ought not to lie", and that may certainly be a moral judgment, but we should remember that the baffled poisoner may say, "I ought to have given her a second dose".'[37] So when we think about the principles that 'ought' to be followed in order to regulate society by law, it does not follow that we are engaged in moral reasoning. Nor does it follow from the fact that we freely talk about how a law 'ought' to be interpreted, that we have found a moral basis to legal interpretation. There are lots of oughts. The 'inner morality of law' falls among the non-moral ones, alongside the oughts of cookery and carpentry.

Fuller need not, however, suppose that the injunction 'Law ought to be promulgated!' is itself a moral norm. He can say that when law conforms to this norm of legal craftsmanship, moral good tends to follow or, more weakly, harm is prevented. Whether this saves (F2) is doubtful. For in order to do good, or even prevent harm, the principles of legality—all of them matters of degree—need to reach a certain threshold, which threshold, for Fuller, coincides with the existence conditions for a legal system. But there is notoriously quite a lot of retrospectivity, vagueness, and normative conflict in legal systems. Unless we are going to say that many actually existing legal systems are

---

[35] Hart, 'Positivism and the Separation of Law and Morals', 624.
[36] See David Lyons, 'On Formal Justice' (1973) 58 *Cornell Law Review* 833; See also Chapter 6, this volume.
[37] Hart, 'Positivism and the Separation of Law and Morals', 613.

not what they appear to be, the threshold of minimal conformity to the desiderata of legality will need to be set quite low, and at such a low level it may not prevent harm, let alone do good. At this point, Fuller may be tempted to rely on one of his wilder theses: that every single departure from the principles of legality constitutes an insult to the dignity of people as responsible beings.[38] So while there may be no harm, there will always be a wrong. That is simply too extreme. It is as unreasonable as holding that any failure to say 'thank you' to the bartender is an insult to their humanity. Disrespect, insults, etc. are all subject to threshold conditions, and minor slights, especially if unintended, do not undermine our dignity as responsible beings. In any case, this idea is inconsistent with Fuller's own view that some retroactivity can make law better, for there comes a point when prospectivity is a block to removing other deficiencies in legality. We may need to fix these right now, but with effect from some date in the past. That may be not only permissible but required if we are to respect all subjects' humanity.

There is something wrong in these arguments. Hart and Fuller both neglect the point stressed above: nothing has instrumental value unless the ends it serves have value. Probably they take this for granted, sharing the common view that all existing legal systems do achieve some good ends, even if only in helping to coordinate road traffic. All the same, that common view is not universally held, and it would not be pointless to offer, or expect, some defence of it. Kropotkin appraised three centuries of the rule of law thus:

> The millions of laws which exist for the regulation of humanity, appear upon investigation to be divided into three principal categories—protection of property, protection of persons, protection of government. And by analysing each of these three categories, we arrive at the same logical and necessary conclusion: the uselessness and hurtfulness of law.[39]

Kropotkin's judgement is swift and harsh. But for the legal instrumentalist, it is the territory on which the (F2) needs to be fought, not amongst 'relative' values, plural 'oughts', or 'inner' moralities. We need to modify (F2) so that it is conditioned on the ends that law actually pursues, and on its actual success in pursuing them.

---

[38] Fuller, *The Morality of Law*, 162.
[39] Petr Alekseevich Kropotkin, *Law and Authority: An Anarchist Essay* (International Publishing Co, 1886) 18.

(F3) If law is an instrument, then there is a generic end that law necessarily serves.

I turn now to the main ground for divorce, or at least separation, between two great families of instrumentalist views. (F3) is a thesis that marks an important division between Fuller and Hart, and between Hart and Dworkin. It is denied by the negative limb of the instrumentalist thesis.

I frame (F3) as if instrumentalism commits one to the existence of a generic end for law. In truth, Fuller only says that it is ironical to affirm that individual laws or statutes can have a purpose while holding that law as such does not.[40] He does not explicitly deny that the irony could result from a correct assessment of the nature of things (as in 'It's ironic that the government's enthusiasm for deregulation led to the nationalization of banks'). And, as I mentioned, one of the difficulties in interpreting Fuller on this point is that he sometimes treats as the end of law what everyone else counts as its typical means: that is, the guidance of human action by norms, rules, or principles of a particular sort. Is it possible that Fuller thought the instrumentalists' error was to take for law's means what is really its end? That would render (F3) true but trivial. We should not impute that view to Fuller, for if he does hold it he would not gamble so much on his fragile claim that there is an empirical correlation between law's means being in good order (inasmuch as they satisfy law's 'inner' or 'internal' morality) and law satisfying its proper ends as identified by 'external morality'.[41]

Possibly, Fuller is here groping for the point we took from Aquinas: 'Whenever a thing is for an end, its form must be determined proportionately to that end; as the form of a saw is such as to be suitable for cutting.'[42] That would accord with Fuller's observation that, when legal philosophers try to distinguish legal order from 'the gunman situation writ large', they fail to see that 'It is ... precisely because law is a purposeful enterprise that it displays structural constancies which the legal theorist can discover and treat as uniformities in the factually given.'[43] The 'structural constancies', for example the fact that all law regulates human conduct by rules and similar standards, that these rules form some kind of system, and so on, are constant only because law is a 'purposeful enterprise' striving for a definite end.

---

[40] Fuller, *The Morality of Law*, 150.
[41] Lon L Fuller, 'Positivism and Fidelity to Law: A Reply to Professor Hart' (1958) 71 *Harvard Law Review* 630, 636 and, less tentatively, in Fuller, *The Morality of Law*, 95–151.
[42] See n 12 above.
[43] Fuller, *The Morality of Law*, 151.

It is curious that Fuller thinks positivists deny this, but a lot depends on precisely what he intends by a 'purposive enterprise', and that is not an idea he makes very precise. Anyone who thinks law is a means thinks it a means to some ends or other. Perhaps Fuller assumes that unless law serves a *generic* purpose—an overall end that distinguishes law from other social institutions, law's *very own* end—then law's means could not be 'constancies' but variabilities. Without a generic end, there would be nothing to explain why law has the means it has, nothing to unify them, and nothing that makes them features of law as such.

Even on such a view, however, we still do not need the hypothesis of a generic end. A set of mid-range ends can do the work piecemeal. For example, law contains the sort of rules that are potentially knowable by their subjects, and this can be explained if we assume that law aims to help a variety of people attain a variety of ends. Other features desirable in the law, and at some modest threshold even necessary (e.g. that laws be clear and prospective) can be explained on the assumption that law is trying to pursue its ends while ensuring that it also conforms to important independent values (such as protecting legitimate expectations, respecting persons, and so on). These are plausible ideals for law, and also for many other forms of social organization.

Hence, the hypothesis of a generic end for law is not needed to explain why all legal systems have common features. That does not prove the hypothesis false. On that issue I shall say only this: it is a warning sign that most of the candidates that have been offered for law's generic end (e.g. protecting human rights, securing respect for persons, keeping the peace) are attractive ideals for law that are neither common to all legal systems nor unique to them, while others (e.g. maintaining order, coordinating activity) are so vague as to be useless to jurisprudence and, when specified more precisely, quickly lose their claims to universality.

Rejecting the hypothesis of a generic end is compatible with accepting that law typically serves (plural) ends. Hart thought that, and he thought that without reference to what he sometimes called the 'minimum content' of natural law, we would be without adequate criteria for distinguishing legal systems from other institutionalized rule-systems in a society.[44] A fully fledged legal system typically aims to regulate violence, property, kinship, and promises. Fuller seems uninterested in this issue, because he denies any significant

---

[44] Hart, *The Concept of Law*, 193–200.

difference between the 'enterprise' of law and the enterprises involved in the internal regulation of clubs, churches, schools, or agricultural fairs.[45] Anyone running such institutions according to rules ought to be concerned about the character as well as the content of those rules: both universities and unions should try to keep their regulations clear, prospective, stable, and so forth. There may be additional requirements that apply to legal systems (e.g. in virtue of the fact that they exercise compulsory jurisdiction over their subjects), and there may be additional urgency to some of the shared requirements (e.g. in virtue of the scope of authority that legal systems claim).

Law is therefore less like Aquinas' saw than it is like a Swiss-Army knife: a multi-purpose tool handy for lots of ends, but not strictly an *all-purpose* tool. Many of these ends have structural ramifications of the sort Aquinas mentions, but the ramifications are complex and variable. Inasmuch as law aims at guiding conduct, its action-guiding rules will need to be laid down in advance of the conduct they are to guide. Inasmuch as law aims at evaluating conduct (as right or wrong, good or bad), its standards cannot be hopelessly vague. And inasmuch law is to educate its subjects about the moral significance of the standards it declares, then the reasons for these standards need to be more transparent than they would if law's aim were simply to secure co-ordination and conformity. What we do not need, and what we will not find, is what (F3) proposes: a generic end of law that explains all leading features of law's means.

(F4) If law is an instrument, then it is a neutral instrument.

Wearying pages have been written proving the non-neutrality of law, especially where what is criticized at such length are the following plainly incorrect theses: (a) law is neutral among all sorts of conduct; (b) law is neutral among all political ideologies; or (c) law is neutrally applied to all its subjects. The first is absurd, the second hovers on the margins of absurdity, and the third is a possible ideal rarely satisfied in fact. I therefore disregard these interpretations of (F4) in favour of one that is at least plausibly linked to the instrumentalist thesis. Raz writes:

> Like other instruments, the law has a specific virtue which is morally neutral in being neutral as to the end to which the instrument is put. It is the

---

[45] Fuller, *The Morality of Law*, 124–5.

virtue of efficiency; the virtue of an instrument as an instrument. For the law this virtue is the rule of law.[46]

This does not make any claim about the neutrality *of law*. The claim is about the neutrality of law's virtue, that is, legality, or the rule of law. That is said to be neutral with respect to law's pursuit of its decidedly non-neutral ends. This suggests that (F4) is ambiguous: is it *law* that the instrumentalist allegedly believes to be neutral, or the principles of *legality* that should govern the creation and operation of law?

Fuller concedes that, over a wide range, his principles of legality are 'ready to serve a variety of such aims with equal efficiency'.[47] That is a qualified endorsement of the instrumentalist thesis. The qualifications are as follows. First, Fuller says that there is a tendency for any instrument satisfying his principles to do good, for example by encouraging open government and public scrutiny, and ensuring that there are certain evils that governments cannot perpetrate.[48] Second, as noted above, Fuller thinks that every departure from his principles is an insult to human dignity. Third, he thinks that law, even when well-ordered, is a limited-purpose instrument. He avers that law is bad at economic allocation. He says that adjudication as a social technique is trustworthy only when confined to the traditional role of deciding cases between two (or a few) parties, avoiding what he calls 'polycentric' issues, moral problems involving complex principles and consequences for many people, including non-parties.

These points are all doubtful. The effective capacities of law as an instrument of governance are hard to assess, but probably vary amongst societies. Law's capacity to produce desirable economic outcomes depends on the content of the law, and on the way it goes about securing those allocations. And the idea that traditional adjudication is somehow insulated from 'polycentric' issues is false in fact and dubious as an aspiration.[49] But the key point is this: no one needs to be converted to (F4) to think we should use law's instruments only when they stand a decent chance of being effective, and that when they are effective, they are not likely to be neutral amongst ends or ideologies.

---

[46] Raz, *The Authority of Law*, 226.
[47] Fuller, *The Morality of Law*, 153.
[48] Strangely, Fuller thinks that racial discrimination is among them, for to *target* a given race for ill treatment requires defining the indefinable, whereas a statute prohibiting discrimination on *grounds of race* is safe from any such vagueness. *The Morality of Law*, 160–1.
[49] See Jeff King, 'The Pervasiveness of Polycentricity' (2008) *Public Law* 101.

I said that law is more like a Swiss-Army knife than like a saw. It is not so much a single instrument as a union of various instruments: mandatory rules, power-conferring rules, individual norms, definitions, and more. However, it is not a union of every possible instrument, and in trying to order one's own affairs or those of others, one may find oneself stuck with a task for which none of the legal instruments are much good. Each of law's tools has its limits, and there are some things that probably cannot be directly achieved by any of law's tools or all of them together. ('You can't legislate love'—which is not to say that you shouldn't try.)

(F5) If law is an instrument, then law is subject only to instrumental evaluation.

The final obstacle we need to remove saddles the instrumentalist with exclusively instrumental standards for evaluating law: the end (and *only* the end) justifies the means.

If L is a valuable instrument, then one important question is how effective L is, compared to the feasible alternatives, in achieving the valued ends. The criteria of effectiveness vary with the instrument and the end: an effective knife should cut well, an effective algorithm should compute well, an effective flute should play well. When an instrument is partly identified by its intended or typical end, the criteria of effectiveness take on a special caste: they are also criteria that must be met (allowing for adjustment or repair) if the instrument is to count as a fully fledged member of the class. A baseball is not an ineffective knife; it is not a knife at all, though a blunt or bent knife certainly is. We can speak of these, if you like, as 'internal' criteria of evaluation: instrumental standards called up by the nature of the instrument itself. Law has such criteria, and Fuller identifies several of them. But as he admits, they do not pick out law as a social institution, for they are mostly criteria that apply to all other rule-governed enterprises.

Importantly, the existence of such internal criteria of evaluation does not establish any of the following propositions:

(1) The internal criteria are the most morally important criteria for evaluating law.
(2) The moral significance of the internal criteria is exhausted by their instrumental contribution to the value of the law.
(3) Moral criticism of law may be ousted by showing that it is not based on one of the internal criteria for evaluating law.

(4) With respect to any internal criterion, any change that improves its effectiveness is morally desirable.

Some of these propositions are more obviously wrong than others. Both (1) and (2) confuse functional importance with moral importance. Proposition (3) suggests the comforting but implausible view that a social institution gets to choose the moral standards that it would like to meet—that it can face an examination board best suited to its own talents. Occasionally, this thought gets reversed, so that from the premise that there is a standard that law must meet (say, that its allocative norms should be just) it is held to follow law must meet that standard in virtue of the fact that it is law.[50] The truth is that law must *answer to* justice, but that is not because a modicum of justice is required for something to count as law (not even Fuller goes that far) but because, as an institution that allocates burdens and benefits among people, law is specially apt for appraisal as being just or unjust. In the same way, a market, whose internal virtue is efficiency, cannot oust appraisals of its foreseeable distributive effects by pleading, 'I wasn't trying to do justice!'

Finally, (4) neglects all other moral constraints to which any valuable instrument must conform. Nothing in the claim that law is a means licenses or encourages such omission. On the way to securing its ends, law must respect all sound deontological constraints; it must treat its subjects with respect, and so on. To the extent that Fuller wants us not only to keep this in mind, but also take it to heart, the reminder is helpful. But it is not as if the instrumentalists named in the indictment express any sympathy for (4), not even Bentham or Ihering, who come closer than any to supposing that 'the end justifies the means'. Kelsen eventually sees that, 'the end cannot "justify" the means, even if the end itself is "justified", i.e., obligatory. The means to a justified end can be quite unjustified.'[51] And Hart's theory of law is, on the normative side, surrounded by non-instrumental constraints: his case for duty to obey the law rests on the principles of reciprocity and fairness; his case for punishment includes distributive constraints on who may be punished; his account of justice acknowledges the principles of legality that Fuller so prizes.

Fuller darkly accuses legal positivism of being 'managerialist', of being a 'one-way projection of authority ... simply acting on the citizen—morally or

---

[50] See, e.g., Robert Alexy, *The Argument from Injustice: A Reply to Legal Positivism* (B. L Paulson and S. L. Paulson trs, Clarendon Press, 2002).

[51] Hans Kelsen, *General Theory of Norms* (M. Hartney trs, Oxford University Press, 1991) 17–18.

immorally, justly or unjustly, as the case may be'.⁵² The final clause intimates, absurdly, that Hart cares less about whether the law acts morally or immorally than he does about the conceptual distinction between the moral and the immoral. The penultimate clause asserts, falsely, that Hart is unaware that law is not only top-down but bottom-up, as seen in the facilities it provides for private individuals to arrange their affairs, but also in the voluntary cooperation of large numbers of people without which law could not exist at all. The leading charge, associating rule-based instrumentalism with something called 'managerialism', is a bare stipulation or an indication that Fuller either misunderstands Hart or misunderstands how managers actually run enterprises.

5. Conclusion

I defended the instrumentalist thesis about law—or at any rate one instrumentalist thesis about law—first, by showing that it belongs to an instrumental conception of law that, if not undeniable, is in any case not denied by most legal philosophers, whether they be positivists or not. I then tried to make it seem a plausible interpretation of that conception by showing that influential charges against it cannot stand. At the same time, not all versions of instrumentalism survived unscathed. We had to abandon the claim that law is essentially a coercive instrument, as well as the claim that law can only have instrumental value. In other respects, however, familiar charges against instrumentalism turn out to be a matter of guilt by mistaken association. This does not prove that law's means contribute more to the identification of law than do its ends—but I think it makes it harder to doubt.[53]

---

[52] Fuller, *The Morality of Law*, 191–2.
[53] Anthony Sebok was a helpful respondent to an early version of this paper delivered at the Australian National University. I am also indebted to Andrei Marmor and others at a USC colloquium in legal theory, and to Dori Kimel, Joseph Raz, and, especially, Julie Dickson for their criticisms.

3
Custom and Convention at the Foundations of Law

1. The Foundations of Law

In modern legal systems, few laws are customary. Most are enactments that came into existence in a flash and could disappear without ever entering the life of the community. Others result from rulings instantly binding on the parties, and normally on others too, which are later reinforced or modified by further rulings and enactments. But underlying all these formal and deliberate activities are informal customary norms without which we could not have the formalities of law at all. These are rules that emerge gradually and exist only because they are respected by key legal actors, especially by judges. Recent attacks on legal institutions, including in Western democracies, make the customs underlying our constitutions suddenly visible, but they are always at work in the background. The existence of law depends on them, and since we cannot have the rule of law without having law, that depends on them too.

Of special importance are the rules that determine which activities in each society make or change the law. Are executive orders law? Departmental guidance notes? Treaties? Tweets? Any of them could be, if were they made so by customary norms in that legal system, or by norms whose use is required or authorized by such norms. This applies also to laws that proclaim their supremacy. The 1787 US Constitution says that it is supreme law; but if American judges and lawyers stopped applying that Constitution and instead applied directives from Deuteronomy or commands of colonists then *those* would become supreme. And it applies to legal systems that restrict the role of custom in law. The 1983 Code of Canon Law says, 'no custom which is contrary to divine law can obtain the force of law.'[1] That restriction rests on

---

[1] Can. 24 §1.

the authority of the Code, and that rests on customs of the church, including its ideas about the existence and content of divine law.

It is a central task of jurisprudence to understand the customs that direct judges and other officials to recognize and apply certain things as sources of law. These are the 'recognition rules' of a legal system, and they provide the ultimate criteria for the validity of other standards in that system.[2] We could call them 'constitutive rules' in John Searle's sense or, as Andrei Marmor puts it, 'constitutive conventions'.[3] These terms strike me as harmless but uninformative. No one who understands that rules provide criteria for legal validity understands any more by being told that they are constitutive of the tests for law. And whether there is anything else that they constitute, in constituting law (the 'spirit of the people', 'social values' . . .) is highly variable. The theory I want to examine advances a special explanation, not a special nomenclature, for the criteria. This is the idea that ultimate recognition rules are *social conventions*: more-or-less arbitrary norms that are self-sustaining owing to the widely distributed benefits conformity to any such rule brings.

Conventions of that sort surround us. We aim to use words as others do, and they aim to use them as we do—but it does not matter whether we all call cats 'cats' or 'mats'. We aim to drive on the same side of the road as everyone else, but it does not matter whether that is the right or the left. We use social media we think others will use and we stop when they do: a fear of losing touch or missing out keeps us together. When people succeed in coordinating their activity in these ways, success tends to breed success and a rule may emerge that makes one way of proceeding normatively salient: what starts out simply being done ends up becoming 'the done thing'.[4] Such informal conventions can become so entrenched that changing them becomes practically impossible—even if everyone agrees that some other rule would be better.

---

[2] These include H. L. A. Hart's 'ultimate rule of recognition': H. L. A. Hart, *The Concept of Law* (3rd edn, Penelope. A. Bulloch and Joseph Raz, eds; Leslie Green, intro, Oxford University Press, 2012) 94–110, 292–4. I prefer a slightly different terminology to avoid any implication that there is only one ultimate recognition rule in each legal system, and as a reminder that there are subordinate recognition rules that are themselves law (e.g., Art. 38 of the Statute of the International Court of Justice (ICJ) lists the sources of international law. That Statute is law.)

[3] John R. Searle, *Making the Social World. The Structure of Human Civilization* (Oxford University Press, 2010); Andrei Marmor, *Social Conventions: From Language to Law* (Princeton University Press, 2009).

[4] I may owe this way of putting it to John Gardner. Or perhaps he owed it to me. (It figured in a long-standing joke in our Oxford jurisprudence seminar.)

The idea that foundational legal norms are conventions of this sort enjoys appeal among legal theorists, including legal positivists, natural lawyers, economists of law, and others. For example, H. L. A. Hart writes:

> [T]he rule of recognition is treated in my book as resting on a conventional form of judicial consensus. That it does so rest seems quite clear at least in English and American law for surely an English judge's reason for treating Parliament's legislation (or an American judge's reason for treating the Constitution) as a source of law having supremacy over other sources includes the fact that his judicial colleagues concur in this as their predecessors have done.[5]

Many other versions of conventionalism have been proposed in contemporary jurisprudence.[6] Apart from a few remarks about Hart's comment, however, I will not examine any particular version of the thesis. My aim is to test the following objections that, if sound, apply to any version:

(a) A social convention rests on a stable but arbitrary consensus of judgement and action. Yet officials, including judges, sometimes deny that their consensus is a matter of convention.

(b) The foundations of every legal system include norms that tell us what we must, may, or can do. How could a convention do that? A social convention is an inert series of events: no 'ought' from 'is' alone. The 'normativity' of a norm must come from some other norm, and there is no norm requiring that every convention be obeyed.

(c) The recognition rules in every legal system are mandatory: they impose obligations that bind officials of that system to apply the law in relevant disputes. No convention does that. Merely unconventional conduct cannot amount to a delict.

---

[5] Hart, *The Concept of Law*, 226–7.
[6] A sample: Lon Fuller, 'Human Interaction and the Law' (1969) 14 *American Journal of Jurisprudence* 1; Chaim Gans, 'The Normativity of Law and its Co-ordinative Function' (1981) 16 *Israel Law Review* 333; Gerald J. Postema, 'Coordination and Convention at the Foundations of Law' (1982) 11 *Journal of Legal Studies* 165; William S. Boardman, 'Coordination and the Moral Obligation to Obey the Law' (1987) 97 *Ethics* 546; Andrei Marmor, 'Legal Conventionalism', in Jules L. Coleman ed., *Hart's Postscript: Essays on the Postscript to 'The Concept of Law'* (Oxford University Press, 1998) 200; John Finnis, *Natural Law and Natural Rights* (2nd edn, Oxford University Press 2011); Gillian K. Hadfield and Barry R. Weingast, 'What is Law? A Coordination Model of the Characteristics of Legal Order' (2012) 4 *Journal of Legal Analysis* 471.

My argument will be that objections (a) and (b) can be answered (on certain assumptions) but that objection (c) holds good and is decisive against conventionalism. The challenge of (c), however, is not the familiar objection that there is no general *moral* obligation to conform to conventions. That is true, but irrelevant. The problem lies deeper and persists even if we have a satisfactory answer to objection (b): we cannot explain even the legally obligatory character of a norm by reference to its conventionality.[7]

En route to these conclusions, I embrace without defence a familiar view about the nature of law: all law is positive law, and wholly a social construction. But the arguments I offer aim to convince even those who disagree about that. It is rare in general jurisprudence, or anywhere in social theory, that everything turns on some One Big Thesis. I conclude with some more speculative remarks on why, and to whom, conventionalism seemed attractive.

2. Norms, Customs, and Conventions

In law, the term 'convention' can be applied to agreements, treaties, nonjusticiable rules, and general legal principles. These may or may not be conventions of the sort that I have in mind. Moreover, one thing that 'convention' means in ordinary language is simply 'custom'. In following other writers, I am using 'convention' in a somewhat technical, but non-legal, sense to pick out norms that are one sort of customary rule. I map the territory as follows:

(A) A *norm* is a guide to belief, desire, action, or emotion. General norms include rules (e.g. 'Everyone must have a valid licence to drive a car'). Individual norms include directives (e.g. 'Show me your licence!').
(B) A *custom* is a rule that exists if and only if it is practised in a group but was not created by any procedure authorized to create that rule for that group. Customs need not be venerable, but they tend to solidify with use and endurance may be evidence of their existence. (C) A *convention* is a custom that exists in a group if and only if those who follow (or apply) it

---

[7] I also take this opportunity to refine some of my earlier doubts about conventionalism and to place it in the context of some wider themes in jurisprudence. For my earlier work on these problems, see Leslie Green, 'Law, Co-ordination, and the Common Good' (1983) 3 *Oxford Journal of Legal Studies* 299; Leslie Green, 'Authority and Convention' (1985) 35 *Philosophical Quarterly* 329; and Leslie Green, 'The Concept of Law Revisited' (1996) 94 *Michigan Law Review* 1687. My paper, 'Positivism and Conventionalism' (1999) 12 *Canadian Journal of Law and Jurisprudence* 35, is the source of several passages in this chapter, but I have tried to improve on that discussion.

do so because each aims to follow any such rule commonly followed by the others, and this dominates any reason to follow some different rule instead. When a rule emerges as a matter of convention it therefore has an arbitrary quality. Of course, conventions are not arbitrary in the sense that they are created wilfully or inexplicably. They are arbitrary because for any operative convention there is at least one other rule that would serve adequately were it followed instead. The reason for following a convention includes an essentially genealogical component: it is the norm that most have come to follow, though things could have been otherwise.

Unlike legislated norms, conventions need not be deliberately created.[8] Unlike other sorts of customary norms, conventions need not be enforced by sanctions or penalties. A convention of the pertinent sort exists only when conformity brings its own rewards and deviation its own costs. This is a key point. It can sometimes be useful to add penalties and sanctions to support existing conventions. The highway code penalizes driving on the wrong side of the road; but even if it did not, most people would still aim to drive on whatever side the others drive on. If penalties are necessary for a rule to emerge or persist, then it is not a convention.

Some philosophers find premonitions of this idea in David Hume's remarks on language and money. In *A Treatise of Human Nature,* Hume writes,

> languages [are] gradually establish'd by human conventions without any explicit promise. In like manner do gold and silver become the common measures of exchange, and are esteem'd sufficient payment for what is of a hundred times their value.[9]

This passage, however, simply contrasts norms created by undertakings ('explicit promise') with those created some other way. It does not specify the character of those emergent ('gradually establish'd') norms. In the *Enquiry* Hume goes a bit further. There, he says that justice depends on convention because it has its origins in a sense of common interest; 'which sense each man feels in his own breast, which he remarks in his fellows, and carries him,

---

[8] Philosophers sometimes treat bare stipulations, as in symbolic systems, as conventions—for example, the rules of Reverse Polish Notation (RPN) (in which the operand follows the operator). I think RPN is now a set of conventions but that when Lukasiewicz invented it, it was a set of stipulations more akin to legislation than to custom.

[9] David Hume, *A Treatise of Human Nature* (L. A. Selby-Bigge ed., rev. 3rd edn, P. H. Nidditch ed., Oxford University Press, 1976) 490.

in concurrence with others, into a general plan or system of actions, which tends to public utility; [and thus] it must be owned that, in this sense, justice arises from human conventions.'[10]

This is nearer what I have in mind, though norms can have the features Hume mentions here without also having the arbitrary and self-sustaining features of the conventions I am interested in. A 'system of actions' might, for instance, be sanction-imposing norms that provide public goods liable to free-riding, or it might be made up of the kind of '*I-will-if-you-will*' assurance norms that support promising.[11] There are other possibilities too. Conventions in the sense relevant here are one special kind of custom that tend to emerge when our dominant concern is to settle on a common way of acting. That is why they play an important role in natural languages as well as other sorts of cooperative activities.[12] According to jurisprudential conventionalists, law is at bottom a lot like language. As we shall see, the similarities are overwhelmed by the differences.

3. Conventions in Law and in Jurisprudence

There can certainly be conventions of this sort *in law* since law may create or recognize conventions for one purpose or another. Conventionalism *in jurisprudence* is the thesis that fundamental legal norms are always conventions. We need to pause over this point about the level of analysis.

That ordinary laws may incorporate or create conventions is clear. Rules of the road, weights-and-measures requirements, retail pricing regulations, formalities of marriage, the law of royal succession, and many aspects of the law of property are conventional. Not all laws are like these, however. The

---

[10] David Hume, *An Enquiry Concerning the Principles of Morals* (L. A. Selby-Bigge ed., rev. edn, P. H. Nidditch (Oxford University Press, 1975) 306.

[11] Hume recognizes customs of various sorts. For example, he holds that ordinary—convention-dependent—justice norms may sometimes be suspended, and we should instead act on constraint norms: 'When any man, even in political society, renders himself by his crimes, obnoxious to the public, the law punishes him in property and in person. In other words, the [ordinary] rules of justice are, with regard to him, temporarily suspended, and it becomes proper, for the benefit of society, to inflict on him suffering which, in other circumstances, would be considered an injustice or violation of his rights.' Hume, *An Enquiry Concerning the Principles of Morals*, 148.

[12] Foundational theoretical works include Thomas Schelling, *The Strategy of Conflict* (Harvard University Press, 1960); David Lewis, *Convention* (Harvard University Press, 1969); Edna Ullman-Margalit, *The Emergence of Norms* (Oxford University Press, 1977); and Christina Bichierri, *Rationality and Coordination* (Cambridge University Press, 1993).

legal prohibition on genocide, the legal right to health care, and the power to create a trust are not arbitrary norms that solve problems of cooperation. Our interest is in the norms that constitute ultimate criteria of validity of *any* such laws in a system. These could be conventional even if the laws they recognize are not. Some *mala prohibita* are conventional, but even among the *mala in se* what makes some but not others unlawful could be a matter of convention.[13]

Jurisprudential conventionalism holds that *there could not be* things like a legal prohibition on genocide, or a legal system capable of producing such a prohibition, unless there were rules determining which acts or events create or change laws and that here, at law's bedrock, various rules would suffice, provided enough officials fall in with them. Law could be created by decree or by enactment, by custom or by ruling, but so long as there is convergence among judges and others on the way(s) to create law, it does not (much) matter what those are. No doubt some law-creating procedures are better than others. Some are morally superior. Some are more efficient. But none is a better *specimen* of such a procedure and, however we might rank their merits, once a law-making procedure becomes effective it is better to conform to it than to risk breach of consensus by doing something inconsistent with that. So argues the conventionalist.

Some hold that an even broader consensus is necessary. Like Hume, they think that those who hope to lead must also follow.[14] My own view is more pessimistic. Whatever the merits of a broader consensus, law can work untethered from the views and values of the community it regulates. This is the downside of a feature that contributes to law's value. Law's institutionalized nature allows officials to create new norms for a society in advance of, and therefore in the absence of, social buy-in. But whatever the precise contribution of wider social attitudes, it is clear that *at least* judges, legislators, and other legal officials need to concur on the sources of law. Without pre-existing sources that judges have a duty to apply to disputes, we could have a system of arbitration or of mediation, but not a system of law-application.[15]

I assume that every legal norm is either practised or else satisfies validity conditions created by a norm that is practised, and that this applies to the

---

[13] For one way the *prohibita* can become *mala*, see David Owens, 'Wrong by Convention' (2017) 127 *Ethics* 553.

[14] Hume, *A Treatise of Human Nature*, 556. Compare Postema, 'Co-ordination and Convention'.

[15] All legal systems are a mixture of these techniques. But a dispute settlement institution that *never* applied pre-existing standards to disputes would not be a legal system. The recognition rules identify those standards.

recognition rules. Some recognition rules satisfy no further recognition rules: they are ultimate in the system. In modern legal systems, the law-making events identified by such rules often include legislative enactments, delegated regulations, administrative rules, judicial rulings, international agreements, and some customary practices: both customary law *in foro*, and a few customs *in pays*. These are our typical 'sources of law'. The recognition rules direct judges as to which materials are to be treated as sources. I say, 'are to be' treated because these rules are not epistemic, unlike, say, a rule for identifying the Canadian Warbler.[16] Neither are they heuristic. If you are in a rush and need the *ratio* of a case, a common heuristic is 'read the headnote'. It is an imperfect procedure: it fails for inaccurate reports and may be misleading for complex cases, but it is a time-saver. What is important, however, is that while one can make a legal error in not applying a relevant *ratio*, one can never make a legal error in failing to follow a useful heuristic. The foundations of law are thus not rules for law-spotters. They are practical rules that regulate decision and action by judges and others.

In the absence of a rule-creating power, all social rules rest on a degree of consensus. It would therefore be impossible to have recognition rules without consensus about the identity and bearing of law-creating events. When such a consensus emerges, 'I can rely on the belief that the others have consulted the same sources and expect that I have done the same'.[17] The value of distributed reliance is one reason people seek a common solution to the problem of what to apply as law. Of course, that reliance cannot provide certainty because no source-creating consensus is fully determinate. Like every customary rule, recognition rules are somewhat vague or ambiguous and, where there are several, they may conflict. The law is always incomplete. Law-appliers—especially judges in higher courts—therefore exercise a law-creating function when they make these rules more determinate through the very act of applying them. The importance of this function is evident in debates about who ought to occupy judicial roles, and about how they ought to approach adjudication.

Our question, then, is whether the foundations of law lie in social conventions of this sort. Those foundations can certainly *involve* conventions, and normally do so at two points. They may draw needed but arbitrary lines

---

[16] 'Known by its necklace of short stripes, the Canada Warbler is a summer resident of moist, shady woods in the East. It usually stays in the understory, feeding in the bushes or on the ground' <https://www.audubon.org/field-guide/bird/canada-warbler>.

[17] Eerik Lagerspetz, *The Opposite Mirrors: An Essay on the Conventionalist Theory of Institutions* (Kluwer, 1995) 76.

around vagueness or ambiguities in the recognition rules, and they may need to be communicated to the law's subjects by a shared language or similar way of signalling intentions.

Consider the first point. Suppose legislative enactments are recognized as law-creating only because there is a widely shared belief that democratically created norms should be applied, together with the further belief (or fantasy) that the legislature's enactment procedures are in fact democratic. Suppose further that each judge holds these beliefs independently and would adhere to them even if others did not. A custom of recognizing enactments could then emerge, but as an 'overlapping consensus', to use John Rawls's term, on the idea that enactments should make law. Since this custom is not the upshot of any effort to coordinate judgement, it is not a convention. Yet conventions may play a supporting role. Possibly some further belief, also widely held on varied grounds, has it that only measures endorsed by a majority of legislators count as enactments. Now: what counts as *endorsing*? Saying 'Aye'? A show of hands? Of *right* hands? This may well be settled purely as a matter of convention. It may need to be: there may be no grounds to choose any alternative apart from whatever the others choose. So we have this: enactments make law because of a custom that emerges from concurring, independent, judgements that law-making by legislative endorsement is justified, but particular formalities count as endorsement by convention.

A second place conventions turn up is where legal requirements are communicated to their subjects. What natural language(s) will the law authoritatively speak? If a law would be invalid or if it would misfire unless promulgated amongst the population, how is that to be done? Here, too, the need for shared means of communication overwhelms the reasons for particular ones, and this too may be settled through mutual adjustment of expectations and conduct. Henry VIII imposed not only English law, but the English language, on the courts of Wales. Henry did not care whether the Welsh understood the Laws in Wales Act (1535); he did care that his imposers understood it, and they cared that they understood Henry. The Welsh courts came to speak English by compulsion; the English courts already spoke it by convention.

Legal systems can thus involve conventions in ancillary ways. We need to distinguish those from the bolder claim that the foundational legal norms are *themselves* conventions, and at their core, not just near arbitrary margins. It would be an error to go from the conventionality of legal formalities or legal language to the conventionality of legal norms themselves. That is a bit like the mistake in going from the obvious fact that the *word*, 'sex' and the *lines between* female and male embodiments, are conventional to the (doubtful) claim that *sex* is a conventional classification picking out nothing of independent biological or moral importance. (That mistake bedevils a lot of work in gender studies, and sometimes leaches confusion into feminist jurisprudence.[18]) Similarly, the conventionality of the words we use to pick out law ('law', '*lagh*', '*cyfraith*' . . .) and the conventionality of any sharp line between laws and norms in other forms of social order ('the laws of cricket', 'transnational law') do not show that the ultimate recognition rules are conventions.

What might be the attractions of the stronger claim? There seem to be three: (a) Conventionalism models how legal norms can be determined by social facts. We do not need to know whether a social convention would be morally or economically justified to know that it exists and what it requires. (b) Conventionalism explains the fact that a society can have shared sources of law that are nonetheless subject to criticism. Maybe judges' rulings or living authors' treatises should not make law—maybe that is undemocratic— but if they actually emerge as solutions to a coordination problem of how to legislate, they contribute to the law nonetheless. (c) Conventionalism explains how it can be intelligible to cite legal rules when accounting, to oneself or others, for one's conduct. The fact that there is an existing convention can be a reason—at least an auxiliary reason—for conforming to that standard. Together with operative reasons (such as the fact that one needs to communicate effectively or to drive safely) these conventions can be reasons because they can contribute to justifications.[19] Moreover, the fact that they can make an independent contribution distinguishes conventions from reasons of general applicability. Most drivers refuel when the gauge approaches 'Empty', but not because each is trying to do as the others do. Their common conduct is a non-coincidental response to common circumstances, not something that figures in any one's reasoning about when to fill the tank. On the other hand, most drivers do keep right (or, in some places, left) because that is a response that is sensitive to other's predicted responses.

4. Non-Arbitrary?

That is a bare sketch of a theory that has been elaborated and refined in many ways. The objections I now consider apply, if sound, to all versions of it. I begin with the idea that the foundations of law are arbitrary.

---

[18] On why it is an error, see Kathleen Stock, *Material Girls: Why Reality Matters for Feminism* (Fleet, 2021); on how it leaches confusion, see Chapter 5, this volume.

[19] On 'operative' and 'auxiliary' reasons, see Joseph Raz, *Practical Reason and Norms* (rev. edn, Oxford University Press, 1999) 33–5.

If fundamental legal norms are conventions, they are arbitrary in the sense that, for any operative convention, there is another that would serve adequately were it generally followed.[20] We could sell turnips by the pound or by the kilo. We could treat rulings by trial courts as changing the law, or only rulings by courts of appeal. As I have stressed, it is a feature of conventions that it can be rational for each to follow the common standard, even if it would be rational for all to follow a different one. That is why, although there is no longer a very good case for pounds or pints, they are not going away any time soon. We fall into such rational ruts because, while each can adjust their own behaviour to the anticipated choices of others, no one can simultaneously adjust everyone else's behaviour as well.

Is that sort of arbitrariness a feature of law's constitutive rules? Here is one reason to be sceptical: few judges or legislators acknowledge it. For example, in their comments on constitutional 'originalism', we do not usually hear American judges say that old, informal, materials are relevant to current law on the ground that they provide one common, salient standard in interpretation, though some other shared standard would do just fine. On the contrary. The case of *The Living Tree v. The Petrified Forest* grinds on precisely because judges think the standards are *not* arbitrary, that it matters which they follow, and that, within limits, some risk breaking ranks to get the constitutional politics that they or their patrons prefer. In extra-curial ruminations, some even argue the moral or semantic *necessity* of the relevance of colonial history to current law. It is easy to make fun of their efforts. But aren't the efforts evidence that the sources of law are not conventional?

That is a significant objection, and it has some weight. But it is far from decisive. Judicial comments on the nature of fundamental legal norms do not determine their nature, and that includes theoretical, meta-juristic, remarks to the effect that recognition rules are not conventions but, let us say, matters of principle, self-evident deliverances of practical reason, or emanations of divine will. So it is with language.[21] People can think that it was Adam that gave the (Hebrew?) names to all the birds of the air; but that does not change the fact that those names emerged by convention. The proof lies in their genealogy and evolution, of which we have evidence. Likewise, judges may think the 1787 Constitution is supreme law in the United States because

---

[20] On arbitrariness, see Federico José Arena, 'Marmor on the Arbitrariness of Constitutive Conventions' (2012) 2 *Jurisprudence* 449; Hanoch Sheinman, 'The Conventionality of Promising: A Defence' (2011) 2 *Jurisprudence* 463.

[21] Cf. Tyler Burge, 'On Knowledge and Convention' (1975) 84 *Philosophical Review* 249.

it creates a framework of justice or embodies the wisdom of great men, but in fact it settled into its role gradually, including among people who loathed its ideas of justice, who distrusted its framers, and many more who had no view one way or the other about these things. We have evidence of all that, too. Conventionality does not depend on an awareness or acknowledgement of conventionality. It depends on history.

Perhaps we nonetheless need explanations for the lack of a frank acknowledgement of conventionality. They are easy to find. Where judicial denials of conventionality are sincere, they may reflect a more complex role for conventions. A sophisticated conventionalism can absorb convention-denying comments as intermediary steps in explaining how conventions arose. For example, historical materials may attract judicial attention because they are thought to have some property *other than* a propensity to attract general attention. Maybe judges think there is special wisdom in statements from the founding era. What makes them law is the impact of that belief on the emergence of recognition rules, not its cogency. On the other hand, denials of arbitrariness may not be sincere at all. Jurisprudence should not discount purely ritualistic statements by judges. Judges may know, in their heart of hearts, that the ground rules of their legal system are arbitrary, or they may half-suspect it, yet they may feel that their professional role or political culture requires them to affirm otherwise. In some countries, judges are expected to say elevated, inspiring things about the norms underpinning their constitutions, and they usually deliver. The fact that such explanations are available does not show that they are correct. It does show that disavowals of arbitrariness do not preclude the possibility that judges are acting on, or acting to create, arbitrary conventions at the foundations of law. To the first objection, we return a verdict of not proven.

5. Not Normative?

I turn now to the second source of doubt: the idea that conventions lack a kind of 'real normativity' that law necessarily has. Social conventions are patterns of conduct that belong to the realm of 'is'; what law needs in order to get normativity flowing through its circuits is special energy from the realm of 'ought'. Hans Kelsen believes something like that, and so do some natural lawyers. I think belief in such energy is the 'cold fusion' of jurisprudence.

I have been freely referring to norms as the genus under which customs and conventions fall, but I have not said much about norms as such. On my view, all legal norms have existence conditions exhausted by ordinary human acts and intentions. As legal positivists put it, the existence and content of law is a matter of social fact. Not all jurisprudents accept that. Some say there are laws that exist at least in part because it is just, fair, or reasonable that they should exist. The existence of social conventions—'*mere*' conventions as they inevitably get called—cannot suffice to make law because social conventions are not *really* or *truly* normative. They might be called normative in some pale, *soi-disant*, 'rule-implying' sense, but not in the robust, blue-ribbon, 'reason-implying' sense that matters for laws whose existence depends on their justice or rationality.[22]

Those who hold that law necessarily has a special, 'real' kind of normativity have convictions about legal systems that I do not share. They also hold views about rules that I do not understand. A normative statement can presuppose the existence of a rule *yet not* presuppose the existence of a reason only if there is a difference between rules and reasons such that it is possible to presuppose that there is a rule without presupposing *any* sort of reason. I think the existence of a conventional rule is a kind of reason. The fact that there is a rule requiring one to yield to traffic approaching from the right is a reason to yield to the right. It may not be one's motivating reason: one may yield out of fear of legal penalties. It may not be a moral reason: in a given intersection, failure to yield may risk no harm and do no wrong. The existence of the traffic law may even be a reason on which there is a reason not to act: it may be a sensible law made by an illegitimate authority whom we should not encourage. But a reason it is. The existence and character of such conventions explain why it is possible on a one-way street to drive not only the opposite way but the *wrong* way, and why non-conformist spelling can be not only surprising but *in error*. In what does the 'normativity' of conventions lie? In the way they are used: as standards for guidance and, derivatively, for assessment.

Something is a norm only if it is offered or taken as a guide to action (or belief, emotion, etc.)[23] Normative guidance has distinctive features.[24] A wall

---

[22] On this formulation of the distinction, see Derek Parfit, *On What Matters: Volume Two* (Oxford University Press 2011) 267–8. Parfit himself holds that criminal laws (and, I imagine, all other laws) are normative in the rule-implying sense.

[23] By 'is offered or taken' I mean is *actually* offered or taken: Leslie Green, 'Escapable Law' (2019) 19 *Jerusalem Review of Legal Studies* 110. That something ought to be used as a norm does not make it a norm. Nor does the belief or judgement that something ought to be used as a norm: that is just someone's idea for a norm.

[24] W. D. Falk, 'Goading and Guiding' (1953) 246 *Mind* 145.

may keep me out of your garden because I cannot climb it. Nothing normative there. On the other hand, even a wall that is but 10 centimetres high may keep me out of your garden if it marks a boundary by which I guide my conduct. Or it may do so by guiding someone else's conduct—yours, or that of the police—who may in turn guide my conduct normatively or change it non-normatively.[25]

A great many things can give that sort of guidance: rules, directives, decisions, whistles, gestures, boundaries, maps, and more. But not everything. For something to function normatively certain conditions must be satisfied. We must be able to know whether the putative norm exists and what it would take to conform to it. There are no parallel conditions to meet before an insurmountable wall can restrain me. I need not know that it is insurmountable or even that it exists. I simply cannot get over it if I try. The boundary is different. If it is to guide my conduct at all, I need to know that there is a line, where it lies, and what it signals. (Keep out always? Except in emergencies?) Since not everything can satisfy such conditions, not everything can give normative guidance. For example, even if there were (as some philosophers think) a sharp boundary surrounding vague predicates—for example, a sharp line between conduct that is reasonable and conduct that is unreasonable, or a sharp line between people who are competent and people who are not—not even those philosophers believe anyone can *detect* the line that, they hold, must exist 'in principle', somewhere. Since we cannot know the location of the alleged dividing line, we cannot guide conduct by it, and it cannot function as a norm. However, someone may be able to 'draw a line', as lawyers say, between the reasonable and the unreasonable, etc., and perhaps we can guide our conduct a bit further by that. So, too, conventions can draw lines for normative guidance, and that can make them valuable.

Some who are willing to concede this much think that any answer to the 'problem of the normativity of law' remains incomplete until it addresses a further question: 'what *makes* legal norms normative?' What sort of answer are they hoping for? If some laws are norms, we can explain their normativity only if we can explain the normativity of norms. But we can explain the normativity of norms only in the way we explain the triangularity of triangles. We say what it is to be that thing and have that property. A triangle is a system of three points lying in one plane; triangularity is nothing other than

---

[25] Or: set things up so that I will then conform to the norm, or get someone to make me conform to it, and so on.

that property. Does anyone feel the urge to ask, 'Yes; but what is it in *virtue of which* triangles are triangular; what *grounds* the triangularity of triangles?' Nothing stands between triangles and their triangularity that could figure in an informative answer. Likewise, nothing stands between norms and their normativity that could figure in an 'explanation of the normativity of norms'. We can certainly ask, 'what *is* a norm?', and can ask *of* a norm whether it is practised or justified, just as we can ask what a triangle is, and of a given triangle whether it is equilateral or beautiful. Perhaps those in search of the 'ground' or 'source' of the normativity of norms are therefore using 'normativity' in a stipulative sense, for instance, to pick out a property of norms that guide conduct necessarily or irresistibly. I am not confident that there are such norms, or what it would be for them to exist. So, I use 'normativity' as the dictionary does: to pick out the property of being a norm. Where there is a norm there is a reason, even if it is a reason we have (some other) reason not to act on.

One could have reservations about this way of looking at things if one held that law necessarily 'gives us' reasons because the existence of law is fused to its justification.[26] There could be various versions of the fusion view. The fusion may be claimed to hold of *all existing* laws, or only the best, *paradigm*, examples of the species. Those who hold that all legal norms are justified can also disagree about the target of justification: some hold that a law exists only if we are justified in *creating* it, others only if we are justified in *obeying* it; for some the requirement is that judges be justified in *enforcing* it. And they may disagree again on the relevant justificatory standards. Some think it enough that a law satisfies ideals of *legality* in order to exist, others say it must also be *efficient*, a few hold that every law, or every law-creating procedure, must satisfy all sound *moral* standards. We can mix and match among these options, so there are probably lots of fusion-type niches yet to be occupied, and we can look forward to still more exotic 'explanations of the normativity of law'.

I assume, instead, that a norm can be a legal norm without satisfying any sort of justification condition, that anything that is actually used for guidance is normative, and that this applies to the most fundamental norms in a legal system, and even in their paradigm cases. I have not demonstrated that; I have only noticed some confusions and complications in competing views. What is more important here, however, is this: those who dissent *only*

---

[26] For ambiguities in the idea of law of law 'giving reasons', see David Enoch, 'Reason-Giving and the Law', in Leslie Green and Brian Leiter eds, *Oxford Studies in Philosophy of Law*, vol 1 (Oxford University Press, 2011) 1.

because they hold a fusion view of the 'normativity of legal norms', have *non-specific* objections to conventionalism, flowing from their conviction that law must satisfy a justification condition, together with the obvious fact that some conventions are unjustifiable. These objections are non-specific because, if sound, they apply to conventions simply in virtue of their positive character. They therefore apply to any theory that finds the basis of law in social facts, whether in conventions, customs, pragmatic presuppositions, or even habits. Thus, the objection is not to conventionalism as such. It is to any theory that does not allow, or does not need, the special conception of normativity they advocate. The next objection is different. It applies to conventionalism in virtue of distinctive features of that theory. Unlike the objection from normativity, it is an objection the most stringent legal positivist should endorse.

6. Not Obligatory

Not all norms underpinning a legal system are mandatory, that is, obligation-imposing. Some create powers. But the ultimate recognition rules are obligation-imposing, and every legal system has such rules.[27] They impose obligations on officials to identify the law according to those very norms and to apply it in relevant fact situations. If these rules are not themselves conventions, then the obligation to apply them will need some other explanation.

To fix ideas, consider an ordinary legal obligation. The following is a norm in the law of negligence: 'Everyone must take reasonable care not to injure his neighbour.' People use that standard not merely to predict or control behaviour, but to guide it. As a norm, it states something people ought to do. But this one goes further. It states something people have a legal obligation (or duty) to do. We know this not from the superficial fact that, in my formulation, it contains the strong modal 'must', but from the exigent way it functions in the practical thought of those who use it. Courts and counsel use that norm to direct or advise that reasonable care is categorically *required*

---

[27] I assume that recognition rules are *at least* mandatory. For an argument that ultimate rules of recognition are hybrids of duty-imposing and power-conferring rules, see Matthew Kramer, 'Power-conferring laws and the Rule of Recognition' (2019) 19 *Jerusalem Review of Legal Studies* 87. To note: the question of whether, and how, recognition rules impose obligations is *not* the question whether there is a moral duty to obey the law, that is, what is usually called 'the problem of political obligation': Leslie Green, 'Law and Obligations', in Jules Coleman et al. eds, *Oxford Handbook of Jurisprudence and Legal Philosophy* (Oxford University Press, 2002) 514–47.

by law, whether or not it serves the interests of the duty-bearer, and even in the face of reasons against taking such care (for instance, the fact that taking care costs money). True, the duty to take care falls only on certain people and only in certain contexts, so it is not absolute: there are exceptions and defences. These, too, are determined by law. Within its scope, however, the norm requires that one take reasonable care. It has an exigency that ordinary reasons lack.

Three families of theories have been influential in explaining this: (1) *Enforcement*: obligations are legal norms breach of which triggers or justifies the application of coercive sanctions; (2) *Weight*: obligations are, or are created by, legal norms to which there is an especially weighty reason to conform; and (3) *Structure*: obligations are legal norms that are peremptory—they require conformity on the part of the norm-subject, notwithstanding the existence of valid reasons for non-conformity. None of these fits the conventionalist picture of norms.

6.1 Enforced Norms

Hobbes, Bentham, and Austin hold that obligations are norms reinforced by coercive sanctions. Kelsen says that obligations are norms requiring that sanctions be ordered if a certain act is performed or omitted. Dworkin says that obligations are norms breach of which gives someone a moral right that a court order coercive enforcement. The theories are more alike than they are different, and they all face insuperable obstacles in explaining the foundational obligations in a legal system.[28] Whether recognition rules have sanctions attached is variable. There are often no legal sanctions for breach of ultimate rules by supreme courts. There can be legal reasons for judges to decline to order sanctions even against those who breach legal obligations, and it can be legally justified for them to exercise restraint and 'underenforce' obligations.[29] Most important, however, there is a fundamental obstacle in conjoining the conceptual role that all these theories assign to coercive enforcement with the view that customary obligations are created or imposed by conventions. If sanctions are necessary to the existence or stability of a

---

[28] Hart, *The Concept of Law*, 26–49, 82–91; P. M. S. Hacker, 'Sanction Theories of Duty', in A. W. B. Simpson ed., *Oxford Essays in Jurisprudence: 2nd Ser.* (Oxford University Press, 1973).
[29] Lawrence Sager, 'Material Rights, Underenforcement, and the Adjudication Thesis' (2010) 90 *Boston University Law Review* 579.

customary rule, then that rule is *not* a convention. If sanctions are an optional add-on, then we are without an explanation of how the custom—the consensus *sans* sanction—is obligatory.

6.2 Weighty Norms

The most successful theory of the second type is Hart's, according to which there is an obligation to V only when V-ing is required by a categorical rule conformity to which is considered (rightly or wrongly) to be of great social importance and is reinforced by serious social pressure to conform. Hart says the rule of recognition is a customary practice among judges and other officials, and that it satisfies the existence conditions for such a rule.[30] Oddly, given its centrality in his theory, Hart never gives a clear explanation of how his 'ultimate rule of recognition' also meets the criteria for obligations, leading some to wonder whether he does, after all, regard it as obligation-imposing.

It is true that the rule of recognition is of theoretical significance because it is of great *structural* importance in a legal system. It helps explain the idea of legal validity and contributes to an understanding of what it is for a set of laws to belong together as parts of one legal system. But that does not show that it is an obligation-imposing rule. The Hartian requirement for an obligation is that conformity to a rule is thought to be of great *social* importance. The judicial duty to apply law may be seen that way, but that is hardly necessary and in some legal systems it may not be all that common. Judges—to say nothing of ordinary subjects—may think all that is socially important in court is wisdom in judging, and that judicial craft requires a willingness to decide in light of justice, efficiency, or common sense. In explaining their

---

[30] Hart, *The Concept of Law*, 94–9, 100–10. Hart uses the term 'practice' in its ordinary, philosophically innocent sense—to refer to what is thought and done. Thus: 'the rule of recognition exists only as a complex, but normally concordant, practice of the courts, officials, and private persons in identifying the law by reference to certain criteria. Its existence is a matter of fact' (ibid., 110). The emphasis is on concordance and facticity, not some kind of ritual called 'a social practice'. Is this the 'practice theory of rules' criticized by Warnock, Raz, and, following them, me? Hart never uses that phrase save in the Postscript, where he replies to those who criticize him for endorsing a theory they call by that name. Whether Hart holds that theory, or any theory, of rules, is open to doubt. It depends on what one thinks a 'theory of rules' amounts to: see Chapter 1, this volume. Thomas Adams, 'Practice and Theory in *The Concept of Law*', in John Gardner, Leslie Green, and Brian Leiter eds, *Oxford Studies in the Philosophy of Law*, vol. 4 (Oxford University Press, 2021) 1–31. What is clear is that Hart's remarks about practices do not purport to offer any sort of moral justification for having or following rules, and do not identify rules with practices.

duty to apply law, judges more often refer to their oaths, or to the judicial role, or to a constitution, than they do to the supposed social importance of applying it. Finally, we have, in Hart's 'serious social pressure' condition, a reprise of the difficulty we found in marrying sanction theories and conventional rules. I am not suggesting that a theory of obligation that requires social pressure collapses into a sanction theory. The point is rather that it is liable to a similar objection: if the rule of recognition is a convention, then widespread social pressure to conform to it would be unexpected unless explained by some further fact. When conformity brings its own reward, social pressure is surplus. An optional extra cannot be the explanation for the binding force of convention.

In the original text of *The Concept of Law*, Hart leaves open all questions about why judges usually run with their crowd. That is a matter for investigation but seems likely to include some mixture of the following: they see it as part of the job, they believe the rule of recognition is justified, and they fear the personal and professional consequences of stepping too far out of line. However, in the passage quoted above from the Postscript to that book, Hart appears to narrow things down: 'surely an English judge's reason for treating Parliament's legislation (or an American judge's reason for treating the Constitution) as a source of law having supremacy over other sources includes the fact that his judicial colleagues concur in this as their predecessors have done.'[31]

Considering Hart's debate with Dworkin, it seems that Hart must intend this as a narrowing condition, otherwise it would not meet the objection that there can be obligations without rules. Hart's reply appears to be, 'Yes; but not in the case of conventional obligations, of which the duty to apply law is one. Here, there must be rules.' Yet the quoted passage states a necessary condition only. An ultimate rule of recognition exists only if it is practised by judges, and it seems plausible that any judge's reason for applying could *include* the fact that others do too without that fact explaining the difference between an obligation and other sorts of reasons. And if the condition is not sufficient, convention may be playing only one of the ancillary roles identified above. If the duty to apply something as law is not a conventional obligation, then it is no help in reply to Dworkin.[32]

Many non-conventionalist scenarios would fit Hart's comment. For example, judges might apply legislation as law if and only if: most of them consider

---

[31] Hart, *The Concept of Law*, 226–7.
[32] See Green, 'The Concept of Law Revisited' and Julie Dickson, 'Is the Rule of Recognition Really a Conventional Rule?' (2007) 27 *Oxford Journal of Legal Studies* 373.

legislation a product of democratic procedures *and* other judges concur in applying it (for whatever reason). Even a judge who considers democratic pedigree the sole source of law's authority might think there is no point in holding out if most other judges allow executive edicts to trump legislative enactments. Or again: a judicial decision might not reliably convey its democratic credentials unless it is embedded in a system of professionally accepted norms, which norms do not themselves prioritize democracy. (On some views of the English constitution, for instance, the democratic authority of Parliament is a gift of the common law.) Or judges may hold that consensus is a precondition for legitimacy *de jure*, on the basis that no authority is legitimate unless it is effective, and that consensus is needed for efficacy. None of these are situations in which the rule of recognition is a 'mere convention', though they all conform to Hart's remark about judges acting as their colleagues do.

6.3 Peremptory Norms

A third account, and one that I find plausible, explains the exigency of obligations in terms of their special role in practical reasoning. A norm is obligatory only if it offers a reason for acting as it requires and a reason for *not* acting on certain valid reasons to the contrary. This follows Joseph Raz's view that obligations are 'protected' reasons for acting.[33] This helps explain why there are legal obligations that are *not* generally seen to be of great significance—they regulate minor concerns, but they do so by excluding from consideration other reasons for acting. Unlike sanction accounts, this can explain how obligatory norms make an independent contribution in practical reasoning: they 'protect' certain reasons for acting from the competition of some other valid reasons.

The difficulty here is that this is not how conventions work. The sort of reasons we have for settling on a common means of exchange, a common calendar, or a common language have nothing to do with placing restrictions on practical reasoning. Conventions emerge and are sustained by the ordinary process of balancing reasons against each other, taking into account all available information and all valid reasons. If I have a preponderant interest in making myself understood to you, and if we both speak French and English, but my French is good and your English poor, then I had better speak to

---

[33] See Raz, *Practical Reason and Norms*, 49–84.

you in French. Even though I might otherwise prefer speaking my mother tongue, I do not prefer it so strongly that I am prepared to forgo communication. My reason to speak to you in English is outweighed; it is not a persisting, valid reason that needs to be excluded from consideration lest it tempt me off course and I fail to make myself understood.

The point is subtle but important. In the situations that give rise to conventions, people are mutually responsive to each other's decisions—they act strategically, not just parametrically. In a strategic environment, the features that are relevant to practical reasoning include the predicted reactions of others to one's own reactions. The fact that, in a parametric decision, I have a reason to prefer one alternative to another does not carry over into the strategic situation. Put simply, a reason which *would have been* valid (cogent, persuasive) had I been choosing for myself alone, or choosing when others' actions may be taken as fixed, is not valid in situations of mutual interdependence. Just as there are matters regulated by legal institutions without rules of any kind but via the sort of individuated, particular attention we used to call 'equity', there are also standards that require weighing all valid considerations, giving each its appropriate due. (Most 'balancing' tests in law have this character and are therefore distrusted by those who want everything governed by obligatory rules laid down in advance.) In the sort of circumstances in which conventions emerge, we would need some kind of error theory to explain the emergence of peremptory norms that have no practical role, and such an error would inevitably call into question the assumptions of mutual rational responsiveness on which the genealogy of conventions depends.

To be clear: where mutual coordination is needed people may well have preferences among possible conventions, but these are dominated by their overarching preference for uniformity. The fact that conformity to such rules is individually and jointly beneficial secures compliance: first-order, strategic reasoning is enough. G. J. Postema suggests that this point was understood already by Bentham:

> Rather than excluding some or all independently relevant practical considerations from the practical reasoning of individual citizens, law, in Bentham's conception, seeks to focus expectations and thereby alter the environment within which rational individual citizens exercise their 'right of private judgment'.[34]

---

[34] G. J. Postema, 'Bentham on the Public Character of Law' (1989) *Utilitas* 41, at 49.

On Postema's reading, Bentham holds that this is true of all law. It is clearly true of some laws, and it is a fair description of how all conventional norms work.

It is true that someone or something can mandate conformity to a convention and that could *make* it obligatory. Your mother can require you to mind your manners. The Weights and Measures Act can require you to sell turnips by the kilo. We then need an explanation for the power of your mother, or Parliament, to create such obligations. On their own, however, conventions provide only ordinary reasons to conform. While you can make a martyr of yourself by breaching convention, if you want to be martyred for breach of an obligation, you'll need the help of something else, for instance, your mother, or the courts.[35]

To sum up: are the norms at the foundations of law conventions? No. They are customary rules that exist if and only if practised by officials but are not created by any procedure authorized to create those rules for that group. But they are not conventions in the present sense. The difficulty in jurisprudential conventionalism, however, is not that conventions lack some special normativity law enjoys, and probably not that some judges deny that the foundations of law are conventional. The core problem is that the foundations of law are mandatory, obligation-imposing rules, and those differ in character from conventional norms.

With respect to law's normativity, custom and convention are in the same boat; but it is a safe vessel. With respect to arbitrariness, there is no reason why a custom must be arbitrary: something could be a uniquely rational or feasible way of doing something (say, of making law) and yet be unable to function that way unless it were generally practised. Consensus would then be the upshot, but not the aim, of conduct that creates customs. What, finally, of obligation? One might worry that the objections to thinking conventions obligatory must carry over to customs—or a pessimist might think the obligatory character of positive norms defies explanation: we simply need to acknowledge it as a primitive feature of the social world. I am not that pessimistic. Here it suffices to note that while the difficulties of sanction-based theories and weight-based theories do apply to customs as much as to conventions, structural accounts of obligation such as the peremptory-norm view can mesh with customary rules. A customary obligation is a standard used to place informational restrictions on practical reasoning and thereby take certain considerations out of the ordinary weighing of reasons in

---

[35] *Thoburn v Sutherland City Council* [2002] EWHC 195 Admin.

considering what to do. Customs can become closed off to general balancing in ways that conventions, owing to their strategic context, never do.

Then how, precisely, do customary rules emerge from conflicts of interest and belief? There is no 'precisely' about it because there is no general theory of customs. Any model we turn to—conventions, constraint norms, assurance norms, internalized habits—can explain only some of the phenomena and then only imperfectly. Still, we know that customs *can* emerge out of conflict because we know they actually *do*. We have customs of showing respect to courts, customs of deferring to one legal institution over another, customs of treating certain classifications of people as presumptively suspect, and so on. None of these emerged out of coordinated efforts to march in step. As we have them, they are results of political and legal struggles of various kinds. We can nonetheless do some theorizing in the area, at least in mapping some important differences: customs vs habits, reasons vs obligations, informal customs vs institutionalized rules, and so on. We can state, in a rough and ready way, existence conditions for certain kinds of customary rules. Whether it is worth calling the sum of such work a 'theory of customs' depends on your expectations of theory. I tend to think it is more honest to describe it as 'theoretical reflections on customary rules'.[36] A misguided desire for a general theory of custom is one of the things that leads jurisprudence down the cul-de-sac of conventionalism. But it is not the only thing.

7. Conflict and Consensus in Jurisprudence

Behind these technical and sometimes fussy arguments lies a wider debate about an outlook that is as much ideological as philosophical. Conventionalism is consensualist. That leaves it liable to an objection that has been put by many legal theorists, in many contexts, from different perspectives: even at its foundations, law is a matter not only of consensus but of conflict. Some consensus on the sources is necessary if we are to have law at all: but it is a consensus that *emerges from* conflict, and often retains marks of its history. The consensus of custom is more like a vector sum of contending forces than like coordination around whatever rule others follow. Thus, we

---

[36] I also think that when jurisprudents talk about, for example, 'the philosophical foundations of tort' they mean 'some philosophical reflections on the law of tort'.

see pulling and pushing at the sources: some contending for more weight to be given to history, others less; some wanting to open domestic law to international or foreign law, others trying to insulate it. Such contention can go unresolved, giving indeterminacy to the foundations of law. No one who thinks that law has social foundations ever denied that.

Conventionalism downplays such conflicts with its implicit assumption that legal life is fundamentally a matter of marching in step to secure a common good. On that sort of view, law addresses what is essentially an informational problem, not a motivational problem. Perhaps that is why so many of the models to which conventionalists appeal come from human language. We use language to express disagreement and disapproval, and our choice of words can give offence—but all that depends on a deeper consensus. The communicative role of language makes it unusual amongst human artefacts, however: it is one of the few places where, at bottom, our common interests and a need for consensus massively predominates. No doubt that that is why a smoothly running communication situation seems, to some philosophers, a kind of utopia.[37]

Law often uses and creates conventional rules in the ancillary ways that I identified above. Perhaps we could say that, at least there, law necessarily serves the 'public interest' or the 'common good'—but only in a very thin sense. The outcomes those rules secure need not be distributively just, for they reflect a balance among expectations, not a balance of interests or rights. They need not be optimal, for someone might be better off and no one worse off under a different convention. They need not be utility maximizing, for some other combination of actions might produce more net benefit than the existing one. They need not even ensure that there is no incentive to depart from the conventional norm—only that convention's incentives outweigh any temptation to unilateral departure. Depending on the prospects for successful collective action, there may be incentive for multilateral departure. Here, we need to bear in mind that legal officials, especially judges in apex courts, form a small community—a thin market, so to speak. A judge may not be a norm-taker if he thinks one or two other votes can bend the rules in a direction he prefers.

This does not mean there cannot be, at a given moment, settled norms about the sources of law. Consensus about legal norms, especially in the law's

---

[37] For example Jürgen Habermas, 'Discourse Ethics: Notes on a Program of Philosophical Justification', in Jürgen Habermas ed., *Moral Consciousness and Communicative Action* (Christian Lenhart and Shierry Weber Nicholson trs, MIT Press, 1990) 43–115, esp. 65–6.

ordinary operation outside the courts, is substantial.[38] It does mean that the consensus is more fragile than are the conventions underpinning language, and that serious conflict may be just over the horizon. That conflict can lead to a new, if temporary, peace among contending parties who support it for different reasons. The peace will always be partial: every consensus leaves some matters unsettled. Yet it can provide a working basis for law provided the unsettled conflicts do not intrude too much in the daily life of the legal system, and provided the tiny proportion of legal conflicts that do end up before the courts are met with some restraint before push comes to shove—for example, by not deciding what we do not need to decide, or by agreeing to differ and finding a way to proceed without relying on law. Every legal system uses such techniques, even at its foundations. Together with the application of customary rules, they play a more important part in understanding law in general than do conventions.[39]

---

[38] Hart, *The Concept of* Law, chap. 7; Frederick Schauer, 'Easy Cases' (1985) 58 *Southern California Law Review* 399; Ken Kress, 'Legal Indeterminacy' (1989) 77 *California Law Review* 283; Brian Leiter, 'Legal Indeterminacy' (1995) 1 *Legal Theory* 481.

[39] I thank Allan Hutchinson, Hafsteinn Kristjánsson, and Denise Réaume for helpful criticisms of an earlier version of this chapter.

4
Realism and the Sources of Law

1. Legal Positivism

We should not make too much of party labels in jurisprudence, including 'legal positivism'. Jeremy Bentham and John Austin were energetic partisans, but the party that energized them was philosophical radicalism, not legal positivism.[1] Nor did H. L. A. Hart write *The Concept of Law* to show loyalty to the positivist tradition in English legal thought; he sought to explain the nature of law and, along the way, appropriated ideas from others, including natural lawyers and legal realists. Perhaps Hans Kelsen wrote in order to produce a positivist philosophy, that is, with the aim of disciplining theoretical reflection on law by strictures he considered methodologically positivist or, as he put it, 'scientific'—but even Kelsen modified those as his thought developed. And today, influential advocates of legal positivism often adopt that label somewhat diffidently or with qualifications: Jules Coleman, Julie Dickson, John Gardner, Matthew Kramer, Brian Leiter, Andrei Marmor, Joseph Raz, Frederick Schauer, Wil Waluchow, and others would probably describe their own theories as 'positivist, but . . .' Their hesitations reflect a reluctance to associate a sound theory of law with distracting, misleading, and even mistaken doctrines that have adhered to it over the years. Thus, it is hard to find any contemporary positivists who still hold that law is the command of a sovereign, that all law is the product of explicit or tacit legislation, that there is a sharp distinction between applying and creating law, or that there are no necessary connections between law and morality—all claims once associated with, or even taken to define, legal positivism. Nonetheless, any theory of law that a positivist would be willing to call 'positivist' endorses some version of the following claim: All law is positive law.[2]

---

[1] See E. Halevy, *The Growth of Philosophical Radicalism* (Faber, 1934).
[2] I ignore the pejorative use of 'positivist' once current in American law schools: a mélange of doctrines no serious philosopher ever endorsed, including the idea that law is always clear, that 'plain meaning' is the only proper approach to interpretation, that judges never make law, and that, however foolish or unjust, the law is to be applied and obeyed. For discussion, see Frederick Schauer, 'Positivism as Pariah', in R. P. George ed., *The Autonomy of Law: Essays on Legal Positivism* (Oxford University Press, 1999).

Nearly everyone agrees that *some* law is positive, meaning that its existence and content are fixed by considerations of social fact.[3] What is distinctive of legal positivism is the claim that this is true of *all* law. Law is positive if and only if it is created by human thought and action: by actual, datable events such as people deliberating, deciding, ordering, accepting, tolerating, conforming, or obeying—whether individually or in concert. As this (incomplete) list shows, not all positive law is created by acts performed with the intention of creating law, so positive law need not be legislated. And, if an artefact is something that is created intentionally, law need not be an artefact either. It can be an *objet trouvé* that someone puts to a fresh, legal use. Law can even be made unintentionally: a custom may emerge by invisible hand mechanisms yet satisfy the prevailing criteria for legal validity in that legal system; a ruling can be made solely to settle a particular dispute but have the upshot of changing the law governing many future cases; a piece of judicial reasoning can silently introduce, en route to its conclusion, a presupposition that is later treated as legally binding. And so on.

Such positive events produce the 'sources' of law in a legal system: the constitutions, treaties, statutes, decisions, and customary practices on which lawyers rely in argument and by which judges are bound in their rulings. Another familiar way of epitomizing legal positivism is thus to say that it is the view that all law has sources, where a source can be identified in a content-independent way, apart from its merits.[4] Many sources involve norms of a general character, rules created under the authority of, or using, other rules. Hence, a third familiar way of characterizing positivism is to say that law is

---

[3] The prominent exception is Ronald Dworkin, who comes close to suggesting that there is no fully positive law, and that anything worth counting as a legal system, and anything worth acknowledging as a law, must satisfy demanding moral conditions: Ronald Dworkin, *Law's Empire* (Harvard University Press, 1986); similarly, Mark Greenberg, 'The Moral Impact Theory of Law' (2014) 123 *Yale Law Journal* 1288. In contrast, neo-Thomist natural lawyers typically affirm the existence of ordinary positive law: John Finnis, *Natural Law and Natural Rights* (2nd edn, Oxford University Press, 2011); Mark Murphy, *Natural Law in Jurisprudence and Politics* (Cambridge University Press, 2006). These theorists do not deny that there is purely positive law; they reject positivists' explanations for that law.

[4] Some hold that all law is *ultimately* source based (but may include non-ultimate, non-source-based materials); others hold that all law is *wholly* source based. This is the distinction between 'inclusive' and 'exclusive' legal positivism: W. J. Waluchow, *Inclusive Legal Positivism* (Oxford University Press, 1994). I do not examine that debate here. My own view conforms to an exclusive interpretation of the idea that all law is positive. For discussion, see Joseph Raz, *The Authority of Law: Essays on Law and Morality* (Oxford University Press, 1979) chap. 3 and Leslie Green and Thomas Adams, 'Legal Positivism', in Edward N. Zalta ed., *The Stanford Encyclopedia of Philosophy* (Winter 2019 edn) <https://plato.stanford.edu/archives/win2019/entries/legal-positivism/>.

a system of social rules. These three characterizations differ in nuance, but here I use them interchangeably. My interest is not in defending a particular version of legal positivism but in exploring the relationships between positivism and its closest cousin in the evolution of jurisprudential thought: legal realism.

Brian Leiter says that legal realists believe that all law is positive law, and, at one point, Hart riskily describes his own theory as a kind of 'descriptive sociology' of law.[5] Yet some realists have thought, or said, that they disagree with legal positivism, and textbooks in jurisprudence still include set-piece 'debates' between positivism and realism. How can this be if realists accept the essentials of legal positivism? I will try to answer that question. Like Leiter and Hart, my conclusion is conciliatory, for I, too, think that the differences have been exaggerated. But I have a different explanation of how the misunderstandings arose.

2. Upshots of Positivism

Legal positivism has been doubted on many grounds, often rooted in what are taken to be inevitable but unacceptable upshots of the positivist thesis. Here are four such claims, each accompanied by a brief remark suggesting how positivists address it. There then follows a fifth supposed upshot of the positivist thesis. I will explain why that one is no mistake, then turn to consider its bearing on the relationship between positivism and realism. Mainly, I have in mind American legal realism—not only the historical variety but also the casual, untheorized 'realism' or 'functionalism' that circulates in many substantive subjects in law schools. Where I need a specific version of legal positivism, I will enlist work by H. L. A. Hart, somewhat inflected by my own views.

Here are four familiar objections (to be read in a *reductio* tone of voice) followed by the replies:

(1) 'If law were wholly positive, law could have no real value since mere facts cannot entail values.' *But*: It is wrong to suppose that whatever

---

[5] H. L. A. Hart, The Concept of Law (3rd edn, Penelope. A. Bulloch and Joseph Raz, eds; Leslie Green, intro, Oxford University Press, 2021) v; cf. Brian Leiter, Naturalizing *Jurisprudence: Essays on Legal Realism and Naturalism in Legal Philosophy* (Oxford University Press, 2007).

value law has must follow—and follow as an entailment—solely from true propositions about law's nature.

(2) 'Law is a purposive activity, so law cannot solely be a matter of fact.' *But*: It is wrong to suppose that a historical, factual activity cannot be identified partly by the purposes for which it is undertaken. An election, for example, is a purposive activity.

(3) 'If law were positive, legal systems could not be identified by their contribution to human goods.' *But*: Institutions and artefacts may have constitutive aims to promote well-being. Nothing is a sewage system that is not oriented to promoting public health, yet the existence (and content!) of a sewage system is a matter of plain empirical fact.

(4) 'If law were positive, there would be no guarantee that there is always a prima facie moral duty to obey it.' *But*: There is no reason to believe in such a duty, as opposed to, say, a duty to give due weight to the requirements of an effective and potentially beneficial institution.

The quoted propositions in (1) to (4) reflect familiar errors about legal positivism. The telegraphic replies could be, and have been, endorsed by both legal positivists and legal realists. But now consider this upshot:

(5) 'If law were positive, then the law would be incomplete and, on some matters, there would be no conclusive law.' No buts about it: This does indeed follow and is true. However, realists and positivists often have had different reactions to it.

There are three related reasons why the consequent in (5) follows from the positivist thesis, together with some other true propositions:

(A) The sources of law are finite. The UK constitution contains all the powers needed to create an infinite number of statutes. But most of those have not been created, including many for which there is an overwhelming moral need. Law provides for, and regulates, the creation of law 'dynamically', as Kelsen puts it: by being used. Hence, if an existing set of legal norms would justify, or even logically entail, further norms, those further norms are not law unless someone were to endorse or presuppose or otherwise use that justification.

(B) All legal sources are somewhat indeterminate, owing to the related phenomena of ambiguity, vagueness, and the fact that there is always more than one permissible way of applying a legal norm, even a mandatory norm.[6]

(C) There are unresolved conflicts among laws. An action that is permissible according to one rule may be impermissible according to another. Legal systems have positive, conflict-resolving rules, but the list of conflict-resolving rules is finite (see A), those rules are themselves indeterminate (see B) and they may never get applied, since a conflict may go unnoticed or not be worth resolving.

Hence, positive law is incomplete, and some legal disputes lack a single right answer in law. Some writers think that consequence is a powerful objection to legal positivism.[7] But legal realists do not think so, at least not those who have mastered the distinction between legal positivism and so-called formalism. Like positivists, legal realists understand that the rule of law cannot be fully realized, not least because it has multiple desiderata that may conflict *inter se*. The law should be stable, but it should also be clear. Often, intolerably vague provisions can be cured only by introducing instability into the law, that is, by changing it. In any case, a society thoroughly ruled by law is not an attractive ideal. It is better to leave judges some discretion to accommodate the equities in a particular case and as a prophylactic against formalistic fantasies of fixing future laws now, in ignorance of what sorts of law we shall later need. Here, positivism and realism are at one.

3. Indeterminacy and Realism

Positivism, as I have described it, contributes to a conceptual explanation of law. By that I mean that it aims to deepen our understanding of law by examining what counts as what; it has only a secondary interest in counting up instances of the various 'whats'. How then could there be any conflict between positivism and a theory that acknowledges that all law is source-based but adds that courts' decisions cannot generally be explained by positive law,

---

[6] 'The higher norm cannot bind in every direction the act by which it is applied. There must always be more or less room for discretion, so that the higher norm in relation to the lower one can only have the character of a frame to be filled by this act.' Hans Kelsen, *Pure Theory of Law* (2nd edn, M. Knight trs, University of California Press, 1967) 349.

[7] Most insistently, Ronald Dworkin, *'No Right Answer?'*, in P. M. S. Hacker and J. Raz eds, *Law, Morality, and Society: Essays in Honour of H.L.A. Hart* (Oxford University Press, 1977). In reply, see Raz, *The Authority of Law*, chap. 4.

though they can be explained by extra-legal considerations (including the court's sense of what would be fair in a case, what common sense or efficiency requires, or what suits a judicial style or temperament)? The positivist thesis is a claim about how law is determined, not a claim about how much of a judicial decision is determined by law. On the latter issue, Kelsen says that '[t]here must always be more or less room for discretion', and Hart insists that, in every legal system, 'a large and important field is left open for the discretion of courts and other officials'.[8] Positivists are not indeterminacy-minimizers. Indeed, as the discussion of (5) shows, the incompleteness of law is intimately connected with its nature as a social institution.

One source of friction between realists and positivists arises this way: positivists hold that law is wholly constituted by social facts, but a realist might ask what use is it to know fact-constituted law if it gets little traction in court? Admittedly, there is such a thing as useless knowledge. Perhaps some realists share Dworkin's view that the only sensible career ambition for jurisprudence is to become a kind of high-brow *amicus curiae*. Felix Cohen wrote:

> Fundamentally there are only two significant questions in the field of law. One is, 'How do courts actually decide cases of a given kind?' The other is, 'How ought they to decide cases of a given kind?' Unless a legal 'problem' can be subsumed under one of these forms, it is not a meaningful question and any answer to it must be nonsense.[9]

Cohen misses something here. Whenever we have two meaningful questions, we perforce have a third: What is the relationship between the first two questions?

According to one view, Cohen's questions are independent. There are psychological and sociological questions about the causes of judicial decisions and there are normative questions—moral or legal—about how such decisions ought to be made. These enquiries do not compete and may not converse. This tolerant view takes no sides in general jurisprudence; it is held by H. L. A. Hart[10] but also by Ronald Dworkin, who not only acknowledges the

---

[8] Kelsen, *Pure Theory of Law*, 349; Hart, *The Concept of Law*, 136.
[9] Felix Cohen, 'Transcendental Nonsense and the Functional Approach' (1935) 35 *Columbia Law Review* 809, 824.
[10] H. L. A. Hart, 'Problems of Legal Philosophy', in H. L. A. Hart, *Essays in Jurisprudence and Philosophy* (Oxford University Press, 1982).

legitimacy of legal sociology but says that it is entitled to its very own concept of law—the 'sociological concept of law'.[11]

Competing with the independence view are two imperialistic ones: for Kelsen, normative questions take conceptual priority over factual ones; for realists, the reverse is true. Kelsen holds that intelligible enquiry into the causes of judicial decisions presupposes a normative (but not moral) theory of adjudication. Legal and political entities are norm-constituted, and, while we can and should aim for a descriptive theory of a normative object, that theory must preserve the character of the object. A legal system is a system of norms directing judges in how they ought to decide cases, not a set of predictions about how they will in fact decide, so the former is the proper object of jurisprudence. Kelsen does think sociological jurisprudence and legal positivism cannot come entirely unstuck. He holds that a legal system exists only if it is broadly effective—only if most of its rules are obeyed or applied, most of the time. He also holds that a particular legal rule, if never applied, is liable to be extinguished by the doctrine of desuetude or by the customary practices of the courts. So, he concludes, '[t]he norms which normative jurisprudence regards as valid are norms that are ordinarily obeyed or applied' and 'the results of a sociology of positive law cannot essentially differ from those of normative jurisprudence'.[12] That is over-optimistic. System-wide efficacy does not guarantee the efficacy of individual norms, and desuetude is but a possible rule of positive law. In many legal systems there are valid laws 'on the books' that have long been ignored or gone unused or are honoured in the breach. (In fact, this weak link between current conformity and continuing validity is one of the things that gives legal systems an edge over kinds of customary social order.)

A second imperialistic view, attributable to some realists among others, is that social science should *replace* normative jurisprudence because the norms found in legal doctrine either do not exist or are causally inefficacious in court. We understand the nature of law—to the extent that law has any determinate nature—the same way we study the nature of political parties, electoral systems, or markets: only by empirical analysis. When the data do not match the norms held out as valid law, the norms that are efficacious in court are the ones that should determine the province of jurisprudence.

---

[11] Ronald Dworkin, *Justice in Robes* (Harvard University Press, 2008) 2–3; but contrast his more Kelsenian view in Dworkin, *Law's Empire*, 12–13, relying on the idea that law is necessarily a normative (because argument-dependent) practice.

[12] Hans Kelsen, *General Theory of Law and State* (A. Wedberg trs, Russell and Russell, 1945) 170, 174.

Brian Leiter once defended a related view, both on its merits and as an interpretation of the leading ideas of the American legal realists, whom he regarded as presaging a kind of 'naturalized jurisprudence', a jurisprudence fit to keep company with the successful empirical sciences.[13] On this view, positivists may have been substantively correct about the nature of law, but they were wrong methodologically: it was just a lucky guess. No armchair analysis of the concept of law can show that law is wholly based on sources. An empirical study of judicial decision-making may reveal that something like positive sources figure in the working assumptions about, or an operational definition of, law as used by lawyers and sociologists. But that definition is revisable. If doctrinal rules have a place in a theory of law, it must be in virtue of their predictive efficacy.

4. Legal Realism and Positivism

On any account, positivists and realists agree about much: that law is constituted by social facts, that judges have and exercise significant powers to make law, and that law is morally fallible and so is to be approached in a realistic spirit in the everyday sense of that term, that is, with attention to facts and without romanticism or mystification. What is there left to disagree about? It proves surprisingly hard to say.

According to H. L. A. Hart, the Scandinavian realists advocate reductivist theories of rules and the American realists lack an adequate account of the rule-constituted institutions of courts and judges that preoccupy them. (He lays the same charge at the door of the imperativalists, especially Austin.) In both cases, there is a failure to pay attention to the character and variety of rules in law. These objections are second nature to contemporary positivists, many of whom first met the realists not in habitat but in chapter VII of *The Concept of Law*. Returning to the sources, Leiter argues that we have been misled: the most important realists hold views that are either compatible with Hart's positivism or, to the extent of any incompatibility, superior. In particular, the realists are not the 'rule sceptics' that Hart made notorious.

---

[13] Leiter, *Naturalizing Jurisprudence*: especially the essays 'Rethinking Legal Realism: Toward a Naturalized Jurisprudence'; 'Legal Realism, Hard Positivism, and the Limits of Conceptual Analysis'; and 'Legal Realism and Legal Positivism Reconsidered'. Leiter's view changed as he lost confidence in the (current) sciences of judicial decision-making: *Naturalizing Jurisprudence*, 188–93.

Realists do not deny the possibility of legal rules and they do not offer a predictive analysis of the concept of a rule—those are forms of conceptual rule scepticism, and the realists eschew conceptual analysis altogether. They are committed only to empirical rule scepticism, the view that, owing to indeterminacy, the decisions of appellate courts cannot be predicted on the basis of (positive) law but they can be predicted by extra-legal considerations, for instance, by 'judges' responses to the underlying facts of the cases', including their beliefs about what would be fair, given those facts.[14] While philosophers like Hart or Kelsen were cogitating, Leiter thinks they should have been counting.

Unfortunately, Hart uses the term 'rule scepticism' in several ways. It covers those who deny that practical rules exist and instead hold that they are theoretical 'prophecies of what the courts will do in fact'.[15] He also uses it to cover jurisprudents who think that those who have final authority to decide must also have unfettered authority to decide. And, most generally, he uses it for all who deny 'that for the most part decisions . . . are reached either by genuine effort to conform to rules consciously taken as guiding standards of decision or, if intuitively reached, are justified by rules which the judge was antecedently disposed to observe and whose relevance to the case in hand would generally be acknowledged'.[16]

These three sceptics are different, but Hart thinks that they are all befuddled by a failure to understand *what it would be* for conduct to be rule-guided. Rules can be loose or crisp, they can have exceptions or be defeasible, they can appear *ex ante* in decision-making or be appealed to *ex post*, when conduct is challenged. So long as they are shared standards of belief or conduct effectively 'accepted' as appropriate from the 'internal point of view', they are rules, they have practical functions, and they constitute both laws and legal institutions.

In Leiter's view, the American legal realists have no stake in any of this. 'Conceptual' claims about the nature of law or rules just leave them cold. Could all the loose talk, in Holmes, Cohen, or Llewellyn, about 'definitions' or 'ideas' of law or rules merely be jurisprudential *obiter dicta*? Leiter seems to think so:

---

[14] Ibid., 61–5.
[15] O. W. Holmes, Jr, 'The Path of the Law', in O. W. Holmes, Jr, *Collected Legal Papers* (Harcourt, Brace & Howe, 1920) 173.
[16] Hart, *The Concept of Law*, 137.

[Theirs] is not a claim about the concept of law but, rather, a claim about how it is useful to think about law for attorneys who must advise clients what to do.... [F]rom the practical perspective of the franchisee, what one wants to know about the law is what, in fact, the courts will do when confronted with the franchisee's grievance. That is all the law that matters to the client. And that is all, I take it, the Realists wanted to emphasize.[17]

Well, some of them seem to emphasize more. Beginning with Holmes, it becomes almost an article of realist faith that there are 'really' no primary obligations in tort or in contract; there are only remedial obligations to pay damages if so ordered by a court. Yet a client—even Holmes' 'bad man'—may think that they have a stake in their reputation for fidelity. They may even care more about what people outside courtrooms think than they care about the likelihood of being ordered to pay damages. Cohen writes that legal realism is 'a theory of the nature of legal roles, legal concepts, and legal questions. Its essence is the definition of law as a function of judicial decisions.'[18] Yet Cohen insists that '[j]udges are human, but they are a peculiar breed of humans, selected to a type and held to service under a potent system of governmental controls. Their acts are "judicial" only within a system which provides for appeals, rehearings, impeachments, and legislation.'[19] To say that judges' acts are judicial only within a system of effective norms is to say no more than Kelsen says in section II of *Pure Theory*. If these realist comments do not actually assert conceptual claims, they do presuppose them.

Of course, the realists are not coming to any of their theoretical conclusions through analysing ordinary language (any more than is Hart).[20] And sorting through the realists' opinions—most of whom had no philosophical training or insight—is a task that calls for an intellectual historian, and a patient one at that. Here, I hazard only two claims.

First, as Leiter agrees, insofar as the realists assert no claims about the concept of law or the concept of a rule, they have no dispute with the essential thesis of positivism. And, as I have stressed, positivists are not

---

[17] Leiter, *Naturalizing Jurisprudence*, 292.
[18] Cohen, 'Transcendental Nonsense', 842. Leiter takes a dim view of Cohen as a jurisprudent and as an exemplar of a legal realist: *Naturalizing Jurisprudence*, 291.
[19] Cohen, 'Transcendental Nonsense', 843.
[20] 'The idea that what demands understanding about law is the concept of law as manifest in ordinary language would have struck [the realists] as ridiculous.' Leiter, *Naturalizing Jurisprudence*, 291. On Hart and ordinary language, see Leslie Green, 'Introduction', in Hart, *The Concept of Law*.

indeterminacy-minimizers, certainly not with respect to decisions of appellate courts: the indeterminacy of law follows from positivism's thesis.

Second, if realists are nonetheless committed to claims about the concepts of rules and law, then the fact that they do not assert them as such does not immunize them from conceptual mistakes. Conceptual error is a strict liability offence. If someone complains to their doctor that 'my arthritis has moved into my thigh', what they say is not, as Cohen might have put it, 'nonsense'. It is grammatical and intelligible English. It may even be diagnostically useful. ('They're feeling the sort of pain in their thigh that their arthritis causes in their knee, therefore...') All the same, it is a mistake, and a mistake about the concept of arthritis. Of course, the patient has some command of 'arthritis' ('it causes an ache and not an itch', 'it is felt in the limbs but not the ears'.) They are getting by, as we all do, with a partial grasp of concepts prevalent in their society. In a similar way, if lawyers say that there are no such things as legal rules but only decisions of courts made by people called judges, they, too, demonstrate a partial grasp of a concept: they see that law stands in internal relation to the positive activities of courts. Moreover, just as the patient's mistake about arthritis may not matter for clinical purposes, conceptual mistakes about law may not matter for advocacy. But they matter for jurisprudence.

I doubt that Hart considers the typical rule sceptic to be committed to absurd denials that any rules exist. He takes the realists' extravagant statements to be 'great exaggerations of some truths about law unduly neglected'.[21] The neglected truth is that source-based law is always somewhat indeterminate and, in the most complex and most studied cases, quite indeterminate. The exaggeration lies in thinking that this is the ordinary run of things in an operational legal system, where people use legal rules to find their way through a roundabout, to enter tenancies, to buy cars, to make wills, or to get married— usually going nowhere near a lawyer, never mind a courtroom. Even in the appellate courts, Llewellyn's idea that 'there is always more than one available correct answer, the court always has to select'[22] neglects the fact that, on some points (e.g. whether the court has jurisdiction), the law may be as determinate as law ever is. And Llewellyn's famous claim that 'there are two opposing canons [of interpretation] on almost every point' does not show them to be in equipoise.[23] It is a reminder that advocates have lots of tools to

---

[21] Hart, *The Concept of Law*, 2.
[22] Karl N. Llewellyn, 'Some Realism about Realism—Responding to Dean Pound' (1935) 3 *Vanderbilt Law Review* 395, 396.
[23] Ibid., 401.

work with. Among contemporary, garden-variety, 'law-school' realists—and especially those teaching American constitutional law—some hold that there is no rule of recognition because courts disagree about the sources of law to an extent inconsistent with the *correct* criteria for the existence of a rule.[24] That, too, rests on a notion of what those criteria are. Unless we are happy with bare stipulations in these disputes, when we wrestle with questions of the form 'What counts as X?' or 'What are the criteria for Y?', we engage with conceptual problems.

Like Kelsen, Hart considers law to be a norm-constituted object, but one that is tractable to descriptive analysis.[25] His arguments against the various characters he labels 'rule sceptics' are cogent but compact. His points about the role of legal reasons in legal arguments, about finality versus the infallibility of decisions, and about how we detect social rules all require expansion and, at points, correction.[26] They do not reach a hard-bitten sceptic who thinks that our entrenched notions of rules, reasons, and judicial mistakes involve explicable errors. Nor are they alert to Goodman-type or Kripke-type anxieties about rules in general. Perhaps Hart does not need more for his purposes, since he mainly wants to show that the errors on which predictivism rests are so gross that we should not treat them as literal proposals for a new jurisprudence but as vivid reminders of important, though modest, truths about positive law.

Any realist who is any kind of rule sceptic faces a challenge in keeping his scepticism under control. A dose is needed in respect of the reasoning of appellate courts; but not so much that it will dissolve those institutions, and not so much that it makes ordinary law—law-in-action, law-in-the-solicitor's-office—unintelligible. Legal institutions, courts, officers, and decisions are rule-constituted things. Holmes says it might be of value if every word of moral significance were purged from jurisprudence, but he is never tempted by the thought that we should also eliminate all reference to institutional facts about courts, judges, or decisions. That is no doubt why Hart says that the only serious form of scepticism acknowledges that rules exist, that they are indispensable to understanding law, including both courts and their decisions, and that statements of rules have non-assertoric, dynamic functions.[27] The sceptic that Hart criticizes accepts all that but goes on to deny that such

---

[24] Dworkin, *Law's Empire*, 10.
[25] As my granny used to say, 'It disnae tak a fat cowherd tae drive fat kine'.
[26] For one correction, see Chapter 3, this volume.
[27] Hart, *The Concept of Law*, 38.

rules ever bind judges to a unique decision. This sceptic thinks that whatever psychological states judges find themselves in, whatever their pretence, however predictable their decisions, it is always false to suppose that they are bound by their own practices to decide cases as they do: 'There is nothing which courts treat as standards of correct judicial behaviour, and so nothing in that behaviour which manifests the internal point of view characteristic of the acceptance of rules.'[28] Did American realists of the early generation think this, or is Hart projecting backwards his own concerns? I am not sure; but some such view became sufficiently influential, not only among untheoretical 'law-school realists' but also in the short-lived critical legal studies 'movement', that it is still worth considering how it should be addressed.

5. Permissive Sources of Law

How could someone understand the boundary between law and non-law (such as custom, convention or instinct) if they were to deny that the law controls decisions in the higher courts, where these boundaries are produced, usually indirectly, by the application of law?

Leiter notices the resonance between the realist argument from indeterminacy and the positivist view about the boundaries of law. Herman Oliphant's idea that the American promise-not-to-compete cases were decided by accepted norms of business practice *rather than* by legal norms and Holmes' idea that broad policy considerations *rather than* legal norms determine outcomes both depend on a distinction between such norms on the one hand and American law on the other.[29] So they accept that law has boundaries and that its boundaries are determined—to the extent that they are—by social rather than moral or metaphysical considerations. Holmes calls law a 'business with well understood limits, a body of dogma enclosed within definite lines'.[30] Max Radin calms the anxious by reminding them of the common culture of legal thought: 'We need not fear arbitrariness. Our Cokes and Mansfields and Eldons derive their physical and spiritual nourishment from the same sources that we do.'[31]

---

[28] Ibid.
[29] Leiter, *Naturalizing Jurisprudence*, 292–3.
[30] Holmes, 'The Path of the Law', 171.
[31] Max Radin 'A Theory of Judicial Decision, or How Judges Think' (1925) 11 *American Bar Association Journal* 357, 362.

What should we make of this? Perhaps the realists *presupposed* something like a positivist view of law without working out whether it could be made consistent with their sceptical views about rules and appellate decisions. Or perhaps they were happy to compartmentalize, to be casual positivists in their court pleadings and hard-bitten sceptics in their graduation addresses. But I think that there is another possibility.

Legal positivists hold that all law is positive law. On Hart's version, the sources of law are ultimately determined by customary social rules that identify them as valid grounds for judicial decision, binding on the courts. But there is a complication in this idea of a 'source': Hart writes:

> [W]hen it is said that a statute is a source of law, the word 'source' refers not to mere historical or causal influences but to one of the criteria of legal validity accepted in the legal system in question. Enactment as a statute by a competent legislature is the reason why a given statutory rule is a valid law and not merely the cause of its existence.[32]

Enactment is both part of the causal history of a statutory rule and also something else, namely, one of the criteria identified as a source of law in that system. Since the ultimate recognition rules in every legal system, even ones with a 'written' constitution, are customary practices of (at least) the courts and other officials, there can be no clear demarcation between an event playing a causal role in the creation of a statute and it being accepted as a criterion of statutory validity. Customary norms emerge higgledy-piggledy out of common practice, not as products of prescription or planning. *Ex post facto*—when a customary norm is well entrenched—courts and others may look back on earlier bits of history as precursors to, or even aspects of, its contemporary acceptance; but that is as much of a fiction as when we say *Donoghue v Stevenson* was the 'beginning' of our negligence standard. (It became the beginning only later, after other courts reacted to it.) That means there will be grey areas in which something may, or may not, be a source; or a source-to-be; or, I will now suggest, a source of a permissive kind.

In discussing the notion of a source of law, Hart remarks that, in addition to the familiar binding sources of enactments, decisions, and customs, a court may draw on the decision of a foreign court, institutional writers, Roman jurists, and even, in some jurisdictions, academics. 'The legal system does not

---

[32] Hart, *The Concept of Law*, 294.

require him to use these sources, but it is accepted as perfectly proper that he should do so. They are more than merely historical or causal influences since such writings are recognized as "good reasons" for decisions.[33] Yet the very same courts might never think it appropriate to cite Rawls' *Theory of Justice* or (thank God) Leviticus. Customary practice makes the difference.

How should we characterize these 'good reasons' for decisions whose normative force turns on practice but that have not crystallized into binding law? Judges sometimes cite treatises or law dictionaries for a pithy statement of the law, believing that the statement is, on independent grounds, correct. They also sometimes cite academic arguments they find convincing on their merits, taking them not as authoritative but as persuasive only. Sometimes, however, the very fact that things *are* generally 'recognized as good reasons' sets them apart. For example, it is a matter of positive practice that Scots courts may cite the seventeenth- and eighteenth-century writers Stair and Erskine. Unlike the way an English lawyer might cite Blackstone, however, the Scots allow their institutional writers some actual, if weak, authority. The very fact that Erskine declares N is some reason for holding that N is part of Scots law—though it is a subordinate reason and one that cannot resist the contrary authority of, say, statute or case law. Still, Erskine can be used to resist common sense or a persuasive argument from a law journal. It may be no legal error to omit Erskine where he could be relevant, yet it may strengthen a case to cite him. (Scots lawyers being canny, they do not waste sources.) In many legal systems, something similar holds for the judgments of foreign courts.

On Hart's account, whether a norm is mandatory (or binding) is a matter of degree.[34] Hence, the distinction between which sources are binding on the courts and which things are not is also a matter of degree—as we would expect in an area of customary obligations. In addition to sources that they are strictly bound to apply, there are sources that courts are by their own customs expressly permitted to apply: practice-based 'good reasons' for decision that are given greater force than they would have had just on their own merits and in the absence of that practice.

A 'permissive source' of law is not, however, a bare permission. Being permitted to V is not normally any sort of reason to V (though it may be a reason for others not to interfere with one's V-ing). Moreover, absent a source, courts are generally permitted to act on any sound reasons relevant to a dispute. It is

---

[33] Ibid., note to 101.
[34] Ibid., 82–91.

not as if we live in a world in which judges have no grounds to decide any dispute until law steps in and provides some. Where judges have a duty to make a ruling, they may rely on any lawful and cogent consideration. The function of the sources in law is often to block reliance on reasons for decision that would otherwise be cogent.[35] We should normally transfer wealth from the rich to the poor—though not when the law of negligence steps in to require a poor negligent driver to compensate the rich one they have injured, thereby blocking reasons of beneficence or charity. A permissive source of law thus differs both from a bare permission and from something that is on its merits a persuasive reason for decision, for example, a consideration of justice, utility, or humanity. Permissive sources get their merit-independent force from the fact that they are recognized and applied as reasons for decision in the practice of the courts, even though they fall short of binding authority.

I conjecture that part of the realists' objection to positivism is that they consider *many* sources to be permissive—not only Llewellyn's canons of interpretation but also case law and even statutes, judicially construed. They do acknowledge the core of rules that constitute legal institutions and elementary procedures; that licences them to speak freely of the boundaries of law and legal institutions all the while thinking that the law does little to constrain judges in tried cases. While sharing positivist claims about the finitude, indeterminacy of, and possibility of conflicts among sources, the realist adds a more radical claim: many 'formal' sources have little more than the weak authority of something like a doctrine of foreign law, or the views of a writer like Erskine or Stair.

On the view I am describing, legal doctrine is a limited menu of socially based considerations that courts are entitled to apply, that are recognized as appropriate to apply, that are distinct from things like ordinary commercial customs and social convention, but that have such weak authority that it is easily overborne by considerations of policy, justice, the equities of the case, and so forth. Legal reasoning is, as the positivists hold, source-based, but the control of those sources over judicial decisions is more limited than most positivists think. That sounds, to me, like the position the moderate realists defend.

If I am correct, then there is an empirical *and* a conceptual dispute between positivists and realists. Hart addresses the empirical point the only way one can: with a plea to look. He does not think that the realists mean to

---

[35] Joseph Raz, *Between Authority and Interpretation: On the Theory of Law and Practical Reason* (Oxford University Press, 2009) 190 ff.

restrict their claim to the American appeals courts only—that would drain a lot of blood from their theory. For a realist should think it an open question to what extent the trial courts follow the high court: The output, not just the input, of appellate cases is legal rules. Hart thinks that, freed of the *a priori* blinders of behaviourism or reductionism, anyone can see the uncontroversial application of rules at some points in the appeal courts, at many points in the trial courts, but, most important, in the myriad ways that law guides daily conduct without the supervision of courts at all. '[B]oth the framework within which ... [judicial decisions] take place and their chief end-product is one of general rules. These are rules the application of which individuals can see for themselves in case after case, without further recourse to official direction or discretion.'[36] This plea is not an argument. But neither is it *ipse dixit*. If someone fails to spot the pigeons and then boldly declares that there are none about, it may be enough to say, 'Just look; over there! Pigeons everywhere!' People sometimes miss fairly determinate legal rules because they are looking in the wrong places, and sometimes because they are wrong about what a fairly determinate legal rule looks like.

To this, Hart adds two arguments for believing that there are mandatory legal norms that bind the courts. These arguments aim to clarify what it is for a standard to be binding. First, even if judges do not experience any special psychological states like 'feelings of compulsion', they may nonetheless have an obligation to decide in a certain way.[37] This point is addressed to the crude behaviourism of Alf Ross or Axel Hägerström's reductionism, or maybe eliminativism, about legal entities.

The second argument is that most judicial decisions are either (a) 'reached by genuine effort to conform to rules consciously taken as guiding standards' or (b) reached 'intuitively'—without conscious effort to conform—but nonetheless 'justified by rules that judges are disposed to observe and whose relevance to the case at hand would be generally acknowledged'.[38] Point (a) reiterates the plea to look. Point (b) invokes the criteria for the existence of rules. It is a mistake to think that one can follow a social rule only if there is *a very high* degree of consensus about what the rule requires over the full range of *possible* applications, if one is *conscious* of it as a rule, and one uses it in *an*

---

[36] Hart, *The Concept of Law*, 136.
[37] 'What is necessary is that there should be a critical reflective attitude to certain patterns of behaviour as a common standard, and that this should display itself in criticism (including self criticism), demands for conformity, and in acknowledgements that such criticism and demands are justified ...' Hart, *The Concept of Law*, 57.
[38] Ibid., 141.

effort to conform. This overemphasizes the degree to which rule-following is articulate and conscious *ex ante*. It leaves too little room for our familiar experience of the inarticulate, unconscious, and instinctive following of rules that are clear enough over their usual range and that are internalized, for example, when we know how to speak our native language, or how to dress for an occasion, or when we know that a certain legal argument 'just won't fly'. Rule-following is also displayed *ex post actu*, when rules are produced in justifications, used in communicating past decisions to others, or used to explain what was decided or to defend it against criticism, actual or anticipated. To downplay all this is to make a mistake about the concept of a rule, a mistake that can infect one's theory of law. It leads to a failure to appreciate the extent to which law works through tolerably clear rules and binding sources.

6. The Displacement of Jurisprudence?

Law is an anthropocentric, mind-constituted thing, and one way to understand such things is to get clearer about their conceptual structure. Once we understand law, we can begin to evaluate it. Llewellyn seems content with that. He contends only for a 'temporary divorce of Is and Ought for the purposes of study'.[39] And Cohen writes: 'When we recognize that legal rules are simply formulae describing uniformities of judicial decision . . . then we are ready for the serious business of appraising law and legal institutions in terms of some standard of human values'.[40] Neither of them thinks that the 'serious business' of judicial decision is insulated from reasoned (if sometimes non-legal) argument.

How far could Cohen's 'formulae describing uniformities of judicial decision' replace the doctrinal aspects of legal argument? It depends, I suppose, on what we expect from a replacement. Compare proposals for a naturalized account of knowledge. Reflecting on the failure of foundationalist epistemologies, Quine writes: 'If all we can hope for is a reconstruction that links science to experience in explicit ways short of translation, then it would seem more sensible to settle for psychology'.[41] 'Seeming sensible' is not an

---

[39] Karl N. Llewellyn, 'Remarks on the Theory of Appellate Decision and the Rules or Canons about How Statutes Are to Be Construed' (1950) 3 *Vanderblit Law Review* 395.
[40] Cohen, 'Transcendental Nonsense', 487.
[41] W. V. O. Quine, *Ontological Relativity and Other Essays* (Columbia University Press, 1969) 78.

entailment relation or even a very compelling reason. That E fails is no reason for thinking that P will succeed, and certainly no reason for thinking that P will succeed at what E was aiming for. Perhaps Quine's observation shows that knowledge defies reasoned inquiry of any kind, and that if you want to study something naturalistically, you will have to settle for the sociology or psychology of belief. In a Quinean spirit, Leiter writes: '[I]f no normative account of the relation [between legal reasons and judicial decision] is possible, then the only theoretically fruitful account is the descriptive/explanatory account given by the relevant science of that domain.'[42] This sounds more like a reason for studying a different domain, one tractable to the methods that 'naturalism' approves. Kelsen makes the same sort of move: He decides he wants to study law 'scientifically', drafts desiderata for such a programme, then gives no further thought to aspects of legal life that are not tractable to his methods.

Why should the psychology of judicial decisions be worth pursuing only on the condition of the *failure* of doctrinal argument to shed light on questions that psychology is not even asking? If Carnap's foundationalism had succeeded, we could still have pursued an independent science studying the extent to which people endorse or follow the principles it constructed. If Bayesianism is the best foundation for decision theory, we can still study how far, and why, people deviate from its prescriptions. Likewise, where law yields determinate answers, we can still ask why some judges and not others are willing to rule as the law requires. Maybe we will discover that some judges misunderstand the law, or misapply it, or even break it? That would hardly come as a surprise. There are judges and courts who make little effort to apply settled law when it is at variance with the wishes of their patrons; there are many more whose wishful thinking makes such variance invisible to them. Kelsen writes:

> To replace this [normative legal] science by legal sociology is impossible, because the latter is concerned with an entirely different problem. As long as religion exists, there must be a dogmatic theology that cannot be replaced by religious psychology or religious sociology; in precisely the same manner there will be a normative science of law as long as there is law.[43]

---

[42] Leiter, *Naturalizing Jurisprudence*, 293.
[43] Kelsen, *Pure Theory of Law*, 89.

The analogy is a bit strained. Some religions did not evolve hand-in-glove with European rationalism, and so were not shaped by its characteristic modes of rationalization through doctrine. Still, Kelsen is on the mark in thinking that a psychology or sociology of those religions would not deepen our understanding of their meaning for their adherents and would involve changing the subject of inquiry. Are we tempted to object: some people study astrology with sophistication and energy, and that gives meaning to their lives? Yes: but in that case there is no evidence that astrology can do what it purports to do, that is predict the future, determine human compatibilities, and so on. Astrology fails *at the very thing it promises*, and its promises are part of its meaning for its practitioners. In contrast, a normative theory of adjudication does not purport to predict how judges will decide cases; it purports to explain how they ought to decide cases according to law. To the extent that 'ought implies can', it will be interested in the sciences of human decision-making. But none of that undermines the relative autonomy of jurisprudence as a subject.

7. Conclusion

The thesis of legal positivism is that all law is positive law—all law has sources; all legal systems are systems of source-based rules. Other legal philosophers doubt that, on various (incompatible) grounds. But, as far as I can tell, most legal realists *do not* doubt it and, in any case, they should not doubt it. Their distinctions between traditional legal materials and considerations of policy or judicial psychology suggest that they presuppose that law rests on sources. They may doubt that the sources generally determine judicial decisions, at least in the appellate courts, but more exaggerated assertions of indeterminacy risk sawing off the branches they sit on—their comfortable, and mostly unexplained, ontology of courts and judicial decisions. Maybe, as Hart holds, realists are exaggerating to foreground a phenomenon they consider under-appreciated. Maybe, as Leiter holds, they are suggesting that we replace, for some purposes, an 'unsuccessful' method with a more useful one. (There is no denying that if one really could predict judicial decisions, there would be good money in it.) Maybe—and this is the idea I have been offering here—they think that court cases often turn on sources that are not binding but are instead permissive. Or maybe there is something in all three explanations: they are partly compatible and, as elsewhere in jurisprudence, the truth may be shared among them. But there is no doubt that legal positivism and legal realism have much in common, and not only in temperament. Let us not make them seem more foreign to each other than they are.[44]

---

[44] I thank John Gardner, Brian Leiter, and Torben Spaak for criticism of earlier drafts of this chapter.

5
Gender and Jurisprudence

1. Law and Jurisprudence

What can feminism contribute to the study of law? A lot. Feminist theories take a special interest in the role of gender in society and, as far as we know, every society that has a legal system also has a gender hierarchy in which women are dominated by men.[1] It would be a miracle if the law was not shaped by gender norms. In turn, law supports and helps constitute those norms: the doctrine of *feme covert* that limited married women's control over property did not merely reflect background misogyny, it gave it shape and force. Feminist scholars have explored such issues in many contexts and found their etiology distressingly similar. This is of academic interest and of practical import: it can help us understand what it is for women to be disadvantaged by law, the ways that happens, and the remedies that might be feasible. These are massively important contributions to the study of law.

What can feminism contribute to the study of jurisprudence? This is trickier. Of course, if 'jurisprudence' *means* law—as when we use the term to refer to case law or general principles of law—we already have our answer. But what if 'jurisprudence' means the philosophy of law and, in particular, the philosophy of law in the analytic style dominant throughout the Anglophone world and in many other places as well?

There is plenty of good feminist writing in the normative branches of jurisprudence that overlap moral and political philosophy.[2] Feminists have tackled issues such as the importance of relationships in morality, free speech

---

[1] There are many feminisms, but none fail to give gender a central explanatory, and sometimes normative, role. For a philosophically informed discussion of feminism in legal analysis, see Denise Réaume, 'What's Distinctive about Feminist Analysis of Law? A Conceptual Analysis of Women's Exclusion from Law' (1996) 2 *Legal Theory* 265. For a helpful treatment of feminism in philosophy, see Alison Stone, *An Introduction to Feminist Philosophy* (Polity, 2007).
[2] The literature is vast, but a beginning would have to include Carole Pateman, *The Sexual Contract* (Polity Press, 1988); Susan Moller Okin, *Justice, Gender, and the Family* (Basic Books, 1991); Martha Nussbaum, *Sex and Social Justice* (Oxford University Press, 1999); and Cheshire Calhoun, *Feminism, the Family, and the Politics of the Closet: Lesbian and Gay Displacement* (Oxford University Press, 2000).

and pornography, and the connection between domestic equality and social justice. There is no harmony here, but we are familiar with a range of well-articulated feminist positions.

Suppose, however, we are thinking of what is usually called 'conceptual' or 'descriptive' jurisprudence.[3] To assess the relevance of gender here we need to take the question in two stages. *General jurisprudence* is audacious in ambition. It addresses the nature of law as such, anywhere and everywhere. Its central topics include the existence, identity, and structure of legal systems, the nature of legal norms, the relationships between law and morality, and the dependence of law on social facts. In contrast, *special jurisprudence* is concerned with conceptual problems about particular kinds of legal systems (e.g. common law, civil law, or Sharia law) or particular doctrines within legal systems (e.g. property, contract, or family law). General and special jurisprudence differ in level of generality—but not only in that. They also differ in the evidence base with which they begin. *Law* is not itself a technical legal concept; it is part of ordinary social and political thought, and general jurisprudence begins with ordinary (lay) knowledge of law and society. Whether, for example, 'indigenous law' or 'Masonic law' count as law is not determined by how any particular legal system regards the rules of indigenous bands or Freemasons' lodges. Whether *according to Australian law* indigenous law is 'really' law has no more importance for general jurisprudence than whether, according to Australian law, German law is really law. A social order is law if and only if it has enough features of the core cases of legal systems.[4] What features those are is not a question that can be answered by consulting the law of some jurisdiction or other. (Which one would we pick?) General jurisprudence is a department of political theory. We should think of its accounts of

---

[3] I treat these as rough synonyms. Ronald Dworkin holds that there is no such thing as descriptive, conceptual jurisprudence: 'Hart's Postscript and the Character of Political Philosophy' (2004) 24 *Oxford Journal of Legal Studies* 1. If that were correct, all conceptual jurisprudence would be normative, and feminism would be relevant to it for the reason I give above. I do not think that thesis is correct, nor is it relied on by any of the feminist arguments mentioned in this chapter. My own views about description and evaluation in jurisprudence are explained in Section 5 below and in the Introduction to this volume.

[4] If indigenous law or Masonic law do not share enough of these features to count as law, they may nonetheless be *importantly like* law for various purposes. The idea that general jurisprudence is interested only in law *sensu stricto*, or that it harbours a secret ambition to police the boundaries around 'law', is false. Even John Austin knew that many things that are *not* law 'are connected [to law] by ties of resemblance and analogy; with which they are further connected by the common name of "laws"': John Austin, *The Province of Jurisprudence Determined* (W. E. Rumble ed., Cambridge University Press, 1995) 51.

the nature of law as being similar to theoretical accounts of the nature of markets, states, or political parties.

Leading concepts in special jurisprudence, in contrast, are law dependent. The evidence base for a theory of restitution need not address 'ordinary' understandings of restitution—there is probably no such thing—nor need the theory accord with some general scheme of what people think they owe each other. It is true that some concepts in special jurisprudence, causation for example, also have a role outside the law, so here we may need to examine relations between causation *as the law thinks of it* and causation as understood in science or in history.[5] But special jurisprudence must be centrally interested in, and answerable to, the law—and especially to the law as applied by the courts. This reflects the fact that special jurisprudence takes as its explananda *concepts within the law*, while general jurisprudence targets *the concept of law*.

2. Feminism and General Jurisprudence

Could there be a feminist *general* jurisprudence? A generation ago, when feminist legal theories began to take shape, we sometimes heard claims such as 'law is male' or 'the state is male in that objectivity is its norm'.[6] These sound a bit like general theories of law and the state. But are they, really? If law is the male of the species, what is the female? If objectivity is male, is subjectivity female? Any philosopher foolhardy enough to subject slogans like 'law is male' to analytic scrutiny deserves everything he gets. Like 'property is theft', 'law is male' is a searing metaphor that incites people to action, not a cool analysis of the concept of law.

The fact that leading feminist writers of the 1980s and 1990s paid no serious attention to any general theory of law suggests they assumed that feminist theory had no stake in general jurisprudence.[7] I think they were right. General jurisprudence is 'normatively inert', and most feminists wanted to

---

[5] H. L. A. Hart and Tony Honoré, *Causation in the Law* (2nd edn, Oxford University Press, 1985).

[6] Catharine MacKinnon, 'Feminism, Marxism, and the State: Towards Feminist Jurisprudence' (1983) 8 *Signs* 635, at 645.

[7] For a sample of their actual concerns, see Ann C. Scales, 'The Emergence of Feminist Jurisprudence: An Essay' (1986) 95 *Yale Law Journal* 1373; Robin West, 'Jurisprudence and Gender' (1988) 55 *University of Chicago Law Review* 1, and many of the essays in the two volumes by Frances E. Olsen ed., *Feminist Legal Theory* (Dartmouth, 1995).

be where the action is.⁸ The best feminist theory took up overtly normative positions, backed with careful doctrinal and empirical research to provide the factual premises of the arguments they advanced. Among academic writers, polemics about the sexed character *of law* proved less productive and ultimately less influential than detailed examinations of gender *in the law*: in feminist studies of family law, criminal law, discrimination law, and so on. Here, researchers took for granted that the statutes, cases, and practices they scrutinized were authentic legal, or legally relevant, materials. They did not pause to ask—or, if you like, did not waste time asking—questions like these: Is sexist moralizing from the bench an application of law or an exercise of discretion? If the principles that best explain and justify settled law harm women is there nonetheless a reason to extend them to unsettled cases? Do men have duties to obey the law that women lack?

Feminist lawyers of the formative generation were not mere casecrunchers or activists, but such theory as mattered for their purposes—principally, normative theory and social theory—did not include general jurisprudence. And, on the flip side, one would struggle to identify anything distinctively feminist in the general jurisprudence used or developed by writers sympathetic to feminism in legal studies.⁹ By the late 1990s, most scholars had come to see feminist legal studies and analytic jurisprudence as different things: not team mates, but not competitors either.

How do things stand, thirty years on? There have been decisive steps forwards, but also the occasional great leap backwards. In her well-regarded book about law and gender, for example, Joanne Conaghan writes, 'the concept of law (to invoke the title of Hart's famous work) has been endlessly interrogated in terms which do not admit the relevance of gender'.¹⁰ This is no

---

⁸ I take the phrase from John Gardner, 'Legal Positivism: 5 1/2 Myths' (2001) 46 *American Journal of Jurisprudence* 199. The point is not unique to positivism; it holds for legal realism, legal naturalism, socio-legal jurisprudence, historical jurisprudence, and all other approaches to law whose aims are descriptive rather than hortatory.

⁹ Among others who can fairly be counted as feminists of one sort or another are: Julie Dickson, Nicola Lacey, Denise Réaume, Connie Rosati, Emily Sherwin, and Seanna Shiffrin. How many of her readers know that Lacey, whose work in socio-legal feminism is indispensable, wrote with precision and insight on the existence conditions for momentary legal systems? (Nicola Lacey, 'The Place of the Distinction between Momentary and Non-Momentary Legal Systems in Legal Analysis', in W. E. Butler ed., *Anglo-Polish Legal Essays* (Transnational Publishers, 1982) 15) Or that Denise Réaume, who taught us about culture, discrimination, and dignity, also did illuminating work on obligation and law? (Denise Réaume, 'Is Integrity a Virtue? Dworkin's Theory of Legal Obligation' (1989) 39 *University of Toronto Law Journal* 380.) That such writers found no incompatibility between general jurisprudence and feminist analysis of law might have given pause to those who think analytic work is ideologically suspect.

¹⁰ Joanne Conaghan, *Law and Gender* (Oxford University Press, 2013) 6.

casual remark: Conaghan labours to show that gender has pervasive relevance, not only to law but also to jurisprudence, including (as this quotation affirms) general jurisprudence. '[I]n the legal conceptual framework gender tends to be understood at best as a matter of content not form', and it is this alleged error that Conaghan strains to correct, by an extended critique of 'The official position . . . that the *idea* of law and legal fundamentals are, and certainly ought to be, gender-independent.'[11]

Now, legal philosophy, unlike law, is a domain without officials, so how could it have any 'official position' on the idea of law? Conaghan's thesis, which I test here, is that shared *methodological* commitments on the part of (analytic) legal philosophers screen out the relevance of gender to the idea of law. For all the vast substantive differences among the jurisprudential views of, say, Hans Kelsen and H. L. A. Hart, Ronald Dworkin and Joseph Raz, John Finnis and Jurgen Habermas, they concur in thinking that the 'idea' of law, or the concept of law, is not in any literal sense 'gendered' because they share a broad commitment to the methods of analytic philosophy.

To know whether that conjecture is plausible, we need to begin by considering what it is for gender to be relevant to a jurisprudential question. I will assume it is for some position about the nature or role of gender relations to make a jurisprudential thesis more or less plausible, that is, for gender to bear on its truth or acceptability. Compare two problems: (A) You are wondering whether the ideal of equality under the law is satisfied provided existing legal rules are applied constantly, without exception, to all and only those who fall under their terms. That is to presuppose that equality is independent of the content of the law and thus independent of whether that law treats women as it treats men. That would be unacceptable on most feminist views of morality (and on most sane views of morality). So, gender is relevant here. (B) You are instead wondering whether, as Hans Kelsen claimed, municipal and international law form parts of one unified and consistent legal system.[12] No view about gender—what constitutes it, what its social importance is, how it shapes law or life—is going to tilt the answer in favour of or against Kelsen's monism. To this question, gender—and, therefore, feminist legal theory—is irrelevant. The difference between (A) and (B) explains why there are feminist theories of legal equality but no feminist theories of legal systems. Likewise, there are feminist theories of discrimination, but no feminist theories of the existence

[11] Ibid., 7, 8.
[12] Hans Kelsen, *Pure Theory of Law* (M. Knight trs, University of California Press, 1967) 328–44.

conditions for rules, feminist theories of the family, but no feminist theories of vagueness, and so on.

We can bring the point into focus by imagining a feminist utopia in which all laws, substantive and procedural, all the attitudes underlying and reinforced by them, and all the people creating and administering them cease being sexist. Books about law and gender come to have only antiquarian interest. In that utopia we would have non-sexist law, non-sexist legal institutions, and non-sexist legal officials. But we would still have law. Or does Conaghan intend to deny that when she avers that 'gender is implicated in the very forms of law;'[13] that it has a role 'in the construction and formal ordering of law'; and that it is expressed in the 'basic forms and underpinnings of law?'[14] These claims supposedly exemplify truths that the analytical tradition in jurisprudence cannot or will not admit. What are they truths about?

An inquiry into 'how law is conceptualized, organized, articulated, and legitimated'[15] cannot show how gender is implicated in 'the very forms of law' since that depends on the content of the law and not on its forms alone. How law is conceptualized, in Conaghan's sense, depends on *how people see law*, including their fantasies and ideologies. (They may think of law as daddy, or of justice as a woman.) How law is organized and articulated is a function of *how the law is used and expressed* by its officials and others. How the law is legitimated depends on the *sort of stories people tell* in defence of the law or its authority. All of these are important but none of them has much bearing on the concept of law. None of them gives us a reason to think that, in fantasy feminist utopia, law would have withered away.

To establish that the very forms of law are 'gendered' would take an explanation of those forms and an account of the sense in which they are masculine (or feminine). Conaghan does not undertake that analysis. That does not prove it infeasible. We do have a rough model of how to go about that sort of project in Evegny Pashukanis' development of a Marxist theory of law.[16] First, he explains the basic forms law: Pashukanis says they necessarily include individual rights. Second, he explains how social class is related to control over property. Finally, he argues that the rights that constitute law are essentially property rights. It follows that law is capitalist, not merely in function or ideology, but in its very form. Pashukanis' theory is liable to objections,

---

[13] Conaghan, *Law and Gender*, 5.
[14] Ibid., 7.
[15] Ibid., 8.
[16] Evgeny B. Pashukanis, *Law and Marxism: A General Theory* (C. Arthur ed., B. Einhorn trs, Pluto Press, 1978).

but it proceeds in the correct way: from an analysis of the forms of law to an argument connecting those forms to class domination. But the first step, the analytical work, is vital. Seeing this sets Pashukanis apart from many other Marxist theorists.[17] He warns: 'If . . . we forgo an analysis of the fundamental juridical concepts, all we get is a theory which explains the emergence of legal regulation from the material needs of society . . . Yet legal regulation itself has still not been analyzed as a form.'[18] Feminist jurisprudence calls attention to sexism in the ways people see, use, and defend the law and to the ways these activities emerge in a gender hierarchy; but that is on a par with Marxist attention to 'the emergence of legal regulation from the material needs of society'. Someone who wants to prove that the 'idea' of law, or the 'concept of law', or the 'very forms' of law are gendered needs to go further and achieve for feminism what Pashukanis attempts for Marxism. That would be, not to transcend analytical jurisprudence, but to do it.

3. Feminism and Concepts in Special Jurisprudence: An Example

In the previous section, I examined the case for thinking feminist legal theory offers an account of the concept *of* law; now I turn to see how it handles concepts *within* the law. In other writings, I examined the legal concept of marriage, motivated by legal and moral questions that arise now that same-sex couples can marry.[19] I do not summarize that work here, though to fix ideas one thesis I defend is that the common law's concept of marriage had less to do with sex than some suppose, and that William Blackstone was essentially correct when he wrote, in 1765, 'Our law considers marriage in no other light than as a civil contract', approvingly citing Justinian's *Digest* on the primacy of *consensus* over *concubitus* in constituting marriage.[20]

Conaghan strenuously objects to this thesis, which she treats as symptomatic of the errors of the whole analytic approach in special jurisprudence. She

---

[17] See Christine Sypnowich, *The Socialist Concept of Law* (Oxford University Press, 1990); and Hugh Collins, *Marxism and Law* (Oxford University Press, 1996). Marxist legal theory went through its own period of hostility to analytic political philosophy, until the 1980s and the emergence of 'analytic Marxism'. Feminist legal theory still struggles to shed its hostility, and for similar reasons.
[18] Pashukanis, *Law and Marxism*, 55.
[19] Leslie Green, 'Sex-Neutral Marriage' (2011) 64 *Current Legal Problems* 1
[20] William Blackstone, *Commentaries on the Laws of England* (G. Sharswood ed., Lippincott, 1893) Bk 1 chap. 15, 433.

says my works offer 'a rare glimpse into how sex/gender is conceived in the analytical jurisprudential mind',[21] a glimpse that reveals the 'methodological limitations which characterize [all such] jurisprudential analysis', to wit:

> the abstraction of legal concepts from the framework in which they operate and the tendency to treat them as having a fairly fixed content over time and space; the unarticulated normative prioritization of some features . . . over others . . . evidencing the presence of evaluative choices which problematize any claim to be rendering a descriptive or value-neutral account; the overlooking, or at least unexplained disregard, of contra-indicative evidence . . .[22]

In sum, the allegation is that an analytical approach in jurisprudence fails to detect the significance of gender *even in marriage*, because the methods of analytic philosophy screen it out: by use of unhistorical abstractions, by a pretence of value neutrality, and by disregard of empirical evidence.

If this diagnosis were correct, analytical jurisprudence would not merely have 'methodological limitations'; it would be a failure. To suppose legal concepts are unchanging flies in the face of the obvious; the law changes and with it so do some concepts. To think we can describe anything without prioritizing some of its features is to misunderstand the nature of description. To overlook or disregard pertinent evidence is incompetence or dishonesty. Unsurprisingly, I do not accept that I made such blunders. Self-defence may not be enough to get the whole 'analytical jurisprudential mind' off the hook, however. Perhaps I am not prone to these vices though everyone else is; maybe I escaped a bad upbringing. If that were all there were to it the matter would be of little interest, even to me. But that is not all there is to it. If these are endemic vices of analytic jurisprudence (or of 'the analytical jurisprudential mind') then law students would be well advised to stay away from it altogether, especially if they are sympathetic to, or just curious about, a feminist analysis of law. That would be a loss to jurisprudence, and to feminism.

Let us focus for a moment on concepts. Conaghan's claim is that if one abstracts legal concepts from their historical and doctrinal contexts, one inevitably isolates them from gendered contexts. To treat concepts abstractly is to treat them as fixed, whereas they change in ways that respond to, and produce, changes in our ideas about gender. Conaghan illustrates this with

---

[21] Conaghan, *Law and Gender*, 169.
[22] Ibid., 176.

reference to my claim that *sex* and *gender* pick out different concepts, sex a biological one and gender a social one. She denies this, maintaining that both are social—'social constructions', as some people say—and thus liable to change over time.[23]

Why assume that if we abstract a concept from a particular context of use, or study it at one point in time, we must obscure the role of gender in explaining that concept? Wouldn't that depend on whether gender is, or is not, needed to explain that concept, at that time? For example, if we try to analyse the concept *woman*—in the context of middle-class, twenty-first century Britain—we may have to mention social norms that apply distinctively to adult human females, if *woman* is, as some think, partly constituted by gender norms. But we would not mention the fact that British women speak fewer languages than Dutch women or are on average 162 centimetres tall. Not everything that is true of most, or even all, instances of C is part of what it is to be C. It is not as if the analysis of *woman* somehow *failed to detect* relative linguistic incompetence as part of *what it is* to be a woman. It would have been an error to include it. Why, then, think that if an analysis of some concept in the law, for example, a *tort* or a *treaty*, makes no mention of gender it must have missed something needed for an adequate account—and missed it as a result of a defective methodology? We would need an affirmative reason to include it.

Maybe none of this bears on what Conaghan has in mind when she complains about the absence of gender in explanations of the concept of law or concepts in the law. People use the word 'concept' in various ways, and she may be using it differently than those she criticizes. I think it is useful to distinguish *concepts* (ideas, notions, senses) of things, our *words* for things (and for concepts), and the very *things* in question. For example, there is *gold*, the element that has atomic number seventy-nine; there is the *concept* of gold, an abstract notion that expresses the sense of terms referring to that element and which may be rendered in necessary and sufficient (or at least typifying) conditions; and finally there is the English *word* 'gold', which has four letters, brings associations of treasure and sunsets, and translates the Norwegian '*gull*' as well as the Irish '*ór*'.

---

[23] It is a hard to retrace why Conaghan thinks that, to disprove my claims about marriage, she needs to analyse the relation between *sex* and *gender*. Possibly, she thinks an argument showing that sex is not constitutive of marriage can be refuted by arguing that sex is not what it appears to be.

FEMINISM AND CONCEPTS IN SPECIAL JURISPRUDENCE   135

If we are interested in the nature of *gold*, we are unlikely to start by studying our concept of gold, let alone the word 'gold'. On the other hand, to understand the nature of *grief*, we do need to understand our concept of grief and its relations to nearby concepts (sadness, depression) as well as remote ones (happiness, joy); we may even need to study the meaning and origin of the concept-word 'grief' in English, or its synonyms in other languages. The fruitfulness of conceptual analysis can depend on how anthropocentric and mind dependent a thing is.

I assume that *law* is thoroughly anthropocentric and mind dependent and that analysis of the concept of law reveals things about law.[24] The same applies to legal relations and entities: crimes, duties, contracts, wills, courts, etc. I also assume that legal concepts can change—has anyone ever denied it?[25] New concepts emerge with new bodies of law, as when contract emerges out of assumpsit. Change can also occur when some elements in a cluster-concept alter their character or salience: marriage once picked out an indissoluble relationship between two people of different sexes, but no longer. It is a nice question how much can change before we are no longer talking about the same thing. A personal relationship whose duration is legally fixed in advance—a three-year deal, say—is not a marriage; yet the conditions that can terminate a marriage did alter over time. Many jurisdictions now allow 'no fault' divorce. That changed the character of marriage, but it would be false (not to say hysterical) to think that it brought an end to marriage.[26] Ditto with respect to sex difference—or so I argue. The fact that same-sex couples can now legally marry is a massive *social* change, and one that required heroic political efforts. But that does not prove that it brought a massive *conceptual* change in marriage. Many concept-defining aspects of the institution remained constant, and that is because sex mattered less to (legal) marriage than some think.

Conaghan thinks this way of approaching things loses grip on the *essentially* 'gendered' character of marriage as an institution oppressive to women (or, I suppose, to at least one ersatz 'woman').[27] Following Judith

---

[24] I am treating this as a sufficient condition for the utility of conceptual analysis in jurisprudence, not as a necessary one.
[25] Can the concept of law *itself* change? Was there a time when law had a nature other than the one it now has? It is difficult to make sense of the questions, let alone answer them. I do not explore the issues here.
[26] Lenore Weitzman argued that no fault divorce was bad for women in her book, *The Divorce Revolution: The Unexpected Social and Economic Consequences for Women and Children in America* (Free Press, 1985). She never argued that no fault divorce *ended* marriage.
[27] Although she seems unaware of it, it follows from Conaghan's view that in a male-male marriage one of the men will have to count as the 'wife'. A similarly disturbing reductionism

Butler and other 'post-modern' literary critics, Conaghan holds that sex basically *is* gender, so it follows that she will see gender difference where others do not. But her defence of the sex/gender equivalence is not Butler's.[28] Conaghan believes sex is gender on the ground that *English law* sometimes treats sex as gender: 'one way of bringing out this point [i.e. that sex and gender are the same] is to look at how sex and gender have been expressly conceptualized in law.'[29] She offers this example: 'it cannot be contended that sex discrimination in law is confined strictly to discrimination based on biological factors alone.'[30] On this basis, she proposes that sex, like gender, is social: 'the bodies are one thing; the meaning and significance we attach to them another. It is in this sense that it is wrong to assert that our understandings of sex (as opposed to gender) are not also socially and culturally imbued.'[31]

The thing it is supposedly 'wrong to assert' is, however, not something I ever asserted—nor did Plato, Augustine, Darwin, or Freud. No one denies that *views about* sex, and even sexual anatomy, can reflect popular understandings (and misunderstandings).[32] My claim is that *sex* and *gender* are different, not that notions of sex difference do not reflect social mores, and certainly not that English law always treats sex and gender as different. In fact, what I say about sex and gender cannot illustrate anything about the hazards in the 'abstraction of legal concepts from the framework in which they operate' because I say nothing at all about the *legal* concepts of sex or gender. The concept I put under scrutiny is *the law's concept of marriage*. Along the way, I use the ordinary concepts of sex and gender, the ones made more precise in biology, psychology, and sociology. And those are the ones we need. We learn no more about the nature of sex from the fact that the

---

infects some feminist treatments of pornography. See Leslie Green, 'Pornographies' (2000) 8 *Journal of Political Philosophy* 27; and Leslie Green, 'Men in the Place of Women, from *Butler* to *Little Sisters*' (2006) 44 *Osgoode Hall Law Journal* 1.

[28] 'If the immutable character of sex is contested, perhaps this construct called "sex" is as culturally constructed as gender; indeed, perhaps it was always already gender, with the consequence that the distinction between sex and gender turns out to be no distinction at all.' Judith Butler, *Gender Trouble: Feminism and the Subversion of Identity* (Routledge, 1989). Notice that the '*perhapses*' leave lots of room to deny the thesis that the final phrase appears to assert.
[29] Conaghan, *Law and Gender*, 178.
[30] Ibid., 183.
[31] Ibid, 178.
[32] See Thomas Laqueur, *Making Sex: Body and Gender from the Greeks to Freud* (Harvard University Press, 1992).

law sometimes treats gender as sex than we would learn about the nature of whales from a Fisheries Act that 'expressly conceptualized' whales as fish.[33]

There is a further, dialectical, point. Feminists who argued for more attention to gender in jurisprudence meant more attention to gender in the ordinary sense of the term, not more attention to gender as 'conceptualized' in English discrimination law or the UK Gender Recognition Act 2014. And they were right to take the broader view. Any legal system's local concept of gender may be profoundly misleading; it may even *conceal* the full significance of gender in the law.

4. How to Distinguish Sex and Gender

It is a fair abbreviation of my view to say that gender is 'a social category superimposed upon a sexed body'.[34] But Conaghan associates that abbreviation with a hodgepodge of other ideas: that sex is immutable; that our ideas about sexual anatomy are not 'socially inflected'; that our attitudes to sex are not socially 'mediated'; and that there is 'a sharp and definitive line . . . between nature and nurture'.[35] She rejects those and, with them, any distinction between sex and gender: 'I do not regard the common distinction between sex and gender in terms of nature and nurture (or body and consciousness) as either useful or tenable. Therefore . . . I will be using "sex" and "gender" loosely and interchangeably . . .'[36]

A reasonably clear distinction between sex and gender need not, however, presuppose any of those things. The distinction rests instead on the idea that gender is partly constituted by *sex*-specific norms and presupposes an independent concept of sex. Gender involves what is conventionally considered appropriate to the sexes. I give this example:

> To know whether it is a violation of any gender-norm for Robin to wear a dress, drive a truck, or have sex with a man, one first has to know Robin's (presumed) sex. If one can't identify norm-violation and norm-conformity,

---

[33] For some reasons why law is of so little help in thinking about the realities of 'sex', see Luis Duarte d'Almeida, 'Legal Sex', in Leslie Green and Brian Leiter eds, *Oxford Studies in Philosophy of Law*, vol. 2 (Oxford University Press, 2013) 277.
[34] Conaghan, *Law and Gender*, 18.
[35] Ibid., 21.
[36] Ibid., 22.

one cannot identify the norms, and shapeless norms cannot be projected onto something else to give it shape.[37]

Conaghan takes this passage to assert that:

> ... such arguments [namely, arguments equating sex and gender] are incoherent because unless sex is to some extent objective and fixed, we have no stable reference point for identifying gender norms and no measure for determining gender non-conformity...[38]

No doubt this is why Conaghan suspects that I think sex (or the concept of sex?) is 'fixed' and 'stable', ignoring the possibility that sex/gender could morph over time, in ways that might make it more relevant to jurisprudence.[39] But the passage under complaint does not say, entail, or presuppose that sex is 'objective' or 'fixed', and nowhere else have I ever claimed that a 'reference point' for gender needs to be stable. Indeed, the fact that gender norms are applied to people in accordance with their *presumed* sex shows that gender's 'reference point' can be both subjective and liable to change. The point is important. I claim:

> people are generally held to the gender norms of the sex they *present*; only when they fail to pass are they held to the gender norms of the sex they actually *are*. (This does not suppose that a person's actual sex is his or her sex at birth; it supposes only there can be a distinction between what someone is and how he is regarded.) One's presumed sex may be determined by gender-presentation, but that does not show that sex is gender.[40]

Compare this with a suggestion in Sally Haslanger's work on the concept of a 'woman'. Haslanger proposes this analysis:

> S is a woman [if and only if] S is systematically subordinated along some dimension—economic, political, legal, social—and S is 'marked' as a target

---

[37] Green, 'Sex-Neutral Marriage', 4.
[38] Conaghan, *Law and Gender*, 177.
[39] She never considers the possibility that conceptual change could render sex, or gender, *less* relevant to jurisprudence.
[40] Green, 'Sex-Neutral Marriage', 4, note 7.

for this treatment by observed or imagined bodily features presumed to be evidence of a female's biological role in reproduction.[41]

Haslanger follows Catharine MacKinnon, Andrea Dworkin, and others who emphasize subordination as part of the concept of a woman. The analysis is open to objections—is it true that an adult human female who is not 'systematically subordinated' is not a woman? Does a man who wants to become a woman want to become a target of subordination? But these are objections to the suggested *content* of gender-constituting norms; they are not objections to explaining gender as constituted by norms that apply to people in virtue of their actual or supposed *sex*. Haslanger and I agree on that.

Any literal suggestion that sex is gender would be extravagant. Conaghan concedes as much when she writes that sexual embodiment is 'often the referent for gender-based evaluations and judgments' and acknowledges that human bodies do 'vary anatomically along the lines we generally interpret according to prevailing understandings of sexual difference'.[42] These comments are all compatible with the kind of distinction between sex and gender that Haslanger or I endorse. An appearance of disagreement is sustained only by the loose talk of 'referents' and 'interpretations'. Gender-based evaluations do not 'refer' to sex; they presuppose beliefs about sex. Suppose someone says, 'Boy George was awful when he was girlish'. The referent of 'Boy George' is George O'Dowd, and the referent of his girlishness is his gender nonconformity. There is no term in this sentence that refers to his sex. The sentence expresses (unjustified) contempt for O'Dowd in virtue of the fact that his girlishness is thought, by the imagined speaker, to be especially awful for someone who is or is held to be male. Our social norms have it that a male should behave and think in certain ways only, and these norms constitute gender.

It is also incorrect to hold that sex is merely a classification produced by the ways we 'generally interpret' the 'prevailing understandings' of our anatomy. Plants and animals are sortable into sexes independently of interpretations or understandings because, to put it crudely, things that reproduce sexually are sexed *anyway*. There were different sexes among the ferns and dinosaurs long before there were any animals with the cognitive capacity to form interpretations of anatomy or anything else. We may now discover a new organism

---

[41] Sally Haslanger, *Resisting Reality: Social Construction and Social Critique* (Oxford University Press, 2012) 230.
[42] Conaghan, *Law and Gender*, 177.

and be unsure whether it reproduces sexually, and thus unsure whether the individual we found is male or female (or both, or neither).[43]

Gender is different. It is a human projection onto the material world. This explains many familiar facts, including these: gender is much more variable across human history than is sex; children gradually learn gender roles; people can reform gender distinctions. Take a famous example. If you are trying to understand gender in fifth-century Athens, you will need to find out what Athenians (and maybe others) thought fitting conduct *for the sexes* in that time and place. Among the things you will discover is that in Ancient Greece it was not necessarily thought unmanly for males to have sex with other males. This is so different from gender norms in nineteenth-century England that nervous translators of the classics routinely bowdlerized perfectly clear passages about homosexual love and sex. Yet there was no relevant difference in sexual biology between the boys in Plato's Academy and the boys in Jowett's Balliol.

Must any of this be denied by someone who thinks, 'a clear line between the material world and the ideas and concepts through which we perceive that world cannot really be drawn'?[44] Or—more radically—that, '[T]he discursive juxtaposition of law and the real, whether in terms of correspondence or divergence, belies the fact that law plays a vital role in constituting what we understand as real . . .'?[45] No. It is a fallacy to think that without clear lines there can be no clear cases. And even if we go so far as to reject any distinction at all between the world and mind (or law!), it will still not show that sex is gender. It will show they are both mind dependent. On any plausible metaphysics, *some* things are mind dependent, for example, constellations and currency. That does not show that constellations are currency.

What then should we make of the claim that 'law plays a vital role in constituting what we understand as real'?[46] If it is an empirical conjecture, it seems implausible. Most people know little of the law and take their cues about what is real from other things: from their own experience, from their peers, from scientists, from priests, from Twitter, and so on. Even a thoroughgoing metaphysical or linguistic idealist can accept a distinction between the way

---

[43] On 'both' and 'neither', see Joanne Roughgarden, *Evolution's Rainbow: Diversity, Gender, and Sexuality in Nature and People* (rev. edn, University of California Press, 2009). Indeterminacy of natal sex in humans is very rare. By comparison, indeterminate gender presentation or 'sense of self' is much more common, and not highly correlated with indeterminacy of sex. 'Masculine' and 'feminine' shade into each other more smoothly than do 'male' and 'female'.
[44] Conaghan, *Law and Gender*, 23.
[45] Ibid., 58.
[46] Ibid.

the world is and the way the world is 'constituted' in law (or in novels, or on Netflix). It would be worrying if someone were to base their understanding of reality mainly on the law—especially in the domain of sex and gender, where law replicates and produces so much error and superstition.

At points, it is uncertain whether Conaghan intends her thesis about the identity of sex and gender to be taken literally. She warns that she will be using sex and gender 'loosely and interchangeably'.[47] What started as a substantive disagreement about the bearing of sex on the concept of marriage now risks becoming no more than a matter of notational variants, or a quirk of dialect. But no one who asserts that sex difference is a *necessary* feature of marriage will be satisfied by the thought that, since we can speak 'loosely', a gender difference between the partners might suffice. No man who hopes to marry someone of the opposite sex will be happy to discover that his fiancée is a male whose dating profile used the concept *woman* 'loosely'.

Analytical jurisprudence, like analytic philosophy in general, tries to use terms precisely when it can. Admittedly, precision can be a fault, for instance when it imposes a misleading clarity on an unclarifiably vague subject matter. Are sex or gender such cases? There is no denying that English usage, and English law, does not always distinguish them. In certain contexts, people use 'gender' to mean 'sex'. Sometimes they do so out of prudishness—sex (the classification) and sex (the activity) are embarrassingly homonymic in English. Sometimes they do so because they are trying to sound bureaucratic or academic. Thus we hear talk of 'the gender imbalance of the judiciary' or 'gender discrimination in law firms'. But this does not mark an ambiguity that cannot be resolved or vagueness that cannot be made more precise. People who use 'sex' and 'gender' loosely and interchangeably in such contexts have not lost the capacity to distinguish them when they need to. They do not tell people who suffer depression because their sex does not match their gender identity that they are just conceptually confused. They do not say that appointing four drag queens to the bench would cure the gender imbalance on the Supreme Court.

A final point on law and concepts: if feminists were to treat law's construction of reality as 'vitally' constitutive, they would lose the resources to distinguish the way the world seems to the law and the way the world really *is*. Along with that, they risk losing another distinction on which the 'analytic jurisprudential mind' famously insists: the difference between law as it is and

---

[47] Ibid., 22.

law as it ought to be. I think reform-minded feminists had better hang on to that one.

5. Description and Evaluation in Jurisprudence

Conaghan's next charge against analytic jurisprudence is that it encourages 'the unarticulated normative prioritization of some features' over others, requiring 'evaluative choices which problematize any claim to be rendering a descriptive or value-neutral account'.[48] This is not simply an observation; it alleges a fault (a 'methodological limitation'). Since Conaghan makes no suggestion that some other kind of jurisprudence offers value neutrality, the fault can only be one of two kinds. It is either *false advertising*—pretending to neutrality that is impossible—or else *bad values*, for example, prioritizing values that lead us to miss the importance of gender in jurisprudence.

Conaghan offers no evidence that I am guilty of false advertising. I have never maintained that accounts of anything of significance in jurisprudence are value neutral. I do think that many conceptual claims are *descriptive*— and this applies to my claim that sex is not gender as much as to my claim that, in common law, consummation was not a validity condition for marriage. By 'descriptive' I mean that these are claims about what the concepts of *sex* and *consummation* actually are in their respective domains, not claims about what it would be good for them to be. It does not follow that descriptions involving those concepts are value neutral: I have long denied that.[49] 'An actual description of something is not a list of all the facts about it; it is a selection and arrangement of facts that are for some reason taken to be important, salient, relevant, interesting, etc. Every description presupposes, or is made from the point of view of, certain values.'[50]

My view is not idiosyncratic; as far as I can see, all contemporary writers in analytic jurisprudence endorse it. But isn't there a live debate about the place of values in jurisprudence? There is indeed, but that is a different debate. I can illustrate it with an example. Suppose a visitor asks how I would describe the English bar, and I reply: 'It is geographically centralized, socially exclusive and systematically sexist.' There are many other facts I could have mentioned

---

[48] Ibid., 176.
[49] Leslie Green, 'The Political Content of Legal Theory' (1987) 17 *Philosophy of the Social Sciences* 1, 14–16.
[50] Leslie Green, 'Introduction', in H. L. A. Hart, *The Concept of Law* (3rd edn, Penelope A. Bulloch and Joseph Raz eds; Leslie Green, intro, Oxford University Press, 2012) xlix.

DESCRIPTION AND EVALUATION IN JURISPRUDENCE   143

instead or as well, so there are 'unarticulated normative prioritizations' behind this reply. But what are they? Without a context there is no way to know, although there are various possibilities, including these:

(a) I think these are *bad* features of the English bar, so I highlight them as a way of condemning it.
(b) I think these are *good* features of the English bar, so I highlight them as a way of commending it.
(c) I think *other people think* these are bad (or good) features of the English bar, so I highlight them as socially salient, never mind what I think.
(d) I think these features are *explanatorily important* in understanding other features of the English legal system, never mind the rights and wrongs, or anyone's perceptions of the matter.

The debate about evaluation in legal theory is about whether every description of law must engage the describer's values *in (a)-type or (b)-type ways*. That thesis is defended by legal philosophers like Ronald Dworkin and John Finnis.[51] It is rejected by H. L. A. Hart and by Julie Dickson.[52] But no one in analytical jurisprudence denies the relevance of values to descriptions in (c)-type or (d)-type ways.

Now to the second possibility: that analytical jurisprudence is guilty, not of falsely pretending to neutrality, but of presupposing bad, or unappealing, values. Conaghan thinks some such presupposition underpins my discussion of marriage. One fear is based on a misunderstanding. In describing traditional Anglo-American marriage law, I note that there was no sexual orientation bar on marrying: gay people could always marry, provided they married other people—gay, straight, or in-between—of the other sex. Unlike many other writers, I think this fact was conceptually significant. Conaghan takes me to be thereby suggesting that in 'a very technical sense', sex-restricted marriage did not discriminate against lesbians and gay men on grounds of sexual orientation.[53] That is emphatically not my claim. I expressly say that sex-restricted marriage laws discriminate on grounds of sexual orientation

---

[51] Ronald Dworkin, 'Hart's Postscript and the Character of Political Philosophy' (2004) 24 *Oxford Journal of Legal Studies* 1; John Finnis, *Natural Law and Natural Rights* (2nd edn, Oxford University Press, 2011) chap. 1.
[52] Hart, *The Concept of Law*, 240; Julie Dickson, *Evaluation in Legal Theory* (Hart Publishing, 2001).
[53] Conaghan, *Law and Gender*, 169.

and I explain how they do so.[54] Moreover, I hold that such discrimination is wrong, and by 'wrong' I mean not that English law *treats it* as wrong (a (c)-type value relevance), or that treating it as wrong *explains* important features of English law (a (d)-type value relevance); I think that sexual orientation discrimination *really is wrong* (that is to say, (a)-type value relevance). I think sexual orientation discrimination is as morally vicious and socially destructive as sex or race discrimination. Thus, I here use the term 'discrimination' in its full-blooded, condemnatory sense and *not* as a descriptive or technical-legal term. To think sex-restricted marriage laws involve wrongful discrimination does presuppose a lot of things (some of which are argued in this work and some elsewhere), but I cannot see that any of them turn on values a feminist should reject, let alone values that are suspect.[55]

The fact that there was no sexual orientation bar to marriage is relevant to a different point entirely. Although the common law of consummation had what I call a 'fixation' with one sex act, the nature of that act shows how little the law cared about sex within marriage.[56] More than anything else, it is this remark that convinces Conaghan that analytic jurisprudence must be up to no good. She writes, 'This tells us more about what Green thinks of as sex than it communicates about the common law.'[57]

What is the implied criticism? To consummate a marriage at common law did not mean to 'have sex'. All sorts of familiar sex acts failed to consummate marriage; the courts were unequivocal about that. Consummation required that a man put his penis inside a woman's vagina, at least for a little while—long enough to please the trier of fact. The law did not require that this act take place between people capable of reproduction. It did not require that the act take place more than once. It did not even require that it be done with the (morally) valid consent of the woman. And importantly, an unconsummated marriage was not void and, though it was *voidable*, it could be voided only at the request of one of the spouses and only under extremely restrictive conditions.

What does that tell us about what I 'think of as' sex? If we are considering 'sex' the classification, it shows that I think anatomy is relevant to it. If we

---

[54] Commenting on the American case of *Goodridge et al. v Department of Public Health*, 798 N.E.2d 941, I write, 'the fact that anyone in Massachusetts could, without regard to sexual orientation, use their marital powers to marry someone of a different sex does not begin to show that the marriage law was non-discriminatory.' Green, 'Sex-Neutral Marriage', 13.

[55] For other elements of the argument, see Leslie Green, 'Sexuality, Authenticity, and Modernity' (1995) 8 *Canadian Journal of Law and Jurisprudence* 67.

[56] Green, 'Sex-Neutral Marriage', 20.

[57] Conaghan, *Law and Gender*, 171.

are considering 'sex' the activity, it shows the following. *First*, I think sexual activity is not exhausted by what the common law counted as marriage-consummating acts. *Second*, since the law tolerated a sex act that I call rape, it tells us that I hold that the doctrine of consummation was morally deficient. *Third*, it tells us that I hold that a same-sex couple who, as a matter of natural necessity, cannot perform the consummating act can nonetheless be validly married. As far as I can see, nothing else can be inferred from my claims about sex in marriage. Are any of these views suspect? Should a feminist reject them and hold, instead, that only heterosexual penetrative intercourse conforms to the proper function of sexual activity, or that the marital rape exemption was right, or that same-sex marriages are not marriages at all? Those would undeniably give sex a central role in the concept of marriage; but it is not the role it actually had, and it is not a role a feminist should welcome.

6. Analysis and Evidence in Jurisprudence

Conaghan's final charge resonates with a criticism familiar from some approaches to the sociology of law and some movements within legal philosophy itself. The methods of analytical jurisprudence, or most of them, seem *a priori*. Legal philosophy does not spend long hours with the law reports, historical archives, or data sets. Analytical jurisprudence takes its methods from analytic philosophy: it examines the nature and structure of the concept of law and legal concepts 'from the armchair', as critics say. These methods are a familiar source of scepticism about analytic philosophy, not only among philosophical 'naturalists' who hope to reconstruct the subject along the lines of a natural science, but also among historically and practically oriented lawyers.[58] They read in a jurisprudence book that legal systems necessarily have courts, but do not necessarily have legislatures. (All law could be customary.) Then they wonder: how could mere *philosophy* make that sort of discovery? Wouldn't a generalization about all legal systems—let alone all possible legal systems—require mountains of evidence and carefully specified and tested quantitative models?

Yes, any empirical generalization would. But the thesis that legal systems necessarily have courts is not an empirical generalization. It is an explanation

---

[58] See Morton J. Horowitz, 'Why is Anglo-American Jurisprudence Unhistorical?' (1997) 17 *Oxford Journal of Legal Studies* 551; Brian Leiter, *Naturalizing Jurisprudence: Essays on American Legal Realism and Naturalism in Legal Philosophy* (Oxford University Press, 2007).

of concepts that such a generalization must use. Think of it this way. If you want to do a sociological or historical study of legal systems, you will need to identify them. You cannot just stipulate that you will use *legal system* 'flexibly and loosely', and then go on to present as some kind of *discovery* that there are legal systems without courts. That only regurgitates your stipulation. The problem jurisprudence addresses is a prior one: among the varied forms of social organization with which we are familiar—markets, religions, clubs, anarchic orders, etc.—what distinguishes legal systems? Yet general jurisprudence does not begin—*pace* Hobbes—with purely postulated premises. Because it is the philosophy *of law* it presumes enough ordinary knowledge of law to get off the ground, and special jurisprudence presupposes specialist knowledge of laws and legal systems. Nonetheless, jurisprudence is a consumer and not a producer of empirical findings. It does not reveal new facts about any matter; it reveals what matters about familiar facts. To look to analytic jurisprudence to replace history or advocacy would be like looking to Plato's *Symposium* to understand how sex evolved or how to get a date. On the other hand, if you care about what love is, and why love matters, the *Symposium* would be a good place to start.

I write, 'The fact that the capacity to marry is already and everywhere neutral with respect to sexual orientation shows how little interest the law takes in sex within marriage.'[59] Conaghan replies, 'Green's conclusion about the insignificance of sex as a core feature of marriage seems so far out of line with the picture of marriage we have encountered up to now as to demand examination.'[60] My argument that a certain kind of sexual activity did not *constitute* a valid marriage is thus met with the empirical generalization that the regulation of sex was a *historically significant* feature of marriage. But the latter is not in dispute. The fact that there could, at common law, be a valid marriage between a gay man and a lesbian who never have sex with each other shows exactly what I say it shows: how little the law cared about sex within marriage. Naturally, it does not show 'legal indifference to sexual matters';[61] but I never suggest anything so silly. I say the law of consummation was *fixated* on one sex act. The law would hardly be fixated on something it regards with indifference.

In what sense then might one say that my view amounts to a denial that sex is a 'core feature' of marriage? In two senses only: (α) *Sex difference* is not

---

[59] Green, 'Sex-Neutral Marriage', 3.
[60] Conaghan, *Law and Gender*, 171.
[61] Ibid., 172.

conceptually necessary to marriage—so same-sex married couples really are married. (β) *Sexual activity* is not necessary to marriage, since a legally valid marriage may be formed, and continue to exist unless voided, without sexual activity between the spouses. There is an important general point here. The necessary features of a legal relation or institution include all of its constitutive features, the features without which it would not be what it is, but they may not include all of its socially important features. Nor are all constitutive features necessarily important. Might I then be correct about the constitutive features of marriage, but have focused on ones that are socially or morally trivial? Not in this case. After all, some people hold that 'conceptually', 'by definition', a marriage must be 'between a man and a woman', the only pair that can perform the marriage-consummating act: (α) denies that. Other people say a sexless marriage is legally void, since the whole point of marriage is to support reproduction: (β) denies that. These are not mistakes made by uninformed lay people who have only a partial grasp of the legal concept of marriage, or by lazy students who did not do the reading. They are ideologically motivated errors whose function is to uphold a heterosexist ideal of human relationships. That is enough to make (α) and (β) important, and important to feminist theory.

Of course, these are not the *only* important facts about marriage law. It is also important to know how marriage was used to regulate sex, property, and labour. There are excellent historical and sociological writings on these topics, and they are not my targets. There is no need to guess at whom my arguments are actually directed: they are the theorists I mention and, by implication, all others who think that the essential nature of marriage is a 'one-flesh union', constituted by a particular sexual transaction between one person with a penis and one person with a vagina. Through strenuous wishful thinking, such writers find their own religious dogma 'reflected in traditional American and British marriage law'.[62] I try to show why they are wrong, and why their errors matter. (Basically, Blackstone was right all along.) Conaghan ignores all this and asserts, 'When we step back and look at marriage in its historical context, we do not see a picture of legal indifference to sexual matters. Rather we see a framework of rules which guaranteed a husband's access—and exclusive access—to the physical person of his wife.'[63]

---

[62] Robert P. George, 'Public Reason and Political Conflict: Abortion and Homosexuality' (1997) 106 *Yale Law Journal* 2475. George is only one of several who, in loyalty to a religious ideology, omit facts about marriage as the law sees it. For a penetrating, and patient, critique of George and others, see Nicholas Bamforth and David A. J. Richards, *Patriarchal Religion, Sexuality, and Gender: A Critique of New Natural Law* (Cambridge University Press, 2011).

[63] Conaghan, *Law and Gender*, 172.

In a final flourish, she declares that marriage 'was all about sex, understood as a hierarchical order based upon male domination and female subjection'.[64]

My arguments are consistent with (but do not entail) her grim view. But when I show how little the common law of marriage cared about sexual activity within marriage, I am not asserting that the law played no role in the domination of women. The law's doctrine of consummation was shot through with sexism of an ugly and obvious kind, in the ways I explain. We are not clear of it even now.

7. Conclusion, Warning, and Invitation

None of Conaghan's claims about the 'analytical jurisprudential mind' is sound, and none of her arguments cast any doubt on the diagnosis I offered at the outset: Gender is highly relevant to law because gender norms shape the content and application of the law. Gender is relevant to several problems in normative jurisprudence and to some problems in special jurisprudence, though that must be shown piecemeal, in each case. But gender is of no relevance to general jurisprudence for, as far as anyone has shown, there is nothing about 'the very forms of law' that warrants calling them 'gendered', and no answer to leading problems in general jurisprudence depends on any thesis about gender. Finally, the methods of analytical legal philosophy are well-equipped to detect the conceptual role of gender where it exists.

Maybe this will provoke a fresh complaint. If general jurisprudence has so little to learn from feminist theory, perhaps we should stop doing general jurisprudence. Or perhaps people should not write about general jurisprudence unless they also write about law and gender, and in the very same book. Was Hart at fault for developing his defence of gay people against criminal oppression, not in *The Concept of Law* but in *Law, Liberty, and Morality*? Should Kelsen have included his defence of a rules-based international order in *The Pure Theory of Law*? I can think of no reason why. Not every omission is an 'erasure', as they used to say. Conaghan offers this comment on contemporary feminist criticism of earlier feminists:

> Not only does this kind of claim often overstate or misrepresent the 'errors' of past feminist scholars, it encourages readings of bodies of scholarship

[64] Ibid., 173.

which were the product of particular times, energies, and concerns against the times, energies, and concerns of later generations.[65]

This is a correct and important point. It applies also to past scholars in analytical jurisprudence. The works of, say, Kelsen or Hart are philosophically rich, intellectually focused, and now also quite old works. They too are the product of particular times, energies, and concerns, and their errors are greatly overstated.

In the end, jibes about the 'analytical jurisprudential mind', like jibes about 'the criminal mind'—or for that matter the 'female mind'—express little more than prejudice. As human vices go, an intellectual prejudice is a minor thing. Nonetheless, it will have victims. The most serious casualties will be among beginning law students, especially young feminists curious about things like the social construction of gender, the evaluative character of jurisprudence, the subordination and silencing of women, or social inclusion and legal equality. Will they learn that some of the best thinking on these themes includes work by analytic philosophers, and even analytic legal philosophers?[66] Will they discover that this work is sensitive to context where relevant, that it is alert to the ways values enter analysis, and that it is literate about social facts? Not if they accept Conaghan's caricature. Students told what the 'analytical jurisprudential mind' *must* think about such issues may not spend time discovering what any particular writer *does* think. They may feel pressed into building walls against gender-excluding abstractions, smuggled-in values, and empirical biases—unlawful migrants to the empire of law and gender, disguised in nit-picking arguments.

In truth, feminist legal scholars have nothing to fear from the best analytic philosophers working on problems that feminists care about, including the ones I just cited. But to discover whether I am right about that, they will need to read them, and read them while open to the possibility that they may know something worth learning. In jurisprudence as elsewhere, acquaintance is a good solvent of prejudice. It is long past time for feminist jurisprudence to risk meeting the neighbours. It may be pleasantly surprised.[67]

---

[65] Ibid., 125.
[66] For example, see on the following topics: social construction of gender—Sally Haslanger, *Resisting Reality: Social Construction and Social Critique* (Oxford University Press, 2012); evaluation in legal theory—Julie Dickson, *Evaluation in Legal Theory* (Hart Publishing, 2001); subordination and silencing—Rae Langton, *Sexual Solipsism: Philosophical Essays on Pornography and Objectification* (Oxford University Press, 2009); social inclusion and legal equality—Elizabeth Anderson, *The Imperative of Integration* (Princeton University Press, 2010).
[67] Chris Essert, Darryl Robinson, and especially Denise Réaume improved this chapter with criticisms, as did the editor and referees of the *Modern Law Review*.

II
LAW AND MORALITY

6
The Germ of Justice

1. Constancy

Beginning with the ancients, people have supposed there to be a connection between inconstancy and injustice. Heraclitus sees it even in nature: 'The sun will not overstep his measures. Otherwise the avenging Furies, Ministers of Justice, will find him out.'[1] Aristotle says lawlessness is one of the modalities of injustice.[2] And lawyers have long held it a serious injustice to deviate from the principle *nulla poena sine lege*—no one is to be punished save for a violation of law.

Lawlessness can bring injustice. Does that mean conformity to law brings justice? Not always. That depends on what the law requires, permits, or empowers. Stricter conformity to laws that make it more difficult for blacks to vote than for whites makes a society not more just, but less just. To improve its justice score we would need to change the laws or apply them less strictly. Change would be best, and probably best achieved by having legislatures make them. But there will be times and places where that is politically impossible, and where the knowledge that things cannot improve through lawful means produces even further humiliation and disengagement of minorities. In such circumstances self-help and other help may be justified. Someone wrongly deprived of the vote may present fake identification to get their ballot. A scrutineer might allow them to vote without identification. A judge might refuse a valid application to review or to annul the result in that district. You may think that in one way this society is getting worse: official deviation from law brings lower rule-of-law marks. But in another way, it is getting better, for more people are getting the rights to which they are morally entitled. We can argue about whether the rule of law or justice should take priority when they conflict, but not about whether a society in which more people get their due is the more just: *suum cuique tribuere*.

---

[1] Heraclitus, *Fragments* (T. M. Robinson trs, University of Toronto Press, 1987) fragment 94, 57.
[2] Aristotle, *Nicomachean Ethics* (T. Irwin trs, Hackett Publishing, 1985), 1129a32-b1.

At this point, many lawyers bridle: Yes, they concede, there is more *substantive* justice when more people get their due. But it is not only the rule of law that counts against inconstancy. When substantive justice is achieved by deviation from law it comes at a price in *formal* justice, the justice of applying laws strictly according to their terms and without regard to their merits. The sympathetic scrutineer or generous judge are neither following the laws laid down nor treating like cases alike (as the law sees them). That is itself an injustice. We can argue about whether formal justice should take priority over substantive justice, but not about whether a society that tolerates official deviation from settled law is, to the degree of that deviation, formally unjust.[3]

Interestingly, it is not only the hard men of jurisprudence—Hobbes or Bodin—who advance such views. Even softies, including H .L. A. Hart, Matthew Kramer, and many administrative lawyers feel the pull of formal justice (Kramer calls it 'procedural' justice).[4] They acknowledge that our ultimate aim should be substantive justice. They may hope, with Lon Fuller, that by strictly applying the rules a society will eventually arc towards to substantive justice.[5] They usually allow that justice-based deviation from law is permissible or required in some cases of conscientious refusal or civil disobedience. They insist only on the following: we must count all the costs. Deliberate failure, however well motivated, to apply pre-existing law is always a cost in terms of justice, apart from any other consequences that may follow. Even a justified sacrifice of formal justice involves moral loss. As Isaiah Berlin puts it in a different context, 'a sacrifice is not an increase in what is being sacrificed . . . however great the moral need or the compensation for it. Everything is what it is . . .'[6]

This view is popular. Hans Kelsen is a moral relativist and non-cognitivist, but even he maintains that one aspect of the otherwise 'irrational ideal' of justice does have rational content. He claims it is a requirement of justice that positive law be consistently applied according to its terms, and whether that has been done is an empirical, non-subjective, fact—the one ascertainable fact among a welter of non-rational justice-claims.[7] Matthew Kramer says

---

[3] We hear parallel claims about 'formal' versus 'substantive' equality. Much of the argument to follow applies also to those claims.

[4] H. L. A. Hart, *The Concept of Law* (3rd edn, Penelope A. Bulloch and Joseph Raz eds; Leslie Green, intro, Oxford University Press, 2012); Matthew Kramer, 'Justice as Constancy' (1997) *Law and Philosophy* 16, 566.

[5] Lon L. Fuller, *The Morality of Law* (2nd edn, Yale University Press, 1969) 152–62.

[6] Isaiah Berlin, 'Two Concepts of Liberty', in Isaiah Berlin, *Liberty* (H. Hardy ed., Oxford University Press, 2002) 172

[7] Hans Kelsen, *General Theory of Law and State* (A. Wedberg trs, Harvard University Press, 1949) 13–14.

that such 'procedural justice' guarantees that official conduct in the administration of law will be no worse (though no better) than what is required by the substantive standards of fairness embodied in the laws themselves, and that respecting such boundaries amounts to 'justice as constancy'.[8] And, most boldly of all, H. L. A. Hart affirms that, 'though the most odious laws may be justly applied, we have, in the bare notion of applying a general rule of law, the germ at least of justice'.[9]

There are differences among these views, but all maintain that law application is an elementary or basic kind of justice, so I will adopt Hart's phrase and call them versions of the 'germ-of-justice thesis': strict application of valid law, without regard to its merits, is one sort of justice. I reject that thesis and offer another in its place. There is a connection between law and justice, but it is not an incident of the strict application of rules. What connects law and justice is not law's rule-like features, but its social task and its institutional features. First, every legal system necessarily addresses questions of justice, so justice is always an appropriate standard of appraisal for law in a way it is not for other rule-governed activities, such as sonnets or sarabandes. Second, while the norm, 'Apply rules strictly!', is no measure of justice, the necessary existence in every legal system of institutions that make binding decisions about the application of rules to individual cases is a practically necessary means to justice. Or at least it is so in the sort of societies that have legal systems.

2. Plato's Challenge, and Some Assumptions

I am not the first sceptic about formal justice. The decisive objection is put already by Plato. In response to the then-conventional suggestion that justice amounts to giving each his due, telling the truth, and returning what we borrow, Plato says these cannot be what justice is because these are 'actions that can be sometimes right and sometimes wrong' and 'justice is the sort of thing that is, by its nature, right'.[10] That undermines all familiar suggestions

---

[8] Kramer, 'Justice as Constancy', 566.
[9] Hart, *The Concept of Law*, 206. Hart uses the 'germ' metaphor on another occasion in *The Concept of Law*. He says that 'in the simple operation of identifying a given rule as possessing the required feature of being an item on an authoritative list of rules we have the germ of the idea of legal validity' (95). I take this to mean a primitive criterion for legal validity, that is, a primitive recognition rule.
[10] Plato, *The Republic* (2nd edn, D. Lee trs, Penguin Books, 1987) 331 c, 65–6.

about the moral basis of formal justice. *Generally* we should respect expectations inculcated by existing laws, *normally* judges should fulfil their institutional roles, and *in most cases* officials should not undermine the rule of law. But none of that supports the conclusion that these injunctions are exceptionless in the way they would be if law application were itself a form of justice. For that to be true, law application would have to be, as Plato puts it, 'by its nature, right'. Sometimes, however, law application is thoroughly wrong. And it is not only that the justice of strict law application can be overridden; sometimes there no justice in it to override. In a pair of influential articles, David Lyons and John Gardner hammer home Plato's point. After allowing for reformulations of the germ-of-justice thesis, both conclude that the very idea of formal justice is flawed.[11] I build on their arguments, add some more, then offer a different proposal about law and justice.

But I want to begin with what is common ground among all writers considered here:

(1) The application of law is a matter of determining the bearing of pre-existing rules (including standards, principles, etc.) on instant cases. Law is not 'whatever the judge says it is'. If that is how things stand, there is no law. In typical cases, however, it is possible to know whether a given decision did or did not apply a legal norm. In atypical cases, where it is seriously doubtful whether or how the law applies, the germ-of-justice thesis is not engaged. The thesis therefore brings no commitments about how indeterminate cases are to be handled since there is, in those cases, nothing that counts as a strict application of pre-existing law. The thesis bears on the application of law, not on the creation of new law.

(2) The germ-of-justice thesis applies to all valid positive law, that is, to all law whose existence and content can be identified without consideration of the law's merits, including any merits of the process by which that law is created or applied. This assumption is important. That there is some reason to apply good laws goes without saying. But the thesis under scrutiny holds that justice is found, not only in the application of substantively just or democratically produced laws, but even in the application of laws that are, in Hart's words, '*the most odious*', laws whose very existence is a blight on society.

---

[11] David Lyons, 'On Formal Justice' (1973) 58 *Cornell Law Review* 833; John Gardner, *Law as a Leap of Faith* (Oxford University Press, 2012), chap. 9.

(3) The thesis holds that constancy in law application is a sufficient condition for formal justice. This differs from Ronald Dworkin's suggestion that the injunction to 'treat like cases alike' rests on a value he calls 'integrity', a sort of coherence among the moral principles that would best fit and justify settled law but which express a virtue that is different from, and stops short of, justice.[12] Dworkinian integrity does not require or presuppose that all valid law is to applied, so it does not bear on the claims I test here. Hart's claim, in contrast, is that a kind of justice inheres in rule-following, via a putative connection between that and the idea that like cases are to be treated alike. Kramer says it follows from the fact that, when strictly applied, law sets limits to how people may be treated, and it is valuable for law to work within limits. Kelsen says conformity to a general legal rule always produces an objective, if rule-relative, value. This is the territory I want to contest.

3. Positive Law and Ideal Justice

The thesis under scrutiny is ambitious. It may seem, however, liable to an immediate objection. It is acknowledged that this thesis applies to *all* positive law, that is, to law that is constitutional and meets all other requirements of validity in the relevant jurisdiction. I assume, with its sponsors, that whether these requirements are met can be ascertained by considering matters of social fact. The germ-of-justice thesis therefore needs to be consistent with legal positivism. But doesn't the thesis call positivism into question? In Hart's version, it establishes a *necessary connection* between law and justice through a feature they both share: they comprise general rules. The presence of such rules 'connotes the principle of treating like cases alike'—though the criteria of likeness are nothing other than what the existing rules specify or presuppose. Nonetheless, he insists, that principle is 'one essential element of the concept of justice', and if a legal system is to be a going concern, its general rules, or a significant subset of them, must be generally effective and therefore actually followed or applied. 'So there is', Hart concludes, 'in the very notion of law consisting of general rules, something which prevents us from

---

[12] Ronald Dworkin, *Law's Empire* (Harvard University Press, 1986) 166–7.

treating it as if morally it is utterly neutral, without any necessary contact with moral principles'.[13]

That comes as a surprise. For Hart also says—and Kelsen and Kramer concur—that 'it is in no sense a necessary truth that laws reproduce or satisfy certain demands of morality, though in fact they have often done so'.[14] But if law can exist with *nothing* to be said in its favour, how could there be a necessary plane of 'contact' between law and morality, let alone one that prevents us from treating law as a morally neutral social phenomenon? And if forced to choose between the contingent, 'no guarantees' thesis and the necessary, 'germ-of-justice' thesis, is any legal positivist not bound to opt for the first?

That conundrum also lurks in the background of Kramer's discussion of constancy in law application. He aims to show that we can endorse strict law application without giving up legal positivism. His solution is to deny that formal justice is like substantive justice in having 'an affirmative moral weight'.[15] This suggests we are not bound to regard law application as in any way good. But if formal justice may have *zero* moral weight we cannot conclude that something of moral value is always lost in deviating from applicable law. Perhaps, then, Kramer has something else in mind by 'affirmative'. Perhaps he means that legal constancy has negative value in the sense that it prevents evils without necessarily doing any good, along the lines of 'negative utilitarianism'. That idea is unhelpfully sensitive to the descriptions under which we consider law's contribution. Would non-application of US voter-suppression laws be an affirmative good or the prevention of evil? Either description is apt. Moreover, the contingencies that break any conceptual link between applying law and doing justice in the positive case do so in the negative case as well. Kramer is correct if he only means that the germ-of-justice thesis is not committed to holding that the value of rule application is invariant. It will be more or less important to treat like cases alike depending on what is at stake. Race-biased selection for issuing speeding tickets is unjust, it is more unjust in stop-and-search practices, and race-biased selection for the death penalty is utterly monstrous. Still, if constancy in the application of law is to be any kind of justice it can never fall to zero. That is Plato's point.

There is a better reply to the worry that the germ-of-justice thesis commits us to anti-positivism. (I mean: a reply other than 'so much the worse

---

[13] H. L. A. Hart, 'Positivism and the Separation of Law and Morals', in H. L. A. Hart, *Essays in Jurisprudence and Philosophy* (Oxford University Press, 1983) 81.
[14] Hart, *The Concept of Law*, 185–6.
[15] Kramer, 'Justice as Constancy', 579.

THE DOMAIN OF JUSTICE   159

for legal positivism'.) There is simply no reason to deny, and no reason *for a positivist* to deny, that there are 'necessary connections' between law and morality. As I explain in Chapter 7, there are many. All a positivist needs deny is that, whatever those connections are, they do not fix the criteria for identifying law. Like fashion, etiquette, and grammar, law is at bottom a matter of ordinary historical facts about what actual people have said, done, directed, approved, tolerated, and so forth. Law whose existence conditions satisfy only non-moral tests may nonetheless bring morally desirable results downstream from the criteria for validity. Hobbes thought something like that: positive law can be identified by consulting the sovereign's intentions, but when sovereignty actually exists it guarantees an exit from the state of nature, and nothing is more morally important. Nor need a connection between positive law and moral value be purely consequential. Perhaps—this is an idea some claim to recover from Kant and Rousseau—law helps constitute values that cannot be realized without positive rules, without the reign of *Recht* or the victory of *la volonté générale*. I do not say these ideas are sound, only that they are coherent, and they demonstrate that there need be no conflict between positivism and the germ-of-justice thesis. Of course, all that matters here is whether the thesis is correct. That depends on what justice is.

4. The Domain of Justice

We sometimes use the term 'justice' in a capacious way. Wars, causes, measures, and criticisms can all be said to be just or unjust, since at its most general the idea of justice involves little more than conformity to some standard of rectitude. David Miller says we are fortunate to have lost the Greeks' sense of justice as virtue in general, or as all the virtues being realized in right relation; but I have a feeling it is alive and well and its persistence explains why usage is so pliable.[16] For almost any wrong you contemplate (including rape, torture, and assault) there is someone prepared to describe it as an injustice. And when people are being raped, tortured, or abused something is very out of kilter; so why not call that kilter 'justice'?

I have no ambitions to restrict usage. But there is no plausible argument that connects the steadfast application of legal rules with moral virtue in general or with a correct balance among the various virtues. The germ-of-justice

---

[16] David Miller, *Social Justice* (Oxford University Press, 1976) 17.

thesis is more modest. It is held to establish a relationship between law and only one kind or aspect of justice, where justice is only one department of morality. There are very serious wrongs (including rape and torture) that are not injustices and steadfast rule application cannot itself prevent or mitigate them. A formalistic attitude to rules may even enable the commission of such wrongs, depending on what the rules permit.

The reason rape or torture are not injustices is not that 'unjust' is too pale to capture the horror. Rather, as Hart says, the concept of justice has its primary application to matters of distribution and compensation from which its other applications, including procedural justice, derive. What these have in common is the maintenance of 'a relative position of equality or inequality' as judged by some baseline or other.[17] That is why rape is not an injustice. Rape does reflect and enforce an inequality between men and women; but that is not what is wrong about it *qua* rape. A rape of a man by another man who is his equal is not a different or lesser wrong. Unconsented sexual assaults would be wrong even if they somehow helped *redress* a background inequality between the sexes. (For instance, by making men as liable to sexual violence as women already are.)

Hart says that the sort of equality he has identified shows that the general concept of justice consists in a constant, acontextual, injunction —'treat like cases alike'—together with variable criteria that determine for the relevant context which cases *are* alike.[18] Many debates about substantive justice can then be understood as debates about which factors properly link cases for common treatment (or distinguish them for disparate treatment). Descriptive jurisprudence offers no advice about that: it calls for substantive moral argument.

Although 'treat like cases alike' is thus offered as the concept of justice, that seems wrong. If in practising arithmetic on Tuesday I count two apples and two apples to make four apples, then on Wednesday I had better count two oranges and two oranges to make four oranges. If I treat these like cases differently, I am not being unjust (nor am I failing to follow precedent!). I am simply being irrational, since neither the day of the week nor the type of the fruit can make any difference to a count. No doubt irrationality can precede moral misjudgement. If I maintain that same-sex marriages are wrong because non-procreative while insisting that deliberately sterile different-sex marriages are licit, my erratic judgement shows me to be inconsistent, but

---

[17] Hart, *The Concept of Law*, 159.
[18] Ibid., 160.

not yet unjust, for that depends on what I intend or what happens on the basis of that judgement. Inconsistency may itself reflect badly on me. It may show me to be unprincipled or lacking integrity. It may support an inference of bigotry, which may become stronger as I twist and turn to distinguish the cases. But it does not yet convict me of injustice. For that, it needs to commend or produce a maldistribution of benefits and burdens. A worry about injustice emerges only when we move from irrational or inconsistent judgements to a disposition to withhold benefits from some people on the basis of those judgements. Justice is a person-affecting consideration: there is no injustice 'in the air', no injustice until someone's interests are set back.[19]

More helpful is John Rawls' suggestion that 'the concept of justice applies whenever there is an allotment of something rationally regarded as advantageous or disadvantageous'.[20] This is more abstract than the special problem of justice that is the concern of his book ('the way in which the major social institutions distribute fundamental rights and duties and determine the division of advantages from social cooperation'.[21]) The special conception cannot delimit the concept of justice, however, for we also care about the distribution of benefits and burdens when they do not result from social cooperation, for instance when we are dividing up manna from heaven or, what amounts to the same thing, the territory and natural resources of the planet. But only when the criteria of likeness and unlikeness specify something we can sensibly regard as an 'allotment' of benefits or burdens is there room for a norm of justice. This accords with the traditional idea that justice is a matter of securing to each their due. It is tempting to say, therefore, that justice is always a matter of distribution, but that idea is sometimes used in narrower ways (e.g. to draw a contrast with commutative or retributive justice, or to pick out what Robert Nozick calls 'patterned' principles of allotment) so it is safer to have a different term.[22] I will follow John Gardner and say that the domain of justice is the domain of 'allocative' principles.[23]

Now: why care so much about allocation—about who gets what, and on what grounds? One familiar reason is that many allocable resources are

---

[19] I am not assuming the setback is narrowly consequential; it may be expressive, and the inequality may be one of status rather than resources. On 'person-affecting' considerations, see Derek Parfit, *Reasons and Persons* (Oxford University Press, 1987) 363.
[20] John Rawls, *A Theory of Justice* (Harvard University Press, 1971) 7.
[21] Ibid.
[22] Robert Nozick, *Anarchy, State, and Utopia* (Basic Books, 1974) 156.
[23] John Gardner, 'The Virtue of Justice and the Character of Law' (2000) *Current Legal Problems* 531. I depart from Gardner's original claim that allocative principles regulate scarcity. (He modifies that claim in John Gardner, *Law as a Leap of Faith*, chap. 9.)

scarce, so that if some get more others will get less. This is the nub of David Hume's explanation of why there is virtue in conforming to the requirements of justice. Hume says that if there were a general abundance, so that my use of an object or resource made no one worse off and crowded no one out, there could be no point to rules allocating control to persons or groups. '[I]n such a happy state every other social virtue would flourish, and receive tenfold increase; but the cautious, jealous virtue of justice would never once have been dreamed of.'[24] Hume acknowledges that norms could exist that do not regulate scarcity, but he thinks they would be 'useless', and would amount to little more than an 'idle ceremonial'[25]—like superstitious taboos about who can wear what sort of cloth or look whom in the eye.

It is wrong to give scarcity that much prominence. Hume overestimates the significance of the link he draws between justice and rules regulating property. Intelligible questions about justice arise in many other contexts, especially in criminal law. Here, we are concerned that the right person is allocated the right penalty, but not owing to any scarcity of lawyers or gaols. Jeremy Waldron offers an apt illustration.[26] Suppose we read that a judge has sentenced five members of a criminal gang to a total of two hundred years in prison. On the basis of that information, we are not in a position to come to any view about the justice of the sentences because, although the information presented is nothing other than the aggregate penalties the individuals are to suffer, we are missing the most important thing, justice-wise: how those penalties are allocated amongst the offenders. What matters to the justice of punishments is who is punished, how severely, and on what grounds. This is not a matter of scarcity, though scarcity of legal resources may compound injustices in punishment.[27] Nor can we bracket criminal justice as a secondary or marginal case. Distribution and proportion in punishment is a central concern of every legal system.

Moreover, were we to restrict the domain of justice to norms governing allocation under scarcity, it would be unlikely that law application would have any special connection to justice, for many legal rules are not

---

[24] David Hume, *An Enquiry Concerning the Principles of Morals* (Tom L. Beauchamp ed., Oxford University Press, 1998), Sec. III, Pt 1, 13.
[25] Ibid.
[26] Jeremy Waldron, 'The Primacy of Justice' (2003) 9 *Legal Theory* 271, 275.
[27] What lawyers call 'access to justice' involves scarcity, and criminal punishments can be unjust not only by prohibiting conduct that is not wrong, or by punishing out of proportion to any wrongfulness, but because they fall too often on those who are too poor to afford lawyers. See F. Wilmot-Smith, *Equal Justice: Fair Legal Systems in an Unfair World* (Harvard University Press, 2020).

scarcity-regulating norms and should not be interpreted as if they were. The formation rules for contract do not allocate any scarce good; they tell us how to make a contract. Nor do laws prohibiting torture—there is no shortage of non-torturing to go around. The justifications for these norms are fundamentally non-allocative.[28] As I have already said, a non-allocative prohibition may be differentially applied. Whether this could give rise to a complaint of injustice depends on the grounds of differentiation. A prohibition on driving over 100 kilometres per hour does not need to be justified in terms of rationing any scarce good. And there is no injustice in stopping a random selection of speeders on the highway, even though one who ends up being stopped may ask, 'Why me?' and we may have no better answer than, 'Why not you? You were speeding.' On the other hand, a valid concern about justice will arise when the selection principle is itself unjust, for example, when mostly black speeders are stopped or, when mostly gay men are charged with public indecency, or when the homeless are disproportionately policed for vagrancy. But here we have substantive injustices in the allocation of enforcement resources, not a mere violation of the principle that like cases are to be treated alike.

5. The Form of Justice and 'Formal Justice'

Although the term 'formal justice' is in common use amongst lawyers, it is unclear. Throughout the law, the distinction between form and substance is highly context dependent. It is one thing to distinguish the formalities needed for a valid will from the substantive disposition it makes of an estate. It is a different thing to claim that corrective justice differs 'in form' from distributive justice. Kramer calls legal constancy 'procedural' justice, and that suggests a third contrast with substance. But whether a legal procedure is any kind of justice procedure depends on what it does. It is a fault in parliamentary procedure to begin the Queen's speech without first summoning the Gentleman Usher of the Black Rod, but it is no injustice. Typical rules of procedural justice are things like the requirement that no one should be judge in their own cause and that both sides to any dispute must be heard.

---

[28] Joel Feinberg distinguishes comparative and non-comparative justice; but it is unclear how we are to distinguish non-comparative *injustices* from non-comparative wrongs of other sorts, for example, cruelty, inhumanity, or infidelity. I will assume that the sort of justice alleged to arise from 'treating like cases alike' is comparative. Joel Feinberg, 'Noncomparative Justice' (1974) 83 *Philosophical Review* 297.

These are requirements that cannot be fulfilled merely by consistent application of a legal system's procedural norms, irrespective of their content. If the law allows the rich twice as much time to present their case as the poor, strict application of the law offends procedural justice.

As we have seen, Hart says the connection between formal justice and 'the very notion of proceeding by rule is obviously very close'. That is not so obvious. However, Hart continues that line of argument with something that may seem more evident: 'it might be said that to apply a law justly to different cases is simply to take seriously that what is to be applied in different cases is the same general rule, without prejudice, interest, or caprice.'[29] Does this mean that justice in the application of law is a matter of whether an official acted 'without prejudice, interest, or caprice?' Is this meant to be an explanation for why consistent rule application always brings justice, or is it a restriction, specifying cases in which it does so? That is: is the idea that constancy is a form of justice *only when* the law is applied in a certain spirit, namely, impartially?

If no one can be said to apply a rule constantly unless they do so without prejudice or interest, then the virtue Hart is trying to capture is not formal. Whether one's motivation in applying a rule is independent of one's prejudices or interests is a matter of moral psychology, not an incident of rule application. Formalists claim to detect an injustice in non-application itself, irrespective of the law-applier's motivation. That suggests the mention of impartiality is non-restrictive. The claim must be that, when a rule falls within the domain of justice by prescribing an allocation of benefits or burdens, to do anything other than enforce that very allocation is already to misallocate, and all misallocations (as judged by the law itself) are formal injustices and *in that sense* failures of impartiality. When we ask *why* there is any kind impartiality here, we are directed, by paths of varying circumference, back to the assertion that this is what formal justice violates. It is starting to sound as if the formalist is claiming that whenever we do something that has *the form of* justice, we are doing something called *formal justice*, and that is a genuine kind of justice. Yet something can have the form of K without being a form of K. A cloud can have the form of a camel.

Kelsen spots one mistake in this line of thought. As I noted, he regards strict norm application as the only *cognitive* aspect of the mainly non-cognitive

---

[29] Hart, *The Concept of Law*, 161.

and relativistic idea of justice.[30] However, there remain the other aspects of justice to attend to. Kelsen writes:

> That a general norm is applied in one case but not in a similarly situated case appears, then, as 'unjust'; and it appears 'unjust' quite apart from any consideration of the value of the general norm itself. According to this usage, judging something to be just is simply to express the relative value of conformity to a norm...[31]

The reason Kelsen says '*according to this usage*' and puts 'just' in scare quotes is that he denies this fully captures the meaning of justice, which purports to pick out a value that is *non*-relative.[32] Now, as far as Kelsen is concerned, that is bad news for justice. He thinks there aren't any non-relative values, so to use 'justice' in its literal, full-blooded sense is always to make an error, and an ideologically loaded one at that. It conceals the way justice-claims advance some people's interests over those of others while pretending they are being calibrated against some (non-existent) universal standard. Norm-conformity, on the other hand—what lawyers professionally but sloppily *call* justice—is a rational and cognitive matter, but that is because it expresses only the relative value of norm-conformity, that is, the value relative to— measured by—that very norm. If a law says, 'the total votes cast by black electors shall count as three-fifths of the total votes cast by white electors' then what we get from strict compliance is more burdens on blacks than on whites—that is, an injustice. And there isn't some extra value called 'formality' or 'strict compliance' that compensates or mitigates for it. Kelsen is aware of this. That is why he thinks formal justice, so-called, is *not* justice, but is a consistency feature we would see *as part of justice*, if only justice existed. If unicorns existed, they would have just one spiral horn, and whether a member of *Equidae* had such a horn is a matter that could be empirically ascertained. But there are no unicorns.

---

[30] There is tension between Kelsen's relativism and his non-cognitivism. If what is just is determined by local customs, the question of what justice requires (there) is a question of fact to be settled by investigating those customs. But if claims about justice are emotive or expressive, there is no reason why they should be anchored in social conventions the speaker may not endorse. I cannot explore these issues here.
[31] Hans Kelsen, *Introduction to the Problems of Legal Theory* (B. L. Paulson and S. L. Paulson trs, Oxford University Press, 1992) 16. The scare quotes appear also in the original German.
[32] 'In its literal meaning, however, different from this legal sense of the word, "justice" stands for an absolute value.' Ibid.

Kelsen is correct to maintain that rule application alone can give us nothing more than the 'relative value' of norm-conformity. If we are to get justice conclusions from conformity, we would need to show that the rule in question is of the right sort, namely, an allocative norm, and we would also need to ratchet-up the value from norm-conformity to some non-relativized value.[33] That cannot be done. Norms of justice do take the form of allocation norms, but not all allocation norms are norms of justice. Gardner puts it in terms of the personal virtues:

> The just person, it goes without saying, is the person who is animated only by *sound* principles of justice. To act on unsound principles of justice— such as 'give black people fewer benefits than white people'... is to be an *un*just person; it is to possess, not the virtue, but the corresponding vice. But sound principles of justice and unsound principles of justice... take the same distinctive forms.[34]

And that is why the idea that there is a kind of justice that is purely formal is purely a myth. *All* principles of justice—including 'natural', administrative, corrective, distributive, retributive, and procedural justice—are justice principles in virtue of their substance. The reason to inspect a norm in point of its form is to distinguish *candidate* allocative principles from other principles of other sorts—prohibitions or powers for example—not to select among the candidates to find which ones are principles of justice. Fuller sees this more clearly than does Hart. He, too, notes the connection between justice and treating like cases alike, but Fuller says that the latter only has 'a certain formal *resemblance to* justice'.[35] He never suggests it is *a form of* justice.

Consider now the other idea we left hanging: that justice emerges when rules are applied 'without prejudice, interest or caprice'[36] or, as Hart puts it in another place, to say that a law is justly applied is to say that 'no prejudice or interest has deflected the administrator from treating them "equally".'[37] As with Kelsen, Hart's scare quotes are red flags. If impartiality (or equality) is associated with stringency in rule application, it cannot be the impartiality

---

[33] Justice could be relative to something else, for example, to its contribution to human flourishing, or conformity to the will of the gods, or the demands of pure practical reason. The stringency of rule application cannot establish anything like that.
[34] Gardner, 'The Virtue of Justice and the Character of Law'.
[35] Fuller, *The Morality of* Law, 215, emphasis added.
[36] Hart, *The Concept of Law*, 161.
[37] Ibid., 160.

of the point of view of Adam Smith's ideal observer, or the impartiality John Rawls models in the 'original position', or the impartiality Brian Barry suggests is fundamental to justice.[38] Those are all substantive ideals that compete with others, including ideals that permit or require us to give special consideration to our own interests or to those of our affiliates. Impartialist ideals cannot be derived from the principle that legal rules are to be strictly applied, or from the requirement that one needs a reason to treat legally similar cases differently. Hart seems alert to this when he concedes, to Patrick Devlin, that there may sometimes be content-independent value in conformity to the customary morality of a society. Notice, however, that this is a 'formal' value in a rather different sense of the term:

> [I]n the practice of any social morality there are necessarily involved what may be called *formal* values as distinct from the *material* values of its particular rules or content. In moral relationships with others the individual sees questions of conduct from an impersonal point of view and applies general rules impartially to himself and to others; he is made aware of and takes account of the wants, expectations, and reactions of others; he exerts self-discipline and control in adapting his conduct to reciprocal aims. These are universal virtues and indeed constitute the specifically moral attitude to conduct.[39]

Two things merit attention here. First, unlike the germ-of-justice thesis, this does not allege any conceptual connection between rule application and justice. To be sure, the 'specifically moral attitude to conduct' *includes* justice, but it does not distinguish justice from all other moral standards, including general beneficence. The specifically moral attitude sketched above is a thick one, comprising attitudes and dispositions that have little if anything to do with willingness to apply rules. Second, the fact that a certain attitude is independent of the content of the norms *it applies* does not show that it is independent of all material features. It shows only that it is independent of the content of *those* norms. Impartiality, for instance, is dependent on norms that bar a predisposition to favour one's own interests or the interests of one's friends or family. If it is right to exclude those considerations in favour of an impersonal point of view, that can only be in virtue of what taking up that

---

[38] See Brian Barry, *Justice as Impartiality: A Treatise on Social Justice, Vol II* (Oxford University Press, 1995).
[39] H. L. A. Hart, *Law, Liberty, and Morality* (Stanford University Press, 1963), 71.

perspective expresses or realizes, and that is no formal matter. We can go further. It is not necessary to follow *any* sort of rule to treat people impartially or to remain steadfast against the pull of self- or party-interest. A single Solomonic act of arbitration need not be the application or creation of a rule, but it should be undertaken impartially, without a predisposition to favour either party.

This points to a deeper divergence between rule application and justice. Whether we should have any rule at all to regulate an allocative problem is a substantive question on which justice bears, not a conceptual presupposition of the applicability of justice. To create a general rule to regulate a class of concerns is a decision that has allocative consequences and that may be assessed on allocative grounds. To allocate by general rule may even undermine justice where that requires a fine-grained sensitivity to the particular equities or interests in a case. As Aristotle says, even good rules get things right only in the general run of things. We do well to reason according to rules when, notwithstanding their coarse-grained and 'sticky' nature, we do better by using a rule than by not using one. We should not decide by following rules if that makes things worse overall, or worse for certain classes of people. Justice itself may therefore require that we decide without the straitjacket of rules, or only according to defeasible rules of thumb subject to adjustment in individual cases.

If, on the other hand, we are thinking of impartiality not as a virtue of a procedure but of a person, then its association with exceptionless rigour is even less plausible. One of the reasons racist judges in the American South found it easy to be steadfast in their application of the Jim Crow laws was that those laws harmonized so nicely with their prejudices. Contemporary judges of similar outlook no doubt find it easier to apply, or to hold as constitutionally valid, voter-suppression laws than do judges who loathe their embedded racism. There need be nothing conscious about this. It is more usually a matter of sub-rational and difficult-to-control processes of cognitive dissonance, wishful thinking, and insensitivity to important facts. People's racism can even be held sincerely and in good faith (rather than, say, as a pose to curry favour with other racists.) We tend to imagine that partiality and prejudice bring injustice only when they lead judges *not* to apply law according to its terms, and instead to give breaks to their patrons and parties. But that is only one side of the matter. Partiality and prejudice are also powerful forces *encouraging* judges to stringently apply laws that favour those they antecedently favour, even if the laws are unjust. A dogmatic racist, sexist, or homophobe may find themselves backsliding into just behaviour when empathy, humanity, or common sense push back against rules that are well-adapted to their blind spots. It is not always easy for normal human beings to be unjust, even on the bench. To be a cool, reliable dispensary of injustice can take a lot of discipline.

Why, then, was anyone ever tempted by the idea that constancy in rule application amounts to equality, impartiality, or justice? The explanation may be epistemic. In the cases of laws that are horrifically unjust—chattel slavery, enclosure of the commons, segregation of races, voter suppression—the evil is so dominant that even if there were a smidgen of injustice in failing punctiliously to apply those awful norms, we might not notice it. It would be buried by the overwhelming and decisive moral considerations on the other side: a negligible needle of 'formal' justice under a Himalayan haystack of 'substantive' justice. Will our formalist now plead, 'Exactly! That is why it is hard to notice!'? That is a plea of desperation. The fact that *if* formal justice were present, we might miss it is no reason for thinking it is really there. There are many haystacks without needles. We need an affirmative reason to believe justice is present whenever a rule is constantly applied, and we have not managed to reverse Plato in our search for one.

What has gone wrong? Formalists may be misled by the fact that inconstancy can compound substantive injustice. When L is unjust, punishing someone under L who is actually in conformity with L is an additional affront. No one should be punished for breach of L, and certainly not those who did not even breach L. To do so would be, in a phrase due to Antony Quinton, a lying imputation of their guilt.[40] But it does not follow that, when L is itself unjust, *failing* to punish someone else under L is also unjust, unless that is a result of the law's attention and application being regulated by substantively unjust selection norms of the sort discussed earlier. To stiffen someone's resolve to do injustice produces yet more injustice. Except when it is part of an indirect strategy that is highly beneficial in terms of justice in the long run or overall, it is wrong to produce more unjust allocations.

Perhaps we should permit constancy of injustice when that is the only way of awakening those with the power and will to remedy it, and it is likely to provoke them to do so. I doubt that we are very reliable at identifying those circumstances or at predicting when the provocation will work. Human nature being what it is, however, people do sometimes complain when others have not been treated as badly as they once were. Hospital specialists moan

---

[40] A. M. Quinton, 'On Punishment' (1954) 14 *Analysis* 133, 137.

when new working-time legislation protects junior doctors from the inhumane conditions previously inflicted on the specialists; senior partners think junior associates in law firms should suffer the drudge and hierarchy that hollowed out their own younger selves. These are not people with a keen sense of justice. But they do have something in common with the just. Those gripped by envious or dog-in-the-manger attitudes are highly attentive to the comparisons and relativities of who gets what. Justice also requires that sort of attention—but only to the right relativities and only for the right reasons.

6. The Measure and Means of Justice

We might just leave things there, with the conclusion that the germ-of-justice thesis is incorrect. Apart from the superficial linguistic fact that, in English, 'justice' sometimes means 'law' (e.g. 'The Ministry of Justice'), there is no affinity between justice as a moral value and law as a political institution. There is no shortage of plausible explanations for why judges and other officials might say or think the contrary. They have been taught to deliver 'justice according to law', and their training and selection make them good at detecting, and alert to the significance of, what their law *regards as* just. And, as I said, it can't be easy for a person of ordinary intelligence and moral sensitivity to apply, in case after a case, without exception, a rule they know to be seriously unjust. That must take special resolve, perhaps made easier by entertaining the fiction that constancy is itself a form a justice. Those who entertain a fiction long enough may come to believe it.

There is also room for an explanation that allows partial truth, if not the whole truth, to the germ-of-justice thesis. That thesis focused on just one necessary feature of law: it involves rules. But law's rule-like nature is not its only important feature. Not every rule is a legal rule, and not every system of rules is a legal system. Other features of law point towards the fact that while law is not necessarily *a measure of justice*, a functioning legal system is often *a means to justice*, and sometimes a humanly necessary means.

One of these features I examine in more detail in Chapter 8. To foreshadow, law has a necessary content. What distinguishes a legal rule from a rule of etiquette or sport is the fact that a legal rule is such in virtue of its membership in some legal system, and every legal system regulates a particular subject matter: a set of important of human interests including limits on the use of violence, access to external resources, support for agreements among people, and for forms of association and kinship. Even if it goes too far to say that this is what law is (teleologically) 'for', we cannot distinguish legal systems from other norm systems without reference to such content. No structural features alone can distinguish law from professional hockey, for example: both have primary and secondary rules, officials, effective jurisdiction, and so on.[41] To be law, a system of norms must regulate particular concerns, and these are the concerns of morality. If you want to think of law as having a job, or performing a service, in society, its most important job is supporting morality. Law may fail at this--miserably. It often does. But unless a rule system is oriented to, or could with adjustment become oriented to, this task it is not a legal system. And to be so oriented, law needs to allocate duties, powers, sanctions, and rewards among its officials and subjects. Morality demands that these allocations answer to justice. Unlike a novel or a movie, a legal system cannot rebuff the charge that it aids or abets injustice by saying 'I'm not *trying* to do justice, I'm trying to educate or entertain!' We worry so much about justice in the law precisely because the subject matter of law is the indigenous territory of justice and injustice.

Justice is therefore linked to law by law's necessary content. Does it follow that law is not only a domain that is especially *apt for* justice, but that law answers dominantly, or even uniquely, to justice? No. There is nothing here to suggest that justice is 'the first virtue of social institutions', as Rawls puts it at the beginning of *A Theory of Justice*.[42] The allocative character of justice may reflect its primacy over certain aggregative considerations, but only at certain points, and justice is not the only non-aggregative principle bearing on the law. *Jus cogens* norms banning genocide, slavery, torture, and refoulement are not properly characterized or justified by considerations of the allocation of benefits and burdens. They serve humanity and dignity, not justice.

It is doubtful that we should always enforce the requirements of justice, no matter how damaging or pointless that would be. Even Rawls, who assigns special priority to justice, allows that some injustices are tolerable, provided they are not too severe and do not always afflict the same people or groups. As with 'micro-aggressions', there are 'micro-injustices' we should be willing to put up with for the sake of toleration and solidarity. Injustice in the allocation of labour in child-rearing is still one of the things that most limits women's freedom and restricts their professional and avocational success. It

---

[41] Should we say that law has and enforces a compulsory jurisdiction, whereas the rules of games only apply to those who choose to play? At best this is true of state law. Canon law does not have compulsory jurisdiction.
[42] Hart, *The Concept of Law*, 7.

needs to stop. Yet spouses who track with actuarial precision the number of times they load the dishwasher or collect the mail are headed for the divorce courts. This is why Hume calls justice 'the cautious, jealous virtue'.[43]

A second affinity between law and justice flows not from the necessary content of law, but the institutions that supervise it. Unlike language and courtesy, legal systems necessarily have agents with authority over the operations of the system. Law regulates its own creation, and also its own application. Law could not do its tasks of identifying which rules are binding or determining compliance or breach without people who have the power and duty to do these very things. Legal systems necessarily have *allocators*.

In view of importance and scope of these tasks, allocators must be produced if they do not already exist. Generally speaking, the reasons for doing a task are also reasons for finding or creating someone to do it. This point is too often neglected in political theory. In the middle of the last century, some thought it an objection to the existence of 'second-' or 'third-generation' rights that there was (they asserted) no one who had the correlative duties or powers. How can we say there is a universal right to education when some countries have no schools or teachers? How can there be a right to clean air when so many countries scheme to externalize the costs of polluting? It is odd that anyone was ever moved by such arguments. The case for a right to education is already a case to find or create a person or institution who will bear the duties necessary to teach children. The right to clean air already makes the case for agencies able to regulate pollution.

These cases may meet countervailing arguments, some of them sound. But my point is that a sound case often goes *from* the rights *to* the duties including, if necessary, to the creation of a duty-holder and perhaps also a duty-enforcer. The right to vote, or more generally to participate in politics, is our fundamental reason for *seeing to it that* there are elections, polling stations, returning officers, etc. It would be ludicrous to say, in a newly independent country, that there is no moral right to participate because there exist no institutions with the authority to make participation count.

This second affinity between law and justice is one lawyers recognize under the slogan 'where there is a right there is a remedy' or, more accurately, 'where there is a right there *ought to be* a remedy'. Sometimes that remedy requires law. Take a simple case. P asserts in good faith that D is unlawfully occupying their land, and D in good faith denies it. If there is no way to resolve this

---

[43] See n. 24 above.

dispute, it is likely to continue and to fester. That is usually bad, not only for P and for D, but for many others too. Each honestly believes they are in the right (or are dealing with someone who has a right.) One of them may even be correct. A conciliator may persuade them to split the difference, an agreed arbitrator may settle it for them. But disputes like this keep coming up, if only by accident, owing to uncertainties about norms and facts, including new facts brought about by unpredicted changes in technologies and the environment. Conciliation and private arbitration help, but they need to be constituted and provided for, and there are huge transaction costs in relying on them alone. Private fora are also over-responsive to differences in bargaining power between the parties, that is, they tend to fail at delivering justice. This grounds a case for having someone with the power and duty to rule on inevitable disputes, in a general way, while aiming at (substantive) justice. The allocator may rarely need to rule; the fact that there is in the background someone who could do so may encourage the parties to come to a successful and fairer conciliation or arbitration. Justice is a reason for creating agents that could deliver justice, and in societies like ours the most prominent of these agents are courts—though their work is not always and never only a matter of applying rules.

That argument is schematic and admits of exceptions. It would be wrong to think that only legal systems with courts and all the rest are capable of sustaining social order, organizing cooperation, and seeing that people get their due. For most of the history of *homo sapiens*, there was no law at all. But it is reasonable to think that over an important range of disputes the case for a just allocation (of rights, of obligations, etc.) is a case for having someone capable of settling one. And in large, mobile societies with complex, recurrent disputes it is a significant part of the case for having law. Without courts to determine what that law requires and whether someone is in conformity to it, it is harder to make and sustain just allocations. This is a familiar argument, with antecedents in Aristotle, Aquinas, Hobbes, Locke, Rousseau, Kant, and Mill. The fact that it is so unoriginal reassures us that it is on the right track.

Where we need someone with the power to decide a dispute as between P and D we need someone to allocate, and their decision should therefore answer (inter alia) to justice. Where courts have the immediate power to bind others beyond the parties, or where they shape legal norms more slowly via customs of interpretation, they create norms that others use and rely on, and this gives rise to waves of further possible disputes and the need for more yet allocative settlements. As Ronald Dworkin puts it, a system of adjudication by courts tends to turn disputes—even disputes which begin over other sorts of issues—into disputes about rights, including the 'right to win a lawsuit'.[44]

So law is after all connected to justice: first by its content, which makes law justice-apt and, second, by its essential institutions, which help make justice possible. Could we go further, and say that together these show that law is not only necessarily a 'justice-seeking' institution, but also a justice-realizing institution?[45] Law requires courts; courts have a justice-task; and justice must be done to be seen to be done? No. That goes too far. To be effective, a legal system probably has to deliver the goods to some people, certainly to the most influential and powerful. But that cannot be inflated to show that it must deliver the goods to all, and in a just way. Laws can do injustice while fully satisfying the minimum content thesis, while aiming at justice, and through the instrumentality of institutions that have the pursuit of justice as one of their necessary functions. But perhaps we can go this far: if we do have law-applying organs, then we have social machinery by which justice could be made effective, and in certain social conditions nothing but such organs stand a chance of achieving justice, or of doing so overall and amongst everyone. And if that is correct, why not express it by saying that we have, in the idea of a society subject to law, the germ at least of justice?

This germ is not a kind, form, or element of justice. A seed may be infertile or may fall on stony ground; it may be eaten by birds or choked by thorns. Should we therefore backtrack, and say there is no significant link between law and justice? Law may give justice, or it may not. It is all contingent. Did we need to study legal theory to learn that? Some philosophers never see the word 'contingent' without imagining it preceded by 'merely'. In social studies, constant dependencies that fall short of conceptual or metaphysical necessity are some of the most important things to discover about institutions. But if we do insist on limiting 'necessary' to some narrow, technical usage, we can nonetheless say that the affinity between effective law and justice is *no accident*. It is not a 'mere' contingency that law is justice-apt or that law answers to justice. And when we have institutions set up to, and able to, perform an allocative task then we have a chance at justice that we would not have without such institutions: institutions with the power and duty to bring settlement to allocative disputes about matters of moral concern. There can be no legal system without such institutions. That is no accident either. It is the germ of justice.

---

[44] R. M. Dworkin, *Taking Rights Seriously* (Duckworth, 1979) 115.
[45] I owe the term 'justice-seeking' to Lawrence G. Sager, *Justice in Plainclothes: A Theory of American Constitutional Practice* (Yale University Press, 2004) 19 ff.

7
The Inseparability of Law and Morals

1. A Difficult Divorce

H. L. A. Hart's Holmes lecture gave new expression to the old idea that legal systems comprise positive law only, a thesis usually labelled 'legal positivism'. Hart did this in two ways. First, he disentangled it from the independent and distracting projects of the imperative theory of law, the analytic study of legal language, and non-cognitivist moral philosophies. Hart's second move was to offer a fresh characterization of the thesis. He argued that legal positivism involves, as his title put it, 'the separation of law and morals'.[1] Of course, by this Hart did not mean anything as silly as the idea that law and morality should be *kept separate* (as if the separation of law and morals were like the separation of church and state).[2] Morality sets ideals for law, and law should live up to them. Nor did he mean that law and morality *are* separated. We see their union everywhere. We prohibit sex discrimination because we judge it immoral; the point of prohibiting it is to clarify and enforce that judgement, and we do so by using ordinary moral terms such as 'duty' and 'equality'. To the extent that it suggests otherwise, the term 'separation' is therefore misleading. To pacify the literal-minded, Hart might have entitled his lecture 'Positivism and the *Separability* of Law and Morals'.[3] That captures well his idea that 'there is no necessary connection between law and morals or law as it is and law as it ought to be'.[4]

---

[1] H. L. A. Hart, 'Positivism and the Separation of Law and Morals' (1957) 71 *Harvard Law Review* 593.

[2] The association of this idea with Hart seems to be a confused interpretation of a thesis that he *did* hold, namely that the law ought not to prohibit harmless deviation from conventional moral standards. See H. L. A. Hart, *Law, Liberty and Morality* (Stanford University Press, 1963). That is a normative thesis about legislation, and not a theory of the nature of law. If positive law necessarily reproduced conventional morality, the recommendation would have been pointless.

[3] Hart sometimes described the thesis that he opposed as making the claim that law and morals are 'indissolubly fused or inseparable'. H. L. A. Hart, *Essays in Jurisprudence and Philosophy* (Oxford University Press, 1983) 50. I think Jules Coleman coined the term 'separability thesis'. See Jules Coleman, 'Negative and Positive Positivism' (1982) 11 *Journal of Legal Studies* 139, 142.

[4] Hart, 'Positivism and the Separation of Law and Morals', 601 n. 25.

Lon Fuller refused to take Hart at his word. He thought that Hart *was* recommending that 'law must be strictly severed from morality';[5] if Hart was not, then why did he say that it is *morally* better to retain a 'broad' concept of law, one that applies even to wicked legal systems? And anyway, if positivists *were not* recommending separation, then what advice *were* they offering politicians who have to design constitutions or judges who have to decide cases?

The obvious answer is that positivists were not offering advice. They were trying to understand the nature of law. Fuller's unwillingness to credit that project flows from his apparent conviction that it could amount to nothing better than 'a series of definitional fiats'.[6]

Fuller is not the last to have doubts about the prospects for an explanation of the concept of law, nor the first to think it more important to change the world than to interpret it. The only surprising thing is that Fuller supposes that world-changing can be brought about by philosophy-changing. He thinks that jurists could improve society by treating philosophies of law not as efforts to understand social reality but as 'direction posts for the application of human energies'.[7] In which direction should they point? Towards a much greater 'fidelity to law'. But that is scarcely the beginning. Fuller also wants general jurisprudence to see to it that constitutions not 'incorporate a host of economic and political measures of the type that one would ordinarily associate with statutory law',[8] and he wants it to give solace to trial judges who have expertise in commerce but find themselves under the thumb of a supreme court with no business sense.[9] Legal positivism's laxity about such things agitates him: 'What disturbs me about the school of legal positivism is that it not only refuses to deal with [these] problems ... but bans them on principle from the province of legal philosophy.'[10]

There are no such bans; positivists simply believe there to be more than one province in the empire of legal philosophy. They think that, say, opposition to having economic provisions in constitutions must be defended within the province of political morality, not dragged into general jurisprudence as a supposed inference from, or presupposition of, some theory about the nature of law. Most positivists think that general jurisprudence itself should have no

---

[5] Lon L. Fuller, 'Positivism and Fidelity to Law—A Reply to Professor Hart' (1975) 71 *Harvard Law Review* 630, 656.
[6] Ibid., 631.
[7] Ibid., 632.
[8] Ibid., 643.
[9] Ibid., 646.
[10] Ibid., 643.

pretensions at all to be a 'guide to conscience'[11] and so are neither surprised nor disappointed when it proves 'incapable of aiding [a] judge'.[12] The mission of legal positivism is not to promote economic liberalism or even 'fidelity to law'. Its aim is not to preserve pieties, but to seek truth and clarity about law—what Hart calls 'a sovereign virtue in jurisprudence'.[13] It is that project, not some other one, that reveals a 'separation of law and morals'.

The victory of Hart's lecture in promoting this slogan was virtually total. People who know nothing else about jurisprudence know that legal positivists are those who maintain the separation of law and morality. The one group amongst which the slogan did not catch fire was the legal positivists themselves. Joseph Raz notices that the separability thesis is logically independent of the idea that legal systems contain positive law only:

> The claim that what is law and what is not is purely a matter of social fact still leaves it an open question whether or not those social facts by which we identify the law or determine its existence do or do not endow it with moral merit. If they do, it has of necessity a moral character.[14]

Jules Coleman describes the separability thesis as undeniable and therefore useless as a demarcation line in legal theory: 'We cannot usefully characterize legal positivism in terms of the separability thesis, once it is understood properly, because virtually no one—positivist or not—rejects it.'[15] John Gardner maintains that the separability thesis cannot characterize positivism for the opposite reason: It is 'absurd . . . no legal philosopher of note has ever endorsed it.'[16] Amid such cacophony, it is unsurprising that some onlookers find the thesis 'hopelessly ambiguous' and the long-standing debates about the separability of law and morals 'entirely pointless'.[17]

In this chapter I offer a different diagnosis. The separability thesis is neither ambiguous, absurd, nor obvious. On the contrary, it is clear, coherent, and false. But it is false for reasons that Fuller does not notice and which

---

[11] Ibid., 634.
[12] Ibid., 647.
[13] Hart, 'Positivism and the Separation of Law and Morals', 593.
[14] Joseph Raz, *The Authority of Law* (Oxford University Press, 1979) 38–9; see also Joseph Raz, *Practical Reason and Norms* (rev. edn, Oxford University Press, 1999) 165–70.
[15] Jules Coleman, *The Practice of Principle* (Oxford University Press, 2001) 152.
[16] John Gardner, 'Legal Positivism: 5 ½ Myths' (2001) 46 *American Journal of Jurisprudence* 199, 223.
[17] Klaus Füßer, 'Farewell to "Legal Positivism": The Separation Thesis Unraveling', in R. P. George ed., *The Autonomy of Law: Essays on Legal Positivism* (Oxford University Press, 1996) 120.

throw into sharp relief, and into question, celebratory views of law like those of Fuller and his followers.

2. What the Separability Thesis *is Not*

The separability thesis is not a methodological claim. It bears only on the object-level domain—that is, on laws and legal systems.[18] Hart's method was to approach the nature of law through what some call a 'hermeneutic' study of the concept of law: he examined the concept as it is for those whose concept it is. He considered this method noncommittal with respect to the moral value of its objects and, in that sense, morally neutral. But that is not the engine of the separability thesis. There is no reason why a noncommittal method cannot discover necessary connections between law and morals should they exist; and to discover that there *are* such connections is not to presuppose or assert that it is a good thing they do exist. Hart's methodological neutrality is no more than the claim that general jurisprudence must not arrive pre-committed to conclusions about the moral value of law. This neutrality does not prompt or preclude any conclusions one way or the other about the value of law, nor does it presume any other kind of value-neutrality.

Does Hart's discussion of the moral reasons for retaining a broad concept of law cast doubt on such neutrality? No: the separability thesis rests wholly on his destructive arguments against the necessary connection thesis. The moral and pragmatic considerations that he mentions respond to something that Hart considers 'less an intellectual argument . . . than a passionate appeal'.[19] The appeal comes from a conceptual reformer who asks us to revise the concept of law so as to deprive wicked legal systems of whatever allure attaches to the label 'law'. Hart is not suggesting that moral and pragmatic considerations *establish* the separability of law and morals. He is arguing that there are no such reasons for pretending that the nature of law is other than what it is shown to be by a neutral method, and no reasons for reforming the concept—if that project even makes sense. This assumes that the concept of law is sufficiently determinate to make intelligible the idea of a conceptual

---

[18] It is therefore what Stephen Perry calls 'substantive', as opposed to 'methodological', positivism. Stephen R. Perry, 'The Varieties of Legal Positivism' (1996) 9 *Canadian Journal of Law and Jurisprudence* 361. For the view that the separability thesis includes at least one methodological commitment, see James Morauta, 'Three Separation Theses' (2004) 23 *Law and Philosophy* 111.

[19] Hart, 'Positivism and the Separation of Law and Morals', 615. For discussion, see Chapter 1, section 5, this volume.

revision—there must be something the revisionist is revising—but it does not assume that law has the nature that it would be good for it to have.

Because the separability thesis is a substantive claim about the nature of law it might be tempting to identify it with one of two influential theories of the nature of law, each of which claims association with the tradition of legal positivism—either the social thesis or sources thesis.

According to the *social thesis*, law must be grounded in social facts and any non-factual criteria for the existence and content of law must likewise be grounded in such facts. Coleman favours the social thesis. He holds that the separability thesis, 'properly understood', is only a claim about 'the *content* of the membership criteria for law', and as such is not open to serious doubt.[20] If the just-quoted phrase means that the separability thesis is only a claim about *what the criteria are*, then it is probably true that no one holds that *the criteria* are necessarily moral—not even a Thomist like John Finnis, who acknowledges that 'human law is artefact and artifice, and not a conclusion from moral premises . . .'[21] Coleman infers that the correct demarcation line between positivists and others turns on the 'existence conditions' for the not-necessarily-moral criteria. He says that positivists maintain, while others deny, that these conditions are conventional or social.[22]

Now, one may with fair warning use 'separability thesis' however one likes—it is just a technical label. But Coleman's thesis diverges from Hart's, for it neglects one of Hart's central teachings: 'There are *many* different types of relation between law and morals and there is nothing which can profitably be singled out for study as *the* relation between them.'[23] Hart's thesis is that *none* of these relations holds as a matter of necessity. Far from zeroing in on one narrow (if important) question about law and morals, Hart's theory is pluralistic to the point of tedium. He canvasses just about everything that anyone ever thought might constitute some kind of necessary connection and then argues, one by one, that 'it ain't necessarily so'.[24] The social thesis that Coleman has in mind is narrower than the thesis Hart seeks to vindicate.

For similar reasons, the separability thesis cannot be identified with the *sources thesis*—that is, with the view that the existence and content of law

---

[20] Jules Coleman, *The Practice of Principle* (Oxford University Press, 2001) 152.
[21] John Finnis, 'The Truth in Positivism', in George, *The Autonomy of Law: Essays on Legal Positivism*, 205.
[22] Coleman, *The Practice of Principle*, 152.
[23] H. L. A. Hart, *The Concept of Law* (3rd edn, Penelope. A. Bulloch and Joseph Raz, eds; Leslie Green, intro, Oxford University Press, 2012) 2, 185.
[24] Though, as we shall see, Hart is of two minds about how to regard relations of 'natural necessity'. See this chapter, section 4.1.

depends on its sources and not on its merits.[25] We have already noticed one way in which this thesis is less stringent than the separability thesis: the sources thesis only excludes the *dependence* of law on morality. As Raz notes, this leaves wide open the question of whether there are other necessary relations between the two (including relations of entailment *from* propositions about law *to* propositions about morality).[26] In another way, however, the sources thesis is more stringent than the separability thesis. It excludes from the criteria for identifying law not only morality but *any* merits—that is, any evaluative considerations that would need to be satisfied for us to conclude that an organization counts as a legal system or that a rule is one of its laws. Hart is interested in all sorts of relations between law and morals; but he never pauses to consider what positivism should hold about, say, the relationship between law and economics. According to the sources thesis, however, the fact that a certain legal rule would be inefficient is no better reason for doubting its existence than the fact that it would be inhumane or unjust. John Austin put it this way: 'A law, which actually exists, is a law, though we happen to dislike it, or though it vary from the text, by which we regulate our approbation and disapprobation.'[27] Austin intends the quantification *for all* 'texts.'

3. Understanding the Separability Thesis

The separability thesis is not the methodological neutrality thesis, not the social thesis, and not the sources thesis. It is the contention that there are no necessary connections between law and morality. Do not mistake the breathtaking sweep of the thesis for ambiguity. It applies to various relata (to individual laws and to legal systems, to positive morality and to valid morality); to various relations (causal, logical, and normative); and to various modalities (including conceptual and natural necessities). It boldly proclaims that,

---

[25] It is the last clause ('and not on its merits') that distinguishes the sources thesis from the social thesis. The social thesis permits the merit-dependence of law, provided that this dependence is itself a consequence of social facts. See Gardner, 'Legal Positivism: 5 ½ Myths'. For other statements and defences of the sources thesis, see Raz, *The Authority of Law*, 45–52; and Joseph Raz, *Ethics in the Public Domain: Essays in the Morality of Law and Politics* (Oxford University Press, 1994) 210–37.
[26] Raz, *The Authority of Law*, 15.
[27] John Austin, *The Province of Jurisprudence Determined* (W. E. Rumble ed., Cambridge University Press, 1995) 157.

among all the permutations and combinations, you will not come up with any necessary connections *at all*.

There are three terms here that we need to clarify: 'connection', 'morality', and 'necessary'. *Connection* is not a technical notion; it is simply any sort of relation. Connections matter because we do not fully understand law until we understand how it relates to things like social power, social rules, and morality. There are external relations between law independently identified and interacting in a variety of ways with the rest of the social world. There are also internal relations without which something would not *be* law—that is, relations that belong to the concept of law. It is not plausible to suppose that law's nature could be hidden to us, to be revealed only in some yet-undiscovered microstructure or as a consequence of some yet-unproven theorem. Law is a human institution; we can study it only in the ways that such institutions can be studied. One fruitful way is to study the concepts through which institutions are structured—concepts implicit in our thought, language, and practice.

Now for *morality*. While the noisiest disputes involve law's relation to valid (or ideal) morality, the separability thesis applies no less to customary (or positive) morality. There is a connection between these, for valid morality is what every customary morality claims (or is taken) to be. The separability thesis rejects necessary connections on both fronts. It denies not only the so-called 'natural law' view that there must be moral tests for law, but also the thesis of 'consensus sociologists' who suppose that all legal systems necessarily embody the spirit, traditions, or values of their communities.

The only complex idea is that of a *necessary* connection. The separability thesis allows for any sort of contingent connection between law and morals. But what, precisely, is the difference? It turns out to be less precise than metaphysicians might like. Hart gives 'necessity' a large and liberal interpretation. Apart from thinking that a necessary relation is one that *in some sense* cannot fail to hold, he espouses no firmer commitment about its nature. In particular, he does not attempt to take any advantage that might be gained from arguing that what is naturally necessary or humanly necessary is not *really* necessary, on the ground that it is not, as the slogan has it, 'true in all possible worlds'. He expressly allows for necessary truths to be contextual—that is, dependent on stable empirical features such as our embodiment, our mutual vulnerability, and our mortality, all of which are 'reflected in whole structures of our thought and language'.[28] Given such intransigent facts, to label

---

[28] Hart, *The Concept of Law*, 192; Hart, 'Positivism and the Separation of Law and Morals', 622.

a feature of law that involves them a 'contingency' would be misleading, for although it could change in tandem with human nature, the fact that it would *take* a change in human nature shows that it is essentially unavoidable. So 'why not call it a 'natural' necessity?'[29] The fact that law has these features is, after all, no accident. As far as jurisprudence is concerned, natural necessities and human necessities are no less necessary than are conceptual necessities, and there are no very firm boundaries setting them apart.

Only three further issues about the modalities need mention. First, an obvious point. 'Necessary' and 'contingent' are not contradictories. From the denial that there are necessary moral tests for the existence of law, it does not follow that there are contingent moral tests. There may be none at all. Thus, the separability thesis lends no support to Hart's other view that, as a contingent matter, in some legal systems the existence of law does depend on it satisfying moral tests.

Second, not all necessary truths are important truths. Rousseau said, 'laws are invariably useful to those who own property and harmful to those who do not'.[30] Suppose that this is neither false nor necessarily true. There is no denying that, although it is a contingency, it is just as important as many necessary truths about law (e.g. the truth that every legal system contains norms). Rousseau's contingency is of obvious moral importance and explanatory power; on the other hand, the fact that law contains norms, though necessarily true, is not a very fecund truth. Moreover, the relationships *between* necessary and contingent truths often contribute to our interest in the necessary ones. Every legal system necessarily contains power-conferring norms that play a role in explaining how law governs its own creation. But power-conferring norms such as the powers to legislate or appropriate are also important because they provide facilities to certain agents, on certain terms. They therefore have a contingent relation to the distribution of social power within a society, a matter of the first importance in legal and political theory.

Finally, we should bear in mind that a necessary connection need not be obvious or self-evident. It may be something that we only come to see on reflection. Nor need it be uncontroversial. One may have an incomplete grasp of the concept of law and thus fail to recognize some of its necessary features. There are also areas of uncertainty. There are respects in which the concepts of law or of a legal system are indeterminate, and thus there are conceptual

---

[29] Hart, 'Positivism and the Separation of Law and Morals', 623.
[30] Jean-Jacques Rousseau, *The Social Contract* (M. Cranston trs, Penguin, 1968) 68.

claims with respect to which there is no truth of the matter. If these indeterminacies generate any controversy that needs to be settled, we can do so only by a stipulation that, while perhaps more or less useful for our purposes, cannot be judged true or false.

4. Refuting the Separability Thesis

Let us now turn to assessing the thesis. On reflection we can see that it is false, for there are many necessary relations between law and morality, including the following:[31]

- (N_α) Necessarily, law and morality both contain norms.
- (N_β) Necessarily, the content of every moral norm could be the content of a legal norm.
- (N_γ) Necessarily, no legal system has any of the personal vices.

Is this just a smart-alecky trick? Does anyone maintain, contrary to (N_γ), that law *could* have, say, the vice of infidelity? Probably not literally. Some philosophers do think it a bad idea, or self-defeating, for certain moral norms to be made the content of legal norms; that does not, however, contradict (N_β). To try to impose a legal obligation to love one's neighbour as oneself might be pointless, but it would not be the first time that the law created obligations pointlessly. A few seem to deny (N_α). Some legal realists write as if law were a set of predictions about what will happen rather than a system of prescriptions about what should happen. I doubt they seriously believe that law is *nothing but* 'prophecies of what the courts will do in fact'.[32] (Do they believe that if a given court is predictably racist it follows that *the law* requires that black litigants lose?) In any event, my point is not that these theses have never been denied in the history of legal philosophy, nor that they are undeniable, but only that they are correct.

Maybe these truths are not so impressive, however. Possibly Hart caught a glimmer of things like (N_α), (N_β), and (N_γ), but thought that they should be bracketed as trivial exceptions. In his very last formulation of the separability thesis he does hedge a bit; he says that 'there is no *important* necessary or

---

[31] Cf. Joseph Raz, 'About Morality and the Nature of Law' (2003) 48 *American Journal of Law and Jurisprudence* 1, 2.
[32] O. W. Holmes, 'The Path of the Law' (1897) 10 *Harvard Law Review* 457, 461.

conceptual connection between law and morality'.[33] Considerations of importance are interest-relative, and I think that (N_α) and (N_β) are rather important truths about law. Moreover, as I explained above, some necessary truths get theoretical interest through their relations to contingent truths. For example, (N_α)—together with some other truths—leads Hart to conclude that there is a necessary—or perhaps *nearly* necessary—relation between law and justice. I argue in Chapter 6 that that conclusion is an error, but it is an interesting one. In any case, there are two other groups of necessary connections between law and morality that no one could think trivial or unimportant to a theory of law.

4.1 Derivative Connections

Fuller holds that 'the fundamental postulate of positivism—that law must be strictly severed from morality'—renders the idea that law always creates moral obligations of obedience not only false but unintelligible: How could there possibly be 'an amoral datum called law, which has the peculiar quality of creating a moral duty to obey it?'[34] Fuller here takes for granted a proposition that many others think requires defence: he assumes that *there is* a moral duty to obey the law. If there isn't, then his claim that the positivist 'postulate' renders that idea incoherent is of no concern.

He makes another rash assumption, and one that may explain why his argument takes the shape it does. He supposes that if law *were* an 'amoral datum', then there would be something peculiar about it creating obligations. Why is that? Perhaps he has unwittingly absorbed from Kelsen and Hart the Humean thesis that there is a fundamental split between fact and value, and that we cannot derive an 'ought' from an 'is' alone. That might explain why Fuller thinks it incoherent to suppose that law is an 'amoral datum'. If there were such a split, then no conclusion about our moral obligations could follow from the nature of law *alone*, unless law itself has a moral nature. So Fuller concludes that law does have a moral nature.

He does not consider two other possibilities. It may be that the split thesis is incorrect and that some moral conclusions do, after all, follow from some factual premises alone. Or it may be that moral obligations do not follow from propositions about law's nature *alone* but they do follow from those together

---

[33] Hart, *The Concept of Law*, 259, emphasis added.
[34] Fuller, 'Positivism and Fidelity to Law', 656.

with other true propositions about morality and human well-being. Even Hume believed that whether a promise has been made is a matter of social fact and, also, that there is an obligation to keep promises. Promises have no 'peculiar quality', but they are morally binding all the same. That is because there can be derivative connections between factually determined practices and full-blooded moral conclusions (whether or not the derivations require the help of other propositions).[35] Important moral conclusions may then follow as a matter of natural, or even conceptual, necessity from the proposition that rule R is law.

We should not make too much of this analogy to promises. The fact (if it is one) that self-imposed obligations result from matters of fact yet are morally obligatory does not show that the *other*-imposed obligations of positive law are obligatory in the same way or for the same reason. And the derivative connections between law and morality might not support any obligation to obey it, in spite of claims to the contrary by philosophers as diverse as Plato, Aquinas, Hobbes, Locke, Hume, and Kant. Yet their general line of argument may be sound even if it does not go so far as to establish a duty to obey. Factually determined law may be good- or right-making in some other way. Legal systems make moral norms determinate; they supply information and motivation that help make those norms effective; they support valuable forms of social cooperation. Human nature being what it is, it is overwhelmingly likely that *some* good comes of all this, at least as a matter of natural necessity.

Hart is both alert to and suspicious of these arguments. He concedes that there are at least two 'reasons (or excuses) for talking of a certain overlap between legal and moral standards as necessary and natural'.[36] The first is his 'minimum content' thesis: legal systems cannot be identified by their structure alone; law has a necessary content.[37] It must contain rules that regulate things like violence, property, and agreements so as to promote the survival of its subjects. The second I examined in Chapter 6. This is the claim that every existing legal system does some administrative or, as he also calls it, 'formal'—justice. How so? Necessarily, every legal system contains general rules; general rules cannot exist unless they are applied with some constancy; and constancy is a kind of justice: '[T]hough the most odious laws may be justly applied, we have, in the bare notion of applying a general rule

---

[35] Raz, *Practical Reason and* Norms, 165–70.
[36] Hart, 'Positivism and the Separation of Law and Morals', 624.
[37] Hart, *The Concept of Law*, 193–200. And see Chapter 8, this volume.

of law, the germ at least of justice.'[38] Hart sympathetically develops both the minimum content thesis and the germ-of-justice thesis and then stops just short—at any rate, I *think* he means to stop short—of concluding that these theses prove there to be necessary connections between law and morals. His grounds for hesitation seem to be that neither argument establishes a moral duty to obey the law and each is consistent with the most stringent moral criticism of a legal system that realizes them. Be that as it may, it does not prove the separability thesis. At most it proves that the values the minimum necessary content and the germ-of-justice contribute to law may be accompanied by serious immoralities, possibly so serious that they undermine any duty to obey the law. Still, if every legal system necessarily gives rise to A and to B, then it necessarily gives rise to A, even though it gives rise to B on the demerit ledger.

4.2 Non-Derivative Connections

The derivative connections rely on the supposition that a legal system is effective amongst people with natures much like our own, living in circumstances much like our own. They are among the contextually necessary connections between law and morality. There are also necessary connections between law and morality that are more direct. Here are four of the more interesting ones:

(N_1) Necessarily, law regulates objects of morality.

Morality has objects, and some of those objects are necessarily law's objects. Wherever there is law there is morality, and they regulate the same subject matter--and do so by analogous techniques. As Kelsen notes, '[j]ust as natural and positive law govern the same subject-matter, and relate, therefore, to the same norm-object, namely the mutual relationships of men ... so both also have in common the universal form of this governance, namely *obligation*.'[39]

This is broader than the minimum content thesis. Some think Hart is too timid in limiting the necessary content of law to survival-promoting rules. I think that unless 'survival' is understood in a vacuously broad way, the

---

[38] Hart, *The Concept of Law*, 206. See Chapter 6, this volume.
[39] Hans Kelsen, 'The Idea of Natural Law', in Hans Kelsen, *Essays in Legal and Moral Philosophy* (O. Weinberger ed. and P. Heath trs, Reidel, 1973) 34.

claim is too bold: There are lots of suicide pacts around these days. (I return to this issue in Chapter 8.) But even legal systems that hinder individual or collective survival for the sake of unrestrained consumption, national glory, or religious purity share a common content: they regulate things that the society (or, more likely, its elites) take to be high stakes matters of moral salience. If we encounter a normative system that regulates only low stakes matters (such as games or courtesies) we have not found a legal system. It is of the nature of law to have a large normative reach, one that extends to the most important concerns of the morality of the society in which it exists. How law regulates these matters varies greatly (whether by enforcing them, protecting them, or repressing them), as does its success and value in doing so. Unlike the derivative arguments, therefore, (N_1) does not show that every legal system necessarily has some moral merit; it shows that there is a necessary relation between the scope of law and morality. This is one of the things that makes law important, and it also explains why normative debates about law's legitimacy and authority have the significance that they do.

(N_2) Necessarily, law makes moral claims of its subjects.

Law tells us what we must do, not merely what it would be advantageous to do, and it requires us to act in the interests of other individuals (or in the public interest generally), except when law itself permits otherwise. Every legal system contains obligation-imposing norms, and law necessarily claims legitimate authority to impose them.[40] Judges speak as if their orders create reasons for their subjects to conform in the first instance, not only reasons to conform if they happen to be followed by a conviction for contempt, obstruction, or resisting arrest. Legislated duties presuppose that their subjects are to conform whether or not it is in their self-interest to do so: they purport to be categorical reasons for acting. To impose duties on others in this spirit is to treat them as morally bound to obey—it is to claim legitimate authority to rule. That claim may be, and often is, unwarranted. Sometimes it is half-hearted or cynical. The necessary connection between law and (claimed) moral authority is a thin one. Yet it is in the nature of law to project the self-image of a legitimate authority.

---

[40] I here abridge arguments in Raz, *The Authority of Law*, 28–33, 122–45; Joseph Raz, 'Hart on Moral Rights and Legal Duties' (1984) 4 *Oxford Journal of Legal Studies* 121; and Leslie Green, *The Authority of the State* (Oxford University Press, 1990) 21–88.

For this reason, neither a regime of 'stark imperatives'[41] that simply bosses people around, nor a price system that structures their incentives while leaving them free to act as they please, would be a system of law. It is true that we can capture something about law by thinking of it as a boss or an incentivizer. Perhaps we can represent some of the content of a legal system as incentives or stark imperatives. (N_2) says that these accounts are necessarily incomplete and that they cannot represent the nature of all laws *without loss* (e.g. loss of the distinction between being obliged and having an obligation, or the distinction between a penalty and a tax on conduct).

While (N_2) says that law necessarily has moral pretensions, it says nothing about their soundness. I am inclined to think that some of law's pretensions are always unsound. Suppose that is so. Is it paradoxical? Could it be of the nature of an institution that it necessarily makes claims that are not valid, or that are typically invalid? Assume all theological propositions are false. This does nothing to undermine the fact that part of what it is to be Pope is to claim apostolic succession from St Peter. Whether or not there really is a succession, a bishop who does not at least put on a show of claiming it, and of claiming his place in it, is not the Pope. The nature of law is similarly shaped by the self-image it adopts and projects to its subjects.

Obviously, there is more to be said here, for (N_2) is an example of a necessary connection between law and morality that is neither self-evident nor uncontroversial. One is brought to see it, if one is, by argument and on reflection. (That is why there is work for legal philosophy to do.) Hart himself denies (N_2).[42] In fact, he is willing to go far to save the separability thesis from (N_2), as far as flirting with the sanction theory of duty that his Holmes lecture laboured to discredit.[43] Perhaps he thinks that the arguments for (N_2) are wrong but he can see no other coherent interpretation of the moralized language of law. Or perhaps he also saw that (N_2) poses an immediate threat to the separability thesis, a thesis to which he still had loyalty.

(N_3) Necessarily, law is justice-apt.

In view of the function of law in allocating and enforcing obligations, it always makes sense to ask whether law is just and, where it is found deficient, to

---

[41] The term is due to Matthew Kramer, who is sceptical of the claim that law need ever be more than such imperatives: *In Defense of Legal Positivism: Law Without Trimmings* (Oxford University Press, 1999) 83–9.
[42] H. L. A. Hart, *Essays on Bentham: Jurisprudence and Political Theory* (Oxford University Press, 1982) 127, 157–60. Cf. Hart, *Essays in Jurisprudence and Philosophy*, 10.
[43] Hart, *Essays on Bentham*, 160: '[T]o say that an individual has a legal obligation to act in a certain way is to say that such action may be properly demanded or extracted from him according to legal rules or principles regulating such demands for action.'

demand reform. This applies as much to the substance of law as it does to its administration and procedures. Law is the kind of thing that is *apt for* inspection and appraisal in light of justice; we might say, then, that it is *justice-apt*. This does not mean that every individual *law* is justice-apt. Considerations of justice apply directly only to those laws that aim to secure or maintain a distribution of burdens and benefits among people. But even laws that have some other purpose can give rise to disputes, all of which the law claims authority to settle—in its courts by judges who must be attentive to the question of who deserves the benefit of winning and who the burden of losing.

The fact that there is this connection between law and a particular department of morality is significant. Not all human practices are justice-apt. Consider music. It makes no sense to ask whether a certain fugue is just, or to demand that it become so. The musical standards of fugal excellence are preeminently internal. An excellent fugue should be melodic, interesting, inventive—we do not expect a fugue to answer to justice. With law, things are different.

One of Fuller's great contributions to legal philosophy is to offer the first fairly comprehensive analysis of the internal excellences of law—the virtues that inhere in its law-like character, its 'inner' or 'internal' morality, a morality, he claimed, that makes law possible. There are indeed such excellences; the difficulty is in explaining their relationship to the existence conditions for legal systems and in keeping their value in proper perspective. Thesis (N_3) says they can never preclude or displace the assessment of law on independent criteria such as justice. A fugue may be at its best when it has all the virtues of fugacity; law is *not* at its best when it excels only in legality. To enhance legality may come at a cost to other values: general laws may do injustice in particular cases; precise laws may be useless as guides to action; prospective laws may leave past injuries without remedy. When a legal system maximally instantiates the inner morality of law, we have law at its *most legal*, but not necessarily law at its best.

While (N_2) and (N_3) are important, we must not overstate their implications. Tony Honoré overstates the case when he says that law, by making moral claims, is always vulnerable to having such claims legally contested in each case. He therefore thinks ideal morality is necessarily a *source* of law, albeit only a persuasive one.[44] Since law is justice-apt, principles of justice will always be among the persuasive sources, whether or not any source-based consideration directs judges to apply them.

---

[44] Tony Honoré, 'The Necessary Connection between Law and Morality' (2002) 22 *Oxford Journal of Legal Studies* 489, 491.

What is a persuasive source of law? Perhaps it is one that is relevant but not conclusive in its application. That is not so unusual, for statutes, decisions, and customs are not always conclusive either. But these have a further feature: the fact that their requirements would, on balance, be morally wrong does not absolve the courts of their legal duty to apply them. It is a feature of the moral considerations mentioned in (N_3), however, that they are to be followed only to the extent that they are sound. Justice does not require or permit a court to do injustice. This shows that it is mistaken to assimilate the operation of justice in law to a kind of 'source', persuasive or otherwise. Morality is neither source-based nor is it a source; and it is present of its own force in adjudication unless it is ousted by some source-based consideration.[45]

It is not law's moral *claims* that open the door to morality in adjudication. It is not the claim to justice that makes some legal norms (and all judicial decisions) answerable to justice—it is the fact that they are, by their nature, justice-apt. An allocative institution that makes no claims at all (such as a price system) is no less exposed to assessment on grounds of morality, including on grounds of justice. The reason that considerations of justice and injustice turn up, time and again, in court is that courts have an allocative task before them and, except where law limits their resources in approaching that task, justice will always bear on an allocative decision.

(N_4) *Necessarily, law is morally risky.*

It is a curious fact that almost all theories that insist on the essentially moral character of law take law's character to be essentially *good*. The gravamen of Fuller's philosophy is that law is essentially a moral enterprise, made possible only by a robust adherence to its own inner morality. The thought that the law might have an inner *immorality* never even occurred to him.[46] It has occurred to others, including Grant Gilmore, whose brilliant epigram is often cited: 'In Heaven there will be no law, and the lion will lie down with the lamb. . . . In Hell there will be nothing but law, and due process will be rigorously observed.'[47]

---

[45] This distinguishes what Honoré calls persuasive sources from the 'permissive sources' I examine in Chapter 4 of this volume. A permissive source is one a court is positively permitted to apply, in virtue of some source-based consideration, for instance a judicial custom. In contrast, it is not any directive or custom that makes judicial decisions answerable to justice.
[46] Füßer does note the possibility in 'Farewell to "Legal Positivism"', 22—though he associates it with anarchism.
[47] Grant Gilmore, *The Ages of American Law* (Yale University Press, 1977) 110–11.

Everyone knows that law can be hellish, but some believe that, in its essentials, legality shines with a heavenly light. E. P. Thompson shocked his fellow Marxists when he wrote, 'We ought to expose the shams and inequities which may be concealed beneath this law. But the rule of law itself—the imposing of effective inhibitions upon power and the defence of the citizen from power's all-intrusive claims—seems to me to be an unqualified human good.'[48] The rule of law is indeed a human good, and Thompson is right to oppose the crude reductivisms that suggest otherwise. But *unqualified*? Is the rule of law really all gain and no loss?

Hart is sometimes suspected of sharing that sort of enthusiasm. After all, he does say that as societies become larger, more mobile, and more diverse, life under a customary social order is liable to become uncertain, conservative, and inefficient.[49] We can therefore think of law as a *remedy* for those 'defects'.[50] Does that not show that Hart, too, supposes that law is all to the good? Stephen Guest thinks it does, by

> openly investing [Hart's] central set of elements constituting law in terms with characteristics showing the moral superiority of a society which has adopted a set of rules which allow for progress (rules conferring public and private powers), for efficient handling of disputes (rules conferring powers of adjudication), and rules that create the possibility of publicly ascertainable—certain—criteria of what is to count as law.[51]

There are two mistakes here, and they are sufficiently common to be worth correcting. First, the fact that law necessarily brings gains does not show the moral superiority of the society to which the law belongs. Such a society might be morally inferior to one that turns its back on law and instead opts for the social conditions that make possible governance by customary rules alone. Consider an analogy: one can hold that fuel-inefficient cars have a defect without thinking that a car-driving society is morally superior to a car-free society. All we are committed to is that *if* we are to drive cars, it is better that they be efficient. Likewise, *if* we are to have large, mobile, and anonymous societies, it is better that we have the forms of guidance that law

---

[48] E. P. Thompson, *Whigs and Hunters: The Origin of the Black Act* (Pantheon Books, 1975) 266.
[49] Hart, *The Concept of Law*, 91–7.
[50] Ibid., 94.
[51] Stephen Guest, 'Two Strands in Hart's Concept of Law', in S. Guest ed., *Positivism Today* (Dartmouth, Aldershot, 1996) 30.

makes available. Whether those are morally superior societies is another question entirely.

The second error is the reverse of one we encountered in exploring the derivative connections between law and morality. There we were interested in the gains that are necessary results of effective law. When we enter the world of legality, however, it is not without cost: 'The gains are those of adaptability to change, certainty, and efficiency; the cost is the risk that the centrally organized power may well be used for the oppression of numbers with whose support it can dispense, in a way that the simpler regime of primary rules could not.'[52] Importantly, this risk is one that cannot exist without law, and one that exists whenever and wherever there is law. And it is not only that there are new possibilities for oppression, there is also the risk that ordinary subjects will be alienated from the rules that govern their conduct:

> In the simpler structure [of a customary regime], since there are no officials, the rules must be widely accepted as setting critical standards for the behaviour of the group. If, there, the internal point of view is not widely disseminated there could not logically be any rules. But where there is a union of primary and secondary rules, which is, as we have argued, the most fruitful way of regarding a legal system, the acceptance of rules as common standards for the group may be split off from the relatively passive matter of the ordinary individual acquiescing in the rules by obeying them for his part alone.[53]

How far the acceptance of common standards gets split off varies; only in really pathological cases is it confined to the official class alone. But where there is 'a union of primary and secondary rules'—that is to say, *wherever there is law*—new moral risks are unavoidable. There are not only more efficient forms of oppression, there are also new vices: the alienation of community and value, the loss of transparency, the rise of a new hierarchy, and the possibility that some may be bought off by the goods that legal order (in some cases, necessarily) brings. Although law has necessary virtues, it also has necessary vices, and this marks a connection between law and morality of

---

[52] Hart, *The Concept of Law*, 202.
[53] Ibid., 117. For an important discussion of this passage, from which we draw somewhat different lessons, see Jeremy Waldron, 'All We Like Sheep' (1999) 12 *Canadian Journal of Law and Jurisprudence* 169, 186.

a reverse kind. There are moral risks that law's subjects are bound to run, and they are risks against which law itself provides no prophylactic.

5. Fallible by Nature

So the separability thesis is false, as shown by (possibly) trivial theses like (N_a) to (N_y) and by nontrivial theses like (N_1) to (N_4). But now we have a puzzle. How could one endorse both (N_4) and the separability thesis with which (N_4) is inconsistent? As we have seen, when Hart must choose between the separability thesis and (N_2), he sticks by his thesis, even at cost to his earlier theory of obligations. With respect to (N_4), on the other hand, he feels no need to choose; it is not even clear that he notices a tension. Why should that be?

Perhaps Hart does not, after all, mean what he says about the absence of any necessary connections between law and morals. Maybe his only commitment is to the sources thesis. That thesis is compatible with every one of the necessary connections between law and morality that I have identified. Do we not hear echoes of the sources thesis when he is adumbrating Bentham's brand of positivism?

> The most fundamental of these ideas is that law, good or bad, is a manmade artefact which men create and add to the world by the exercise of their will; not something they discover through the exercise of their reason to be already in the world. There are indeed good reasons for having laws, but a reason for a law, even a good reason, is not a law, any more . . . than 'hunger is bread'.[54]

Were Hart speaking in his own voice here, there would be less talk of 'will' and more talk of the varied ways by which the artefact of law is made. With that amendment, this passage comes as close to the sources thesis as Hart gets. The fact remains, however, that when he expressly considers the sources thesis, he rejects it in favour of what he calls 'soft' positivism, which allows for laws that are not made by anyone, provided only that they are entailed or presupposed by laws that are.[55] Hart's reason for rejecting the sources thesis is that some constitutions contain moral provisions that guarantee things like 'equality before and under the law' and 'human dignity'. On that basis, he

[54] H. L. A. Hart, '1776-1976: Law in the Perspective of Philosophy', Hart, *Essays in Jurisprudence and Philosophy*, 145, 146-7.
[55] Hart, *The Concept of Law*, 250-4. For discussion of this issue, see Chapter 1, this volume.

holds that the existence of law can depend on its merits, provided that the fact that it depends on its merits depends only on social facts.

That is a poor argument. First, what Hart takes as evidence for the merit-dependence of law is universal amongst legal systems: even where there is no express constitutional reference to moral principles, notions of fairness and reasonableness pervade ordinary adjudication. The jurisprudential dispute is not about these facts, but about their explanation. Second, because of his willingness to allow contextual necessities, Hart is open to the charge that the social facts that allegedly make morality a test for law obtain as a matter of natural necessity—if not in constitutions, then in the ordinary moral considerations present in adjudication. By his own lights, he must show not merely that it is conceivable that there could be a legal system in which morality is not a test for law; he must show that this is humanly possible in view of the necessary structure and content of law. Hart never attempts this.

Perhaps Hart should not have rejected the sources thesis. But the fact remains that he did, and we are thus stuck with the problem of (N_4). I think there is a simpler explanation. Hart is not worried that law should turn out to have necessary moral *defects*; he is worried about a misunderstanding and overvaluation of law's moral merits. Hart does not see much risk of his interlocutors undervaluing law and the virtues of legality. He thinks instead that the standard defences of a necessary connection between law and morality systemically *overvalue* them. We see this time and again, not only among judges and their academic apologists, but also among jurisprudents.

Hart's briefest definition of positivism is this: '[I]t is in no sense a necessary truth that laws reproduce or satisfy certain demands of morality, though in fact they have often done so.'[56] This definition is narrower than the separability thesis; it is narrower even than the social thesis (which says nothing about 'reproducing' moral demands). All of (N_1) through (N_4) are compatible with it. Even if law must try to achieve moral ends, or must achieve them minimally, or must contain the germ of justice, or must be apt for justice— each of these is 'compatible with very great iniquity.'[57] What this definition wants us to grasp is not some ambitious thesis about the connections between law and morality, and not even a narrower thesis about the nature of legal validity. Its point is that there is no guarantee that law will satisfy those moral standards by which law should be judged. Law, the definition minds us, is morally fallible.[58]

---

[56] Hart, *The Concept of Law*, 185–6.
[57] Ibid., 207.
[58] See ibid., 185; David Lyons, *Ethics and the Rule of Law* (Cambridge University Press, 1984) 63. Note that this is not Füßer's weaker 'fallibility thesis', according to which 'under certain

The fallibility thesis is correct and important. Positivism has no patent on it, however. Moral fallibility is a feature of law for which any plausible theory must account.[59] Still, it would be a mistake to suppose that whenever two theories both assert a proposition P, it follows that there is no difference between them. That depends on their grounds for asserting P and on the place of P in the web of explanatory propositions within the theories. For Fuller, law's fallibility is, to adapt one of his favourite metaphors, the result of something *external* to law, a result of someone's failure to apply the good means proper to law or to pursue the good ends with which those means reliably cohere—or maybe just a run of brute bad luck.

Hart goes further. The perversion of law to seriously wrong ends is, he says, compatible with the *full* realization of the inner morality of law; legality is compatible with 'very great iniquity'.[60] Fuller will not buy this, though he is well aware that he has no argument against it: 'I shall have to rest on the assertion of a belief that may seem naïve, namely, that coherence and goodness have more affinity than coherence and evil.'[61] There is also a further difference between the two with respect to the basis of law's fallibility. While Fuller thinks law's vices typically result from *too little* legality, Hart maintains they can also result from *too much* of it, for instance, when defective rules are constantly applied with all the 'pedantic impartiality' of the rule of law.[62] Owing to law's nature as an institutionalized system that does not require anything like public acceptance of its rules, law is endemically liable to become alienated from its subjects: that is the lesson of (N_4). For Hart, the fallibility of law is *internally* connected to law's nature and is not merely a result of some kind of pollution or accident.

This recalls a theme in Aristotle's constitutional theory as presented in Book 3 of the *Politics*. He identifies modes of degeneration native to specific forms of governance. The virtuous form of government known as kingship has a shadow version in tyranny; when kingships degenerate, they turn into tyrannies, which are kingships gone wrong.[63] Aristotle was not so pessimistic

---

counterfactual circumstances the law would not be morally valuable': Füßer, 'Farewell to "Legal Positivism"', 128. It is instead the claim that under actual conditions, there is no guarantee that law satisfies the moral standards by which it is properly appraised.

[59] Lyons calls it a 'regulating principle', by which he means that it imposes a presumptive justificatory burden on those who deny it. (See Lyons, *Ethics and the Rule of Law*.) My claim is stronger: No acceptable legal theory may deny it; explaining the moral fallibility of law is an adequacy condition of a successful theory of law.
[60] Hart, *The Concept of Law*, 207.
[61] Fuller, 'Positivism and Fidelity to Law', 636.
[62] Hart, *The Concept of Law*, 81. This is difficult to square with Hart's views about the relations between law and 'formal' justice: See Chapter 6, this volume.
[63] Aristotle, *Politics* (E. Barker trs, Oxford University Press, 1962) 1279a–80a; 113–16.

as to think that degeneration is necessary. That depends on the character of the king, his subjects, the political and economic context, and so forth. But when kingship goes wrong it does so in ways shaped by its specific nature. A bit like unstable isotopes, political institutions have distinctive patterns of decay that are explained by the nature of the thing that is decaying. That is why the degenerate form of kingship is tyranny, rather than oligarchy or democracy.

How does the analogy go here? *Kingship* is to *tyranny* as *legality* is to— what? We have already encountered the vice in our discussion of (N_4); we now need only name it. The vice internal to law is, unsurprisingly, *legalism*.[64] It has two main dimensions: the over-valuation of legality at the expense of other virtues a political system should have (including other virtues law should have), and the alienation of law from social life. Of course, this is not news. That legality has a way of becoming legalistic is something we could have learned from Marx or Weber, Tocqueville, or Dickens. What is original, perhaps, is Hart's identification of the specific contribution that law's institutional character makes to this. Without law, social order requires considerable buy-in from the general population: they are regulated by norms that are more or less accepted. It would be going too far to suggest that widely accepted norms are always morally acceptable, but some kinds of injustice are less stable in those circumstances. With the emergence of law, however, people are also regulated by norms that meet official criteria of validity and that are enforced by specialized agencies. This division of labour can alienate people from the most important rules that govern their lives—rules that threaten to become remote, technical, and arcane. That is one more reason why the rule of law is not an unqualified human good: it is in the nature of law to pose such risks, and more fealty to rule of law cannot eliminate them. The rule of law subjects law-making and law-application to more *law*.

Underlying Hart's mistaken separability thesis lies the correct fallibility thesis. Perhaps this is not surprising, as it is common ground amongst legal philosophers. But his distinctive spin on that thesis is that some of law's failures are necessarily connected to law's nature. Fuller is interested in the morality that makes law possible; Hart is also interested in the *immorality* that *law* makes possible. When the rule of law is under threat from official

---

[64] Cf Judith N. Shklar, *Legalism* (Harvard University Press, 1964).

illegality and popular indifference, it is natural to be receptive to Fuller's concerns. We are wise to remain vigilant; lawless power is a terrible thing. At the same time, however, this fear makes some wish for a more perfect and complete penetration of legality into political life. Hart reminds us to be careful what we wish for.[65]

---

[65] For instructive comments on earlier drafts of this paper, I thank John Gardner, Chris Morris, Denise Réaume, Jeremy Waldron, and Wil Waluchow.

8
The Morality in Law

1. Drawing Lines

The single most important thing to know about the relationship between law and morality is that there is no single thing to know. 'There are many different types of relation between law and morals and there is nothing which can be profitably singled out for student as *the* relation between them', H. L. A. Hart reminds us.[1] There are, for instance, questions about how law is and should be created, and about how law is and should be regarded:

(A) How far is law influenced by a society's moral beliefs and attitudes?
(B) How harmful does an activity have to be, and to whom, before we have a moral justification for regulating or prohibiting it by law?
(C) Do most people believe the law is morally binding?
(D) How far do we owe the law a moral duty of respect or obedience?

There are also questions about the nature of law, including the demarcation between laws and other kinds of standards, and between legal systems and other kinds of institutions, for example:

(E) Where does ethics or decency end and legal duty begin?
(F) What are the differences between legal systems on the one hand, and markets, or systems of arbitration, or sets of social customs on the other?

These six questions are different, but they are inter-related. For one thing, until we know what law is, and have at least working answers to (E) and (F), we aren't likely to make headway with (A) through (D). If you didn't know, at least roughly, what law is how could you know what sort of things shaped it historically, or how could you decide what policy would be the right one

---

[1] H. L. A. Hart, *The Concept of Law* (3rd edn, Penelope. A. Bulloch and Joseph Raz, eds; Leslie Green, intro, Oxford University Press, 2012) 185.

to take towards its demands? Of course, you don't need an explicit *theory* of (E) and (F): making things explicit and revealing the connections among them is a job for philosophers, and with respect to these questions, for philosophers who work in general jurisprudence.

My interests here are mainly in (E) and (F).[2] I will try to answer a question posed by Hart: 'Must some reference to morality enter into an adequate definition of law or legal system? Or is it just a contingent fact that law and morals often overlap ... and that they share a common vocabulary of rights, obligations, and duties?'[3] Hart's own answer is that there is a third option. There are things that are not quite definitional elements of law but aren't contingent overlaps either. I think there is truth in that conclusion, but that Hart's arguments for it need repair. After attending to that, I examine some general worries about the project of distinguishing law and morality, whether in Hart's way or in any other. But first, a comment on exercises in jurisprudential line-drawing, including this one.

Like all interesting social demarcations—the line between religion and conviction, or between pressure groups and political parties, or between rebellions and revolutions—jurisprudential distinctions are somewhat indeterminate. There are clear cases of legal systems, things that are clearly not legal systems, and things that are arguably legal systems.[4] The indeterminacy has two related sources. First, many social kinds are multi-criterial clusters of properties; they are made up of various features and properties. For example, political parties are social organizations; they recruit and socialize members; they shape and articulate interests; they compete for power. But there are no precise rules that combine these criteria, and there can be disagreement about whether each is necessary or about the weight it has in determining whether something does amount to a political party. Second, none of the criteria is itself very precise. (How organized do people need to be before they are an organization? What do they need to do to be actually competing for power?) Laws and legal systems are no different, and the definitions legal theorists offer are no sharper.

So we should not understand jurisprudential questions of the form 'Where does ... ?' as asking '*Exactly* where does ... (a set of customs end and a legal

---

[2] I assume with Kelsen that all laws are members of legal systems, and that 'legal system' has explanatory priority over 'law' and 'a law'. The question whether law must have a certain content is thus the question whether legal systems must, so (F) takes some priority over (E).

[3] H. L. A. Hart, *Law, Liberty, and Morality* (Oxford University Press, 1963) 2.

[4] There are no borderlines between the clear and the arguable cases, for some cases are arguably arguable. And so on.

system begin, a matter of moral obligation become a legal obligation, and so on)?' The correct answers will be inexact answers to the extent that the phenomena we are trying to understand are unclear.[5] But clear cases do not need to be bounded by clear lines, so such questions should be taken as invitations to specify as best we can the necessary features of the clearer, standard cases of law. I think that if one reads most legal theorists, if not charitably then at least without malicious intent, one will find their views consistent with this way of proceeding.[6] At any rate, that is how I try to proceed here.

2. Content and Structure

Our question is whether law has a necessary content as well as a necessary structure. The terms 'content' and 'structure' are not perspicuous and legal theorists use them in various ways. I use them in the following way. Laws that require, permit, or empower us to do things are norms. The content of a legal norm is the action that, according to it, must or must not, may or may not, can or cannot, be done. I will focus mostly on laws that require things of us—mandatory norms—but much of what I say can be extended to the other types as well. The content of a legal system at any given time is the sum total of the content of all the norms of that system at that time.[7] Every legal system contains norms that empower people to create and vary legal norms, for instance, by legislative enactment or by judicial decision. As these powers get used, the law is set in motion. Hovering between modesty and pretension, old textbooks used to say things like 'the law is stated as at 27 November 1956'. A perfect snapshot, taken on a still and sunny day? But every day a legal breeze is blowing and clouds are gathering, for even without statutory changes material is constantly being added to and subtracted from the law as judges make rulings, distinguish cases, reverse decisions, and so on. So 'the English legal system' is a dynamic entity that stays the same while changing. Explaining how that is so is as difficult as explaining how, or in what sense, an adult is the same person as the teenager they used to be. Luckily, we can

---

[5] This remark disavows 'epistemicism' about vagueness. For an accessible treatment, see Timothy Endicott, *Vagueness in Law* (Oxford University Press, 2000) chap. 6.
[6] Bentham, Austin, and Kelsen are often read as if they were utterly ignorant of this. A fair reading of their works will not bear this out.
[7] 'Sum total' is meant to take account of the fact that some norms derogate from other norms, and that some conflict with other norms.

bypass this problem, for if law does have a necessary content, it will appear in every snapshot.

In addition to whatever content they have, legal systems also have structural features, that is, ways their norms relate to each other and to other norms in society. For example, it would be a structural feature of a legal system if all of its norms were created by the same people, or by using the same powers, or were mutually consistent. Many legal theorists think certain structural features are necessary if a collection of social norms is to constitute a legal system. Hart, for example, says that nothing is a legal system that does not have both norms regulating people's conduct ('primary rules') as well as other norms determining how the conduct-regulating norms are to be identified, changed, and applied ('secondary rules'). With reservations, I think that is correct. At any rate, I shall assume that an adequate structural account of legal systems can be developed along such lines.

But that is not enough to constitute a legal system. The Marylebone Cricket Club (MCC) has a collection of rules to guide the conduct of players and others. The rules are promulgated in a code called *The Laws of Cricket*.[8] Being in that code is one test for ascertaining whether a rule is in fact a rule of cricket. The rules are changed from time to time, using rules of the MCC Laws Sub-Committee. There are also rules establishing officials—umpires— and empowering them to render binding applications of the rules. Does this show that the cricket rules are laws or, to be clear, *legal* laws? It does not. Things are missing: everyone knows that the MCC norms are just rules of a game. This does not mean there is anything amiss in calling them 'the laws of cricket'. The Oxford English Dictionary reports that 'laws' are something cricket can grammatically have; also that there is a 'law of the jungle' and a 'law of honour'. The issue is one of theory, not vocabulary. Moreover, when I deny that cricket rules are laws or are parts of a legal system, I do not mean they have nothing in common with laws, or that there is nothing to be learned about legal systems by studying the rules of games, or even that lawyers should not study them while on duty. All kinds of things, including games, folk 'law', soft 'law', transnational 'law', etc., can cast light on law even though they are not law.[9] Karl Llewellyn says that 'the social sciences are not

---

[8] Somewhat missing the point, the MCC has also begun to encode the 'spirit of cricket': <http://www.lords.org/laws-and-spirit/laws-of-cricket/>. It can only be a matter of time before they find a need to encode the *spirit* of the spirit of cricket.

[9] For reasons that are obscure to me, scholars in some areas of legal studies seem to grasp the functions '*counts as*' and '*is a kind of*' yet cannot master, '*is quite a bit like*', or '*can fruitfully be compared to*'. This produces a lot of bad jurisprudence.

staked out like real estate',[10] and that is correct if taken as a disciplinary comment. As far as legal studies go, we should let a thousand flowers—and even a hundred weeds—bloom, intermingled. Nonetheless, the question remains, *what is law*, if not just any sufficiently complex system of social rules?

Intuitively, the difference is this: cricket rules, even when highly systematized and institutionalized, are special-purpose norms that regulate a restricted aspect of social life. Legal systems are not special-purpose institutions in that way; they contain norms that regulate all kinds of things. Moreover, the law claims authority to regulate, and actually does regulate, the MCC, whereas the MCC does not even claim authority to regulate the English legal system. John Rawls elaborates such differences thus:

> What distinguishes a legal system is its comprehensive scope and its regulative powers with respect to other associations. . . . the legal order exercises a final authority over a certain well-defined territory. It is also marked by the wide range of the interests it is designed to secure.[11]

Joseph Raz refines Rawls' idea. It is not so much the regulative powers that law actually *has*, but the regulative authority it *claims* that sets it apart from limited-purpose normative systems. A legal system can limit its own regulative powers, and limited governments do, by constitutions, bills of rights, interpretive presumptions, and so forth. But, as Raz says, they still claim comprehensive authority, that is the 'the *authority* to regulate all forms of behaviour, . . . they either contain norms which regulate it or norms conferring powers to enact norms which if enacted would regulate it'.[12] It follows that legal systems claim a kind of supremacy, that is, the 'authority to prohibit, permit, or impose conditions on the institution and operation of all the normative organizations to which members of its subject-community belong'.[13] Raz further argues that legal systems are to some degree 'open': they contain norms whose purpose is to give effect *within* that legal system to norms that are not norms *of* that system.[14] Conflicts-of-laws rules do this by giving

---

[10] Karl Llewellyn, 'A Realistic Jurisprudence—the Next Step' (1930) 30 *Columbia Law Review* 431.
[11] John Rawls, *A Theory of Justice* (Harvard University Press, 1971) 236 (§ 38). I have suppressed Rawls' remarks about law monopolizing coercion, because I think there can be law without any coercion. Some think that monopoly of coercive force is a necessary feature of *state* law.
[12] Joseph Raz *Practical Reason and Norms* (2nd edn, Oxford University Press, 1999) 151.
[13] Ibid., 152–4.
[14] Ibid.

effect to the laws of foreign countries; contract law does this by giving effect to norms created by private parties, and so forth.

Notice that with one exception, the Rawls–Raz conditions are structural. The exception is Rawls' claim that legal systems are designed to protect a wide range of interests. That is not a matter of how legal norms relate to each other; it is a matter of what they require, permit, or authorize. Law is designed to secure, or at any rate comes to have the function of securing, many important human interests. The view I defend here is a version of that claim.

3. May Law Not Have 'Any Kind of Content'?

The claim that law has a necessary content is not novel. Aristotle and Aquinas advance it, so do Locke and Hume. We have just seen that Rawls holds it as does Hart. One legal theorist who appears to deny it is Hans Kelsen: 'Legal norms may have any kind of content', he says.[15] What does he mean? One thing he does *not* mean is that any possible normative set-up could be a law. Quite the contrary. Kelsen thinks a norm could be a law only if it authorizes someone or other to deploy coercive force—a 'sanction'—on the condition that a certain act (the 'delict') is performed or omitted. Every law therefore needs a coercive sanction for its breach, a power on someone's part to authoritatively determine whether there was a breach, and a power (and also generally a duty) to order that a sanction be applied. Hence, 'Love thy neighbour as thyself' which, in England, is not an actual law, taken by itself is not even a possible law. On the other hand, 'Honour thy father and thy mother: that thy days may be long upon the land which the LORD thy God giveth thee . . .' is a possible law and, on some metaphysical and jurisprudential views, is an actual law.[16]

Is the need for coercive norms in law a matter of structure or content? In favour of viewing it as content is the fact that Kelsen cannot define 'sanction' save by reference to matters that are substantive, and not only by relations among norms. Sanctions have to be coercive acts, whether punishments or

---

[15] Hans Kelsen, *General Theory of Law and State* (A. Wedberg trs, Harvard University Press, 1949) 113.
[16] Interpreting the second clause as an implied threat, rather than an offer or prediction, and taking the reference to God as presupposing the existence of an adjudicative and punitive authority. If the love-directive were indirectly backed by force—eternal hellfire, say—we could reconstruct it as part of the delict of a law, and that is basically Kelsen's strategy for dealing with legal material that has the form of a legal directive but lacks a sanction. (Whether that would be a sane way to think of the love-directive is another matter.)

civil remedies, and must 'consist in the forcible infliction of an evil or, expressed negatively, in the forcible deprivation of a value'.[17] With Foucauldian relish, Kelsen lists as paradigms: killing, blinding, amputation, imprisonment, deprivation of property or loss of an office or of political rights.[18] Since something of this sort is always present, the assertion 'law may have any content' must be 'read down' to mean something like 'any sort of *coercive* content'. On the other hand, law *may* have 'any content' in the sense that the coercion *triggers* (the 'delicts') can be any conduct whatever. A sanction could be triggered by homosexual conduct, or by discriminating against those who engage in homosexual conduct. Neither trigger involves a clearer example, or a more central case, of law than the other. The second law is morally better than the first, but it is not a better specimen of law. And as the law sees things either would be equally entitled to obedience. The law presents its directives to its subjects, not as things they should do only on the merits, for example, because that would be just, efficient, or noble, but as things they are *to do*. The reasons that legal norms provide are in this way 'content-independent', and this is one of their more interesting features.[19] Law holds itself out as, and is often used as, a standard for guidance and evaluation of conduct without regard to the merits of the acts it requires, permits, or prohibits.

Kelsen therefore thinks it is not to any particular ends we should look to understand the nature of law, but instead to its means:

> [W]e can contrast it sharply with other social orders which pursue in part the same purposes as law, but by quite different means.... Law, morality, and religion, all three forbid murder. But law does this by providing: if a man commits murder, then another man, designated by the legal order,

---

[17] Hans Kelsen, *Pure Theory of Law* (Max Knight trs, University of California Press, 1967) 108. In contrast, the Kelsenian delict *is* a structural feature of law, for it is defined, *not* as conduct that the officials disapprove or want to repress, but simply as whatever stands in the logical position of coercion-trigger: 'The behavior which is "commanded" is not the behavior which "ought" to be executed.' Ibid., 25.

[18] Ibid., 109.

[19] The idea of 'independence of content' was introduced in H. L. A. Hart, 'Legal and Moral Obligation', in A. I. Melden ed., *Essays in Moral Philosophy* (University of Washington Press, 1958) 82–107. It is developed and supported in Joseph Raz, *The Morality of Freedom* (Oxford University Press, 1986) and in Leslie Green, *The Authority of the State* (Oxford University Press, 1990) 36–42. For criticism and further discussion, see P. Markwick, 'Law and Content-Independent Reasons' (2000) 20 *Oxford Journal of Legal Studies* 579 and N. P. Adams, 'In Defense of Content-Independence' (2017) 23 *Legal Theory* 143.

shall apply against the murderer a certain measure of coercion, prescribed by the legal order.[20]

One striking feature of this passage is the fact it mentions only to pass over in silence: 'Law, morality, and religion, all three forbid murder.' Why? Is that some kind of coincidence? If it is, there are many others. Law, morality, and religion, all three enjoin the keeping of promises. Law, morality, and religion, all three require that children be cared for. Law, morality, and religion, all three command respect for the authorities. And on it goes. Kelsen seems to feel no need to explain this.

One might reply that, on Kelsen's account, law does have a necessary purpose and, in that sense, a necessary content: it aims at social peace and must therefore contain norms suitable for that. By its features of supremacy and efficacy law is the ultimate coercive regulator of coercion. Hence, law of its nature limits the use of force in every society and brings a minimum of peace. Kelsen will not go even that far: 'the peace of law is only a relative peace.'[21] In principle, law could authorize only self-help as a coercive sanction, and it could authorize it very broadly. That might be no better than the war of all against all—it could be worse, given that vendetta and revenge would then be sanctified with a halo of authorization. Whatever the empirical tendency of societies under law, 'the securing of peace, the pacification of the legal community, cannot be considered as an essential moral value common to all legal orders: it is not the "moral minimum" common to all law'.[22] Indeed, there *is* no 'moral minimum', no 'essential moral value' that law, as law, must embrace—thinks Kelsen.

4. The Moral Minimum

Hart dissents. There *is* a 'moral minimum' essential to law, in one sense of moral and one sense of essential. The pertinent sense of moral is that there are essential moral *obligations* that every legal system must impose. The pertinent sense of essential is that these norms must be part of any *humanly possible* legal system—not just every actual one. So here is a further reason

---

[20] Kelsen, *General Theory of Law and State*, 20. We should read 'sharply' in light of my remarks in Section 1, above.
[21] Kelsen, *Pure Theory of Law*, 38.
[22] Ibid.

why the rules of cricket are not legal laws. Not only do they lack some of law's structural features, they also do not impose the range of obligations that law imposes. None of them individually nor all of them collectively regulate the range of human interests that law does. In short, the cricket rules are not *about* or *for* enough of the right things.

Now, Hart is well known as one who takes a social view of law; he thinks law is wholly a social construction.[23] There is no law or legal institution that was not made, whether deliberately or accidentally, as aim or as by-product, by actual human beings living and acting in groups. It is not so well known that he also takes a social view of morality, or at least the part of morality that has to do with obligations or duties. And this is quite a lot of morality, since we cannot explain moral powers without reference to their capacity to create or vary duties, and we cannot explain moral rights without reference to their capacity to justify the imposition of duties.[24] According to Hart, to have a moral obligation is to be subject to a social rule requiring one to V, where: (a) V-ing is generally believed to be important to human life, or to some valued aspect of it; (b) breach of the V-ing norm is met with serious, if diffuse, pressure to conform; and (c) there is a standing possibility that being required to V may conflict with one's own interests, at least as one sees them.[25] This is a social theory of obligation because of the nature of the factual conditions: obligations are marked by a group's beliefs about the importance of certain norms, by its response to breach of those norms, and by the relation between what individuals value and what the group norm requires of them. So the morality of obligation is always a social morality, or a 'positive morality' to use John Austin's term. What then is correct, ideal, or valid morality? *That* can't be purely positive, can it? Hart's reply is essentially Bentham's. Ideal morality is the social morality that we *ought* to practice. But this second 'ought' is not an 'ought' of obligation, for obligation is the output of the preceding analysis. How should we understand it? We never get from Hart an explicit account of what sort of reasons could make a social morality an ideal morality, but we do get some examples and those, together with the Humean tenor of Hart's argument, suggests that the relevant considerations are eudemonistic: ideal morality is the social morality which, were we to practice it, would best promote human flourishing.[26]

---

[23] See Chapter 1, this volume.
[24] But it does not cover individual ideals, the virtues, or the sources of moral value.
[25] Hart, *The Concept of Law*, 85–91.
[26] Hart sometimes uses the term 'utilitarian' when writing of the possible justifications for social morality, especially in his early work. This will not mesh with his explicit value-pluralism. The term should probably be understood broadly, without any commitment to commensurability or

With all this emphasis on groups and rules, the morality of obligation is starting to sound uncomfortably like law. There are similarities. But there is also a distinction between them that turns on four features:

(1) Morality involves only matters that are thought to be of great importance to human life; legal obligations can involve trivia. The test is not whether moral obligations *actually are* important for human flourishing. Parts of social morality amount to little more than socially organized fears, hatreds, and superstitions. Many common sexual prohibitions, for example, have no sound rationale: they make human life go worse, not better. 'Yet it would be absurd to deny the title of morality to emphatic social vetoes of this sort; indeed sexual morality is perhaps the most prominent aspect of what plain men think morality to be.'[27] It is a measure of how important a social view of morality is to Hart's theory that he insists on it notwithstanding the fact that it puts him at a polemical disadvantage in his argument with Patrick Devlin over whether it is permissible to criminalize sexual immorality 'as such'.[28] Having adopted such a broad view of morality, Hart cannot then help himself to the Dworkinian short-cut against meddlesome moralists. He cannot say, 'Never mind whether it is permissible to criminalize morality "as such"; hatreds and phobias simply don't amount to *morality*.'[29]

(2) Unlike law, morality is immune to deliberate change. We can repeal a legal prohibition on homosexual conduct or a legal permission to force sex on one's wife, but once supporting social attitudes have solidified around those norms, and especially once they become entrenched by religion and ideology, we cannot somehow 'repeal' the gut feeling that gay sex is wrong, or that a wife has a duty to submit to her husband's sexual advances. Conventional moral attitudes like these can change, sometimes quickly; but not as a result of any act authorized and intended to bring about that change. This is a point of

---

aggregation, much as Hume flexibly uses the 'public utility' to cover any human interests the security or promotion of which justifies institutions, practices, etc.

[27] Hart, *The Concept of Law*, 175.
[28] See Hart, *Law, Liberty, and Morality* and Patrick Devlin, *The Enforcement of Morals* (Oxford University Press, 1968).
[29] 'What is shocking and wrong is not [Devlin's] idea that the community's morality counts, but his idea of what counts as the community's morality.' Ronald Dworkin, *Taking Rights Seriously* (Harvard University Press, 1979) 113.

immense frustration for legal reformers, since much reform cannot succeed without a tandem change in social conviction, or at least social convention.[30]

(3) Offences against moral standards must be voluntary. The plea, 'But I couldn't help it' is, when true, always morally relevant and often excusatory—but not necessarily in law. Some who truly could not have done otherwise are nonetheless called to legal account and required to pay damages or even punished. Many consider strict liability, certainly in criminal law, to be a bad idea or at least something that calls for a very special justification. In morality, Hart thinks strict liability would not just be a bad policy, it would be a conceptual absurdity.

(4) Finally, when moral norms fail to motivate, Plan B is resort to a diffuse, decentralized, social pressure that appeals to the intrinsic rightness of conformity and tries to trigger self-criticism via the shame and guilt that often adheres to breach. Law can sometimes help itself to analogues of these, but usually only among habitual law-abiders. For the rest, law has other plans, involving police, courts, prisons, and so on. A judge might not even think it pertinent to tell an offender that their action was, in the eyes of the law, morally wrong—they are as likely to say that, 'rightly or wrongly' the law requires abstention from the prohibited action and punishment will now be meted out for the reason that the law was violated.

Insofar as these four features demarcate legal and moral obligations there are limits to the candidate explanations for the fact that certain obligations turn up in both law and morality, in society after society. That is unlikely to be explained by the nature of morality, for the features do not fix a determinate content for morality.[31] The consequences of this are far-reaching. Suppose law mirrors morality. In every society, then, law would contain what its morality contains. But this will not explain the common content *across* all legal systems, until we have an argument to show that all *moralities* have a common content. The four features do not do that. Yet Hart thinks it is true. He says, 'there are certain rules of conduct which any social organization must contain if it is to be viable': rules that promote people's 'vital interests', including

---

[30] Sometimes law can encourage beneficial changes in morality: Chapter 10, this volume.
[31] Hart says the four marks of morality are 'in a sense *formal* criteria' (*The Concept of Law*, 180–1). This contrasts with the view of someone like Warnock, who holds that morality must contain ameliorative norms that improve the human condition by limiting the general tendency of things to go wrong: Geoffrey Warnock, *The Object of Morality* (Methuen, 1971).

rules about 'persons, property, and promises'.[32] Hart never gives us a crisp list of these rules, but his comments suggest that they include at least these:[33]

(N1) Do not murder anyone.
(N2) Do not lie.
(N3) Keep promises.
(N4) Establish a system of mutual forbearances and comply with it.
(N5) Establish a system of property and respect it.
(N6) Establish a system of for enforcing (N1) to (N5) and use it.

Taking my cue from Hart's suggestion that these might be understood as a sort of 'minimum content of natural law'—natural law 'lite', purged of wishful thinking and dubious metaphysics—I am going to label this set of norms N. The following should be noted:

First, N is not a set of positive norms. These are abstract norm-types, identified by their content, tokens of which can turn up in various places: in social morality, in law, in a story, in religion, or elsewhere. Put another way, N is an *ideal* (for) morality, a set of norms that *ought* to be practised and, perhaps less directly, an ideal for law. (Less directly because law must also answer to law-specific ideals including administrability and the rule of law, and these requirements affect the way, and perhaps the extent to which, N can be realized in law.) But Hart thinks it is an ideal that must be realized in all 'viable' social organizations.

Second, the norms of N fall into two groups.[34] (N1) to (N3) are mandatory norms directed at individuals (or groups acting as individuals) and are satisfied when individuals do as they require. (N4) to (N6) are different. They call for setting up systems of social cooperation that define, require, and support the relevant norm-acts. Thus (N5) directs people to make arrangements to regulate the use and control of external resources, and then to conform to those arrangements. Individuals acting independently cannot set up such norms.

---

[32] Hart, *The Concept of Law*, 193.
[33] Ibid., 181, 195–7.
[34] The groupings are untidy because each of (N1) to (N3) has to be realized somehow or other, and that may involve some of the cooperative norms (N4) to (N6). Also, the classification is open to debate. Some philosophers, notably Hume, think that the promising norm belongs in the second group. Maybe there are even contractarians who think that the murder norm is agreement dependent.

Third, N is incomplete. Some important norms have been missed. Following David Hume,[35] Neil MacCormick plausibly suggests we need to add child-rearing norms (e.g. parents have a duty see to it that their infant children are fed).[36] Then there are norms not included but which are derivable from N.[37] Some can be obtained by what Kelsen would call 'static' derivation: roughly, they are norms entailed or justified by norms on the list.[38] 'Do not murder anyone' entails 'Do not murder (even) terrorists'. Whether a society needs a separate norm of that sort depends, inter alia, on how it tends to regard terrorists. (Are terrorists seen as human? Does that society conceive that some terrorists could be morally innocent?) Further norms can be 'dynamically' derived, via the powers provided or presupposed by N: (N4) is a whirring engine of dynamic derivation. It can generate all sorts of obligations, depending on what schemes of cooperation and forbearances we set up. Some of these will not form part of the minimum content since they are historically and socially variable. Our own legal system needs mechanisms to regulate access to and use of fossil fuels and radio frequencies; but it was not always so. Other forbearances need to be organized universally. Every society needs rules for war that extend beyond the prohibition on murder but which are binding only on condition that they are defined and supported by an effective cooperative system (e.g., prohibitions on the sort of weapons that can be used in conducting wars).

5. The Viability Thesis

The moral minimum, then, is a set of rules it would be good for anyone to have and practise. Why are they rules that must always be found *in the law*? Hart offers two answers, neither of which is compelling.

The first I will call the 'viability thesis'. We have already met it: 'there are certain rules of conduct which any social organization must contain if it is to be viable.'[39] Now viability, as Hart intends it, means providing for individual

---

[35] '[S]uppose the conjunction of the sexes to be established in nature, a family immediately arises; and particular rules being found requisite for its subsistence, these are immediately embraced...' David Hume, *An Enquiry Concerning the Principles of Morals* (Oxford, 1975), III.1.
[36] Neil MacCormick, *H.L.A. Hart* (2nd edn, Stanford University Press, 2008) 117 ff.
[37] Notice how many further 'laws of nature' Hobbes manages to generate from his big three: *Leviathan* (C. Brooke, ed., Penguin, 2017) chap. XV.
[38] Kelsen, *Pure Theory of Law*, 195–7.
[39] Hart, *The Concept of Law*, 193. I take the quoted passage at face value, and on its face 'any social organization' includes law and other organizations as well. Could 'social organization' just be literary variation for 'society', that is, a complete human society? That is unlikely, and in any

THE VIABILITY THESIS 211

survival, and that is provided for when people can continue to *live* at some minimally adequate level (as Hobbes puts it, when they can persist 'in motion'; *perseverare in esse suo*).⁴⁰ Why does viability come into it? First, it is a contingent fact that (almost) everyone does value their own survival, and that is a fact that pervasively shapes concepts central to morality, including those of harm, benefit, need, and injury.⁴¹ So survival is a common human aim that is conceptually entrenched at a deep level. Second, survival is a pragmatic presupposition of our inquiry: 'We are committed to it as something presupposed by the terms of the discussion; for our concern is with social arrangements for continued existence, not with those of a suicide club.'⁴²

A few comments on survival may prove helpful. First, Hart is not saying that survival is the only thing that matters in life. He does not deny and, as a value pluralist he is committed to accepting, that there are other objectively good things.⁴³ John Finnis thus goes astray when he complains that Hart's 'list of universally recognized or "indisputable" ends contains only one entry: survival.'⁴⁴ The minimum content thesis offers no such list. It maintains only that, beyond survival, any other indisputable or universally recognized final ends are either not necessarily compatible with each other, or not necessarily *good for* all who could recognize them *as* goods. This is obviously true with respect to items on Finnis' own list, including 'religion' which, if it is a good at all, is good only for people with particular sensibilities and which, in its central cases, conflicts with other basic goods, including the pursuit of knowledge.⁴⁵ Hart's point, as he puts it more clearly in his Holmes lecture, is simply that 'above this minimum the purposes men have for living in society are too conflicting and varying to make possible much extension of the argument that some fuller overlap of legal rules and moral standards

case the fact that a society needs such rules does not show that it needs them in its legal system. I pursue this point below.

⁴⁰ Hart is interested in the implicit teleology of *individual* human action, the elementary ends that people share with other animals, not in the survival of social forms or structures: *The Concept of Law*, 193–4.
⁴¹ Ibid., 192.
⁴² Ibid. I discuss suicide clubs below, 213–4.
⁴³ Hart, *The Concept of Law*, 157, 204, 205. On Hart's (occasionally unnoticed) pluralism, see Leslie Green, 'Jurisprudence for Foxes' (2012) 3 *Transnational Legal Theory* 150.
⁴⁴ John Finnis, *Natural Law and Natural Rights* (2nd edn, Oxford University Press, 2011) 82.
⁴⁵ Finnis includes under the good of 'religion' inquiry into *whether* there is a god, *whether* there is an ultimate meaning to life, etc. (ibid., chap. 13). That is not religion; it is philosophy. The central cases of religion are marked by commitment to, not merely inquiry about, theism. The conflict between pursuit of religion and the pursuit of knowledge need not arise in non-theistic doctrines. (See the Buddha's 'Kalama Sutta' (*Anguttara Nikaya*, 65.) But are these religions?

is "necessary" in this sense.[46] So survival is not the list of all the objectively good purposes there are, but the list of the mutually compossible common purposes '*that men have*'.

Second, the connection between individual survival and the viability of social organizations is indirect. Consider Hart's remark that legal rules are not the rules of a 'suicide club'. What are the typical suicide club's rules? Americans may think of a phrase attributed to Abraham Lincoln. At the outset of the Civil War, Lincoln thought it better to suspend habeas corpus without the consent of Congress rather than risk the whole Constitution which, he supposedly said, is 'not a suicide pact'.[47] But the viability Hart has in mind is not about the continued existence of a constitution or even a country. It is the survival of individuals, and whether it attempts to provide for individuals' survival is what determines whether a legal system satisfies the minimum content thesis. Remember that it is a mark of this presupposed aim that it is entrenched in 'whole structures of our thought and language'.[48] That may be true of individual survival, but it is not true of constitutional or political continuity. There are constitutions that provide for not only, as most do, their own (repeated) amendment, but even for their own demise, and for the demise of the polity whose constitution they are.[49] Our interest in the rules an organization must have if *it* is to be viable is derivative of our interest in the conditions for individual survival. It is of no independent concern whether English law helps ensure that 'there will always be an England'.

Third, the contrast with 'suicide clubs' might suggest that members of such clubs have no interest *at all* in survival and thus that such clubs would not be expected to share the common content of law and morality. That is too sweeping. Setting aside the common moral prohibition on suicide (which, it is worth noting, is *not* included in N), the clubs and their members do have an interest in most of the fundamental moral rules. At any rate that is suggested by Robert Louis Stevenson's short story 'The Suicide Club'.[50] Stevenson's tale has it that, even in a club set up to organize suicide, elements of N prove

---

[46] H. L. A. Hart, 'Positivism and the Separation of Law and Morals' (1958) *71 Harvard Law Review* 592, 623.

[47] There is no good source for the traditional attribution of this to Lincoln. A less pertinent source for a similar phrase is Justice Jackson's dissent in *Terminiello*, maintaining that the Bill of Rights is 'not a suicide pact', and thus that First Amendment to the US Constitution should not be interpreted to permit speech that might incite riot: *Terminiello v Chicago* 337 U.S. 1 (1949). However, killing someone in a riot is not 'suicide' and a pact that risks such killings is not a suicide pact.

[48] Hart, *The Concept of Law*, 192.

[49] See *Reference re Secession of Quebec* [1998] 2 S.C.R. 217 (Supreme Court of Canada).

[50] Robert Louis Stevenson, *The Suicide Club* (first published 1878; Dover, 2000).

necessary, including the now awful requirement that promises made are to be kept, and that once a system of cooperation has been set up its obligations are to be respected. There is even a version of (N1), for while the members include people who want others to kill them in specified circumstances, they do *not* want them to kill them *outside* those circumstances. That would not be an (indirect) act of their own will; it would be murder. This suggests that we should understand the rules of N as rules, not only for those who can be supposed to want to survive, but also for those who want to be able to control the temporal extent of their own lives.

The viability argument might then be rendered like this:

(1) (We may presuppose that) each values his own survival.
(2) On plausible assumptions about the world and human beings there is a set of rules N that conduce to individual survival.
(3) Every viable social organization provides for individual survival.
(4) Therefore, every existing social morality must instantiate N.
(5) And every existing legal system must instantiate N.
(6) And thus every existing legal system must contain some of what morality contains.

The argument needs elaboration and gap-filling: (3) is either doubtful or begs the question, and (4) and (5) can be derived from (3) and the other premises only with further claims about the character of law and morality. We could doubtless patch up, or give a better reconstruction of, the argument and avoid these problems. There is, however, a more architectural worry. The viability argument pictures the relations among law (L), morality (M), and the necessary content as being like those illustrated in Figure 8.1.

On this view, the fact that morality and law share something with each other is an artefact of the independent relation that each of them has with N. The fact that N is in L is not explained by the fact that it is in M; it is explained by a more general hypothesis, namely, that *any* viable social order requires N. But that hypothesis is not correct. There are many existing sets of rules

Figure 8.1 A spurious correlation between law and morality

practised by and among individuals who wish to survive, but which rules do not contain **N**: the MCC rules of cricket, or the rules of The Royal Scottish Country Dance Society, or of the Congregation of Oxford University. The explanation is not far to seek. These rules and the institutions that implement them do not exist in an autonomous realm beyond law and other forms of social organization. They are rules *of* and *for* people who want to survive; but they are not *survival rules*. Other institutions are already attending to those. As Hobbes says, when survival rules are not well implemented, many rule-governed activities cannot emerge, and there are 'no arts; no letters; no society'.[51] When the survival rules are in place, other rule-governed activities can emerge without having to worry about providing the requisites for survival.

Hence, we cannot safely assume that because **N** is necessary to human life it will be realized in every viable form of social order, *and thus* in law as much as in morality. A quick fix would be to add the premise '*and law is a socially necessary institution without which these rules could not exist and we could not survive*'. But that is plainly false. *Homo sapiens* may have emerged some 200,000 years ago, and other members of our genus who had similar survival needs and at least some of our symbolic capacities long before that. Yet we have no reason to think there were any legal systems at all before 3000 BCE, and for millennia people survived without them. Every human society needs rules, but the special kind of institutionalized rule-systems that characterize law are 'not a necessity, but a luxury'.[52]

6. Voluntary Compliance

Hart mentions a second consideration in favour of the minimum content thesis, and I will treat it as an independent argument. This one turns on institutional features of law. All legal systems contain norms that set up institutions like courts and tribunals. Indeed, this institutionalized division of normative labour is a mark of the emergence of law. One role of these institutions is to administer and, when necessary, order enforcement of the rules. How much enforcement goes on depends on how much voluntary compliance there is, but the power to enforce is always limited. Enforcement is slow and expensive, and at some level of non-compliance it is unaffordable.

---

[51] Hobbes, *Leviathan*, chap. XIII.
[52] Hart, *The Concept of Law*, 235.

Moreover, some of the enforcers may themselves be recalcitrant, so there will need to be people to enforce the rules against them. Then what about *those* enforcers? Coercion cannot rest entirely on coercion, all the way down. Law needs to be able to count on some compliance without coercive back-up. This is the root of Hart's second idea: '[W]ithout a minimum of co-operation given voluntarily by those who find that it is in their interest to submit to and maintain the rules, coercion of others who would not voluntarily conform would be impossible.'[53] That suggests a second line of thought:

(7) A legal system could not exist without a minimum of voluntary compliance of its subjects.
(8) Subjects will comply voluntarily only if they believe it is in their interest to do so.
(9) Only if a legal system contained N would enough subjects believe voluntary compliance to be in their interest.
(10) So every (existing) legal system must contain N.

As with the viability thesis, the bracketed term in (10) suggests that a need for compliance goes to the existence rather than identification of law. A model legal system, for instance one drafted by a legal philosopher, may never exist so it is going to be difficult to know what sort of compliance it might need, and how that might be provided.

Maybe we can learn something from the fact that it is a model for a legal system rather than for a cricket club. For example, it will need the compliance of subjects who did not voluntarily join up, so maybe it will need special ways to motivate the recalcitrant. Even so, there are possibilities that raise doubts about (7). We are told by Hobbes that 'the weakest has strength enough to kill the strongest either by secret machination or by confederacy with others', for even the tyrant has to sleep.[54] But could a tyrant with a doomsday device and a secure redoubt not rule a whole population by terror alone, requiring the voluntary compliance of no one?[55] Offhand, it seems possible. Perhaps some will insist that such an arrangement would not amount to a legal system and the tyrant's orders would not amount to laws. Maybe not. But there is another problem.

---

[53] Ibid., 193.
[54] Hobbes, *Leviathan*, chap. XIII.
[55] As mooted in Gregory Kavka, 'Rule by Fear' (1983) 17 *Nous* 601.

The compliance case depends on the assumption that people will not *believe* it is in their interest to comply voluntarily unless *it is* in their interest to comply, which is what instantiating N achieves. This assumption neglects the complex, yet essential, distinction between what people believe to be in their interests and what is in fact in their (real) interests. It is the former, not the latter, that determines the prospects for their voluntary cooperation. There can be slippage between belief and reality in both directions. The fact that its norms satisfy N is not sufficient for people to believe their legal system serves their interests. Nothing is commoner than for people to be unaware how dependent they actually are on the effectiveness of a legal order they disparage. Some think they would be safer without the system of mutual forbearances provided by a system of gun control: they fail to notice the n-person prisoner's dilemma. Others fail to see that legal constraints can make them less likely irrational to discount their own future interests, for example, in health care or income support in their old age.

The slippage between subjective and objective interests goes the other way too. Social rules satisfying N may be unnecessary to secure the requisite degree of voluntary compliance. Ideology, in the pejorative sense of that term, can suffice.[56] Ideological beliefs are suspect in a variety of ways, but in ordinary cases they do not turn people into zombies or subject them to manipulation so severe as to call into question the voluntary character of their willingness to go along with the law. More typically, ideology leads people wrongly to discount certain options, to entertain fantasies about the feasible set, or to misidentify those who share, or will defend, their interests. In the face of these elementary truths of political sociology, what jurisprudence has tended to offer is some version of Dicey's nostrum:

> [T]he power of imposing laws is dependent upon the instinct of subordination, which is itself limited. If a legislature decided that all blue-eyed babies should be murdered, the preservation of blue-eyed babies would be illegal; but legislators must go mad before they could pass such a law, and subjects be idiotic before they could submit to it.[57]

---

[56] Raymond Geuss, *The Idea of a Critical Theory: Habermas and the Frankfurt School* (Cambridge University Press, 1981) 12 ff.

[57] Albert Venn Dicey, *Introduction to the Study of the Law of the Constitution* (Liberty Fund, 1915) chap. 1. Dicey takes the 'blue-eyed babies' example from Leslie Stephen, *The Science of Ethics* (2nd edn, Smith Elder, 1907) 143.

VOLUNTARY COMPLIANCE 217

Dicey did not live to see the Nazi holocaust; but had he never read of the Massacre of the Innocents?[58] And even if he was correct, it would show only that there are some things that all but the most 'idiotic' will recognize as meriting non-compliance. That may establish that the de facto authority of law is always limited. Yet a legal system can exist though there are things it couldn't get away with if it tried. It exists by learning not to try. It does not follow that the *other* things, all the things it *can* reliably get away with, serve the real interests of those whose voluntary compliance is needed.

The division of normative labour that characterizes law may seem to weaken this conclusion. Isn't it ideology that ensures acquiescence of the broad mass of subjects who could, anyway, have been coerced? Hart sets a low compliance baseline: 'Only if the rules failed to provide these essential benefits and protections *for anyone* . . . would the minimum be unsatisfied and the system sink to the status of a set of meaningless taboos.'[59] Now, a set of meaningless taboos can exist, but laws are not like that. They are meaningful norms that people use to guide conduct. Ideology reduces enforcement costs, but it does not explain the voluntary compliance of those officials at the centre of the system, one might argue. If legal systems can manage with the 'acceptance' and voluntary compliance of a *very* small group, what about them? I see no reason to doubt that even their allegiance could be secured by ideology rather than by security for their real interests. The Inner Ring may itself be attached to the law only by an illusion of its sanctity, or by the idea that it is somehow an expression of their own personality: *l'état c'est nous*. Perhaps compliance cannot rest on coercion all the way down; but compliance can rest on ideology all the way down.

Some think that law couldn't get *that* far adrift: everyone could no more be mistaken about their real interests than all native English speakers could be mistaken about the rules of English grammar. But the question whether a given legal system serves any of its subjects' interests, whether defined as a function of individual survival or otherwise, is not like grammar. These interests are (mostly) not convention constituted. This is consistent with the thesis advanced by E. P. Thompson in his attack on Marxist instrumentalism.

---

[58] Matthew 2:16–18.
[59] Hart, 'Positivism and the Separation of Law and Morals', 624, emphasis added. Hart here assumes what he elsewhere argues, namely, that a legal system cannot exist unless at least some people, including some of the officials, take 'the internal point of view' towards its rules and thus 'accept' them in his special sense of that term (*The Concept of Law*, 55–7). It is, admittedly, hard to tell how far he thinks the class of real beneficiaries and the class of voluntary compliers coincide. But he is clear that one can 'accept' a rule without benefiting from it.

Thompson thinks that the ideological power of law depends on its at least occasionally living up to its own declared standards of justice (and maybe also to *sound* standards of justice). He denies that the pomp and flummery of the English courts and the supporting apparatus of church and state could have been enough to distract people from the objective ferocity of eighteenth-century law: 'The essential precondition for the effectiveness of law, in its function as ideology, is that it shall seem to be just. It cannot seem to be so without upholding its own logic and criteria of equity; indeed, on occasion, by actually *being* just.'[60] If Thompson is right, there is some level of provision for justice that ideologically effective law must always meet. That does not show that every legal system must satisfy the minimum content thesis.

7. The Institutional Support Thesis

Neither the viability argument nor the compliance argument succeeds in establishing a common content to morality and law. But the ways they fail suggest an alternative argument that is more promising. Law and morality share a content because conforming to the norms of **N** is universally valuable, **M** instantiates **N**, and **L** is a kind of instrument *apt for supporting M* and is therefore used to do that. People have generic reasons to support **M**—the reasons given by Hobbes, Hume, and many others—and where there is law they have reasons to use law to support it. To the extent that the human predicament in all societies is similar, similar remedies can help, and law is such a remedy. Indeed, it is a remedy whose features make it especially apt for helping with that predicament.

The revised picture I have in mind is, in relevant part, like Figure 8.2:[61]

Unlike the morality–law correlation produced by Hart's viability thesis this one is non-spurious: it exists because law aims to, or is standardly used to, support morality. It does not rest on any assumptions about the sources of compliance with law. Like both of Hart's theses it yields a 'natural necessity', which is necessity enough for these purposes.

We might summarize the institutional support argument by saying that law and morality have a common content because securing that content is

---

[60] E. P. Thompson, *Whigs and Hunters* (Penguin, 1975) 263.
[61] I am omitting a possible direct connection between **N** and **L** to focus on the mediating role of M, which law supports. Figure 8.2 means to suggest that a direct connection, if it exists, is less important than the one via M: references and appeals to morality in law are overwhelmingly appeals to social morality.

N

↓

M

↓

L

Figure 8.2 Law as supporting morality

what law *is apt for*. We need to interpret that idea with caution, however. Aquinas famously compared law to a saw: a saw is for cutting, and the fact it has that function explains why saws have the structures they do: thin blades, jagged teeth, and so on. These are design features that serve the purpose of saws, which purpose partly constitutes what it *is* to be a saw. Many instruments have constitutive aims: coffee grinders are for grinding coffee. Some institutions have particular aims amongst their constitutive features: universities are for the pursuit and preservation of knowledge and culture. (That is why training schools or seminaries are not universities, not even when they parade the title.[62]) Some legal theorists regard laws and legal systems as aim constituted in this strong way, but law is not as crisply functional as a university, let alone a saw or a coffee grinder. Law is multi-functional, and the ways it performs its functions are important to its nature. There is no function common to all legal systems that explains why legal systems have the structural features they do, and no function unique to legal systems. The minimum content thesis does not therefore depend on the idea that supporting morality is what law *is for* in the sense of 'constitutively for'. Law's important structural features of institutionalization, systematicity, comprehensiveness, etc. are not design features that exist *in order* to enable law to support morality. The connection runs the other way round. It is law's having such features that explains why law is so apt for supporting morality (among other things). Law's comprehensive claim to authority means that it claims power to regulate whatever needs to be regulated; its openness to other norms means that it can give effect to the requirements that people behave with good faith when

---

[62] 'Since its inception, training at Hamburger University has emphasized consistent restaurant operations procedures, service, quality and cleanliness. It has become the company's global center of excellence for McDonald's operations training and leadership development.' <http://www.aboutmcdonalds.com/mcd/corporate_careers/training_and_development/hamburger_university.html>.

in cooperative associations, and so forth. Where law exists and is effective, it is apt for supporting moral norms, which norms instantiate (imperfectly) the minimum content of morality.

What is it to 'support' morality, and how does law do it? Law supports morality, first, by making it more effective at guiding conduct. It does that in two main ways: by authoritative and non-authoritative communication— informing people of what is required—and non-communicatively, by changing their decision-environment and options so that, whether or not they recognize what morality requires, they will tend to conform to it anyway. We sometimes associate these two modalities with just two ways of acting: the issuing of general directives and the imposition of penalties. But law has many other techniques, including giving authoritative examples of how to 'go on' (the typical case-law method) and also by modelling desirable behaviour.[63] We should often treat others impartially: legal institutions contain not just directions for, but also models of, impartial conduct, as in (ideal) judicial decision-making. We should treat others as our moral equals: as in (an ideal) jury of peers. And so on.

The instrumental support thesis does not make *success* at supporting morality constitutive of law. A degree of success may be among law's legitimacy conditions.[64] Making and applying law is a way of governing, and governing is an activity no one should undertake if they are bound to fail at it. What about law's failed efforts to support morality? Do they, if pervasive, show that the legal system in question is only marginal, *ersatz* members of the kind, in the way one might say that an 'invalid proof' is no proof at all? That depends on why law fails. Compare the difference between a jammed, disabled, or ill- engineered rifle on the one hand and a toy rifle on the other. The first three are rifles because they have enough of the structural and functional features of rifles (and their dysfunctions are among the species-typical ways that rifles fail). The second is not a rifle; it is just a toy. A system of primary and secondary social rules that aim to secure the wide range of human interests proper to law can fail in dramatic ways. Laws can be pointless and inefficient; they can be unjust and ignoble. Such failures are common as dirt. If pervasive they undermine the legitimacy of the legal system; but they do not call into question the fact that it is a legal system. That would take more extensive

---

[63] Kimberly Brownlee and Richard Child notice this important feature in their paper 'Can the Law Help us to be Moral?' (2018) 9 *Jurisprudence* 31.

[64] Why only 'may be'? (1) Bear in mind that M, on the analysis here entertained, is only the morality of obligation, understood as a social morality. (2) I assume that the legitimacy of legal authority is always partly dependent on the outcomes it produces.

kinds of failure, ones that also undermine the structural features of law so as to render it utterly inapt for doing any of the things it characteristically does, including supporting morality.

8. The Nature of an Artefact

I now ascend, or possibly descend, to a methodological issue. I have been treating Hart's discussion as an effort to explain the nature of law by specifying its necessary and sufficient features, including its necessary content, at least in its standard cases. Necessity poses problems for any empiricist. Sense experience, with or without the help of instruments, will fail to turn up what is necessary. It must fail, because our experience, individual and collective, is finite while the features necessary to law are those found not only in all existing and historical legal systems, but in all possible ones—or all humanly possible ones—and those are numberless and unobservable. So how to proceed? The only way we can. We begin with the most reliable knowledge we have of actual legal systems, then we test conjectures about which of their universal features are necessary by seeing whether they can resist contrived but intelligible counterexamples. The method is fallible. Our conceptual powers are among our evolved capacities, and it may be that we do not have the power to conceive all pertinent counterexamples. The only ground for optimism is Giambattista Vico's: in the realms of human artefact and history, we may have a better chance of understanding what we have ourselves made than we do in the world of fundamental physics which began and will go on without us, as indifferent as the stars.

Brian Leiter takes a sceptical view. He thinks anyone looking for 'necessary' features of law is heading the wrong way down the one-way street of science.[65]

> [E]ven at the dawn of the 21st century, legal philosophers set conditions for a successful analysis of the Demarcation Problem—to identify the 'necessary' and 'essential' properties of law that distinguish it from morality in all cases—that would strike most philosophers in other fields, even 30 years ago, as wholly incredible.[66]

---

[65] For an earlier critique, see Brian Leiter, *Naturalizing Jurisprudence: Essays on American Legal Realism and Naturalism in Legal Philosophy* (Oxford University Press, 2007).
[66] Brian Leiter, 'The Demarcation Problem in Jurisprudence: A New Case for Scepticism' (2012) 32 *Oxford Journal of Legal Studies* 4.

It is incredible, Leiter thinks, because laws and legal systems are artefacts, and anyone who is up to date knows that artefacts cannot be identified in terms of necessary and sufficient conditions: they have no essential attributes.[67] Informed people came to that view years ago, with the collapse or exhaustion of the so-called 'demarcation problem' in the philosophy of science.

I have reservations about that analogy. Whatever the state of play in the philosophy of science, no sensible legal philosopher, today or thirty years ago, is looking for properties of law that will 'distinguish it from morality in all cases'. That is because they know that law cannot be distinguished from morality *in all* cases. As I explained in Section 1, the demarcation lines around law and legal systems are not bright ones. When we seek necessary and sufficient conditions for the existence of law, we limit ourselves to trying to make precise only the standard, paradigm case. But Leiter holds that, even here, artefacts have no such natures and they elude any account in terms of necessary, never mind sufficient, conditions. (Perhaps he thinks it is in the *nature* of artefacts to have no such natures.)

Now, rarely are legal systems intentionally created artefacts, so we cannot define them in terms of their creators' ambitions.[68] Not even individual laws need be such artefacts; the contribution of a legislative (or law-applying) act to the legal system often depends on its uptake: how it is received and used by courts and others. Customary law is thoroughly accidental; but so too are parts of the common law, and even some parts of statute and constitutional law, as judicially construed. At the systemic level, the role of individual intention is more dilute still. The judges of the King's Bench went out intending to discipline local courts and subject them to Henry's will; but they did not go out trying to make a new legal system—the common law—though that is what emerged as the unintended and unforeseen upshot of all their activities. We can nonetheless define 'the common law' well enough to distinguish it from civil law, Sharia law, or canon law.

Some artefacts can be defined functionally: micrometres and mousetraps, theatres and theodolites, belong to their types in virtue of their capacity to be

---

[67] Ibid., 5.
[68] Leiter once held that: 'The concept of law is the concept of an artefact, that is, something that necessarily owes its existence to human activities intended to create that artefact' ('The Demarcation Problem', 5). That would produce a demarcation between law and ideal morality, which does *not* necessarily owe its existence to such activities. His later work acknowledges that law is not an artefact of that sort: law can be created without the intention to create law (and, at its most basic level, normally is). His considered view is set out in 'Legal Positivism about the Artefact Law: A Retrospective Assessment', in L. Burazin et al. eds, *Law as an Artefact* (Oxford University Press, 2018) 5.

THE NATURE OF AN ARTEFACT 223

used for certain things. Leiter does not think we can approach law that way either: the idea of function is too fuzzy here, and anyway there is no function that all and only legal systems share that makes them of their kind. I agree with that: as I argued in Chapter 2, law is more a modal kind than a functional kind.[69] But law is still an artefact in the way custom, money, language, and etiquette are: it is a social construction with a cluster of non-specific but typifying functions, distinguished from its near neighbours (e.g. custom or religion) by structural and modal features, some of them necessary to legal systems.

What Karl Popper and others hoped for by way of 'demarcation' was not merely a criterion that would enable us to tell science from not-science, but one that would also enable us to tell science from *pseudo-science*. They wanted one criterion to do two jobs. But a pseudo-science is not just a classificatory error, it is a fraud. Popper hoped the 'falsifiability criterion' could be both classifier and fraud-detector. But why should one demarcation be able to do both a conceptual job and a normative job? After all, there is nothing wrong or deficient with something being not-science; there is only something wrong with it being pseudo-science. Music is not-science and neither is formal logic, yet both are wonderful and valuable. (Logic is even valuable *to science*.) On the other hand, polygraph analysis, homeopathy, and graphology are pseudo-sciences, and dangerous ones. Sailing under false colours, they mislead people about their cargo. They pretend to techniques that can show which witnesses are lying, or how to cure diseases, or how to predict people's characters. They can't do any of these things. Pseudo-sciences hold themselves out as sciences; they invite others to use them as sciences; they try to get their adherents qualified, and paid, as expert witnesses; and so on. The demarcation criterion itself is not going to explain that, or what is wrong with it.

Possibly the philosophy of science will never come up with one criterion for science-hood that succeeds at both the classificatory task and the normative task. Be that as it may, there is no analogous pair of tasks waiting to be solved by jurisprudence. What distinguishes legal systems from non-legal systems is a matter for legal philosophy, and, since law is a mind-dependent artefact, explaining the concept of a legal system goes hand in glove with explaining legal systems (and, therefore, laws). But there is a different demarcation between law and *pseudo-law*. In every jurisdiction there are invalid

---

[69] See also Leslie Green, 'The Functions of Law' (1998) 12 *Cogito* 117.

statutes, false precedents, and people impersonating police. These can be as dangerous as any pseudo-science. But it is not the task of legal philosophy to distinguish law from pseudo-law. That is the task of the recognition rules. And, unlike philosophical 'demarcation criteria' which apply to all sciences, recognition rules vary enormously amongst legal systems. That is because the rules that identify the fundamental sources of law aren't philosophical theories; they are actually practiced, implicit, dynamic, and somewhat vague, customary rules. They are among the most important artefacts in a legal system, and they normally arise as a by-product of judges and others doing, not legal philosophy, but something more mundane: settling legal disputes.[70]

---

[70] I thank the Oxford Jurisprudence Discussion Group for the invitation to give the talk from which this chapter descends, John Gardner and Brian Leiter for many instructive discussions of these issues, and Thomas Adams and Luis Duarte d'Almeida who greatly improved an earlier draft of this chapter and prevented unwarranted backsliding on my part.

9
The Role of a Judge

1. Judging and Law

Every society that has law also has people who perform the role of judges. They need not be called 'judges'; they may be 'priests', 'elders', 'kings', or something else. Nor need they be thought of specifically as judges. The society may not distinguish between, say, a judicial role and a priestly role: in religious legal systems it is common for these to be fused. But it is a feature of legal systems of any kind that they have officials who settle disputes by applying pre-existing standards. That marks an important difference between law and things like bargaining, trial by ordeal, or arbitration. When there is a legal system, there are not only people who can make people do things and settle disputes, but people with a duty to do so by applying law.

Legal theorists are in wide agreement that law stands in an important relation to the judicial role. What that relationship is has been disputed. Among historically influential theories we find claims that laws are generalizations that predict the decisions of judges, that laws are norms addressed to judges, that laws are norms judges are entitled to enforce, or that laws are norms that those subject to judicial decisions are morally obliged to obey. The thesis I examine here is different. According to it, laws are norms that judges have a moral obligation to apply. Some jurisprudents propose a negative version of that thesis: they say that a norm that is morally defective—for example, one that is intolerably unjust—is not a legal norm at all, or not a standard case of a one: *lex injusta non est lex*. That tells us what judges may not apply in the name of law. I am interested in a more ambitious, positive, thesis. In this version, not only do some kinds of immorality disqualify standards as law, but good moral credentials stand as affirmative qualifications for something being law. Michael Moore defends a version of that thesis, so I will take his account as the springboard for my inquiry. He says, 'jurisprudence should tie law strictly to judicial obligation, so that if a standard does not give a judge an obligation it is not part of the law'.[1] So far, this seems like a version of the negative thesis. Things get more interesting as he goes on to assert: 'Not only is law conceived as whatever obligates judges, but the role of judging is conceived in terms of decision-making constrained by those standards we think of as law.'[2] Thus, law is whatever morally obligates judges in judging, and judging is a role constituted by the application of all and only those standards that are obligation-imposing.

To forestall misunderstandings, let us notice a few initial points about the thesis under scrutiny. First, it does not merely hold that laws are such that judges have a legal obligation to use them; they have a moral obligation to do so. Second, the claim is not that all legally binding standards are obligations—the law also contains norms that confer powers or permissions, as well as things that are not norms of any kind, for instance, definitions and titles. The claim is that these are law if and only if there is a moral obligation to use or apply them in the way a law of that kind is to be used or applied. Third, there is no suggestion that law necessarily imposes moral obligations on its (non-official) subjects. That judges have a moral obligation to apply the law does not presuppose or entail that its subjects have a moral obligation to obey it. It is consistent with Moore's thesis that ordinary subjects owe law nothing at all and may blamelessly treat it as a price system. (Moore does not endorse that view, but he expressly leaves open the issue of political obligation.) Finally, although the obligation binds people in their role as judges, the morally obligatory standards have a mutually constitutive relationship to that role. Recall the passage I quoted above, 'the role of judging is conceived in terms of decision-making constrained by those standards we think of as law', and the standards we think of as law are all and only those that are morally binding on judges.[3]

Now, Moore thinks of this as amounting to a kind of 'natural law' position, no doubt because it conditions the existence of law on the satisfaction of tests of moral propriety. I will set that aside. It is more important to know whether the view is correct than whether it is loyal to any tradition of natural law. Anyway, Moore makes clear, in an ecumenical spirit, that he does not think this is the only possible theory of law. The view just described he calls an 'internal' jurisprudence; a theory that approaches the nature of law from within

---

[1] Michael S. Moore, *Educating Oneself in Public: Critical Essays in Jurisprudence* (Oxford University Press, 2000) 96.
[2] Ibid., 95.
[3] Ibid., 95.

what is already assumed to be a legal system and identifies its law in terms of standards that officials in that system have reason to think morally binding. He acknowledges an independent project of trying to figure out what sorts of institutions amount to legal systems in the first place. That would be 'external' jurisprudence; the sort of project undertaken by Aristotle or Aquinas, Bentham or Kelsen, who ask, from a general point of view, what the nature of law is as such. External jurisprudence has no ambition to instruct judges in a particular legal system how to decide cases; its ambitions are to explain and evaluate familiar social institutions.[4]

What then are we to make of the claim that, within anything that is undeniably a legal system, the law is the set of all and only those standards that are morally binding on its judges, as judges? Both natural lawyers and legal positivists have rejected that thesis, and I rely on some of those arguments here.[5] But I try to advance the discussion by examining in closer detail what the judicial role amounts to and how law-application figures in it. To anticipate, I argue: (1) Some standards that a judge is morally obligated, *qua* judge, to apply are not law. (2) The role of a judge is not exhaustively constituted by the duty to apply the law, or by any other single duty. (3) Other moral obligations of a judge are related to the obligation to apply the law, but they do not arise from principles of law. The judicial role includes creative powers anchored in principles of the rule of law. These principles do bind judges as judges, but they are not principles of law.

2. A Simple View

Let us begin with a simple view according to which any standard whatever that a judge has a moral obligation to use in deciding a case is part of the law. This is not Moore's stated view; I will introduce that in Section 3. But it is helpful to begin by seeing what is wrong with the simple view. It is vastly over-inclusive. Here are some counterexamples.

---

[4] I say 'explain and evaluate' because general jurisprudence addresses both descriptive and normative questions, including whether certain evaluative standards apply to law in virtue of the nature of law as a social institution. The idea that general jurisprudence is restricted to the 'definition' of law is historically inaccurate and philosophically implausible.

[5] Especially E. Philip Soper, 'Legal Theory and the Obligation of a Judge: the Hart/Dworkin Dispute' (1977) 73 *Michigan Law Review* 473; and Joseph Raz, 'Incorporation by Law' (2004) 10 *Legal Theory* 1 (reprinted in Joseph Raz, *Between Authority and Interpretation: On the Theory of Law and Practical Reason* (Oxford University Press, 2009)).

I take the first from the law of damages. In a personal injury case, English judges must determine what a successful claimant is owed by combining damages suffered under various 'heads': medical expenses, travel costs, loss of future earnings, pain and suffering, loss of amenity, and so forth. How to determine the total owed under any head? Easy—just add up the relevant costs; take the sum. The same goes for the damages overall. The sums are determined by ordinary principles of arithmetic. Someone who could not do arithmetic (or who could not get it done) would be a very poor judge. Of course, what a judge needs in this department is arithmetic 'know-how', not any kind of 'knowing-that'. They need to know how to add; they do not need to know the unique-factorization theorem. But if in reckoning damages a judge did anything other than add—for instance if they awarded only the amount under the category that registered the highest loss, or if they multiplied the individual components together—it would not merely be an arithmetical error. It is immoral to short-change the claimant or to fleece the defendant; a judge has a duty to get the sums right. Nonetheless, principles of arithmetic are not laws of England. When Korean children learn arithmetic, they have not learned a little English law. Arithmetic is universal in application; its content is unconnected with the activity of any English political institution; it is known and understood in a way different to the law. Contrast the principle that damages must be reckoned as a single lump sum payment, or the principle that pension contributions are to be deducted before calculating an employee's actual loss of earnings. These principles are law. They are not binding everywhere; they have not always been in force in England, and their existence and content is dependent on decisions of courts and others.[6]

What holds for arithmetic holds for language and its syntactic, semantic, and pragmatic principles. In every jurisdiction, the law has at least one mother tongue—its official language. In England the law speaks in English. Judges and lawyers in that jurisdiction therefore worry a lot about what English words, sentences, and whole documents mean. It would be wrong to appoint English judges who are illiterate in English or whose command of the language is poor. We depend on the law being intelligible to us, and our lawmakers speak so as to be understood, if not by laypeople, then at least by the lawyers who must advise them. Still, the rules of English grammar are not English laws. Does the literal or 'plain' meaning rule of interpretation suggest otherwise? Isn't that what makes the stop sign at an intersection mean 'Stop!'?

---

[6] *Wells v Wells* [1998] 3 All ER 481 (lump-sum principle); *Dews v National Coal Board* [1987] 2 All ER 545 (pension deductions).

(Instead of, say, 'Stare!') Of course not. English makes it mean that. The plain meaning rule functions in the context of other legal rules. It directs that when the ordinary meaning of a provision is clear, unambiguous, produces no absurdity, and serves some intelligible purpose, then it is to be construed in accordance with that meaning, notwithstanding other available principles of interpretation. But it is not the plain meaning rule that *provides* the ordinary meaning of English words. Like the lump-sum and pension-deduction principles, the plain meaning rule rests on legal sources; its popularity has waxed and waned over time; its merits are arguable.[7] Legislatures and courts control and shape it; they have no similar control over the plain meaning of ordinary English words.

Finally, consider ordinary moral principles. Judges should protect rights, do justice, serve the public good, and decide humanely. Other things being equal, they ought to conform to all such standards whenever and wherever they apply the law. But not because these standards are law, and not because of anything that someone thought, said, or did that made them relevant to legal decisions. 'Why are judges, and humans generally, subject to morality?' This is due to the nature of morality. It has no doctrine of jurisdiction setting out its conditions of application. It applies universally to all agents capable of understanding it.[8] Joseph Raz is correct: if morality applies anywhere, it applies also in court. Special features of adjudication may make certain moral principles—such as the requirement for impartiality in decisions, or for consistency among decisions—more stringent than they are in other departments of life. It is also true that the law may direct or permit people to do something other than what morality would require in the absence of legal institutions. Where the authority of law is legitimate this may be morally justified. But it is misleading to think of any of this as law incorporating morality by reference, or somehow making morality relevant to decisions on which, but for the say-so of some court or legislature, it would not bear.

Like principles of arithmetic or grammar, moral principles apply their own force to the activities to which they are relevant. Sound moral principles do not vary among legal systems except where there is variation in facts on which they supervene. They are not enacted or repealed by legislation. Owing to the nature of the interests that law regulates, and to the allocative and expressive upshots of judicial decisions, moral principles are inevitably relevant in court. No plug-in or adapter is needed to connect them to judicial

---

[7] *Sussex Peerage Case* (1844) 11 Cl & Fin 85; *Fisher v Bell* [1961] 1 QB 394.
[8] Raz, 'Incorporation by Law', 2.

230 THE ROLE OF A JUDGE

decision-making. Morality is already connected unless it gets (legitimately) disconnected.

In pointing to these analogies between the legal relevance of arithmetic, grammar, and morality I am not suggesting that they operate in the same ways in the law. For one thing, judges give much more explicit attention to moral standards, and legislators frequently make explicit mention of them when they make law. Arithmetic and grammar, on the other hand, operate quietly in the background, being used without being mentioned, save in cases of doubt about what they might require. Legislators felt no need to explain multiplication, division, addition, and subtraction when they said:

> There may be deducted from the amount deemed by subsection 146.3(6) to be received by an annuitant out of or under a registered retirement income fund an amount not exceeding the amount determined by the formula A × $[1 - ((B + C - D) / (B + C))]$[9]

They did not need to say anything about arithmetic because, well, everyone already knows how to add, subtract, multiply, and divide (and, if they do not, instructions in the 'Interpretation' section of the Income Tax Act are unlikely to help).

With respect to morality things are often different. Here, legislators and judges become articulate and sometimes garrulous. Statutes and constitutions prescribe ideals such as 'equality before and under the law'; they expressly prohibit 'inhuman and degrading' punishments; they assert all sorts of 'human rights'. Judicial decisions then comment at length on what these standards require in particular circumstances. Even without any invitation from statutory language, judges explain what they think would be 'reasonable', 'fair', or required by 'common sense' in the case before them. If morality is like arithmetic or grammar, then why does law mention it so much more often? Is knowing how to use the concepts of 'equality' or 'degradation' trickier than knowing how to calculate compound interest?

Sometimes—but not always. Even when the force of moral requirements is crystal clear, however, there are several reasons we hear so much about them in court. First, moral standards may remain relevant to a case even after considering the bearing of positive law, and ordinary moral argument is articulate about the reasons for its conclusions. If we want to hold that a certain procedure is oppressive, or that a penalty would in the circumstances be unjust, we normally do so

---

[9] Income Tax Act RSC 1985, c. 1 (5th Supp.) s. 146 (Canada).

using those terms and explaining why they apply. Second, not all moral language in court is what it seems. Some moral terms have legal homonyms. 'Equality' is a very broad moral principle; but in court it sometimes picks out a technical, legal principle subject to source-based tests for what it demands: equality before or under the law, 'formal' but not 'substantive' equality, or the reverse, but in any case equality as the law sees it. Or again: 'harm' is a moral notion; but judges who rule that films are criminally obscene only if 'harmful' sometimes look to community standards, not to moral arguments, to decide what is harmful.[10] Third, some overt references to morality in the law are there to counteract the effects of legal standards. For example, the Canadian Charter of Rights and Freedoms empowers those whose rights are violated to apply 'to obtain such remedy as the court considers appropriate and just in the circumstances'.[11] Does this make justice a principle of Canadian law? Would it have been fine for judges to grant inappropriate and unjust remedies if that clause had not made it into the final draft of the Charter? Of course not. The quoted provision reclaims space for justice by limiting the impact of legal principles including, here, an express constitutional provision for judicial review together with a long-standing judicial prejudice in favour of striking-down as the sole proper remedy for unconstitutionality. The remedial provision reins in a legal provision and a legal prejudice and allows moral principles to reclaim their natural place in crafting remedies. Unless modified by law, these principles bind all judges everywhere, and we know they are binding before we learn anything else about a given legal system. We need to study the law of that system in order to know what is binding there *as well as*, or *instead of*, what morality already permits and requires.

3. Roles and Obligations

These three examples show that the simple view is incorrect. They appeal to our ordinary understanding of law. They can also be supported by theoretical considerations that I have not mentioned.[12] But perhaps all this misses the

---

[10] For example, *R v Butler* [1992] 1 SCR 452 (Supreme Court of Canada). For discussion, see Leslie Green, 'Men in the Place of Women, from *Butler* to *Little Sisters*' (2005) 43 *Osgoode Hall Law Journal* 473.
[11] Canadian Charter of Rights and Freedoms, s. 24(1), Part I of the Constitution Act, 1982, being Schedule B to the Canada Act 1982 (UK), 1982, c. 11.
[12] H. L. A. Hart, *The Concept of Law* (3rd edn, Penelope. A. Bulloch and Joseph Raz, eds; Leslie Green, intro, Oxford University Press, 2012) 200–12; Joseph Raz, 'Authority, Law and Morality' (1985) 68 The *Monist* 295. Moore criticizes the second line of the argument: *Educating Oneself in Public*, chap. 5.

point? The counterexamples rely on the fact that it would be wrong for judges not to apply ordinary standards of arithmetic, grammar, or morality in contexts where they are applicable and where legal authority has not intervened to change that. Judges are obligated to use these standards, in the phrase I quoted from Raz, 'because judges are humans': humans who need to calculate, humans who want to be understood, humans who want to conform to moral principles. However—and this is what suggests the counterexamples may miss their target—Moore does not say that whatever is morally binding on a judge (*qua* human) is part of the law. He says that, 'Law obligates judges in their role as judges . . .' by which he means law is 'that which binds the occupant of [an] office': law is 'binding on legal actors qua legal actors'.[13] Does this qualification make a difference? Perhaps the counterexamples involve standards that judges are morally obligated to apply, but not standards they are morally obligated to apply *as judges*. To know whether this makes a difference, and if so what difference it makes, we need to investigate the relationship between social roles and moral obligations.

Some obligations are binding only on people performing certain roles. Only the dog-catcher has a duty to catch stray dogs. Other obligations bind everyone, but they bind people within roles in a different way than they bind people outside them. Anyone is owed an explanation if reprimanded for poor job performance, but the Dean must reprimand an instructor in writing and give an opportunity to respond.

A social role, like the closely related notions of a 'station' or 'office' or even 'job', picks out a set of norms, values, and expectations that apply to people in virtue of the fact that they hold that role. Obligations that come with a role are in some ways like philosophers' 'special obligations' that bind people standing in a particular relationship or performing a particular activity. Yet not all special obligations are role obligations. Consider an ordinary promise. It creates a paradigmatic special obligation: it binds the promisor in particular and does so in virtue of the fact that they made a promise. Nonetheless, 'promisor' is not the name of a role; it is merely the logical subject of a promissory obligation. We do not assume the role of promisor and then get a duty to keep our promises; we just promise. In this respect, 'promisor' is like 'tortfeasor'; it is no more than a name for someone who did a certain morally relevant thing. It is a mark of roles, in contrast, that they consist of norms that cohere in a way that warrants us thinking of the role as a unity different from its

[13] Moore, *Educating Oneself in Public*, chap. 5.

occupant, and one that might in principle have another or a different occupant. Legal systems are replete with roles like that: judge, juror, police officer, bailiff, legislator, sovereign, and so on. Unlike 'promisor' or 'tortfeasor', these are not just names for the subjects of special obligations or powers; they have a deeper legal and moral existence.[14]

Four features characterize such roles:

(1) A role is cluster of norms (e.g., obligations, permissions, powers) that apply to its occupant, together with virtues and expectations that support those norms.
(2) Role-norms apply to the occupant of the role at least partly in virtue of the fact that they occupy that role.
(3) A role can have more than one possible occupant, either at the same time or sequentially.
(4) Role-norms typically function together as a package: some are binding only because others are; some support conformity to the others; some influence the interpretation of the others.

This characterization attempts to explain, while sharpening, our familiar notion of a role. It does not offer any account of why role-norms are valid, that is, why they are binding on their occupants. It is important to be clear about that. Point (2) is often misunderstood. A role identifies the obligations of its occupants, but this is not enough to justify those obligations. For that we need to appeal to moral considerations external to the role.[15] What can be misleading is the fact that to someone who asks, 'Why do I owe that client a duty of confidentiality?' we can informatively answer, 'Because you are their lawyer.' That will be informative whenever someone knows they are a lawyer but has not yet grasped all that it entails. In such cases, the explanatory 'because' does not give the ground of a duty, it merely identifies it as one of a lawyer's duties. The identificatory function is also present in roles that are morally repugnant and should not be performed at all, not even by those who voluntarily assume them (Mafia capo, Guantanamo torturer, etc.). In such

---

[14] How far special obligations are embedded in roles is variable. Is 'father' the name of a social role, or only of a special relationship? It is unclear, and it probably varies culturally and historically.
[15] See Michael Stocker, 'Moral Duties, Institutions, and Natural Facts' (1970) 54 *The Monist* 605; A. J. Simmons, *Moral Principles and Political Obligations* (Princeton University Press, 1979) 16–23; Leslie Green, The Authority of the State (Oxford University Press, 1990) 193–215; Michael Hardimon, 'Role Obligations' (1994) 91 *The Journal of Philosophy* 333; A. J. Simmons, 'External Justifications and Institutional Roles' (1996) 93 *The Journal of Philosophy* 28.

cases we can informatively say that it falls to the capo to give orders to the sgarrista, or that it falls to the torturer to keep the water-tanks full. What we cannot say is that, just because these things are in their job descriptions, the capo or torturer have a moral duty to perform them. On the contrary, they have a moral duty not to perform them.

The problem of justifying role obligations is, however, more complex than merely identifying reasons for holding people to be subject to the obligations that their roles include. Point (2) entails that we need reasons to think those obligations are binding in virtue of the fact that they help constitute a role.[16] What does that mean? The English philosopher F. H. Bradley believed in the centrality of roles. Against moral individualists, Bradley defended the importance of understanding people's duties in light of their 'stations' in life. He wrote: '[A]lthough within limits I may choose my station according to my liking, yet I and everyone else must have some station with duties pertaining to it, and those duties do not depend on our opinion or liking.'[17] I am unsure whether everyone has, let alone must have, a station, unless that is understood in an unusually wide sense. Bradley's second point, however—that the duties of a station do not depend on our option or liking—is correct. But he mistakes its significance. It is a general characteristic of all obligations that one must perform them whether one likes to or not. That is true even of voluntary obligations: the obligation of a promise also does not depend on our 'opinion or liking'. Role obligations have a feature beyond this: they bind as parts of a role—in a package deal, so to speak. So it is not merely that role duties do not depend on our liking: which duties constitute a given role does not depend on our liking either. When we assume or fall into a role, we take it as we find it.[18] To justify role obligations one reasons why obligations should ever bind in that holistic, package-deal, kind of way.

I do not think there is a general explanation for that feature of roles; but three types of reason are often found (and found in combination). First, because roles can have multiple occupants, it is often important that a new entrant be bound at once by all its obligations, at the point of entry. The unity

---

[16] It need not be the only reason. A witness ought to tell the truth (a) because of a natural duty: everyone should tell the truth; (b) because of a special obligation: he took an oath to do just that; and (c) because of a role obligation: it falls to him as a witness.
[17] F. H. Bradley, *Ethical Studies* (2nd edn, Oxford University Press, 1962) 176.
[18] Throughout I am considering only social roles, like that of a judge. One could take a piece of paper and write at the top, 'My Role', and list below a set of personal duties for oneself, putting down only those that one would like to perform. If that is a role, it is not the sort of role judges occupy. Some social roles do come with individual powers to reform that very role. When one assumes such roles one assumes those powers, too—whether one likes it or not.

of a role facilitates learning what it requires and stabilizes the expectations of those who depend on it being performed. We want the new professor to have all the obligations and powers of a professor, and we want students to know they have them as soon as they take on the job. Second, there are often reasons for several obligations to be in one set of hands: we want the lawyer who owes us a duty of loyalty also to avoid putting themselves in a conflict of interest, and we want them to hold in confidence things that we tell them. These obligations are mutually supporting. It is hard even to make sense of a duty of loyalty where conflicts of interest are permissible, and hard to fulfil such a duty without keeping certain information confidential. Third, many roles have a wider significance in the community; they have a valuable social aspect precisely because they are roles. There are few, if any, obligations of a spouse that could not be negotiated separately through ante-nuptial agreements. If there were no common role of 'spouse' in our society, different intimate relationships would emerge, depending on the wants and needs of couples, and also on the individual's bargaining power. There could be advantages to that arrangement, but also losses. Only when most spouses owe each other similar duties is the status of 'spouse' available and generally understood, and only then can people interact on the basis of shared expectations without need for inquiry, possibly an intrusive inquiry, into others' domestic and intimate arrangements. This is not to deny the value of the many creative variations we already have on the themes of 'husband', 'wife', or 'spouse'. But you cannot have a variation on a theme until you have a theme. It is one of the things that helps sustain a common culture, and a common culture helps us live together in comfort and mutual tolerance.

Such considerations interact with the wider question of why any package of duties ever binds. There are multiple answers here, too, and they vary with the nature of the role. As it is not my aim in this chapter to explain why the judicial role is binding on those who perform it, let me bypass the issue with some brief observations. Sometimes it is important that a role, such as that of spouse or lawyer, be voluntarily assumed. Allowing people control over the incidence of role-packaged obligations has a protective function: it gives them the power to shape their lives to suit their own ambitions and characters, and it helps secure their commitment to the role and their motivation to perform its duties. Such considerations explain the importance of judicial oaths. On the other hand, some important roles are non-voluntarily binding, especially when others are dependent on the role being performed, such as the duties of parenthood on which young children depend. In our legal systems, the role of juror is a familiar example. In smaller and more stable societies, the same was probably true of being a neighbour, and possibly of being an elder called on to settle disputes. In such cases, considerations of 'natural duty' argue in favour of the obligations being binding without actual or even implied consent. No doubt there are other possibilities as well.

4. The Role of a Judge

Consider now, in a general and abstract way, the judicial role as we have it.[19] Judges have an obligation to apply the law. That is not in doubt. It is also widely agreed that this obligation is not absolute and can sometimes be cancelled or overridden. Moore shares that view. He says: 'Law obligates judges in their role as judges; that does not mean that sometimes judges will not be justified in stepping out of the judicial role because other values are more important than those (rule-of-law) values that normally justify conformity to the judicial role.'[20] Thus, if something is law, judges have a role-obligation to apply it, unless they are justified in 'stepping out' of their role. We do not need to think of 'stepping out' as a matter of 'stepping down'. It is doubtful that resignation is a morally necessary precondition for any justified refusal to apply odious laws. Stepping out of role is more like a change of perspective that brings responsiveness to various considerations that need not, or even may not, be attended to whilst immersed in the role—for instance, in the way a professor might need to step out of the role of teacher in order to help a student in personal distress. In any event, the idea that judges *can* step outside their role, and may be justified in doing so, presupposes that there is something out of which to step: some kind of boundary—not necessarily sharp—between what falls to judges as judges and what falls to them as moral agents who have immense power over other people's lives.

Many features of a judge's role are fixed by law and political convention and vary by jurisdiction. In one legal system, a judge may have a duty to strike down unconstitutional legislation; in another they may have no power to do so. In one, a judge must stand ready to rule on the meaning of any constitutional provision if so asked by the Attorney General; in another they may have to await an actual case or controversy. Such local variations do not help us understand how, or which, principles are binding on judges as judges, for

---

[19] Throughout this chapter, I am discussing the judicial role as it now is in familiar legal systems. The judicial role can change, and has changed, over time. Perhaps it should change in various further ways. I make no claims about these matters here.

[20] Moore, *Educating Oneself in Public*, 96.

THE ROLE OF A JUDGE 237

they are simply consequences of the judicial duty to apply the laws of their jurisdiction, including the laws that regulate their own powers. Some law-dependent features of the judicial role are so familiar that we forget that they do have such sources. In Number 78 of *The Federalist*, for example, Alexander Hamilton says the judicial power to strike down Congressional legislation is on a par with the judicial power to decide which of two conflicting laws should prevail. With respect to the latter, Hamilton writes:

> The rule, which has obtained in the courts for determining their relative validity, is that the last in order of time shall be preferred to the first. But this is a mere rule of construction, not derived from any positive law, but from the nature and reason of the thing. It is a rule not enjoined upon the courts by legislative provision, but adopted by themselves, as consonant to truth and propriety, for the direction of their conduct as interpreters of the law.[21]

In fact, Hamilton is wrong to say that the rule that priority is to be given to the newer law—*lex posterior derogat priori*—is 'not derived from any positive law', unless he only means it was not imposed by legislation.[22] *Lex posterior* was a positive rule of the civil law and of the common law and, so far from being obviously mandated by 'the nature and reason of the thing' or being 'consonant to truth and propriety', the merits of *lex posterior* are unclear and have been frequently debated by the courts.[23] (And the same is of course true of the power Hamilton hoped to establish by his strained analogy: judicial review of legislative enactments.)

To make progress here, we need a broader characterization of the sociopolitical role of a judge, one that is not derivative of the requirements of positive law. Although Moore disclaims any interest in 'general' jurisprudence, he does need some general jurisprudence, at least of the judicial role, in order to know what would count as judges stepping outside it, and thus what principles are binding on them just in virtue of that role. As far as I can see, however, the only direction Moore gives us is the following: 'judges are always obligated (in their role as judges) to follow the law and nothing but the law.'[24] I argue below that this is incorrect. Be that as it may, the direction is

---

[21] *The Federalist No. 78* 'The Judiciary Department' (1788).
[22] Sometimes, *lex posterior* is imposed by legislation, e.g. in the Vienna Convention on the Law of Treaties, Art. 32 (1155 UNTS 331).
[23] In the United Kingdom, see *Nwogbe v Nwogbe* [2000] 2 FLR 744 (Court of Appeal); and *BH and Another v The Lord Advocate and Another* (Scotland) [2012] UKSC 24 (20 June 2012).
[24] Michael S. Moore, 'Four Reflections on Law and Morality' (2007) 28 *William and Mary Law Review* 1523, 1537–8.

of little help. First, it presupposes rather than explains the idea of a judicial role. Second, it is a single decisional norm alleged to bind all occupants of that role. As we have seen, however, a genuine role is a cluster of norms and related phenomena. 'Law-applier', like 'promisor', is not a role in the relevant sense. There is more to being a judge than that.

Let us grant then that it falls to a judge, as judge, to apply the law, and also to do other things that are instrumentally necessary to the application of law. What else is in the job description? Here is a suggestion derived from some remarks by H. L. A. Hart. Hart holds that where a case cannot be settled by law (e.g. owing to indeterminacies caused by vagueness or conflicts in the law) judges usually have discretion to settle it; but they do not have a free hand. Their discretionary powers are limited: by deference to the proper authority of other institutions, by considerations of judicial craft, and also by something Hart calls the 'characteristic judicial virtues'. Judges do and should exercise their discretion, he says, while displaying 'impartiality and neutrality in surveying the alternatives; consideration for the interest of all who will be affected; and a concern to deploy some acceptable general principle as a reasoned basis for decision'.[25] I do not think we should make heavy weather of the word 'virtues' here, as if these are desirable dispositions for a judge but not matters of obligation. A judge who acts with partiality or bias, who gives no consideration to the interests of those with a stake in a decision, or who utterly fails to decide on the basis of reasons, does not only exhibit a weakness of character, he is in breach of moral obligations (and, in most jurisdictions, also of legal obligations).

The question arises, however, how far these virtues involve obligations that are not only 'characteristically' judicial, as Hart puts it, but also constitutively judicial: part and parcel of the role itself. The first two—impartiality and due consideration—are important, but they do not identify the judicial role. They are general features of moral decision-making that become more exigent whenever one has effective authority to rule on matters affecting people's interests. Arbitrators and mediators, for example, also ought to work impartially and with due consideration for the interests of those they serve. Unlike judges, however, they are not bound as part of their role to apply pre-existing standards in coming to a decision or in issuing advice—it is perfectly acceptable, and even typical, of them to try to bring the parties to a fresh agreement, or to split the difference between them, or to do justice as they see it without

---

[25] Hart, *The Concept of Law*, 205.

THE ROLE OF A JUDGE   239

regard to what they had done before or what they might do next. Admittedly, obligations of a role do not need to be unique to a role in order to constitute it. A distinctive role can be a distinctive combination of several non-distinctive obligations. Both professors and physicians have a role-based obligation to keep current on research in their field; it is their other obligations and the ways those combine that distinguish these roles. My worry is rather that Hart's first two virtues simply fall to judges as moral agents, something not true of the professor or physician's duty to keep up. There is no general moral obligation to know the latest in numerical analysis or in molecular medicine, not even if these are among your hobbies. The specifically professorial and medical duties to keep current flow from the dependence of others on the skilful performance of the role.

The third virtue, the judicial 'concern to deploy some acceptable general principle as a reasoned basis for decision', is different. Understanding the requirement of generality to be not just logical but temporal—a decision is to be applicable not only without reference to proper names, but also to future similar cases—and understanding the reference to 'acceptability' to bridge moral correctness as well as some sort of fit with existing law, this *does* capture a characteristic duty in the role of a judge.[26] Anyone should decide on the basis of reasons, but judges must decide on the basis of reasons of a particular kind. The requirement to use and articulate general principles applies to judicial decision-making in virtue of the fact that rulings will be used to guide others. The rulings themselves guide the parties and, if necessary, other officials; but rulings can also immediately constitute, or eventually contribute to, general rules of conduct. Providing guidance through such rules is one of the main functions of law. As Lon Fuller stressed, law cannot serve that function unless it contains general rules; rules that are also reasonably clear, consistent, stable, prospective, and effective in legal proceedings.[27] Judges are in control of many of the conditions that determine how far those requirements are satisfied, and they stand in a special position to be able to protect the law from the conduct of people who might undermine them.

This points the way to a more complete understanding of the judicial role, one that includes but goes beyond application of valid law, and that draws on

---

[26] Stripping out some distracting polemics and purely parochial concerns, this is the sound idea in Herbert Wechsler's 'Toward Neutral Principles of Constitutional Law' (1959) 73 *Harvard Law Review* 1. (And it applies not only to constitutional law, but to all judicial decisions.)
[27] Lon L. Fuller, *The Morality of Law* (rev. edn, Yale University Press, 1969) 46–91.

the connection between Hart's third virtue and the ideal of the rule of law. So conceived, the judicial role consists of three families of obligations:

(II) Law-applying obligations: Judges have an obligation to apply valid law in making rulings, and to do other things necessary for the proper discharge of that duty. For example, they have a duty to make correct findings of fact, to know what the law is, to keep their knowledge of the law up to date, to rule intelligibly so that those to whom the ruling applies know what to do, and so on.

(II) Law-improving obligations: Judges have an obligation to keep the law 'legally in good shape'.[28] Not every improvement in law falls to judges as judges, but many of those required by the rule of law do. If judges find the law unclear, they have a duty to clarify it; if there are conflicts in the law, they should try to resolve them. More generally, they should improve the law's capacity to guide the conduct of its subjects.

(III) Law-protecting obligations: Judges have obligations to regulate their own processes and the conduct in their courts, and to protect the rule of law and the integrity of their jurisdiction from those who would attack it by undermining judicial independence, by using the legal process oppressively or abusively to subvert the law, or by undermining the effectiveness of the courts in applying the law.

None of these obligations is absolute, and the law-applying obligations are defeated where the laws are egregiously immoral or the law-creating institutions lack the legitimacy to create law at all. The obligations may also conflict. A judge may need to choose between applying existing law and improving it, between clarifying it and keeping it stable over time. But, painting in broad strokes, these obligations characterize the judicial role and help distinguish it from other political roles in our societies.

This account has the following notable features. First, it is not tied to any particular jurisdiction or type of legal system: these are duties of judges in common-law courts, in civil courts, in courts martial, in religious courts, and so on. Second, it describes an authentic role constituted by several norms, a role that can be occupied by various people. Third, key aspects of the role are unified by the fact that judges have an obligation and power to apply the

---

[28] I borrow this apt phrase from John Finnis, *Natural Law and Natural Rights* (2nd edn, Oxford University Press, 2011) 270.

law. The obligations falling to ordinary subjects in respect of the rule of law are mostly limited to not undermining it: we must not bribe judges, take frivolous lawsuits, break the law without compelling reason, and so forth. But judges, owing to their control over their own procedures and decisions, also have further law-improving and law-protecting duties in the service of that ideal. Fourth, there are reasons for a judge's role-obligations to be jointly binding as a group. It is important that those who apply the law do so in ways and under conditions that help the law guide the conduct of its subjects, and it is important for those in judicial office to be bound by these obligations immediately on assuming the office. They are binding primarily because of the way they serve the rule of law, and secondarily because of the moral force of judicial oaths or their willingness to undertake the job. Fifth, judicial obligations to clarify the law or protect the judicial process are not dependent on the existence of laws imposing those obligations and, like principles of morality, they are unlimited in their jurisdiction. They bind all judges everywhere. As Philip Soper puts it, 'Some standards bind judges, not because they are law, but simply because they are part of what it means to be a judge'.[29] If this is correct, as I think it is, then the fact some moral principles bind not because judges are humans but because they serve in a particular role does not, after all, change the conclusion of Section 2. Many judicial obligations are binding because the law imposes them; to know what they are we need to know what the law requires. Others are binding in virtue of what 'raw' morality requires, or in virtue of what morality requires of people performing a judicial role. These too are invariant among legal systems; that is why they bind judges as such—as *judges*. They are not principles of general morality, but like principles of general morality they apply of their own force and without regard to jurisdiction or any connection to particular social or political institutions.

5. Understanding Judicial Creativity

It will not have escaped notice that, on my account, the obligations of judges are not only applicative but creative. Complying with a judge's law-improving and law-protecting obligations may require bold rulings that go beyond what pre-existing law requires. Moreover, a judge's obligations under points I and III are often imperfect, leaving them latitude to decide how and when

---

[29] Soper, 'Legal Theory and the Obligation of a Judge', 477.

to fulfil them. They may, or may not, decide to distinguish a case; they may choose to overrule earlier decisions; they may instead interpret settled law in new and surprising ways. How should we think about these, and other, creative aspects of the judicial role? Moore is clear on how we should *not* think about them:

> Common law distinguishing or overruling, together with purposive interpretation of statutes, are well-accepted aspects of the judge's role as we know it. If we freed law from its close tie to judicial obligation, we might think of these judicial activities as proper but as going against the law.[30]

To think of these tame and familiar activities as proper yet 'going against' the law would be very strained. It is true that overruling 'goes against' the very law (*in sensu diviso*) that it overrules, as would legislative repeal of that law; but it does not go against the law (*in sensu composito*)—it is not a violation of legality. Each of these activities uses powers that properly fall to any judge, or at least to any judge working in a common-law system. Moore's proposal is that to avoid the absurd conclusion that use of these powers 'goes against the law' we need to 'conceptualize the law as always having been that which the overruling/distinguishing/purposefully interpreting court has discovered for the first time'.[31] Not so. If a legal system had a general norm to the effect that judges may never create law by distinguishing, overruling, or interpreting, then those activities would go against the law in that system. I am not familiar with any legal system, common-law or otherwise, that contains such a norm. It is not clear that it would be even possible for a legal system to wholly lack judicial powers that have law-creating effects, not even one that pledges allegiance to the myth that judges never make law. There will always be cases not determined by existing law, and judges will have duties to settle some of them. The Benthamite fantasy of referring every doubtful point back to the legislature for resolution is a fantasy, not least because it can be doubtful whether a point *is* doubtful.[32] The unavoidable judicial settlements will be both binding and new. Moreover, whether or not there is a formal doctrine of precedent, repeated judicial interpretations of law, including incorrect ones, can over time build up customs that also change the law. All legal systems are dynamic in character, and all judges have (some) creative powers.

---

[30] Moore, *Educating Oneself in Public*, 97.
[31] Ibid., 97.
[32] This is, in fact, the normal case of legal dubiety, and it precludes the use of any sort of 'tennis-line' rule to dispose of all doubtful cases.

To the extent that judicial activities create new law with retrospective effect, they do compromise one aspect of the rule of law, namely the principle that laws should be prospective in force. But that ideal is not itself a law, and violation of it does not lead to the invalidity of a law, unless there is some special legal requirement for prospectivity. And no one thinks the requirement of prospectivity dominates all other aspects of the rule of law, any more than they think that the requirement that the law should be stable over time means that inconsistency or vagueness in law should never be cured by courts or legislatures.[33]

So, these familiar techniques do not 'go against the law'; they use legal powers *provided by* the legal ground rules, whether constitutional norms or, more fundamentally, the rules of recognition and adjudication of that system. In using these powers to shape law, a judge no more goes against the law than does the UK Parliament when it makes valid use of its powers to enact new statutes. Parliament does not deduce or infer statutes from the UK constitution, as if they were already somehow latent in it, just waiting to be discovered or derived. Parliament takes decisions; it acts. If it acts in one way the law will be one thing; if it acts in another it will be something different. That is why it matters who is elected to Parliament. The same is true of judges and, although their legal powers are much more limited and subject to many more constraints, that is why it matters so much who is appointed, or elected, to the bench.

Should we say that judges may be justified in acting creatively if they are also acting non-judicially, that is, outside their role? There is no such place, in a Moore-style theory. I have argued that the role is bounded by obligations to apply law and certain obligations to improve and protect it. Although Moore mentions the possible justifiability of stepping outside the role, he has left no space for it. He says that in every case, even the easiest one in the most benign legal system, where a judge could apply obvious law to the clearest of facts, the judge always has a duty as a judge to consider whether that should on balance be done:

> The omnipresence of the question whether the obvious law should be followed means that one cannot confine the values justifying a limited judicial role to outside-of-role, 'Sunday' musings. Rather, such values enter into each application of the obvious law by a judge, for each application requires

---

[33] See Stephen R. Munzer, 'Retroactive Law' (1977) 6 *Journal of Legal Studies* 373; Charles Sampford, ed., *Retrospectivity and the Rule of Law* (Oxford University Press, 2006).

a balance of those values against the potential injustice of applying such obvious law to the case before a judge.[34]

In this passage, the province of justice seems to be what the ancients called 'general' justice: the realization of all sound moral values in their right relations. (That is, not limited to distributive, corrective, or procedural justice in particular.) Indeed, we should just say 'all sound values', for elsewhere Moore signs up to the view that, 'morality includes everything that is otherwise a valid and relevant reason within the overall balance of reasons that determines the rightness of our actions.'[35] Now, it is true that in the preceding extract Moore explicitly says the values that cannot be consigned to outside-of-role 'musings' are those that justify a limited judicial role. But if a judge must, as he also says, always *consider whether* such values outweigh the possible injustice in applying 'obvious' law, then *within* their role the judge must always assess the justice of every law. So, every valid reason that could be relevant to that issue applies in virtue of the fact that the assessor is a judge. It follows, then, that a judge is never actually justified in 'stepping outside the role'. If the considerations in favour of doing so were justificatory, they would not lie outside the role, for they bear on the pervasive moral question of whether the law should be applied. Since these values bear on every application of law (and bear as law—though not as 'obvious' law) there can be no difference between what a judge is morally obligated to do as a judge and what a judge is morally obligated to do, full stop. This account of the judicial role thus turns out to be a fuel-wasting detour on a road back to the unacceptable simple view: scenic, but circular.

Let me emphasize that I am not denying that judges should attend to morality, or that they should remain alert to the question whether they should be applying law at all. Of course they should: the law is morally fallible and judges exercise great power. The mistake is in thinking that this duty is distinctively judicial, and in thinking that it helps us demarcate what is, from what is not, law. If the law is whatever standards judges are obliged to apply as judges, and 'as judges' they are required to attend to all moral values, we are back with the simple view and its obvious defects. In contrast, the view of the judicial role that I have defended is more complex, but it coexists with a narrower view of the law that judges must apply as one, but only one, of their obligations.

---

[34] Moore, 'Four Reflections on Law and Morality', 1536.
[35] Moore, *Educating Oneself in Public*, 155.

6. Jurisprudence and Conceptual Choices

I conclude with a thought about how we approach questions like these. Moore counts four ways that judges ought to use moral principles in deciding cases: judges ought to apply moral principles when those principles are 'incorporated' by 'obvious' law; judges ought to test the authority of law against those principles; judges ought to use moral principles to settle undetermined cases; and judges ought to use moral principles to decide whether and how to overrule immoral laws. For reasons explained in Section 5, it is a feature of his account that conforming to those norms is inevitably discovering what the law (already) requires. Moore knows that his is a controversial view that faces competition. Other legal philosophers, including me, hold that the law can and does use all sorts of standards without incorporating them into the law, that judges have powers to change and create law even if they do not own up to them, and that there are things that judges must do, as judges, apart from applying the law. Surprisingly, Moore concludes that, as between his view and one like mine, it is a close call. He writes:

> We thus face a conceptual choice that is not obvious. The positivist keeps our notion of law simple—law consists of all and only the obvious stuff; but the ethics of obligation then becomes complicated because judges (even in their role as judges) are not always obligated to follow the law, nor are judges limited in their judicial decisions to the law alone. The natural lawyer keeps our ethics simple: judges are always obligated (in their role as judges) to follow the law and nothing but the law; but their notion of law now becomes complicated, because law is not only, and not always, what we take to be obviously law.[36]

Moore favours simple ethics and complicated law, though he does not think the case for that is obvious. He says jurisprudents have a 'conceptual choice' to make.

What is a conceptual choice and what grounds could be relevant to making one?[37] Some legal concepts, like 'fee simple', are complex but at the same time fairly sharp. Others, like 'reasonableness' are simple but pretty vague. We work all the time with vague concepts, making them more precise only

---

[36] Moore, 'Four Reflections on Law and Morality', 1537–8.
[37] See also the discussion in the Introduction, section 3, this volume.

when we need to. That does pose choices, for there is no single way to make a vague concept more precise: how best to sharpen it depends on our purposes. Perhaps precisification is a conceptual choice.

Like all our social concepts, the concept of law is vague to some degree and in some respects. Bu is it vague in the respects Moore has in mind? He does not show that. All he shows is that there are contending positions in legal philosophy, and he claims it is not obvious which of them is correct. Perhaps not. But it is no measure of the vagueness of a concept that it can attract philosophical disputes, or that it can be difficult to see a clear path through those disputes. There has been a legal philosopher willing to deny almost any proposition about law you can think of, no matter how obvious. The nature of the subject, to say nothing of the profession, encourages that, for the rewards in advancing a thesis that is new, even if crazy, can be greater than the rewards in advancing a thesis that is (merely) true. Moreover, at least since Kant we have known that one of the liabilities of free inquiry is that reason sometimes gets above itself. How best to respond to that and rein in the philosophical tendency to generate nonsense is itself a matter of philosophical dispute. Jurisprudence probably contains no greater proportion of nonsense than do other areas of philosophy, but the fact that there are divergent philosophical opinions about the nature of law does not set up any problem of 'conceptual choice'. It merely sets up a problem for philosophy.

Choices about concepts can arise in a second way, however: not in sharpening vague concepts but in reforming existing concepts, however sharp. We have a deeply entrenched concept of 'race'. It is not difficult to grasp—children learn racial classifications easily and early—and though it admits of indeterminacy it is not so vague that we cannot, for example, ban discrimination 'on grounds of race'. We understand 'race' well enough for that. There is nonetheless no scientific or moral value in what we might call the first-order use of the concept: to sort and rank people into ethno-genetic kinds. There is nothing in the world that answers to our concept of a 'race'. Using the concept in a first-order way has led to grave moral and theoretical errors; so we should live without 'race' if we can, and reform it if we cannot. Some philosophers think there are similar hazards in 'law.' They do not normally advise us to abolish the concept of law, but some do think we should re-shape it with attention to the alleged practical benefits of operating with one concept rather than another.[38]

---

[38] For discussion of so-called 'normative positivism', see this volume, 52–6.

It may be that by 'conceptual choice' Moore has in mind something along those lines: a pragmatic case reforming our concepts of law, the judicial role, etc. He does claim that 'The main virtue of internal jurisprudence is its practicality.'[39] So perhaps it is in a practical light that we should assess his suggestion that 'judges are always obligated (in their role as judges) to follow the law and nothing but the law', a view that supposedly 'keeps our ethics simple'. What would be the value in that simplicity? And why would that be a good way to reform our concept of law—why not instead reform it so that only democratic laws, or just laws, or efficient laws henceforth count as laws? We hear from so-called 'legal pluralists' who maintain that there is no important distinction between legal norms and other social norms. We also hear from some inter- and trans-national legalists that jurisprudence is hung up on an outmoded 'Westphalian' statist view while law is changing all around us, evolving into something bigger and better. If all important international norms are now law, and our familiar juristic distinctions are as phoney as the supposed 'races' of our single species, maybe it is time to retire 'law' too?

I do not think Moore accepts that. But neither does he present any case for reforming the concept of law along the lines he proposes, and I am not sure how one would go. Maybe we could take a lead from something J. S. Mill says about justice. Mill observes that to save a life we may be not only permitted but also obliged to steal food or medicine; we may even be required to conscript an unwilling doctor to help us. Mill then suggests:

> In such cases, as we do not call anything justice which is not a virtue, we usually say, not that justice must give way to some other moral principle, but that what is just in ordinary cases is, by reason of that other principle, not just in the particular case. By this useful accommodation of language, the character of indefeasibility attributed to justice is kept up, and we are saved from the necessity of maintaining that there can be laudable injustice.[40]

Now, this passage is frustrating because it is hard to tell how far Mill is maintaining ironic distance from a habit of speech he thinks misleading—a *mere* keeping up of appearances—and how far he holds that the 'accommodation of language' actually is useful. Perhaps we might say that practice is one thing and theory another, and the norms by which we should guide our

---

[39] Moore, *Educating Oneself in Public*, 97.
[40] J. S. Mill, *Utilitarianism*, chap. V. (*Collected Works*, vol. X, 238) (University of Toronto Press, Toronto, 1969)

lives differ from the underlying structure of morality.[41] You can see why Mill might think it playing with fire to acknowledge that some injustices can be justified. So he may hold that we should try to put some things beyond decision, to the extent that we can, by putting them beyond thought and speech, to the extent that we can. Perhaps that gives us a moral reason to speak as if justice is indefeasible: in the normal circumstances of moral decision-making, we cannot trust ourselves to operate with a more complex, if more accurate, judgement.

I am not sure how far Moore's enthusiasm for 'moral realism' permits him to go down a line like that. If it does, might he invoke analogous considerations about law? I cannot see how. In ordinary life there may be value in working with simple rules such as 'Never lie', 'Keep all promises', or 'Always be just'. But what value would there be in charging our judges to work with the rule, 'Apply the law and only the law'? Bear in mind that, in Moore's view, they need to understand 'the law' as including not only positive law, but also principles of the rule of law, the values underlying them, and any moral reason that might count against applying a law. If judges fail to do the right thing, then they will have failed to conform to this norm. But there is no reason to think that in attempting to conform to it they would be more likely to do the right thing. For that to be plausible, judges would need an independent test for whether they are conforming to the norm, and Moore's capacious idea of 'law' deprives them of one. It is a bit like being told that you would do best to follow the simple rule 'Keep all promises' only to be further instructed that, 'What you promised is determined by all moral considerations relevant to the decision about whether to do what you said you would'. That may not set back our moral reasoning, but there is no way it can improve it.

There are fewer 'conceptual choices' in jurisprudence than some imagine. The concept of law is vague, but not all *that* vague: not vaguer than, say, the concept of a state or the concept of custom. We can certainly make the concept of law more precise—that is one task of a general jurisprudence—and we could try to reform it if there were reason to do so. To succeed in that sort of campaign, however, we need a lot more than philosophical argument. We would also need to change the way we normally talk and think, and, probably, the way we live. (That is why 'race' has been so hard to budge.) But we

---

[41] Perhaps along the lines of R. M. Hare, *Moral Thinking* (Oxford University Press, 1981).

need a better reason to try than that doing so would, by a useful accommodation of language, allow us to keep up the idea that all sound judicial decisions apply the law and only the law, and that that is the beginning and the end of a judge's job. That really is just keeping up appearances. The law is much smaller than that, and the judicial role much larger.

10
Should Law Improve Morality?

1. A New Question

Lawyers and philosophers have long debated whether law should *enforce* social morality. No, says J. S. Mill, unless doing so prevents harm to others. Yes, says James Fitzjames Stephen, so that intentionally inflicted suffering can affirm and validate the community's moral judgements. H. L. A. Hart replies: never, unless doing so attains some good that outweighs the loss of liberty and happiness that come with enforcement. Patrick Devlin rejoins: on the contrary, provided what is at issue is a moral standard whose breach an average person would regard with intolerance, indignation, and disgust, we should enforce it. Ronald Dworkin dissents: but that would be to give force to bare hostilities and prejudices, and those do not even count as moral views. Joseph Raz mediates: it is permissible to uphold social morality when the morality enforced helps constitute a valuable form of life and the 'enforcement' makes no or minimal use of coercion.[1]

The debate about the enforcement of morality represented in these well-known arguments is far from settled. Disputes continue at the theoretical level, for none of the above doctrines is entirely satisfying and, as with all philosophical arguments, when debate progresses it transforms the questions and our sense of the conditions an adequate answer must meet. And the enforcement of morals is not just a problem that persists for theory; it continues to be controversial in practice. In Anglo-American political cultures, the appetite for enforcing social morality remains healthy and on some issues is ravenous. It is an obstacle to reform of unjust and ineffective systems of criminal punishment. How to address this confounds even sophisticated

---

[1] J. S. Mill, *On Liberty* (Penguin, 2010) [f.p. 1859]); James Fitzjames Stephen, *Liberty, Equality and Fraternity* (R. J. White ed., Cambridge University Press, 1967 [f.p. 1873]); H. L. A. Hart, *Law, Liberty and Morality* (Oxford University Press, 1968); Patrick Devlin, *The Enforcement of Morals* (Oxford University Press, 1968); Ronald Dworkin, *Taking Rights Seriously* (Harvard University Press, 1970), chap. 10; Joseph Raz, *The Morality of Freedom* (Oxford University Press, 1986) chaps 14–15.

legal actors. In the law of obscenity, for example, courts can in one breath disown moralistic interpretations of what is obscene, declaring that it is to be defined not by violations of community standards but instead by reference to harmfulness, but then in the next breath affirm that what counts as 'harm' is whatever the community regards as harmful.[2] The controversies also spill across national boundaries. Moral views that were once an unremarkable part of our own cultures and then became minority, even pariah, outlooks, are being given new life. It was not so long ago that our societies held it morally unproblematic that men should be entitled to control women's lives; that family honour should trump individual well-being; that children are vassals of their parents; and that law should support the true religion. Our moral consensus against such attitudes is destabilized by the mobility and migration of peoples who take a different view. Liberal societies have not always reacted well to such fresh encounters with their own moral pasts. Much of the backlash against 1980s-style 'multiculturalism' was bound up with frustration, or perhaps weariness, at having to confront these views all over again, and now not as philosophical hypotheticals but as the actually held values of neighbours and co-workers.

So the theoretical and practical issues about the enforcement of morality remain hugely important. Here, I poach a few ideas and arguments from that debate, but only in service of a different project. I focus instead on a problem that has been almost entirely neglected by legal theorists. The issue of the enforcement of morals begins on the footing that a society's morality is already established—no doubt including diversity and complexity and open to interpretation—but nonetheless in a relatively stable existence. The enforcement question asks how law should respond to that actually existing morality. But that image is inaccurate if it is anything other than a freeze-frame, artificially holding things constant while we inspect various details in the picture. This can mislead because social morality is not frozen or fixed; it is fluid and dynamic. Like any set of customary norms—for example, the rules of grammar, or fashion, or etiquette—a society's morality is in flux. What is more, one of the forces that moves and shapes that morality is the law. Or so I shall argue. And if that is correct we have a further issue to consider: how, if at all, should law attempt to *shape* our morality?

In contrast to the very rich literature on the enforcement of morality, contemporary legal philosophy has almost nothing to offer us on this question.

---

[2] The Supreme Court of Canada made famous errors along these lines: see Leslie Green, 'Men in the Place of Women, from *Butler* to *Little Sisters*' (2005) 43 *Osgoode Hall Law Journal* 473.

Here, I make a start on it, looking to some work in legal sociology for help. I begin with some general observations about social morality. Next, I consider how such a thing could change, and—what is different—how it could *be changed*, including through the instrumentality of law. If morality can be changed, we need to consider whether it *should* be changed, and if so how. There is, obviously, no general answer to this last question, save the formally correct but empty one: law should attempt to change social morality for the better. But to exemplify the sort of analysis I think worth pursuing, I conclude with some less empty, but more conjectural, reflections on a case for changing aspects of our social morality about sex. I choose the example because it is the area in which the debates about the enforcement of morals were fought out, and also because it is where we now find some of the sharpest conflicts between liberal and more 'traditional' moralities.

2. On Social Morality

The question, 'What should our morality be?' sounds ill-formed. Surely we don't get to choose what morality requires of us: morality just is what it is. If it is wrong to lie, or to cheat, or to abuse others, that cannot be because we have chosen to sign some pledge of allegiance or abstinence. For one thing, we have not signed any such pledge; for another it makes perfectly good sense to ask which pledges we ought to sign, and the natural way to interpret that question is to take it as asking which pledges we ought morally to sign. If morality distinguishes good from bad pledging, we cannot understand the demands of morality simply in terms of what we do, or would, choose to sign up for.

Law is different. We do get to choose what our law requires of us. Legislatures choose in making statutes; courts choose in making rulings. Of course, not all law is chosen in such deliberate and punctual ways. Some law is the unplanned upshot of uncoordinated decisions by courts and other officials, some is the unintended result of courts standing ready to apply as law whatever emerges from certain social customs. So our law can surprise us. Nonetheless, if a surprising and unwelcome law emerges we can always fix it, for we have general powers of amendment and repeal that work even on unintentionally created laws.[3] Not fixing something is not the same as enacting

---

[3] The results of deliberate intervention are also subject to less deliberate forms of law creation, so the process is iterative.

it, but our idleness is consistent with the fact that law is always *subject* to deliberate choice.

Whatever we think about the metaphysics of morals, morality is not like that. We cannot enact morals and we cannot amend them either. We could repeal all legal prohibitions on homicide, but nothing we say or do could make it morally permissible deliberately to kill innocent people. Nor is this only a feature of those moral norms that are considered absolute or indefeasible. An ordinary promise is open to being defeated by a variety of contrary considerations. Still, we cannot choose that the moral principle that promises must be kept will no longer be binding around here. Perhaps we can change our circumstances or natures so that the promise-keeping principle would be useless to us. That is not repealing the principle; it is changing the factual conditions under which it has normative force. Similarly, if we were no longer dependent on being able to trust what others say, it would no longer be wrong to lie. But the principle '*those who depend on each other's word should not lie*' would still be valid.

This leaves us in a pickle. If morality cannot be changed, how can we make sense of the question whether law should change it? To find our way through this we can take advantage of some ground-clearing done long ago by H. L. A. Hart, in *Law, Liberty and Morality*.[4] Hart points out that when we ask whether it is *morally* right to enforce *morality*, the idea of the moral sounds in two different registers. There is the morality that a society *does in fact* endorse and practice—he calls that its 'social' or 'positive' morality—and there is the morality that it *ought* to endorse and practice—an 'ideal' or 'critical' morality. So when we ask, 'What should our morality be?' we are asking, from the point of view of ideal morality, what social morality we ought to have.

That distinction resolves one point in the enforcement debate. Some people argue that there is no issue about *whether* morality should be enforced by law, there is only an issue about *which*, or whose, morality should be enforced. The distinction shows why that is wrong. It treats as settled precisely what is under dispute: is it proper for law to lend the force of steel to the moral views of some group or other, because they *are* its views? The position usually characterized as a liberal one—for example Mill's or Hart's claim that we should not enforce morality as such—is not the view that we should enforce the (social) morality of liberals. It is the view that violations of a social morality—liberal or otherwise—do not justify coercive legal response

---

[4] Hart, *Law, Liberty, and Morality*, 17–24.

unless they are also violations of some ideal moral principle. What makes the view liberal is not that it enforces the liberals' morality, but that it gives special weight to the value of liberty in the decision about whether to enforce *anyone's* morality.

That is why Hart says, 'what is crucial to the debate in its modern form is the significance to be attached to the fact that certain conduct, no matter what, is prohibited by a positive morality'.[5] That 'no matter what' is the crux. Hart takes Stephen and Devlin to be maintaining that the fact that something is socially prohibited is always a reason for it to be prohibited also by law. And that is no misprision: Devlin takes pains to stress that law should uphold the actually existing, social morality of a community and not some gaseous ideal dreamt up by philosophers.[6] That shows his position is not empty; it also shows why it is problematic. There is no guarantee that the requirements of social morality will not be repugnant, superstitious, absurd, or confused.

We are morally fallible and so are all our customs and practices. Thus, to think that the fact social morality provides adequate warrant for its own enforcement is to think that there are features of social morality that justify enforcing it *even when* it is repugnant. If we are contemplating the use of force against people, those considerations had better be clear and compelling. We could moderate the Stephen–Devlin view somewhat. We could allow that the enforcement-justifying features are matters of degree, and that in lesser degrees they do not warrant enforcement. We could also say they are defeasible in light of other values. At points, Stephen and Devlin do qualify their view along such lines. They have to, or they would be moral monsters. After all, the Nazis and the Taliban had social moralities they enthusiastically set about enforcing. The qualifications do not still the controversy, however. Mill and Hart reject the view that a social prohibition provides even a prima facie or defeasible reason in favour of criminalizing (or coercively rendering less eligible) the conduct that social morality abhors.

We can make use of this distinction between social and ideal morality to explain how we can coherently ask whether law should improve morality. The morality whose improvement is mooted is social morality; the 'should' is a should of ideal morality. We are not out of the woods yet, however. While it is clear what we could do to go about enforcing morality—we could copy its prohibitions into the statute book—it is not so clear what we could do to improve morality, and even less clear what we could do to improve it by use

[5] Ibid., 24.
[6] Devlin, *The Enforcement of Morals*, 90–3.

of law. Here is one obstacle: not only ideal morality, but also social morality, is immune from the sorts of deliberate change by which we shape law.[7] This thesis is not causal but conceptual. Law gives us tools to enact morality into law, but it does not give us any similar tools to reach beyond law and adjust morality itself. Nor could it: 'immunity from deliberate change' is one of the criteria Hart offers as a test for whether some norm is a moral norm in the first place: 'it is inconsistent with the part played by morality in the lives of individuals that moral rules, principles, or standards should be regarded, as laws are, as things capable of creation or change by deliberate act.'[8]

I will return to that obstacle in Section 4. For now, let us focus on the underlying conception of morality. It is agreed that morality has to do with values and norms, with what is good and worth pursing in life, and with standards that should guide our conduct. This is also true of other areas of human thought and practice, including aesthetics, etiquette, and law. What makes morality different? Without suggesting there are bright-line distinctions to be found, Hart proposes that morality is the domain of standards that are in a special way highly salient or important.[9] This is marked by its immunity from deliberate change, and by three other features: moral standards are believed important for social life or some valued aspect of it; conduct is thought morally wrongful only if it is also thought voluntary; and morality is upheld by appeals to conscience or the intrinsic wrongness of what was done. These criteria offer some plausible distinctions between morality and law, for law in contrast *is* liable to deliberate change; some legal rules are of trivial importance; in law *there is* the possibility of strict or absolute liability; and law's characteristic means of enforcement involve resort to trials and sanctions, not appeals to rightness and conscience. Occasionally, officials apply and enforce the law without even expecting its subjects to think it right, and in frank acknowledgement that it is morally defective: 'rightly or wrongly', as English judges sometimes say. What judges claim or presuppose of the law is not that it is morally sound, but that it is legitimately binding.

These features of morality are formal ones. They identify morality not by its content, but by its social role. Admittedly, this is 'formal' in a rather informal sense of the term. It does not mean that moral norms must have logical features such as being representable in propositions that are universally

---

[7] H. L. A. Hart, *The Concept of Law* (3rd edn, Penelope A. Bulloch and Jospeh. Raz eds; L. Green intro, Oxford University Press, 2013) 175–8.
[8] Ibid., 175.
[9] Ibid., 173–80.

quantified, or speech-pragmatic features such as being expressed in imperative utterances. Nor need moral norms satisfy any of the more substantive requirements some philosophers like to call 'formal' (for instance, that they are principles that could be willed universally without contradiction or agreed to by a group of free people determined to live together as equals). Still, the four conditions are formal-ish in the sense that they can be satisfied by norms of various contents, if not any content whatever. That distinguishes Hart's theory from more substantive understandings of the nature of morality. Here are some familiar examples. In Aristotle's view morality must conduce to *eudemonia*, to a good and flourishing life in community. The Buddha says moral norms (*sila*) clear the path so that people can by their own efforts attain liberation from the bonds of attachment and illusion. Hume says moral norms are general conventions that promote the common good, or what he calls 'public utility'. And, in our day, a pessimistic Geoffrey Warnock says that moral norms are those which, if generally practised, ameliorate the standing tendency in life for things to go badly.[10] According to all these views, nothing qualifies as a moral standard unless it in some way aims at or tends to promote some good or other. In contrast, Hart's concept of morality is 'broad' in the way the concept of law is also 'broad'—both laws and morals can include standards that are pointless, irrational, and seriously wrong. How can morals be wrong? Because social morality is a genuine kind of morality, and it exists among groups of morally fallible people who can treat as morality, and use as morality, standards that are immoral. Naturally, a social morality does not *present* itself as wrong. Probably, every existing social morality presents itself as, or is taken to be, correct.[11] But that does not make it so.

3. Which Social Morality Exists in a Society?

Assuming that is what morality is, it could be changed by either being brought into existence in the first place or by having its existing terms altered. An existing social morality is one that is 'actually accepted and shared by a

---

[10] G. J. Warnock, *The Object of Morality* (Methuen, 1971).
[11] And that would make for a fifth contrast between law and morality. The law does not necessarily present itself as correct, *pace* Robert Alexy, *The Argument from Injustice: A Reply to Legal Positivism* (R. Paulson and S. Paulson trs, Oxford University Press, 2002). The law presents itself as morally binding *whether or not* it is correct. For discussion, see John Gardner, 'How Law Claims, What Law Claims', in John Gardner ed., *Law as a Leap of Faith* (Oxford University Press, 2012) 139–45.

WHICH SOCIAL MORALITY EXISTS IN A SOCIETY? 257

given social group'.[12] It is hard to say precisely what that requires and I do not try to make it sharper here. But I do want to touch on what makes the problem difficult, and to clarify and adopt a couple of points relevant to the present question.

The existence conditions for customary moral norms need to allow for all of the following facts:

- A norm can exist though it is implicit in practice and has no explicit or canonical formulation.
- A norm can exist though it conflicts with another norm that also exists in that society.
- A norm can exist though it is quite frequently breached.

You can see how these make it complicated to state conditions for the existence of a social morality. Our morality prohibits murder, but not because people go around reciting a formula such as 'Thou shalt not kill'. Our morality requires that we respect other's property, and it also permits us to save our own lives by stealing food from someone who will never miss it. Our morality condemns sexual infidelity, and such infidelities are common. The idea that a morality exists only if 'accepted' needs somehow to accommodate all these cases.

Hart says the acceptance of norms 'consists in the standing disposition of individuals to take such patterns of conduct both as guides to their own future conduct and as standards of criticism which may legitimate demands and various forms of pressure for conformity'.[13] 'Acceptance' is a technical term that Hart defines primarily for the case of mandatory, that is, obligatory, moral rules. Such rules are accepted by a group when (a) there is in that group a standard constituted by convergent conduct of some sort; (b) deviations from that standard are considered as faults and occasions for justified criticism; and (c) 'at least some ... look upon the behaviour in question as a general standard to be followed by the group as a whole'.[14] This last point is the famous idea of the 'internal aspect' of rules, or the 'internal point of view' with respect to a rule. Note that the willingness to treat a rule as a standard does not depend on *approval*; one can be willing to use a norm one despises

---

[12] Hart, *Law, Liberty and Morality*, 22.
[13] Ibid., 255.
[14] Hart, *The Concept of Law*, 56.

and which one would replace if only one could.[15] Sometimes Hart hints at a further condition: a norm is accepted only if it also functions as a *shared* standard, for example as a matter of 'common knowledge' among us: I know that you accept it; you know that I do; I know *that*; and so on.[16]

There are difficulties with all this as an account of customary rules, and further difficulties in treating it as a necessary condition for the existence of obligation-imposing rules. The only points we need here, however, are less controversial. The existence of a morality depends not only on a degree of behavioural conformity but also on the actual beliefs and attitudes (towards both beliefs and conduct) that prevail in a community of people. Norms of social morality within that community change only when those beliefs and attitudes change.

One further point. Like law, morality contains obligations, but like law it also contains other kinds of norms, including directives, permissions, and powers, and some of these are norms that regulate the operation and enforcement of the other norms. A social morality is not just a long list of do's and don'ts. It includes norms telling us when it is permissible to enforce the norms on its list. Every social morality has its own doctrine of tolerance, be it mean or generous. So we should not think of social morality as a set of imperious commands accepted as binding in a community. A tolerant society is one with a tolerant social morality, and if that is what ideal morality requires of that society, there can be cases in which moral improvement is a matter of removing or limiting the effect of norms of social obligation.

4. Can Law Change Social Morality?

Everyone acknowledges that changes in social morality can change the law. In democracies, the halting conveyor belt of elections and plebiscites transmits public opinion in ways that try to direct and constrain legislators. Social morality also reaches the law through judicial decisions—an even less reliable mechanism. Although judges may not know the price of a pint of milk,

---

[15] Hart suggests, at ibid., 61, that acceptance can be shown in one's *acquiescence* in a standard, but that is not consistent with 'using' it as a guide to conduct. This is a slip—at 117 the obedience of the masses is contrasted with acceptance, not offered as a possible example of acceptance.

[16] E.g. ibid., 102. On this sort of condition, see David Lewis, *Convention* (Harvard University Press, 1969). I put 'common knowledge' in scare quotes: it suffices for there to be nested mutual beliefs. They need not be true, and thus what is held in common need not be knowledge.

they do seem able to reckon the cost to their own prestige of getting wildly out of sync with public attitudes.

The reflection of social morality in law is generally imperfect, however, for a more structural reason. A legal system can exist without much popular buy-in; a social order composed only of customary norms cannot. A particular legal rule can exist provided only that it is identified as valid by basic ground rules accepted and practised by a fairly small group, that is, judges, legislators, police, and other officials. If they accept the ground rule that all validly enacted statutes are law, then such enactment is sufficient for law to exist. That is why there can be laws most people haven't heard of, and laws binding from the moment of their coming into force, before people are aware of them or have had a chance to form any attitude towards them. None of this holds for customary norms. There are no recognition rules validating customs: they exist only if they are practised. The social morality of a group must be something that many people, if not everyone, are aware of. Hence, there may be, and in most societies there is, a gap between the requirements of social morality and those of the law.[17] But the gap is variable and there are plenty of cases where it is narrowed by morality's influence on law. Albert Venn Dicey did not much like the common law's abandonment of the nineteenth-century virtues of Benthamite individualism nor its moving, and sometimes being shoved, towards the collectivist ideals of an emerging democratic society. But Dicey was right in thinking that part of the explanation for the transformation he deplored was a change of public morality in England.[18]

It is probably accepted that popular morality can cause such changes in the law. But what about the reverse? Can law bring changes in morality? I shall assume that law cannot change *ideal* morality except by changing social facts which, together with principles of ideal morality, justify positive norms. For example, it is not merely illegal to drive south down a one-way street that runs north; it is immoral, since it puts the lives of others at risk. Law can make any one-way street two-way, however, and then it would no longer be immoral to drive south. Here, law is not changing the moral principle that it is wrong needlessly to put other's lives at risk; it is changing which activities put other people's lives at risk. In social morality we see this kind of change all

---

[17] For evidence of a large gap between social morality and criminal law in the United States, see Paul H. Robinson and John Darley, *Justice, Liability, and Blame: Community Views and the Criminal Law* (Westview Press, 1995).

[18] Albert Venn Dicey, *Lectures on the Relation between Law and Public Opinion in England during the Nineteenth Century* (Richard Vande Wetering ed., Liberty Fund, 2008 [f.p. 1905]).

'87	'89	'90	'93	'95	'98	'99	'00	'03	'05	'06	'07	'10
75	69	69	65	56	52	50	47	41	40	34	38	30

Figure 10.1 Percentage who say homosexual relations are always or mostly wrong, by year (BSA)

the time. It is part of English social morality to give special respect to certain members of the royal family, but who counts as a member of the royal family has varied over the centuries and, after considerable bloodshed, is now regulated by statute. That is why Franz, Duke of Bavaria, gets no respect: even if he is in fact (as the remaining Jacobites suppose) the legitimate heir of James II, the claim of his Catholic ancestors to the British throne was terminated in 1701 by the Act of Settlement.

There are also more interesting sorts of moral metamorphosis. There can be changes to the evaluative and normative principles themselves. This is simply obvious. Modern moralities differ enormously from the tribal worlds of Leviticus and Deuteronomy or the heroic societies of the Odyssey and Beowulf. We have gone from thinking that an insult to familial honour is adequate justification for killing another, to thinking that would be plain murder; from thinking slavery is permissible and even natural, to holding it a grotesque assault on human dignity. These are not merely changes in the social facts on which morality operates, they are changes in social morality itself. Such changes can be dramatic and rapid. The British Social Attitudes survey records the following trend in contemporary moral attitudes towards homosexual conduct and relations.[19]

These figures show a steady and significant decline in the proportion of those that think that homosexual conduct and relationships are wrong, from three-quarters to less than one-third. Note that this is not a rise in British *tolerance* of homosexuality: to tolerate something is to think that it should be permitted notwithstanding it is wrong or deficient. Figure 10.1 shows a decline in the belief that homosexuality *is* wrong or deficient. This and other changes in attitudes to sexual conduct are among the most prominent moral innovations of recent times. So it is not open to doubt that social morality changes. What causes that? At the proximal level, people's morals change when they come to have different beliefs and attitudes and are thus disposed

---

[19] The raw data are available at <https://www.bsa.natcen.ac.uk/>.

to act (and judge) differently in response to actual or hypothetical situations. But what causes *that*? All sorts of things. We lack a general account of the springs of moral change, but the growth of scientific knowledge, the wider circulation of information, transformations in the means of economic production, increasing population density, and the mobility of people must all be high on the list. What about changes in the law?

The idea that law might change the hearts and minds of its subjects, and not merely incentivize their conduct, is sometimes met with derision. (Or at any rate it is when people have in mind changes for the better; it seems easier for them to believe that law can change attitudes for the worse.) But I am aware of only three grounds for thinking law *must* be morally inert: there is an argument from the socially constitutive character of morality, an argument from the necessary content of law, and an argument from the lack of a normative power of moral change. Let me dispose of them in turn.

At points, Devlin hints that every society is strongly constituted by its core moral values, so that were they to alter, it would bring a change not in, but *of*, a society.[20] If that were true, law could not change social morality because that is always the morality of some group of people, and on the strongly constitutive view any change in their morality would mean they were no longer the group they used to be. It is like the necessity for you to have had the very biological parents you actually had. If your parents had been different people, none of their children could have been you. Now, I do not know what all of the identity conditions for a human society are, but it is not plausible that *any* change in its accepted values must bring that society to an end. For one thing, the existence of a society also depends on things like the continuity of its population, its territory, its political institutions, and its sense of a common history. These can anchor its existence as its morality drifts. For another, a change in moral values would presumably bring the birth of a new society only if the values that changed were somehow central to the identity of that society. Perhaps a non-Zionist Israel that rejected the idea that it should be, in the words of its Basic Law, a 'Jewish and democratic state' would in *some* sense no longer be Israel. But whether or not this is true, it is incredible to suppose that, say, the United States would no longer be the same society without its familiar religiosity or attachment to free enterprise. The further one gets from values associated with established religions and ethnonationalisms the less plausible the constitutive case becomes. Does anyone

---

[20] Devlin, *The Enforcement of Morals*, 14–15.

really think that Figure 10.1 records the end of British society as we knew it? If those who occasionally indulge that rhetoric took it seriously it would be hard to see why they care about the change in the special way they do, for it happened to a society other than their own.

The second argument appeals not to the nature of a society but to the nature of law. An institutionalized set of norms is a legal system only if it regulates certain important human interests.[21] One of the reasons the rules of the National Hockey League do not amount to a legal system is that they are not *about* the right things. The hockey rules regulate one game, not the full range of morally significant interests that law addresses. Legal systems attempt to regulate these interests by supporting morality. For example, the law of homicide is there to prevent and punish murder, which is a serious moral wrong we have an interest in repressing. A system of rules that failed to regulate homicide (or agreements, property, the resort to violence, and the raising of children) would not be a legal system, or it would be a marginal case of one. But if law necessarily has a minimum moral content, how can it get away with changing morality? I do not think we should say that changing something is a way of supporting or securing it. The solution is simpler. The minimum content thesis requires that law attend to certain core moral interests by regulating the relevant conduct *in some way or other*. It does not require that it regulate it in a particular way, or in a good way.[22] The necessary content of law is a minimal content and is satisfied by a wide variety of legal regimes we actually find with respect to things like property, homicide, and familial obligations. It must be, for regimes encompassing these variants are undeniably legal systems: there is plainly law in societies as morally diverse as England, China, and Saudi Arabia. A legal system can change the way it regulates moral matters, and perhaps that can change what people in that society regard as morally acceptable with respect to those things. The minimum content thesis is no obstacle to this.

The third argument is Hart's. Social morality is composed of customary norms and, as we have seen above in Section 2, those are immune to deliberate change. 'It is characteristic of a legal system that new legal rules can be introduced and old ones changed or repealed by deliberate enactment... By contrast moral rules *cannot* be brought into being or changed in this way.'[23]

---

[21] See Chapter 8, this volume.
[22] It may be necessary that it *aim* or *attempt* to regulate these things well, but it can attempt and fail.
[23] Hart, *The Concept of Law*, 175.

CAN LAW CHANGE SOCIAL MORALITY? 263

There is no 'deliberate enactment' process for social morality; it has nothing on a par with legislative power. There is for social morality no act or omission the performance of which brings about a change in morality because it is undertaken with that intention and is generally known or accepted to have that effect. Unlike the first two claims this one is, strictly speaking, true. There is indeed no such power.[24] But what matters to our case is something else. Customary norms can shift gradually in response to intentional actions that change incentives or help create new meanings of certain acts. To push or nudge a society's morality along a new path is not to 'repeal' or 'overrule' its previous morality; but nothing of that order is needed in order to bring about moral change. Indeed, it is not even needed in order to bring about moral change intentionally. There is plenty of space for intentional influence in the gap between deliberate enactment on the one hand and simple mutation or random moral drift on the other. Hart is correct to say that customary norms cannot be changed *forthwith* by any act intended to produce such a change. However, they can and do change predictably, if gradually, in response to various intentional acts, including legislation. Nor does Hart deny that 'the enactment or repeal of laws may well be among the causes of a change or decay of some moral standard'.[25] He is sceptical only about how common this is, for he thinks 'very often, the law loses such battles with ingrained morality, and the moral rule continues in full vigour side by side with laws which forbid what it enjoins.'[26]

One thing that is not in doubt, however, is that law often *attempts* to shape social morality, and nowhere more overtly than through criminalization. Excepting perhaps for some regulatory offences, the creation of crimes normally aims to make people accept, or to take more seriously than they already do, the idea that the relevant delict is not only prohibited or officially disapproved, but wrong. (It would be bizarre, as well as unjust, to criminalize conduct while insisting that there is nothing at all wrong with it.) Here are just two current examples.

In the United States and elsewhere, lawmakers are trying to make people believe it is seriously immoral to infringe the artificial monopolies of

---
[24] In an inversion of Hart's argument, Neil MacCormick concludes that there must be informal rules of moral change, since there are rules of social morality and they change. He seems driven to this conclusion by an artificially narrow ideal of what social rules are (they must be crisp, clear, have canonical formulations, and so on) together with the implicit supposition that it would *take* a rule of change to change rules like that. Neither view is correct. See Neil MacCormick, *H.L.A. Hart* (2nd edn, Stanford University Press, 2008) 67–71.
[25] Hart, *The Concept of Law*, 176.
[26] Ibid., 177.

copyright. This attempts to shape social morality, not merely through the indirect effect of disincentives, but through the stigma that adheres to criminality. In the case of copyright infringement, the association of ideas they establish is striking. Monopoly-breaking is said to be *piracy*, an idea bearing allusions to marauding and violence, from the Caribbean to Mogadishu. Until legislators started pushing this line, it is unlikely that anyone thought of copyright infringement as theft, let alone piracy. Now, children eager to watch *The Lorax* must first endure this unskippable hectoring: 'the unauthorized reproduction or distribution of this copyrighted work is illegal. Criminal copyright infringement is investigated by federal law enforcement agencies and is punishable by up to 5 years in prison and a fine of $250,000.' There follows the military-looking logo of the National Intellectual Property Rights Coordination Center, and of the FBI, then finally the screaming banner, '*Piracy is not a victimless crime*'.

A second example. In Uganda, repressive and discriminatory legislation was introduced in its notorious Anti-Homosexuality Bill (which, before execution was dropped as a penalty, commonly went by the name 'The Kill the Gays Bill'). Even by local standards, the ferocity of Uganda's attack on gay people was barbaric. It had an interesting history. While it would be going too far to say that homophobia had no indigenous roots in that country, its character and virulence was cultivated, intentionally, by earlier colonial legislation. Moral attitudes in various countries fossilize a brutal period in the British law of sexual conduct, first transmitted via the Indian Penal Code and then extended to other imperial jurisdictions in Asia and Africa. 'Colonial legislators and jurists introduced such laws, with no debates or "cultural consultations," to support colonial control', a credible history comments. 'They believed laws could inculcate European morality into resistant masses.'[27]

In such ways—and of course in many more beneficent ways as well—lawmakers attempt to change social morality. They may end up disappointed, but they are not systematically deceived in what they are about. It may be that law sometimes loses its battles with ingrained morality on certain topics. Paul Robinson and his collaborators offer some evidence of which topics these are likely to be.[28] They find that some values relevant to crime and punishment

---

[27] Human Rights Watch, *This Alien Legacy: The Origins of 'Sodomy' Laws in British Colonialism* (Human Rights Watch, 2008) 5.

[28] Paul H. Robinson and Robert Kurzban, 'Concordance and Conflict in Intuitions of Justice' (2007) 91 *Minnesota Law Review* 1829; Paul H. Robinson and John M. Darley, 'Intuitions of Justice: Implications for Criminal Law and Justice Policy' (2007) 81 *Southern California Law Review* 1.

are invariant among different demographic groups. Here is a trivial example: men and women, the native-born and immigrants, the young and the old, the atheist and the fundamentalist, all pretty much agree that murder is wrong and deserves the most serious criminal sanction. More interestingly, there is social agreement on the *relative* blameworthiness of a range of offences, especially those involving physical aggression, theft, or deception in business dealings. Amid moral diversity and flux there is an area of homogeneity and stability. Perhaps this provides support for Devlin's claim: 'the Englishman's hundred religions about which Voltaire made his jibe gave rise to no differences in morals grave enough to affect the criminal law.'[29] Robinson's conjecture is that, if moral views remain invariant in the face of what are ordinarily powerful social forces pressing in various directions, the chances of them being either reasoned in origin or malleable by law are not very good. His normative recommendation is that law reformers had better reconcile themselves to these facts.

This evidence is suggestive, though the interpretation may exaggerate fixity even with the 'core' area. The existence of a demographically invariant, synchronic core of values does not show that there can be no law-induced *diachronic* change in those values. It shows that we should expect any such change to affect demographic sub-groups in similar ways. It would take a more historical study to exclude that possibility. And agreement on a relative ranking of the seriousness of wrongdoing does not show that people concur on *how* wrong these things are in cardinal terms, and it is the absolute wrongness of conduct, not its wrongness relative to something else, that is relevant to whether it should be criminalized in the first place. Most would agree that it is worse for referees to lie about the merits of university applicants than it is for them to break lunch dates, but neither should be a criminal offence. People's moral views about the propriety of criminalizing conduct can change while leaving their relative rankings of seriousness intact.

In any event, the Robinson–Darley studies also show that there are many moral issues of which the criminal law takes charge that are *not* in the core and *are* subject to demographic variation.[30] This is true of the perceived permissibility of abortion, which in almost all Western countries is tightly correlated with religious affiliation. It also proves true of many sexual offences

---

[29] Devlin, *The Enforcement of Morals*, 87.
[30] Robinson and Kurzban, 'Concordance and Conflict in Intuitions of Justice'. And see further evidence of cross-cultural variation in Donald Braman, Dan M. Kahan, and David A. Hoffman, 'Some Realism about Punishment Naturalism' (2010) 77 *Chicago Law Review* 1532.

266 SHOULD LAW IMPROVE MORALITY?

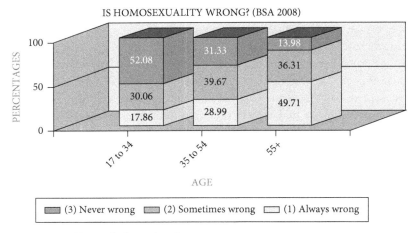

Figure 10.2 Homophobic values by age

that do not involve aggression or violence.[31] Attitudes to the nature and validity of consent to sex, to the permissibility of homosexual conduct, to prostitution, and to the wrongs of obscenity vary systematically by a number of demographic and cultural characteristics. One simple but striking illustration, using the same data as in Figure 10.1, is the age-cohort effect exhibited in Figure 10.2.

Figure 10.2 shows that in Britain, as in many Western countries, moralized hostility to homosexuality is increasingly a trait of the old.[32] This marks a dramatic change in our social morality, for people now often say that being gay is simply 'not a moral issue'. They see no more moral significance in people's preferences in the sex of their romantic partners than in the way those preferences vary by race or wealth.[33] Attempting to revive the sense of *wrongdoing* that used to attach to homosexuality would now be like trying to breathe life

---

[31] And also drunk driving, alcohol, and drugs offences: Robinson and Kurzban, 'Concordance and Conflict in Intuitions of Justice'.
[32] Teenage boys are notorious for bullying gay youth, but this does not show they think homosexuality *immoral*. A more likely explanation is that they find it threatening to their emerging psycho-sexual identities. See Carissa M. Froyum, '"At Least I'm Not Gay": Heterosexual Identity Making among Poor Black Teens' (2007) 10 *Sexualities* 603; and, more optimistically, Mark McCormack and Eric Anderson, '"It's Just Not Acceptable Any More": The Erosion of Homophobia and the Softening of Masculinity at an English Sixth Form' (2010) 44 *Sociology* 843.
[33] On the loss of salience, see Leslie Green, 'Sexuality, Authenticity, and Modernity' (1995) 8 *Canadian Journal of Law and Jurisprudence* 67. This shows, by the way, why disagreement about the law of abortion is different: neither those who favour a permissive regime nor those who favour a restrictive one regard control over pregnancy and childbearing as 'not a moral issue'.

CAN LAW CHANGE SOCIAL MORALITY? 267

into the moral attitudes that once attended violation of the sumptuary laws. (So as not to attract bad luck, I should make clear this is meant to suggest counter-reformation is unlikely, not impossible.)

How far should we impute causal responsibility for the changes recorded in Figures 10.1 and 10.2 to law and, especially, to the decriminalization of homosexual conduct? Robinson and Darley suggest that: 'Criminal law is perhaps unique in its ability to inform, shape, and reinforce social and moral norms on a society-wide level.'[34] Law is assuredly not the only thing that had an effect: scientific discoveries, the increased visibility of gay people, sympathetic media portrayals, and wider knowledge of the history of our moral attitudes were also important. Still, the idea that law had nothing to do with it is a bare dogma. The decriminalization of homosexual conduct beginning in the late 1960s, the rise of anti-discrimination law protecting gay people in the 1980s, and the massive changes in family law by the new millennium or so proved remarkably contagious among liberal (and putatively liberal) societies. By 2013 even right-wing Republicans in the United States had come round. It is widely conceded that criminalization can stigmatize an activity; why doubt that decriminalization can do the opposite?

It is worth bearing in mind here the point noted in Section 3 above: a social morality does not depend for its existence on general *compliance* with that norm. It is enough that there is a disposition to certain kinds of critical response to breaches of the norm, possibly including internal criticism. A drug or alcohol abuser demonstrates their loyalty to the norm that one should remain clean and sober, not by abstinence, but by secrecy and guilt whilst abusing. Similarly, there is an important transformation of social morality when homophobic or racist jokes are no longer felt to be publicly acceptable, even if some still laugh at them in private or, more usually, in secret. And the willingness to indulge these slurs now marks someone as socially marginal—for instance, as not *ministrable*—a mammoth change in our social morality.

These conjectures about the moral impact of law need more evidence than I can offer, and they do not overturn the sensible view that law sometimes leads and sometimes follows. But before leaving the general point I want to underscore one further thing. Nothing I have argued assumes that decisions

---

[34] Robinson and Darley, 'Intuitions of Justice', 28. See also the seminal study by Nigel Walker and Michael Argyle, 'Does the Law Affect Moral Judgments?' (1963) 4 *British Journal of Criminology* 570; and, more recently, Eric A. Posner, *Law and Social Norms* (Harvard University Press, 2002), and the sources cited therein.

of *appeals courts* are the only or best place to look for evidence of law's power to shape morality. Their role varies amongst countries and according to the prestige of the particular court. Gerald Rosenberg argues that looking to the American courts as agents of social change (let alone moral change) is a 'hollow hope': they work within institutional and political constraints that make them inherently conservative.[35] Madison called the judiciary the 'least dangerous' branch of government, and that is because he thought his judiciary was the least powerful branch. The other branches may well have more independent moral influence, though courts could also have influence indirectly, through their influence on those who are more independently influential. But the influence of American judges and litigators is not our issue. Which legal actors are most influential in an area of morality (and, as I shall argue, which laws are most influential) are matters that vary a lot amongst societies and historical periods.

5. Should Law Change Social Morality?

The fact that social morality can be morally deficient and that law may be able to change it does not show that it should do so in a general or in a particular case. There are conservative arguments against law-induced moral change, and we should test their force.[36] I am going to reject one utilitarian argument for conserving social morality as well as two arguments based on values in the neighbourhood of legality or the rule of law. Some other conservative considerations prove more plausible but are only weak constraints.

If you are willing to endorse the thesis that any desire whatever has a claim to satisfaction, you will probably find something in favour of upholding existing moral practices whatever they may be: people want it. Indeed, because a social morality requires buy-in from many people, upholding what exists is likely to find a lot of favour. We need not go so far as Devlin's hysterical worry that unless we enforce all fervently held moral norms we are headed

---

[35] Gerald N. Rosenberg, *The Hollow Hope: Can Courts Bring About Social Change?* (2nd edn, University of Chicago Press, 2008).

[36] By 'conservative' I mean morality-conserving, not 'right-wing'. As Karl Marx saw, many right-wing views are morally revolutionary. The first chapter of the *Communist Manifesto* memorably proclaims that as the bourgeoisie revolutionize production, 'All fixed, fast-frozen relations, with their train of ancient and venerable prejudices and opinions, are swept away, all new-formed ones become antiquated before they can ossify. All that is solid melts into air, all that is holy is profaned, and man is at last compelled to face with sober senses his real conditions of life, and his relations with his kind.'

SHOULD LAW CHANGE SOCIAL MORALITY? 269

for social disintegration. The fact that a society's values are generally thought important and enjoy broad support will produce a headwind in the face of moral change.

Perhaps there are still a few utilitarians and economists who approve without qualification the satisfaction of any desire whatever, but there can't be many. Desires based on fantasy and error, and desires to hurt and humiliate others, are desires that we desire to eliminate, not satisfy. A more plausible view acknowledges that we need to consider the origin and character of our desires, and that in some cases we should decline to satisfy them.[37] Even if the crude utilitarian thesis were acceptable, however, it would be of little assistance here. For there are also *other* people to consider—people outside the moral majority—and their desires may conflict with those of the consensus. We have no reliable way to measure whether the setback to one person's desire-satisfaction is outweighed by the advance of another's. Nor do we think that a minute gain to each of a sufficiently large number of people always justifies imposing enormous losses on a few. In mundane, single-person cases, we do normally allow people to satisfy their own desires, but when they are expecting legal help in realizing their ambitions, the standard is commensurately higher. We need only suppose that existing social morality is bad *enough* to have a justification for improving it by any effective means.

A different conservative argument appeals to rule-of-law values, either through judicial obligation or through the conditions for the perceived legitimacy of the legal system. Courts have a duty to settle cases by applying existing law—this is the most elementary idea of what it is to be ruled by law. In some legal systems, this may require that they apply (existing) social morality for it, like any other social custom, can be a formal source of law, certified as such by the rule of recognition. Even when morality is not a binding source it is often a permissive one, as illustrated in abundant judicial references to 'our values' and to 'common sense'. These ideas lie behind much of Devlin's argument. In one of those passages that infuriate philosophers but strike many judges as unremarkable, Devlin writes, 'after centuries of debate, men of undoubted reasoning power and honesty of purpose have shown themselves unable to agree on what the moral law should be, differing sometimes upon the answer to the simplest moral problem'.[38] A judge should therefore give

---

[37] For theories of this sort, see Richard B. Brandt, *A Theory of the Good and the Right* (Oxford University Press, 1979) 110–29 and Robert E. Goodin, *Utilitarianism as a Public Philosophy* (Cambridge University Press, 1995) 132–48.
[38] Devlin, *The Enforcement of Morals*, 93.

weight to positive morality because, 'as a guide to the degree of definition required by the law-maker the method [of appeal to ideal morality] is valueless'.[39] But the scope and significance of moral disagreement is itself a matter of disagreement, and positive morality can itself be equivocal. Where social morality becomes part of the law, it usually does so through the recognitional practices of judges. If that social morality is seriously defective, judges should change their recognitional practices if they can and violate their judicial obligations if they cannot. This suggestion elicits horrified reactions from those so devoted to the ideal of legality that they think judges should always apply existing law *no matter what*. But that view is unacceptable, and pretence of accepting it is sustained only by fancy arguments that purport to show that, properly interpreted, the law is always worth applying. A more plausible view is that legality is one value among others, not to be discarded lightly, but neither to be pursued at the expense of all other things law should attend to. If judges did not accept that, we would not want them on the bench. When social morality is radically defective, it should not be applied at all. Over time, judicial refusal to do so can lead to a change in the rule of recognition, and even to a change that retrospectively validates the initial refusal.

What is at stake here is an essentially sound idea: people should not have to consult a lawyer to get through daily life, and they should not be subject to too many conflicting demands. Other things being equal then, law and social morality should speak with one voice. The presumption that everyone knows the law rests on a fiction, but the idea that people can be expected to know what their morality requires of them rests, as we have seen, on the nature of social morality: were it not generally known (and, thus, knowable) it would not *be* the accepted morality of a group. So that is a reason to avoid law-morality gaps where we can, and a reason for law to track norms people can be expected to know independently of the law. But, again, this is not an absolute requirement. When the demands of social morality are sufficiently immoral, we should either learn to live with the gap or try to close it some other way.

This point is, I think, given insufficient weight by Paul Robinson and John Darley.[40] Reviewing a range of empirical evidence, they find that, although there is a core of social agreement about the seriousness of offences, American law does not always match it. What to do about the divergence?

---

[39] Ibid. Here, 'law-makers' include judges who apply general rules to particular cases, and who settled doubtful points by the exercise of their discretion.
[40] Robinson and Darley, 'Intuitions of Justice'.

Bring the law into line, they suggest. They think it is good for law to be able to regulate without a lot of enforcement, so they favour it matching social morality at least in 'core' areas. The criminal law in the United States does not now do this: electoral politics, they argue, and not social morality, produces disasters like the 'three strikes' statutes, draconian penalties for drugs offences, and vast over-criminalization. It would be better to go with people's intuitive judgements about criminal deserts: 'The criminal law can most effectively maximize its moral credibility and thereby minimize resistance and subversion by adopting criminal rules that track shared community intuitions of justice.'[41]

What is the 'moral credibility' of law, and why should we try to maximize it? I assume they mean the de facto authority of law, or its legitimacy in the Weberian sense: the willingness of its subjects to take the law as binding. What Robinson and Darley do not explain, however, is why we should care about *that*. The nearest they get is in their claim that 'effective long-term control of crime' requires doing justice as the community sees it, 'thereby building the criminal law's moral credibility in order to harness the powerful forces of internalized norms and social influence'.[42] But this just arcs back in a circle. Controlling crime is an important goal only when the conduct controlled was appropriately criminalized in the first place. If law is morally decent then it is good that it enjoy credibility. If law merits the authority it has, then we do want it to be stable and to function without much coercive intervention. This holds also where the law, though defective, is morally tolerable. But where the law is seriously defective, the last thing we want to do is shore up its moral credibility—we want to undermine it. Where social morality is morally much worse than the law, we should not fix a credibility deficit by making the law worse; we should try to make morality better. Since Robinson and Darley do not deny, and indeed they stress, the power of law to shape norms, it is unclear why they think that maximizing law's moral credibility by matching social morality should be an independent general aim.

I do not want to leave this issue by giving the impression that there is nothing to be said on the conservative side. There is: but it is a more modest case than either the utilitarian argument or rule of law arguments suggest. It rests on two main considerations:

---

[41] Ibid., 28.
[42] Ibid., 43.

(1) Law may have the power to improve morality, but only at a morally unacceptable cost. We need not think of anything as dramatic as tyranny or mind-control. Resort to the ordinary machinery of government, including law, comes with costs and opportunity costs, and these can overwhelm the expected benefits. Moreover, law can leave a legalistic imprint on the morality it shapes and that can be regrettable. We do not want people thinking of all promises as contracts, or of their spousal obligations being only those that family law enforces. We do not want people thinking that anything that is not unlawful under the tax code is perfectly fair. Where there is a tendency for people to take minimally lawful behaviour as establishing a social norm, we should be cautious in trying to improve social morality by mapping law onto morality.

(2) An actually existing social morality, though imperfect, may nonetheless be morally adequate.[43] Since change normally has costs associated with it, and since success is rarely guaranteed, there is nothing wrong with leaving alone what is good-enough. And even if what exists is inadequate, the requirements of social morality may fall within a margin of appreciation that acknowledges that social groups, like individuals, can have rights to do things that are to some degree wrong. Devlin's suggestion that all (strongly held) norms of a morality are worth supporting is incorrect, but a more limited deference seems sound, at least when it is a tolerable part of the fabric of a society. It would be a mistake to make the perfect the enemy of the good-enough, especially when the good-enough actually exists and is an environment that gives structure and meaning to people's lives, while the perfect is just somebody's theory.[44]

It is obvious that these considerations will have force at the margin, but also that they are only weakly conservative. They do not add up to a general case for satisfying the desire to preserve social morality, or for maximizing the 'moral credibility' of law by bringing it into line with popular morality. Where that morality can clearly be improved by law, and where the two conservative conditions do not hold, there is no further reason for restraint.

---

[43] Understood as fully adequate, not as barely adequate.
[44] For a speculative general argument for the sort of the conclusion I have in mind, see G. A. Cohen, *Finding Oneself in the Other* (M. Otsuka ed., Princeton University Press, 2012) chap. 8. See also Chapter 2, this volume, on non-instrumental value in the instruments of law.

6. How Law Could Improve Sexual Morality

That completes the theoretical claims I advance here. They involve a mixture of conceptual and empirical points. We have seen something of what social morality is, of how it exists in a society, of how it can (and cannot) be changed, and of what role law could and should have in attempting to bring about such change. I conclude with an example, with one case where law could, I wager, significantly improve social morality, and where there are no good reasons against trying.

Hart and Devlin worked out their arguments in the territory of sexual offences. They did so in reaction to the UK Wolfenden Report of 1957, which recommended that private homosexual conduct between consenting adults should cease to be a criminal offence, and that prostitution, not itself illegal, should be regulated in its nuisance aspects, by increasing the penalties for soliciting, in order to 'clean up the streets'. These offences were a fair test case for the issue that divided them: whether the law should enforce social morality where the conduct deplored is not harmful. However, we are exploring, not the legal enforcement of morality, but the legal improvement of morality and, at least with respect to homosexuality, our social morality has already improved—thanks in part to the law. So let me instead venture some ideas about our social morality regarding consent to sex. The importance of the issue is evident: the only difference between ordinary sexual activity and intercourse on the one hand, and sexual assault and rape on the other, is consent. And consent can work this magic only when it is valid, that is, when there are moral reasons to hold that it works as advertised. The law has its views about the nature of consent, and about those reasons; so does our morality.

We will need a standard by which to assess our social morality of consent, and that requires nothing less than working out a theory of consent. I could not begin, let alone complete, that task in these concluding conjectures. So I will present a view, somewhat dogmatically, that I think is sound and hope that it will not seem implausible. If it strikes you as misguided, perhaps you can make adjustments so that at least the structure of my claims about how law could help will be intelligible if not, in that case, correct.

Here is what I take to be a sound account of consent to sexual activity.

- *Consent is agreement:* Consent to sex should be understood as a permission to engage in sexual activity, given by a performative utterance (or

other act or omission) that is undertaken with the intention of giving that permission.
- *Consent is given by publicly understood means*: What count as signs of consent, and the conditions under which consent is valid, should be matters of common knowledge between and among those engaging in sexual activity. A good way of ensuring that they are mutually understood by the parties is if they are publicly understood throughout the society.
- *Consent is valid only if voluntarily given by one with the capacity to agree*: Consent is a moral power whose function, here, is to allow people to shape their lives, so it should be regarded as invalid (and thus as not giving the relevant permission) when it cannot do that, for example, when it is procured by coercion, significant manipulation or deception, or from one who cannot understand the nature of sexual activity.

Each of these conditions requires elaboration and interpretation, and the first has sometimes been doubted. The most I can do here is clarify some features of each that will, I hope, suggest the attractions of the view and allay certain worries.[45]

The fact that consent is performative means that attitudes of approval on their own (e.g. the fact of enjoying sex) are not sufficient for consent, though of course they are normally concomitant with it. Consenting to sex is agreeing to it.[46] This also means that those who lack the capacity to perform the relevant act, or other acts which could give an omission performative significance, do not consent.[47] The publicity requirement ensures that those consenting are on the same wavelength about what they are doing. Consent norms should minimize crossed-signals and misunderstandings, whether or not these are culpable. This does not itself require shared understandings among the whole community—two people may have their own mutually understood signs of permission—but sustaining community-wide norms is important to people who do not yet have an established relationship, and as

---

[45] For a more substantial performative account, see Alan Wertheimer, *Consent to Sexual Relations* (Cambridge University Press, 2003).
[46] And I do mean agreeing, not forming *an agreement* in the sense of striking a bargain. What I have in mind is recognized in English law: 'a person consents if he agrees by choice, and has the freedom and capacity to make that choice.' Sexual Offences Act 2003 (UK) s. 74.
[47] This does not mean that consent must be 'expressed through behaviour' or that consent cannot be given in secret, as Douglas Husak seems to assume, in 'The Complete Guide to Consent to Sex: Alan Wertheimer's *Consent to Sexual Relations*' (2006) 25 *Law and Philosophy* 267, 264–77. Under special conditions, silence can give consent. I return to this below.

a default for everyone else. The final condition, requiring certain cognitive capacities and voluntariness, is the site of familiar controversies. In its essential spirit, however, it is unavoidable if we value our capacity to make our own lives, to engage, as Mill put it, in 'framing the plan of our own life to suit our own character'.[48] Some people want a life that includes a lot of sex; some want a life that includes none; but whoever wants sex wants enough control over who they have sex with, when they have it, and what kind of sex they have; so that it fits their plan of life, and suits their character. This is what the final condition aims to secure.

As I said, that is an ideal for sexual morality and it needs a proper defence. But if it is even close to right, as I think it is, our social morality of sex is multiply defective. And this is not news. Whether or not our societies actually embody a 'rape culture',[49] their moralities are flawed in ways that are obviously sexist and, because of that, significantly limit the power of women to plan their lives. The asymmetrical character of the flaws is important. Apart from men in prison and boys under the control of religious institutions, it is girls and women who are most at risk of rape and sexual victimization.[50] Women who have not been, and may never be, victims of rape nonetheless modify their lives for fear of it, or because their parents fear it. They feel obliged to avoid certain places, to be careful going out at certain times, to give thought to how their dress and manner will be received—in general, to remain unwillingly vigilant. Few men have experiences that are remotely similar.

It is easy to see how our social morality fails to prevent much of this and, in some respects, actually supports it. Our morality associates consent to sex and enjoyment of sex. People often project onto others their own feelings about what is or would be enjoyable. A man who thinks he would enjoy having sex with a particular woman may imagine she would enjoy having sex with him. He may think that, once sex is initiated, she will enjoy it and will therefore have consented to it. Ordinary social morality is also too casual about whether there is any shared understanding about the signs of consent.

---

[48] Mill, *On Liberty*, chap. 1.
[49] Catharine MacKinnon, *Towards a Feminist Theory of the State* (Harvard University Press, 1989) 148. And more generally: Susan Estrich, *Real Rape* (Harvard University Press, 1984) and Stephen J. Schulhofer, *Unwanted Sex: The Culture of Intimidation and the Failure of Law* (Harvard University Press, 1998).
[50] My comments in this section are restricted to the heterosexual context. Gay men, and women, are raped or sexually assaulted by people of the same sex, yet we still need to think differently about sexuality and its morality in homosexual contexts. I defend that view in Leslie Green, 'Pornographies' (2000) 8 *Journal of Political Philosophy* 27.

Thirty years of public argument about date-rape and 'token refusal' have scarcely changed our mores. Even in the face of vigorous debate and education campaigns we still lack settled public norms about how these situations should be understood. Yet except for the rarest cases, men can avoid raping women with a simple question. Is it really the context-dependence and complexity of words like 'No' that prevent this? More often it is nothing more than embarrassment or fears about what might 'kill the mood'. Finally, our social morality is insufficiently attentive to the voluntariness of consent. The point has been made many times: far too much coerced or manipulated sex is socially tolerated. (Recall that a social morality includes not only norms of obligation, but also norms of restraint and tolerance.)

It is tempting to think that if other social forces had so little effect on our morality law is likely to do no better, and that the most we can hope for is decent rape laws seriously enforced. I am not so sure. Although the law of sexual assault varies significantly, in many jurisdictions it still shows the influence of the old common law view that found rape only when there was also force or the threat of it, and which was willing to excuse many mistaken beliefs as to consent, some of them ludicrous. So our first thought may be to reform those laws, and the hope that the stigma of criminalization will eventually and indirectly shape our morality. Rape shield laws restrict evidence of the complainant's past sexual history; we may hope that eventually supports the norm that consent is to be an actual agreement, on every occasion. So too of evidentiary presumptions, for instance that those who were subject to threats, or who were drugged, abducted, or unconscious did not consent, and also the requirement that only reasonable mistakes as to consent can exculpate.[51] And to the extent that decent legal standards can be made widely known, we can hope they will support the requirement that standard signs of consent be publicly known.

I do not think we know how effective rape reform law is, or even could be, in changing our social morality of sex. But thinking that *only* rape law stands a chance of shaping attitudes to rape is no better than jurisprudential homeopathy. In fact, it may be that the most influential laws in shaping our social morality here will not be the laws of rape at all. For example, since consent functions through performatives, other laws could protect what are sometimes called the 'felicity conditions' for those acts. They could help ensure, for instance, that refusals are taken seriously, and are actually heard as refusals.

---

[51] Sexual Offences Act 2003 (UK)

The law of obscenity is sometimes charged with this task. Rae Langton argues that the availability of pornography silences women, because it has the power to change the very ground rules of communication so that men will not even recognize 'no' as a refusal.[52] I doubt that pornography has that much power, or that kind of power, but the general idea that we should look beyond the law of rape for resources to improve our sexual morality about rape seems promising. We should not assume that only like cures like: a wide variety of legislative initiatives can shore up the background conditions we are concerned about, including discrimination laws, workplace harassment laws, and fairer work–family policies. (I would bet on equal pay legislation having greater power to mould our social morality of sex in desirable directions than I would on anything in the law of obscenity.)

Dan Kahan finds some experimental evidence that the variation in people's perceptions of facts, including facts about the interpretation of terms like 'no', is closely related to their moral outlooks.[53] The influence of these outlooks seems powerful, for people will judge hypothetical fact situations as showing consent or not by appeal to those outlooks, even in the face of express instruction to apply a particular normative standard. Perhaps judicial instructions to juries are no more successful. This may make us worry that these aspects of morality will not budge, certainly not by dint of orders to budge them. We already knew that, however: the very idea is too close to the notion that there are rules of change for customary morality, and we saw in Section 3 that there are none. But here we should keep in mind the Robinson–Darley point: demographic variation suggests that moral views do respond to social forces. We know that legal change produces moral results in at least one area. Nothing is more condemned by our morality than a sexual interest in youth under the age of consent. That age has varied historically, and in step with it our understandings of exploitation, perversion, and so on.[54] Interestingly, our attitudes respond less to variations in the average age of sexual maturity

---

[52] Rae Langton, *Sexual Solipsism: Philosophical Essays on Pornography and Objectification* (Oxford University Press, 2009). For some doubts, see Leslie Green, 'Pornographizing, Subordinating, and Silencing', in R. Post ed., *Censorship and Silencing: Practices of Cultural Regulation* (Getty Research Institute, 1998) 285–311.

[53] Dan M. Kahan, 'Culture, Cognition, and Consent: Who Perceives What, and Why', in Acquaintance-Rape Cases' (2010) 158 *University of Pennsylvania Law Review* 729. In an experimental setting what matters most in determining whether people will judge that 'no' can mean 'yes' is what Kahan calls their 'cultural style'—roughly, how conservative and sexist they are. The results are as one would expect, except perhaps for the fact that older, sexist *women* are the group *most* likely to think 'no' sometimes mean 'yes'.

[54] Matthew Waites, *The Age of Consent: Young People, Sexuality, and Citizenship* (Palgrave Macmillan, 2005).

(which has been falling) than they do to the legal age of consent (which has been rising). That is at least one case where the law clearly shapes our morality of consent, by drawing lines to which our morality stands ready to assign huge significance.[55]

So much for empirical guesswork. What of the moral objections to attempting to change morality by legal intervention? In this case they are weak. The law of rape belongs to the 'minimum content' of a legal system, and to what Robinson and Darley call the 'core' offences: if there are costs associated with properly regulating it, they are costs a decent society must pay. A more frequently voiced objection is a concern about making our sexual morality too legalistic. We hear that proposed reforms to rape laws that provide wider definitions of rape, add categories of sexual assault, create evidentiary presumptions and all the rest, will render ordinary, spontaneous sex impossible. We will feel it unsafe to kiss without a contract, preferably in writing and witnessed. Of course, this is just a crazy exaggeration; but it comes from a sensible source. Whatever our morality of consent should be, it needs to work in the ordinary circumstances of human sexual interaction. But the hope that law can nudge morality towards a greater publicity in signs of consent is consistent with this. We are aiming for circumstances in which it 'goes without saying' what 'no' and 'yes' mean—and if we do get to that point then consent can sometimes go unsaid. In the right context and subject to the right conditions, silence can give valid consent and an omission can be as good a performative as an act. The catch is in securing the right conditions.

The other valid conservative argument has it that we should preserve a good-enough morality that is part of the fabric of our society. Our ordinary morality of sexual consent is *nowhere* near good enough for this to hold; it is scarred by intolerable sexism. Nor are there any sane arguments for group sovereignty that could sustain this as a kind of collective right to do wrong. For example, so far as I am aware, there are no longer any rape-tolerant religions—at least not officially–who claim rape as among their rights of conscience.[56] There are, it is true, religions that repudiate the ideal of autonomy

---

[55] And this affects teens themselves. The Sexual Offences Act forbids anyone under 16 *any* sort of sexual activity; not only sexual intercourse but also 'sexual 'touching' ('with any part of the body' or 'with anything else', and 'through anything'.) Guidance to the Crown Prosecution Service, however, suggests that under-16s should not be prosecuted for consensual sex. The unenforced prohibition is therefore presumably supposed to 'send a message'. But what, and to whom?

[56] Why 'no longer?' See Deuteronomy 22:28–29; Numbers 31:18, Judges 19:2. Why 'not officially?' That question answers itself, as tens of thousands of raped and sexually abused children could testify and, we may hope, someday will.

that underpins the view of consent I sketched above. They provide some of the most overt and powerful support for sexist moral norms in the modern world. All the assertive metaphors some philosophers like to deploy about the 'authority' of pornography to command the allegiance of men, or to 'silence' women, are literal truths when it comes to these religions. And this brings us back to the cultural and moral conflicts I mentioned at the outset.

Law can and should improve morality, though it will often have to do so by indirection. Those who remind us that none of this can be counted on are correct. But there is evidence of occasional success, so perhaps we may allow ourselves a little optimism. After all, the most important changes in our morality in the last century or two—the repudiation of chattel slavery, the rise of the view that individuals have rights even against their lawful sovereigns, and the idea men and women are moral equals—were not mere 'changes' in our morality, on a par with the evolution in spoken English or shifts in fashions of dress. They were changes *brought about* intentionally if indirectly by people who protested, boycotted, wrote pamphlets, preached sermons, and organized unions—but also by people who voted, legislated, and litigated. In doing so they changed the law, and in changing the law they helped change our morality. It could happen again.[57]

---

[57] For comments and criticism, I thank Michelle Dempsey, Antony Duff, Massimo Renzo, and especially Donald Dripps, whose question provoked me to write this paper.

III
THE DEMANDS OF LAW

11
Hume on Allegiance

1. Facts and Principles in Politics

David Hume offers two contrasting thoughts about the bearing of empirical facts on principles of political morality. One is his famous idea that there is some sort of gap between 'is' and 'ought'. Hume says writers move silently from premises about what is the case to conclusions about what ought to be case without giving any reason for 'what seems altogether inconceivable, how this new relation can be a deduction from others, which are entirely different from it'.[1] Hume's second thought is different. He says that empirical facts about common opinion constitute a decisive standard of correctness for moral principles:

> though an appeal to general opinion may justly, in the speculative sciences of metaphysics, natural philosophy, or astronomy, be deemed unfair and inconclusive, yet in all questions with regard to morals, as well as criticism, there is really no other standard, by which any controversy can ever be decided.[2]

It is not obvious how these thoughts can be reconciled. Admittedly, there is logical space between them. The idea that common opinion is the only standard of correctness in morality does not say that moral conclusions can be 'deduced' from premises about opinions. Their relation could, for example, be evidential.[3] However, Hume's thesis is not merely that general

---

[1] *Treatise* 3.1.1.27, References to Hume's works are given as follows: *Treatise* = *Treatise of Human Nature* (L. A. Selby-Bigge ed., Clarendon Press, 1967); *Original Contract* = 'Of the Original Contract', in *Essays, Moral Political, and Literary* (F. Miller ed., Liberty Classics, 1985); *Enquiry* = *Enquiry Concerning the Principles of Morals* (L. A. Selby-Bigge ed., 3rd rev. edn by P. H. Nidditch, Clarendon Press, 1975).

[2] *Original Contract*, 486.

[3] Compare J. S. Mill: 'the sole evidence it is possible to produce that anything is desirable, is that people do actually desire it. If the end which the utilitarian doctrine proposes to itself were not, in theory and in practice, acknowledged to be an end, nothing could ever convince any person that it was so.' *Utilitarianism*, chap. V (*Collected Works*, vol. X, 238) (University of Toronto Press, Toronto, 1969).

opinion is *some* sort of evidence in favour of a moral principle but that it is unique and decisive evidence. In 'natural philosophy, or astronomy' we appeal to empirical evidence, but we also know it is fallible and that theories answering to experience are underdetermined by experience. We give weight to things like coherence, consilience, and simplicity in judging their merits. Hume, who is aware of the infirmities of empirical observation, nonetheless gives one sort of observation, facts about 'general opinions', extraordinary weight in political morality. Consider his famous and much-admired criticisms of social contract theory.[4] In the *Treatise of Human Nature*, he writes:

> it being certain, that there is a moral obligation to submit to government, because everyone thinks so; it must be as certain, that this obligation arises not from a promise; since no one, whose judgment has not been led astray by too strict adherence to a system of philosophy, has ever dreamt of ascribing it to that origin.[5]

Similarly, in the essay, 'Of the Original Contract', Hume reaffirms that, 'nothing is a clearer proof, that a theory of this kind is erroneous, than to find, that it leads to paradoxes repugnant to the common sentiments of mankind, and to the practice and opinion of all nations and ages'.[6]

These are not the views of one who thinks common opinion is to political morality as fallible observations are to astronomy. Yet Hume's certainty about the failure of consent theory found favour with many empirically minded philosophers and political theorists. In this chapter, I dissent. Hume's great reliance on general opinion and his hostility to consent theory are mistaken. My criticisms nonetheless reflect an attitude to political philosophy that, like Hume's, is intended to be fact-sensitive and alert to the contingencies of political life. I will try to show that Hume's opposition to consent theory is an unforced error in his doctrine. I conclude with some thoughts about how far Hume really is an opponent of consent theory—there are some intriguing hints of a friendlier view.

---

[4] I shall refer to 'social contract theory' and 'consent theory' as rough equivalents, and set aside doctrines of hypothetical consent, which Hume did not consider. I also follow Hume in referring interchangeably to a duty to obey the rulers and a duty to obey the law.
[5] *Treatise*, 547.
[6] *Original Contract*, 486.

2. The Allocation of Authority

In his illuminating study of Hume's political thought, David Miller distinguishes four questions about political authority.[7] Three are normative: (1) What is the general justification for political authority? (2) What justifies the claim of particular people to authority over others? (3) What are the moral limits to anyone's authority? One is genealogical: (4) How do political authorities emerge? Here, I explore Hume's treatment of the allocation, justification, and genesis of authority, leaving to one side (as Hume himself largely does) questions about its limits.

I begin with allocation. It is here that Hume's theory is at its most perceptive and most radical, for he sees that many allocation rules in political morality—rules about who gets what, who is to suffer what, and who is entitled to do what—are at least partly arbitrary. In the contexts that Hume often has in mind, the question of *who* is entitled to rule is especially prominent. Charles I was not executed by extreme libertarians; James II was not deposed by an anarchist commune. The religious and dynastic conflicts of the seventeenth century were pre-eminently conflicts over who should rule, lethal conflicts among people who nonetheless agreed that their societies needed political authority, and sometimes even agreed on why that was so.

Hume's treatment of the rules allocating authority parallels his treatment of the rules of justice. Reason and experience are needed to understand why we need justice at all, but the particular rules we settle on are mostly creatures of sub-rational processes of imagination and fancy. The same applies to authority. The case for obedience to *someone or other* is susceptible to rational justification in terms of the benefits of a general disposition to obey. *Particular* rulers, however, are authorized by considerations not susceptible to that sort of justification:

> When we have been long accustom'd to obey any set of men, that general instinct or tendency, which we have to suppose a moral obligation attending loyalty, takes easily this direction, and chuses that set of men for its objects. 'Tis interest which gives the general instinct; but 'tis custom which gives the particular direction.[8]

---

[7] David Miller, *Philosophy and Ideology in Hume's Political Thought* (Oxford University Press, 1981) 78–9.
[8] *Treatise*, 556.

The relevant customs Hume considers are long possession, present possession, conquest, familial succession, and legislative designation. Two rules that appear in Hume's discussion of property, namely, accession and transference by consent, are absent in his discussion of authority. Have they no application here?

If accession is something like annexation it will be hard to distinguish from conquest, so maybe Hume considers it covered by that. The absence of consent is more difficult. Miller observes that one analogy to the transference of property by consent might be the case of a governor giving or bequeathing some of their territory to someone else. (This is close to Locke's idea that, when one inherits land, one inherits it encumbered with liabilities to those with authority over it.[9]) While this would be allocation of authority by consent of the governor, it would not be authority with the consent of the governed.

So the question arises: why shouldn't a consensual allocation of political control, by the governed, not be as much a 'law of nature' as the consensual transfer of property? Hume rejects the idea with a special ferocity. Not only is consent not even relevant to the justification of authority, express *dissent* is never sufficient to free one from a duty to obey. If one emigrates, one's original sovereign will continue to claim authority—and rightly so. If one wishes to be an independent hunter-gatherer in a remote forest, one will still be ruled—and rightly so. And if one wishes to replace the existing rulers with those to whom one is prepared to pledge fealty, one will be prosecuted for treason—and rightly so. Why are these consequences, on which Hume insists, right?[10] They are not certified by empirical evidence. Perhaps common opinion of the day knew that these things were *likely* to befall dissenters, but Hume offers no evidence to show that they were commonly believed *legitimate*. Exiles did not generally flee oppressive regimes thinking that, in attempting to escape, they were doing something wrong.

Hume's treatment of the allocation rules for authority has two independent weaknesses: (a) He fails to carry over to his analysis of authority an important (and, I think, correct) claim from his analysis of justice, namely, that the arbitrary character of many of the rules does not exclude, and may presuppose, a role for consent. (b) Hume's best reason for thinking that common opinion is

---

[9] John Locke, *Two Treatises of Government* (P. Laslett ed., Cambridge University Press, 1963) II, s. 73.
[10] *Original Contract*, 476; *Treatise*, 548.

decisive in answering the question of who should rule is a reason for thinking that consent is likely to emerge as such a rule.

2.1 Property and Authority

Hume holds that unless we could transfer property by consent, the institution of property would be defective and the virtue of justice less valuable. Ownership must be governed by general rules that guarantee stable, exclusive, individual control of resources. But allocation rules are arbitrary: they are largely determined, not by any calculation of private or public benefit, but by imagination and fancy. As a result, property is often ill-distributed from the point of view of human welfare: 'As these depend very much on chance, they must frequently prove contradictory both to men's wants and desires; and persons and possessions must often be very ill adjusted. This is a grand inconvenience, which calls for a remedy.'[11] The remedy is 'that obvious one, that possession and property shou'd always be stable, except when the proprietor consents to bestow them on some other person'. Transference by consent is justifiable because it allows for efficient redistribution of property; it keeps transaction costs low by avoiding violence; and it facilitates the division of labour. 'All of this requires a mutual exchange and commerce; for which reason the translation of property by consent is founded on a law of nature, as well as its stability without such a consent.'[12]

Jonathan Harrison is among Hume's contemporary admirers, and an astute commentator. He says that Hume's defence of ownership by consent 'is extremely straightforward, and can scarcely be quarrelled with', but also that Hume's criticism of authority by consent is 'absolutely conclusive'.[13] There is no contradiction in that pair of judgements. Still, Harrison does not consider whether Hume is entitled to treat property and authority differently in the way he does. Hume's case for being able to vary ownership by consent relies on the fact that without voluntary control a conventional allocation of property would leave resources 'ill adjusted' and 'contradictory to men's wants and desires'. Imagination and custom fix the customary allocation rules, but at the end of the day even the regime of property must answer to utility. I think we can go further. Without contractual powers to vary ownership it is doubtful

---

[11] *Treatise*, 514.
[12] Ibid.
[13] Jonathan Harrison, *Hume's Theory of Justice* (Oxford University Press, 1980) 112.

that we would tolerate some familiar acquisition rules (such as first possession), and doubtful that they would have emerged in the first place. This is an empirical conjecture. A society in which finders are fated to be keepers, and can never abandon or exchange their findings, is not a society in which a rule of first possession is likely to emerge or persist. Similarly, a society in which the right to rule cannot be deliberately assigned or re-allocated is not a society likely to develop a rule of authority by inheritance. (What if the next-in-line is demented?) Consistently with the general tenor of Hume's theory, consent to authority could function, as it does in his analysis of property, as a backstop presupposition that shapes and gives force to other rules.

2.2 Consent and Salience

Hume thinks that no principle for selecting authorities will stand up to rational scrutiny: descent, conquest, and divine right are all, in a way, fictions. A fiction can make a good allocation rule, however, if it secures popular support. This is the basic foundation for the view that common opinion is and ought to be the decisive factor in determining who should rule. But as Miller explains, custom or convention cannot give adequate direction unless there is a consensus on what it requires.[14] Each of the rules for allocating authority is subject to serious indeterminacy in itself and, when they conflict *inter se*, there is no rational ground for giving any of them priority. For these to be useful fictions it is necessary that they be commonly shared. Hence, the wise (philosophers, let's say) who are alert to their fictitious and indeterminate character should generally follow the more numerous opinions of the vulgar, both as to which rules for selecting authorities are binding, and also as to what those rules require in any particular case. Miller comments: 'It is no use the wise giving their allegiance to one man and the vulgar to another. So the main advice which Hume offers to the wise is that they should acquiesce in the beliefs formed by the vulgar, no matter how flimsy their basis may seem to be.'[15]

What this does not easily explain is why the numerous vulgar will not disagree amongst themselves about which rules pick out those whom we are to obey. One might suppose that, if the wise are few and the vulgar are many, the odds of homogeneity among the wise might be better, or that an elite

---

[14] Miller, *Philosophy and Ideology in Hume's Political Thought*, 90–1.
[15] Ibid., 91.

consensus on authority might be easier to sustain than a mass consensus. There are reasons the proletariat was thought to need a vanguard. In any case, if we are to indulge in *a priori* sociology, we should also consider whether any of the allocation rules has, owing to the intersection of its nature and human nature, a better chance of becoming a focus for common opinion than the others. Hume denies that people actually consent to the rule of their governors. Nonetheless, there are Humean reasons to think that, *if general consent were given* to the rule of a particular person, then that would prove an especially salient way to establish authority. Consent, in the relevant sense, is a deliberate, performative undertaking, and normally a public one. As such, it is likely to have a psychological immediacy and social power that, for example, a legalistic argument about someone's place in the chain of inheritance may lack. It is also likely to have greater salience than any philosophical argument about who, from the point of view of justice and right reason, deserves to rule. If we add to these empirical conjectures the normative thesis that only those who can actually perform the functions of governance have any right to rule, we are not far from the conclusion that only those who enjoy the consent of the governed have a right to rule—not via a transference of right, but via the creation of social salience.

3. Opinion and the Justification for Authority

Hume appeals to common opinion at two different points and in two different ways. He invokes it positively to establish the existence of an obligation to obey the rulers, and he invokes it negatively to undermine one competing justification for that obligation. Essentially, he argues:

(1) Everyone believes there is an obligation to obey.
(2) So everyone has an obligation to obey.
(3) But no one believes their obligation to obey rests on their own agreement.
(4) So everyone has an agreement-independent obligation to obey.

The move from (1) to (2) is the positive argument from common opinion, the move from (3) to (4) is the negative argument. Each consists of a factual premise—(1) and (3)—and some suppressed steps in support of a normative conclusion—(2) and (4). Let's begin with the more convincing of the two arguments.

3.1 The Negative Argument

The transition from (3) to (4) rests on a sound idea about voluntary obligations. They arise from acts intended to assume obligations. A voluntary obligation is not only an obligation that *results from* a voluntary action; it is an obligation *undertaken voluntarily*. If I (voluntarily) punch you in the nose, I get a duty to compensate or apologize. These are not voluntary obligations. A promise, on the other hand, is not merely a voluntary act that is a trigger for some other (non-voluntary) obligation of repair. The fact that a promissory obligation is undertaken, and known to be undertaken, in the belief that it will give rise to an obligation is essential to the reason for thinking it does that.[16] Why? Because it is valuable for people to be able to shape their world by conditioning certain obligations on their own desires and intentions. Exercise of this power leaves a trace among the beliefs of the agent. Someone unaware of having promised has not exercised the power to promise. True, they may have negligently or recklessly led others to rely on their conduct and may in consequence be bound to make good that reliance. But that may occur without the intention to incur obligations and even while planning to avoid them. Those are not voluntary obligations either: they are more tort-like than contract-like. Hume is therefore correct to say that 'no man can either give a promise or be restrain'd by its sanction and obligation unknown to himself.'[17]

It is true, of course, that voluntary obligations must rest on non-voluntary foundations: the duty to keep promises is not the result of any promise. Moreover, what counts as signs of consent need not be, and generally are not, themselves the products of consent. So it is possible for someone to give what is generally and correctly taken to be a promise yet be unaware that they have done so. Whether people should be held to such utterances may be open to doubt. But those who defend actual consent as a basis for political authority do not think subjects stumble unwittingly into a duty of obedience. They take it as essential that such commitments be given knowingly, and normally in a public, ritualized, way (a fact that counts against most versions of 'tacit' consent theory). Many public officials, most naturalized immigrants, and perhaps some others knowingly undertake to obey, if only in vague and abstract terms. So (3) is an overstatement. But on any reasonable amendment of it, the proportion of those who (validly) consent to authority will be a minority and

---

[16] See Joseph Raz, *Morality of Freedom* (Oxford University Press, 1986) 80–2.
[17] *Treatise*, 549.

yet, says Hume, all have an obligation to obey. His positive reason for holding this is that everyone believes it to be so.

3.2 The Positive Argument

In general, 'Everyone believes p' neither entails nor provides any ground for 'p'. As I explained above, while the absence of the first-person belief that one has consented undermines the claim that one has a consensual obligation, the presence of a belief that *there is* a non-voluntary obligation has no obvious connection with the existence of one. Non-voluntary obligations may be belief-independent, so why should common opinion have any relevance here at all? We are back to facts and principles.

I said at the outset that one of the ways facts could bear on principles is evidential. As Miller notes, however, it is unclear what it would be for a fact to count as evidence for a moral principle.[18] Suppose such principles are evaluative (stating what is good) or normative (stating what is to be done). Common opinion may be evidence that some such principle is popular, or has survived the test of time, or is part of our common culture; but that is not enough to show that the principle is correct or acceptable as an evaluative or normative standard. We need some further claim about the relevance of those factual features to the cogency of the standard. We might try to close the gap with a kind of sentimentalist utilitarianism. That is suggested by this passage:

> The distinction of moral good and evil is founded on the pleasure or pain, which results from the view of any sentiment, or character; and as that pleasure or pain cannot be unknown to the person who feels it, it follows, that there is just so much vice and virtue in any character, as every one places in it, and that 'tis impossible in this particular that we can ever be mistaken.[19]

One might argue on this basis that the ultimate foundation of authority rests on its utility, and since opinions about pleasure and pain are decisive, there can be no government that is widely believed to be justified but is in fact not

---

[18] David Miller, *Justice for Earthlings: Essays in Political Philosophy* (Cambridge University Press, 2013) 30.
[19] *Treatise*, 547.

justified. A widespread belief in a certain obligation is not a criterion for public utility but might be evidence for it.

This would not be a safe conclusion. Even if we accept the incorrigibility of judgements of one's own pleasure or pain, there is no similar reliability to our judgements about other's pleasure and pain, let alone what might produce the most overall or long-run balance of pleasure over pain. Hume himself shows how difficult it can be to trace the channels of indirect benefit, and how surprising is the thesis that what he calls the 'artificial virtues' are all reducible to it. Mistakes of fact and errors of logic can easily creep into such complex reasoning. Hume thinks that people do not always know their long-run interests in justice and are not always adequately motivated to pursue them when they do. That is why to grasp moral truths requires 'reflection and experience', 'judgment and observation',[20] and 'argument and reflection'.[21]

Miller has an interestingly different proposal, still in a Humean spirit, about how facts might bear on principles.[22] He suggests that facts can be among the background presuppositions that explain the bearing or relevance of political principles. That is how he understands Hume's claim that, unless there were moderate scarcity, principles of allocative justice would be pointless; they have a normative function only on the presuppositions that there are goods that can be allocated and that it matters how we allocate them. If we also think of political philosophy as John Rawls does, as pointing the way to a kind of 'realistic utopia', its recommendations must answer not only to such general facts about human nature, but also to local facts about our particular societies and their institutions:

> If political philosophy aims to give practical guidance to citizens, it must propose principles that it is feasible for them to act on, where feasibility in turn depends not just on physical and sociological laws, but on what, empirically, they would regard as an unacceptable outcome.[23]

This sounds like an empirical version of contractualism. The usual contractualist holds that it is a validity condition on moral principles that they cannot *reasonably* be rejected; Miller proposes that they should not *actually* be rejected, at least in the sense that they do not have consequences

---

[20] *Original Contract*, 480.
[21] *Enquiry*, 201.
[22] Miller, *Justice for Earthlings*, 25 ff.
[23] Ibid., 38.

that would be regarded, by those to whom they apply, as utterly unacceptable. Might there be something (actually) unacceptable about conditioning authority on consent?

One claim of this sort has it that, in so far as consent gives each a kind of veto, it will produce an unacceptably low level of compliance, especially with respect to public goods that can be produced only with general coordination or individual constraint. Hume thinks a society runs well only when nearly everyone obeys the government in all but the most exigent circumstances: 'I shall always incline to their side, who draw the bond of allegiance very close, and consider an infringement of it, as the last refuge in desperate cases, when the public is in the highest danger, from violence and tyranny.'[24] It seems unlikely that consent can itself be counted on to draw 'the bond of allegiance' that tight.

The 'bond', however, can be produced in various ways: by recognizing the authority of the leaders, by acting on independent reasons for doing what they command, for fear of sanctions, and more. In contrast to the specific target that Hobbes or Locke have in mind—establishing conditions under which subjects *have a moral duty to obey* the sovereign—Hume casually lumps together various attitudes that tend to support a de facto government. Sometimes he says everyone acknowledges 'a moral obligation to submit to government',[25] sometimes a 'blind submission'[26] or a duty of 'exact obedience'[27]; sometimes he says they all accept the rulers' right to punish dissent.[28] Hume treats these as more or less interchangeable. Yet they differ in exigency and in ground. Locke, in contrast, holds that one is sometimes entitled to coerce others without any positive authority over them, under the 'executive power of the law of nature'.[29] Hobbes maintains that the state is entitled to coerce people who have no duty to submit, since the necessity for self-preservation voids all positive obligations.[30] I have explored these issues elsewhere.[31] The key point is this: many who conform to *what* their law requires do not treat as salient *the fact that* the law requires it of them. Instead

---

[24] David Hume, 'Of Passive Obedience', in *Essays, Moral Political, and Literary* (Eugene F. Miller ed., Liberty Classics, 1985).
[25] *Treatise*, 547.
[26] Ibid., 554.
[27] *Original Contract*, 480.
[28] *Treatise*, 548.
[29] Locke, *Two Treatises of Government*, II, ss. 8–9, 312–3. See n. 9 above.
[30] Thomas Hobbes, *Leviathan* (C. Brooke ed., Penguin, 2017) Pt. II, chap. 14, 199.
[31] Leslie Green, 'Law and Obligations', in J. Coleman et al. eds, *Oxford Handbook of Jurisprudence and Legal Philosophy* (Oxford University Press, 2002) 514–47.

of recognizing a general obligation of obedience, they are sensitive to the content and character of the law, to how far others conform to it, to the consequences of non-compliance, etc. When such considerations are operative, people tend to do what law requires, but not because the law requires it. Very probably, this is the typical case.[32] If the law is generally decent and reasonably just (a much higher bar than Hume imposes), many will conform for such reasons, whether they have consented or not. People do not normally regard themselves as having a reason to ignore or breach every norm they have not undertaken to obey.

A related worry is expressed by John Rawls in *A Theory of Justice*. Considering allegiance to the basic ground rules of a society, he says that there is an inherent risk in conditioning it on any principle of voluntary obligation.[33]

> [That] would complicate the assurance problem. Citizens would not be bound to even a just constitution unless they have accepted and intend to continue to accept its benefits. Moreover this acceptance must be in some appropriate sense voluntary. But what is this sense? It is difficult to find a plausible account in the case of the political system into which we are born and begin our lives. And even if such an account could be given, citizens might still wonder about one another whether they were bound, or so regarded themselves. The public conviction that all are tied to just arrangements would be less firm, and a greater reliance on the coercive powers of the sovereign might be necessary to achieve stability.[34]

Rawls' speculations are well-hedged ('it is difficult'; 'might still wonder'; 'might be necessary'), and we should similarly hedge his own suggestion that in the original position everyone would recognize a natural duty to comply with reasonably just institutions that apply to us.[35] Even so, just as there are sources of compliance not noticed by the first objection, there are benign sources of assurance not noticed in Rawls' objection. We have adequate

---

[32] For doubts about the prevalence of a belief in law's authority, see Leslie Green, 'Who Believes in Political Obligation?', in W. A. Edmundson ed., *The Duty to Obey the Law* (Rowman and Littlefield, 1999) 301–17. For a study of the varied grounds of conformity to law, see Frederick Schauer, *The Force of Law* (Harvard University Press, 2015).

[33] Rawls has in mind the principle of fairness, but his objection applies even more directly to any principle of consent.

[34] John Rawls, *A Theory of Justice* (Harvard University Press, 1971) 296 (Internal footnote omitted).

[35] Ibid., 293.

assurance that people will all drive on the same side of the road, accept legal tender for debts, and respect property in most cases, even if the fact that law requires these things is not among their motivating reasons, and even if the law rarely applies sanctions to the recalcitrant. In a morally decent state, there are enormous benefits in conforming to the law. This applies not only to particular requirements, but also to the more basic laws that validate them. The fact that authorities exist and require what they do may be part of the causal history of a convention of driving on the left or regarding the executive as having certain prerogative powers. In some cases, law may be needed to establish such conventions. But once established, the conventions are self-reinforcing and opaque to their origins. This provides assurance that is independent of a whole-hearted acceptance of the basic authority structures and also of the purely coercive power of the state.

Clearly, there is more to be said on these issues, and in Chapter 3 I examine in greater detail the possible roles of custom and convention in law. But we have seen enough to conclude that it would be hasty to think that it is obviously unacceptable to endorse the norm, 'regard yourself as bound to obey only those to whose rule you consent'. The contrary is probably true. The idea that legitimate government rests on the consent of the governed is now more firmly entrenched in common opinion than is any competing account of political obligation. Perhaps Hume's theory has itself been controverted by the evidence?

4. Foundations for Fidelity

It is rarely noticed that, in his most important criticism of consent theory, Hume shuns any appeal to common opinion. He demands of the consent theorist a *theoretical* account of why promises bind, and he offers an influential (and partly convincing) one that makes no appeal to common sense. This is often reckoned to be a sign of his originality. Annette Baier says that 'no one before Hume saw obligations arising from prior promises or contracts to be just as problematic as any others . . .'[36] Even so, Hume's thinks his theory of promises establishes more than it does. Hume challenges defenders of consent to account for the moral obligation to obey:

---

[36] A. Baier, 'Hume's Account of Social Artifice—Its Origins and Originality' (1988) 98 *Ethics* 762.

Your answer is, *because we should keep our word*. . . . I say, you find yourself embarrassed, when it is asked, *why are we bound to keep our word?* Nor can you give any answer, but what would, immediately, without any circuit, have accounted for our obligation to allegiance.[37]

There are two lines of thought here: that consent theory is incomplete because it lacks an account of why we are bound to keep our word, and that it is redundant because such an account would itself justify the duty to obey. Neither is compelling.

4.1 Incompleteness

Hume thinks a consent theorist must be embarrassed by the question 'Why do undertakings bind?', to which they will have no answer. But that is not true of Hume's main opponents. Locke maintains that promise-keeping is a natural duty whose binding force ultimately depends on fear of God.[38] We may think that a bad or unilluminating answer—it would not satisfy Hume—but it *is* an answer, and it is independent of Locke's case for political authority. Moreover, Locke knows there are competing answers, and mentions some in the *Essay Concerning Human Understanding*:

> That Men should keep their Compacts, is certainly a great and undeniable Rule in Morality: But yet, if a Christian, who has the view of Happiness and Misery in another Life, be asked why a Man must keep his Word, he will *give* this as a *Reason*: Because God, who has the Power of eternal Life and Death, requires it of us. But if an *Hobbist* be asked why; he will answer: Because the Publick requires it, and the *Leviathan* will punish you if you do not. And if one of the old *Heathen* Philosophers had been asked, he would have answer'd: Because it was dishonest, below the Dignity of a Man, and opposite to Vertue, the highest Perfection of humane Nature, to do otherwise.[39]

---

[37] *Original Contract*, 481.
[38] John Locke, *Essays on the Law of Nature* (W. von Leyden ed., Oxford University Press, 1958) 183; John Locke, *A Letter Concerning Toleration* (J. H. Tully ed., Hackett Publishing, Indianapolis, 1983) 51.
[39] J. Locke, *Essay Concerning Human Understanding* (P. H. Nidditch ed., Clarendon Press, 1979) I.3.5.

A moral rule may thus be of 'undeniable' validity though its basis is open to dispute. The reason Locke does not defend his particular view of the basis of promising in the *Second Treatise* is not that he thinks the principle self-evident, but because that argument does not require it. There, Locke only needs an account of the limits on any *possible* practice of promising. If there are promissory powers that we necessarily lack, we can never be held to have exercised them. Locke maintains that the power to enslave oneself falls into that class and concludes that absolute governments are therefore always illegitimate. He expresses this in a juridical metaphor: no one can transfer a better title than he has, and we are not our own property, but God's. Having no title to our own lives, we cannot transfer it to others: *nemo dat quod non habet*. Agreeing to absolute authority always violates this principle, Locke thinks.

Now, the scope of valid promising is not entirely independent of the justification for having voluntary powers; but it must have a relative independence or else promises would lack their function of creating new obligations by one's very say-so. A successful theory of promising must show, not only that we have a reason to do what we promised, but that *the fact that we promised* is among our reasons for performing. Locke may be unconvincing when he says that promise-breaking, as such, attracts divine sanction; but the account does have the right structure. One is punished for breach of one's word, not for failure to do whatever it was that one undertook to do. The force of promises is at least partly content-independent.

4.2 Redundancy

Hume's second point is more interesting. He says there are no considerations that would justify keeping promises that would not 'immediately' be sufficient to justify obedience to law. His general name for that class of considerations is 'public utility', by which he means the 'apparent interests and necessities of human society'.[40] We must keep our promises only because

---

[40] *Original Contract*, 481. David Gauthier suggests we should not read this in a utilitarian spirit: it is not that the benefits outweigh the costs, rather, there *are* no costs because, measured against a baseline of anarchic non-compliance, each person is a net beneficiary: David Hume, 'Contractarian' (1979) 87 *Philosophical Review* 3. I find the texts indecisive on this point. For example, we find this in the *Enquiry*, 'When any man, even in political society, renders himself by his crimes, obnoxious to the public, he is punished by the laws in his goods and person; that is, the ordinary rules of justice are, with regard to him, suspended for a moment, and it becomes

promising is, in general and in the long run, a socially necessary and individually beneficial institution. But the very same is true of government, and government cannot exist without 'exact obedience'.[41] We therefore have a duty to obey whether or not we have consented. The two interests are 'on the same footing';[42] the two virtues 'stand precisely on the same foundation'.[43] Thus, 'being of like force and authority, we gain nothing by resolving the one into the other'.[44]

For Hume, promise-keeping and obedience are both 'artificial virtues' distinguished by the fact that they belong to conventional practices performed from a sense of obligation and which promote our mutual benefit by restraining our primary impulses. Although all artificial virtues have one deep function, they serve it in different ways, and it is by reference to these that we distinguish them. The virtue of fidelity serves mutual benefit in one way, by sustaining trust in the performance of future actions; the virtue of allegiance serves it another way, by sustaining compliance with the law.

To show that promise-keeping is an artificial virtue will undercut any doctrine that depends on promising being 'natural' in one of Hume's senses of that term, that is, resting on a principle that is either self-evident or supported by our primary impulses.[45] But it would be a mistake to think consent theorists assume that. As we saw just above, promise-keeping is Locke's example of a rule whose moral force is *not* self-evident. Locke also agrees that our primary impulses are inadequate to sustain promising. That is why he insists, in one of those passages that embarrass modern liberals, that 'those are not at all to be tolerated who deny the Being of a God. Promises, Covenants and Oaths, which are the Bonds of Humane Society, can have no hold upon an Atheist'.[46]

Even if promise-keeping and allegiance are both artificial virtues, nothing follows about their normative relations. The fact that two practices have the same ultimate foundation does not prove that one is not necessary for the other, any more than the fact that two rooms are resting on the foundations of one house proves that one can enter the second without passing through the

---

equitable to inflict on him, for the *benefit* of society, what otherwise he could not suffer without wrong injury' (*Enquiry*, 187). That sounds utilitarian.

[41] *Original Contract*, 480.
[42] *Treatise*, 544.
[43] *Original Contract*, 481.
[44] Ibid.
[45] In the *Enquiry*, Hume says that the issue of whether justice and fidelity are natural virtues is 'vain' dispute, a 'merely verbal' question (*Enquiry*, 307).
[46] Locke, A Letter Concerning Toleration, 51.

first. Hume says the public utility involved in allegiance is no less important and no less a source of obligation than the kind involved in fidelity. 'As there are here two interests entirely distinct from each other, they must give rise to two moral obligations, equally separate and independent.'[47] Then he says that so far as there is any relation of subordination here, it runs the other way around: had we not invented promising, we should still have to invent the virtue of allegiance, for without the support of legal sanction promises would have little force.

All of this is terribly unclear. The Hobbesian thought that 'without the sword' promises are not binding is at odds with Hume's explanation of the pre-political existence and value of promising. And the claim that distinct interests must give rise to distinct obligations is not entailed by the artificiality thesis. Relations among interests and obligations may be criss-crossing and untidy.[48] Moreover, the separate-interests/separate-obligations thesis is consistent with relations of dependence *between* obligations. A consent theorist need not think that the obligation to obey the law and the obligation to keep promises serve fundamentally different interests—certainly not when those are described at a high level of abstraction, such as 'public utility' or 'the interests of society'. Society, and not just the individual, has an interest in individuals having the power to create obligations by promising.

I think that Hume's substantive theory of the interests that promising serves is more important to his view that consent is redundant than is the artificiality thesis alone. Hume holds that the main function of promises is to grease the wheels of production and exchange between parties at arm's length, or with respect to future or abstract goods.[49] Promising promotes the 'commerce of mankind'.[50] And here 'commerce' means the exchange of goods and services; Hume expressly distinguishes this from the wider sense of 'commerce' that comprises all forms of human reciprocity. Promising emerges as a distinct practice precisely in order to distinguish 'the self-interested commerce of men' from 'the more generous and noble intercourse of friendship and good offices' in which mutuality flourishes 'without any prospect of advantage'.[51]

---

[47] *Treatise*, 546.
[48] Some interests give rise to no obligations whatsoever; a cluster of distinct interests may be promoted by a single obligation, and some human interests are served by more than one obligation. The obligation to respect property, for example, promotes economic efficiency, stability of expectations, social peace, and a variety of other things. None of these is uniquely protected by the obligation to respect property.
[49] *Treatise*, 519–20.
[50] Ibid., 520; *Original Contract*, 481.
[51] *Treatise*, 521.

This is an emaciated view of promising. The range of outcomes Hume contemplates—commercial exchange and its analogues—is too narrow. On this basis, it would be hard to explain the difference between promising and the obligation not to frustrate those who legitimately rely on one's non-promissory inducements. An interest-based account of promising needs to explain why it is valuable to be bound by a particular *route*: what is of value is not just the end (securing expectations) but also the means (by pledging one's word).

Compare the role of consent in marriage. We subject the validity of marriage to the consent of the parties, not because that best ensures an optimal distribution of spouses, lowers transaction costs, or expands the range of mutually beneficial partnerships. It is not even the only way to generate duties of mutual support and fidelity—these may bind without marriage. Rather, consent to marry operates as an important expression and constitutive part of a valued relationship, because it bears a certain social meaning. When a couple exchange marital promises they mean to 'plight their troth' and it is understood that they mean to do so. To defend the necessity of consent to marriage one does not need to show that consent and marriage serve fundamentally different interests, or that it is more urgent to keep one's promises than to be faithful to one's spouse. One needs to show that promising plays a special role in creating and marking such relationships.

Hume sees the point when it comes to marriage. He thinks the foundation of marriage is nothing other than the general interests and necessities of society.[52] Yet Hume never suggests it is possible to be married without one's own consent, or that to refer to the exchange of promises would be a 'needless circuit' in explaining why spousal obligations bind. The form of the institution of marriage answers at the tribunal of public utility, but in all his examples the incidence of marital obligations depends on the consent of the parties, just as divorce follows from their dissent. Had Hume thought less about commercial contracts and more about other forms of promissory obligation he might have come to understand why, and when, actual consent is important.

---

[52] David Hume, 'Of Polygamy and Divorces', in *Essays, Moral Political, and Literary* (F. Miller ed., Liberty Classics, 1985) 181.

5. Fact and Superstition in Politics

If my arguments to this point are sound, one can accept sentimentalist ethics, the view that promising is an artificial virtue, give weight to facts about common opinion, yet still endorse the moral principle that government should rest on the consent of the governed. Of course, freely given consent is a poor theory of the *origins* of government. Is this any obstacle to consent theory?

Hume believes that common opinion holds governments to be legitimate, not just in Holland and England but also in France, Spain, or Persia.[53] No one could imagine that the latter governments enjoyed the consent of their people—but neither (in Hume's view) can they suppose them to lack legitimate authority. Many of Hume's eighteenth-century readers disagreed. They said these were despotisms, without legitimate authority over their people, and were proud that England was, they thought, different. That Hume should think France of the *ancien régime* or Persia count against consent theory is as odd as if someone should today offer Iran or China as a counterexample to a claim that justified authority requires respect for human rights. Is Hume here confusing, or identifying, the genealogical question with one of the normative questions about authority?

That would explain why Hume's emphasis on the role of force, violence, custom, imagination, etc. in forming beliefs about authority often sounds like an argument *against* the legitimacy of the governments in question: 'Time alone gives solidity to their right, and operating gradually on the minds of men, reconciles them to any authority, and makes it seem just and reasonable.'[54] And in a passage that almost reads like a *reductio* of his position, Hume writes:

> a man living under an absolute government, wou'd owe it no allegiance; since, by its very nature, it depends not on consent. But as that is as *natural* and *common* a government as any, it must certainly occasion some obligation; and 'tis plain from experience, that men, who are subjected to it, do always think so.[55]

---

[53] *Original Contract*, 470.
[54] *Treatise*, 556.
[55] Ibid., 549.

Here, Hume is playing fast and loose with the term 'natural', and is enjoying it. The fact that people can get psychologically reconciled to almost any regime, and that in this sense an absolutist tyranny can emerge 'naturally', is not something his Whig opponents deny. They know that is true: they have seen it in action, and they deplore it.

Group loyalties activate powerful passions that are encouraged and reinforced by rulers. Hume knows that in some places one can be jailed or executed for defending the view that government owes its legitimacy to the consent of the people.[56] He knows that some rulers who really do depend on consent put about other fictions (genetic, meritocratic, or technocratic) to justify their authority. He knows that propaganda, manipulation, and oppressive socialization sustain and entrench these fictions. He should not say that this turns fiction into truth.

In the *Enquiry*, Hume observes that, by association and habituation, religious superstitions invest events and objects with fictitious and magical qualities. Anticipating an objection, he asks whether 'there enters a like superstition into all the sentiments of justice'. He denies that on the basis that 'there is this material difference between *superstition* and *justice*, that the former is frivolous, useless, and burdensome; the latter is absolutely requisite to the well-being of mankind and existence of society'.[57] Religious superstitions are unnecessary, and people do not come to believe them just as a result of mistakes; 'they are surely obstructed by education, prejudice, and passion'.[58]

Hume should say that similar obstructions can block our understanding of political morality, and that these can be well-entrenched in common opinion. It is plausible to think that, in modern circumstances, law is a necessary institution; but it is a superstition to believe that all laws are necessary laws, or that our laws form a seamless web so that to break one is to put all at risk. It is plausible to think that law cannot function unless the legal system is broadly effective; but it is a superstition to believe that law's efficacy requires the 'exact obedience' of every subject, or a general belief in a duty to obey the law. These fictions are not made true by the fact the authorities are quick to

---

[56] In the *History of England* (Vol. VI), Hume calls the 1683 execution of Algernon Sidney 'one of the great blemishes of the present reign'. David Hume, *The History of England from the Invasion of Julius Caesar to the Revolution in 1688* (W. B. Todd ed., 6 vols, Liberty Fund, 1983). Lacking a second witness against him for treason, Sidney's *Discourses on Government* were offered instead: a book which defended 'the original contract, the source of power from a consent of the people, [and] the lawfulness of resisting tyrants . . .' (ibid.).
[57] *Enquiry*, 198, 199
[58] Ibid., 198.

propagate them when they sense trouble, nor by the fact that there are apologists for authority (including philosophical apologists) who defend them.

Miller writes, 'by allowing empirical claims to influence the way these principles are formulated, we run the risk that our political philosophy becomes too conservative, adapting itself to aspects of human existence that may be contingent, and therefore potentially alterable'.[59] Hume ran that risk and it materialized in his theory of authority. But the conclusion to draw is not that political philosophy is to be purged of what some writers archly call 'merely' contingent, empirical claims. It is that we need to get these claims right and come to a sharper understanding of how they interact with, and sometimes underpin, political principles.

6. A Show of Consent

If I am right, a Humean need not be as hostile to consent theory as Hume is. But how hostile is he, finally? When not in the harness of his philosophy, he is surprisingly friendly. I conclude with some evidence.

Hume's *History of England* is written for different purposes and for a different audience than his philosophical writings. Still, his discussion of the 1688 revolution is not wholly inconsistent with his temper in the *Treatise*, *Enquiry*, or *Essays*. William's military defeat of the Jacobites left the problem of how to re-establish stable government in a divided society. Acquisition of authority by conquest was a well-understood and accepted constitutional norm. Hume explains why William looked beyond it. The explanation is worth having at length:

> The prince seemed still unwilling to act upon an authority, which might be deemed so imperfect: He was desirous of obtaining a more express declaration of the public consent. A judicious expedient was fallen on for that purpose. All the members, who had sitten in the house of commons during any parliament of Charles II (the only parliaments whose election was regarded as free) were invited to meet; and to them were added the mayor, aldermen, and fifty of the common council. This was regarded as the most proper representative of the people, that could be summoned during the present emergency. They unanimously voted the same address with the

---

[59] Miller, *Justice for Earthlings*, 19.

lords: And the prince, being thus supported by all the legal authority, which could possibly be obtained in this critical juncture, wrote circular letters to the counties and corporations of England; and his orders were universally complied with. A profound tranquillity prevailed throughout the kingdom; and the prince's administration was submitted to, as if he had succeeded in the most regular manner to the vacant throne.[60]

Plainly, Hume does not think that William really *enjoyed* 'public consent' for his rule; but Hume thinks he really *sought* it, and that he did so by means that, in the circumstances, came as close to consent as 'could possibly be obtained'. This fiction of consent honours the ideal. And Hume applauds it. He says William was wise to ignore 'some lawyers' who proposed that he simply assert his right to rule by conquest, or that he should summon a new parliament and have it ratify his authority retroactively. Either would fall within the rules of governance accepted at the time. But Hume joins William in turning his back on those, and he cautions that to found the new regime on such principles would violate the rule of law and be 'destructive of the principles of liberty, the only principles on which his future throne could be established...'.[61]

On matters of substance if not method, Hume has here come around to something close to Locke's view. And this gets corroboration in a 1753 revision of his essay 'Of the Original Contract', to which Hume now adds, in a footnote, this intriguing qualification: 'My intention here is not to exclude the consent of the people from being one just foundation of government where it has place. It is surely the best and most sacred of any.'[62] It is pleasing to think Hume believed that, and reassuring to know that his philosophical works leave room for it.[63]

---

[60] Hume, *History of England*, Vol. VI.
[61] Ibid.
[62] *Original Contract*, 474.
[63] I thank Daniel Butt, Sarah Fine, Sam Kukathas, and Zofia Stemplowska for comments, and especially David Miller, in whose company I first learned the importance of Hume's political theory.

12
Associative Obligations and the State

1. Introduction

Some of our moral obligations hold irrespective of local conditions and arrangements. It is not as members of a particular community that we ought to tell the truth or refrain from harming others. These duties bind us as members of the human community or, to put it another way, of no specific community. In contrast, our obligations as Canadians, or Catholics, or chiropractors are more particular in their force. People associated with these smaller groups have special duties which come, as F. H. Bradley said, with their stations. Legal and political theorists have become interested in such associative obligations. Membership in ethnic, religious, or occupational groups is rarely a matter of free choice and, even when it is, any duties that brings are not themselves freely chosen. Associative obligation thus seems a possible model for the relationship between citizens and their states.

Ronald Dworkin challenges sceptics about political obligation to 'either deny all associative obligations or show why political obligation cannot be associative'.[1] I am going to pursue the second alternative. I explain why political obligation is not associative in Dworkin's sense, and how one version of consent theory is able to respond correctly to social dimension of political life, although it cannot show that every citizen does in fact have an obligation to obey the law, not even in a just community. I conclude by explaining why jurisprudents would be wrong to count that as some kind of objection to consent theory.

2. Legitimacy and Consent

The law is a realm of obligation and duty; it acts not as our advisor but as an authority which must be obeyed. Whether we are justified in accepting

---
[1] Ronald Dworkin, *Law's Empire* (Harvard University Press, 1986) 207.

law's self-image is the problem of legitimacy. The liberal tradition has long favoured consent as the best answer to that problem. But it has sometimes been uncertain what consent theory amounts to. In particular, the tradition equivocates between two different claims:

(1) Only if someone consents to obey the law do they have an obligation to obey it.
(2) Everyone has an obligation to obey the law because everyone has consented to obey it.

These differ in ground and force. The first is a critical moral thesis, the second an explanatory, partly factual, one. However, the second is so obviously false that, as David Hume said, it would take a philosopher to believe in it. Many people do nothing that amounts to consent. The fiction that by living peacefully within the territory of a state we tacitly consent to obey all of its laws is one of the embarrassments of the democratic tradition. In Chapter 11 of this book, I am critical of Hume's rough treatment of consent theory, but on this point he is correct.

By consent theory, I intend only (1). This is stronger than (2) and not supported by it: the latter is consistent with there being any number of grounds of political obligation so long as everyone has happened to invoke one of them. The former requires consent but leaves it open who has given it. Notice three further points. First, (1) is a claim about moral obligations only; it does not deny that there are other reasons for obeying the law, including self-interest, courtesy, and fear. Second, its content is an obligation *to obey* the law, where that is understood to be the law of one's own state. This is a prima facie obligation in that it may have to be weighed against other urgent considerations and may, in the end, yield to them. But before yielding it makes a special claim. It asks us to take the requirements of the law as reasons for acting as law requires and for *not* acting on some otherwise valid reasons for disobeying.[2] The supposed duty applies to all of law's subjects, on all occasions on which the law applies, and to all laws that claim our obedience—not only to the good laws, or the laws that promote social cooperation, or the laws that guarantee rights. Finally, (1) does not say that consent is sufficient for legitimacy.

---

[2] Which other reasons? We do not need to decide that here, but I shall assume they include at least: the fact that it would be expensive or annoying to obey, or that doing so would get in the way of plans or projects one hoped to complete. Ordinarily, these are perfectly good reasons for not doing something. When legal officials claim our obedience they need not deny that; they require that we not act on such reasons.

Other necessary conditions must be fulfilled: consent must be free and informed. And the undertaking must be one that it is within our moral powers to give. No one could have gotten an obligation to obey the Nazi regime by making a free and informed promise to do so. Consent binds only if there are reasons for holding that the actions which are signs of consent create duties because they are performed in the belief that performing them does create such duties. The power to create duties for ourselves is worth having, but only in certain circumstances and only within certain limits.

How then might (1) be defended? I state an answer in Section 5 below, but I want to motivate the discussion by showing how hard that task is and thus giving succour to the kind of position that Dworkin defends.

We might interpret (1) as a specification of a more general claim:

(3) For any action V, one has an obligation to V only if one consents to V.

If that is correct, then the obligation to obey the law must be voluntary because all obligations must. This thesis might appeal to those with a highly individualistic outlook, but it is implausible. It is repugnant to suppose that parents have no duty to see that their children are cared for unless they agree to it, or that we have no duty not to discriminate against minorities unless we promise not to. There is also something problematic about (3) on its own terms. Like (1), it only states a necessary condition for obligation. Yet it does not explain why any consent binds. Suppose agreement creates obligations. Why is that? Because there is an obligation to keep our agreements. As Hume already knew, this obligation cannot without circularity itself be grounded in agreement; it must be a non-voluntary obligation. And if there is one, why not others? That undermines (3).

In reply to this objection, some theorists set up a picket-line around obligations. 'There are many kinds of moral reasons', they concede, 'including reasons for keeping agreements, but these are not obligations properly so called. They are urgent moral considerations, or perhaps natural duties. Promises give rise to obligations, but one only has a natural duty to care for one's children.' The distinction can be drawn coherently, but here it is not substantively important. It is not correlated with other morally significant differences between duties and obligations. The natural duty to keep promises is no less urgent than the obligation to keep a particular promise, nor is the duty not to harm others less urgent than the obligation to return what one borrows. Does the difference between obligations and natural duties correlate with directionality? No, because not all obligations are personal and not all duties are general. The obligation not to assault others requires that we refrain from assaulting everyone, while the natural duty to care for one's children is normally thought to bind parents only to their own children. In the political realm, rulers are not going to be disappointed to hear that while there is no obligation *strictly speaking* to obey them, their subjects nonetheless have a natural duty to do so that binds with the exigency of obligations.[3] Nor will subjects be alarmed to learn that other subjects have no obligations to obey laws that protect rights or supply public goods, though they all have a natural duty to comply which ensures that rights are protected and goods are provided.

A third defence of (3) argues the other way round. It attempts to assimilate non-consensual obligations to consensual ones by arguing that they are grounded in hypothetical consent. Suppose as John Rawls argues, that if we had been among the rational but uninformed parties in the original position, we would have agreed to bear a non-consensual duty to obey the law. (Rawls thinks that they would not agree to make obedience consent-dependent, for that would give rise to endless doubts about whether others were indeed bound to obey, and that would undermine confidence in public institutions.) To justify the obligation to obey the law or to keep promises on the ground that it would be rational to make such undertakings does not show that we undertook them. If anything, it suggests that the fact that we made no such undertakings does not matter. A consent-based theory, in contrast, assigns moral significance to actual agreement as the exercise of a normative power. It may allow one to incur binding obligations that it was *not* rational to agree to. A consent theorist must therefore show that there is special value in empowering people to create duties for themselves *by* agreement, not just that it would be valuable to be bound by those duties.

Thus, (3) is wrong and a quick defence of (1) fails. If consent is necessary for the obligation to obey the law, it is not because of the nature of obligations, but because of the content of this obligation in particular. This is the point at which the doctrine of associative obligation begins to seem appealing. Political association is in many ways like other non-voluntary relationships in which we acknowledge moral obligations without a need for prior consent. Friends, for example, owe each other special duties of loyalty, respect, support, etc. which partly constitute their relationship, but which do not, or need not, arise as a matter of undertaking or agreement. As Aristotle

---

[3] John Rawls, *A Theory of Justice* (Oxford University Press, 1971) 114.

saw, there are different kinds or levels of human community, and friendship, unlike a business deal, is marked by deep and intrinsically valuable relations among people. Similar obligations are often thought to bind people to their neighbourhoods, families, partnerships, professions, religions, or ethnic groups. Suppose that something like this is correct. Does the state belong on this list?

There are enough analogies to make the proposal worth entertaining: people rarely choose their states, they do not agree with all their laws, nationality structures their identities, political relationships grow organically, and membership in a state may, ideally at least, have intrinsic value. But there are also stark disanalogies, of which the following are the most important.

States are huge organizations, binding together millions of people who have varied backgrounds and interests. The intensity and depth of social relations familiar in smaller associations are likely to be absent in the state. As Rousseau puts it, 'The more the social bond is stretched, the slacker it becomes'.[4] Moreover, as scale increases, the ability of any individual citizen to control the association dwindles. Though they are structured by social custom, there is more responsiveness to individual will in relationships like friendship, marriage, partnership, etc. than there is in any state. Even in a direct democracy, individual citizens are *law-takers* in the way individual consumers in a competitive market are price-takers. Popular control of government is collective control. To exercise it requires organization and the ability to bear substantial transaction costs. The modern state is thus quite unlike the family, tribe, neighbourhood, or other face-to-face communities. The state claims obedience from individuals who can only control the state in groups. And apart from its physical reach, the state is imposing in its normative ambitions. In all modern states, the law claims supreme authority over our most vital interests. Even a minimal constitutional regime claims power to regulate personal relationships, property, and the terms of membership in any other association. It is not that law requires absolute obedience; on the contrary, it usually recognizes exemptions from its rule. But even a state that takes rights very seriously and promises in good faith that there are things it will never require of its citizens, rests only on its word. The scope and supremacy of the state's claim to authority mean that the stakes here are the highest. Together, these features are sufficiently distinctive for us to

---

[4] Jean-Jacques Rousseau, *The Social Contract* (M. Cranston trs, Penguin, 1968) Bk. II, chap. 9, 90.

require something more compelling of a theory of state authority than the vague suggestion that politics is a bit like friendship and therefore gives rise to friendship-style duties. We need a positive account of the ways in which a modern state could count as a community.

3. Obligations of True Community

Dworkin says we have 'a duty to honour our responsibilities under social practices that define groups and attach special responsibilities to membership . . .'[5] These duties are not consent-based; their content and liability is said to depend on group practices rather than on individual agreement. This dependence is normative. It is vital to distinguish the claim that group membership *identifies* our obligations from the claim that group membership *justifies* or validates them. A lawyer has professional duties that come with the role, but that does not show that those duties are moral ones.[6] A profession may make demands which no one should concede. This does not rest on any sharp distinction between facts and values, as if the character of the group's practice were a matter for the sociologist and its binding force a matter for the moral philosopher. But any theory for identifying associative obligations must allow that they may be unjustified, even prima facie.

How then can associative obligations be validated? What, for example, could turn one's duty as neighbour into a moral duty? That depends on the character and point of neighbourly relations, on the way the duties in question serve that point, and on whether there are good reasons for regarding the fact that someone lives in the neighbourhood as a ground for thinking them bound by the duties. If the point of neighbourhood is to facilitate social contact and local cooperation, one might be able to defend an associative duty to welcome new neighbours as instrumental to its point. Other duties may be non-instrumentally justified. Courtesy does not only facilitate neighbourly relations, it partly constitutes or expresses them. Neither sort of argument can validate everything a neighbourhood might require. A new neighbour who votes differently in local elections has no obligation—not even prima facie—to switch allegiance to fit in to the community, nor can the neighbourhood impose duties on its members to shun minority ethnic groups. It would

---

[5] Dworkin, *Law's Empire*, 198.
[6] See the discussion of role duties in Chapter 9, section 3 this volume.

be wrong to give in to such demands, even if to do so strengthened neighbourly community.

That is just one example. What if we were to seek 'not just an interpretation of a single associative practice, like family or friendship or neighbourhood, but a more abstract interpretation of the yet more general practice of associative obligation itself'?[7] Immediately there is a problem. What is the point of association in the abstract or in general? What duties serve or express its point? There is no point to *association as such* and no generic responsibilities attach to it. One can no more find moral reasons for the general act-type *doing-what-is-required* than one can explain the point of *being-associated*. We justify associative obligations locally, by reference to the points of particular associations. This is not the relativistic claim that each association gets to define moral obligations morally binding for itself. Each must satisfy sound general principles, but those principles operate on the points and characters of actual associations. Any general truths about associative obligations follow only as generalizations from cases, not as deductions from some general theory of association 'as such'.

Fortunately, Dworkin's claims about association in general are defended in the only way they could be, by considering moral relationships in groups like families or friendships and generalizing from those. His move from the family to the state begins with minimal conditions for group life ('bare community') then looks for lessons in familial obligations and elsewhere to help us understand what a 'true community' is entitled to expect from its members. A bare community is defined by social practice.[8] In a true community, members must think that their obligations are *special*, holding in a distinctive way amongst the group members and not holding in that way amongst everyone in the world. Their responsibilities must also be *personal*

---

[7] Dworkin, *Law's Empire*, 197.
[8] Ibid., 207–8. Dworkin says disappointingly little about this. He thinks that political practice adequately defines the boundaries of the United States and the United Kingdom (excepting Northern Ireland). This places too much emphasis on law and not enough on practice. In the United Kingdom it oversimplifies position not only of the Northern Irish, but also of the Scots, the Welsh and, under right-wing governments, those in the North of England. These are all members of one community only in a tenuous sense. With respect to the United States, Dworkin takes the several states each to be political communities. This is another misleading convenience. New York is a community in a very different way from Utah (to say nothing of communities that are not states, like Puerto Rico). And one does not have to look far beyond Britain and America to find still more complex communities, such as Canada. And everywhere there are resident aliens, illegal immigrants, prisoners, and perhaps even future generations to consider. The notion that we can begin by treating existing constitutional jurisdictions as 'bare' communities is far-fetched.

in that they are owed to members of the group as individuals rather than to the group as a whole. And they must also derive from a more general duty of *concern* for the well-being of its members, which concern is *equal* in the sense that the group's role-distinctions and distribution of benefits are held to be in the interests of all and are compatible with the assumption that the well-being of each member is of intrinsically equal value. When held in the correct spirit, these mark a sort of reciprocity so that people 'share a general and diffuse sense of members special rights and responsibilities from or toward one another, a sense of what sort and level of sacrifice one may be expected to make for another'.[9] Together, these add up to the conditions of true community, at least in intimate settings like a family: 'If the conditions are met, people in the bare community have the obligations of a true community whether or not they want them . . .'[10]

Although Dworkin says these conditions reflect beliefs or attitudes of the members, his considered view is that they are interpretive properties of the group: 'practices that people with the right level of concern would adopt - not a psychological property of some fixed number of the actual members.'[11] That is to say, a bare community becomes a true community if a certain complex philosophical argument holds about it, irrespective of its members' beliefs and attitudes:

> Political obligation is then not just a matter of obeying the discrete political decisions of the community one by one, as political philosophers usually represent it. It becomes a more protestant idea: fidelity to a scheme of principle which citizens have a responsibility to identify, ultimately for themselves, as their community's scheme.[12]

Perhaps this helps turn Rousseau's objection. If group life is independent of real affective ties, then any set of people might be involved in it, even when related by nothing more than the anonymous and bureaucratic machinery of

---

[9] Ibid., 199.
[10] Ibid., 201. Here, Dworkin presents these as sufficient conditions for associative obligations. At 204 and 207 what he says is consistent with them being necessary, or necessary and sufficient. At 213–14 they seem sufficient once again.
[11] Ibid., 201. In this passage, 'fixed number' must mean 'any number'. It follows from Dworkin's theory of interpretation that the community believes that *p* provided there is some proposition *q* which some of its members do believe and *p* coheres the best theory justifying their belief that *q*. Thus, *p* can be an 'interpretive property' of the community's belief even although no actual member of the community believes it.
[12] Ibid., 190.

a large modern state. There is therefore nothing in these conditions for true community which limit associative obligations to small, close-knit communities, like a family or tribe. So far, so good.

How do these conditions play out when we ascend to the state? Dworkin thinks we can apply lessons from familial duties. It is significant, he says, that the virtue of fraternity is the one taken as a model for the political realm.[13] Ordinarily, however, we think the content of fraternal or sororal obligations is something like mutual aid and respect—not obedience. That is why the associative model generally deployed by earlier political theorists was not in fact the horizontal association among siblings, but the vertical hierarchy in which children were thought to owe a duty of obedience to their parents. And this was not chosen because parents and children were believed to be more truly associated than siblings, but because two common justifications for authority relations were held to apply here.

First, there is an instrumental argument based on the need for obedience in child-rearing. Children need parental authority to guide their development because they are not yet fully competent judges of their own or others' interests.[14] Suspending their own judgement about certain matters and acting instead on their parents' directives will better promote children's moral education and the proper ends of family life. A second line of argument is set out by John Locke: parents need a right to obedience because they are charged with a duty of caring for their children and thus require the normative powers necessary for the exercise of that duty.

Assuming the conditions of true community meet Rousseau's objection, there is now another to address. Political theory must apply to adults of mature judgement. Is the authority of the state justified because we all need to be treated like children? A reply to this might run as follows. Even in the state, there are nonetheless areas in which even adults do need authoritative guidance. For example, certain questions of social policy turn on knowledge which only state officials have, or on which only they can be relied to act in

[13] Ibid., 437, n. 20.
[14] This point is often neglected. The authority that parents typically claim over their children would not, I think, be justified by paternalistic considerations alone. Children can be taught to act prudently in their own self-interest through exhortation and reward. Parents need authority to command their obedience in large part because children do not give sufficient weight to the interests of others, within and without the family, and because exhortation and reward are often less effective here. Political theorists often wrongly jumped from the correct observation that parents' authority lapses when children mature, to the conclusion that it does so merely because the children have become capable of looking out for themselves. Equally important is the fact that this is when the child's moral sense should develop as well.

good faith. The state can also take a broader view and ensure that the public interest is served through the coordinated activity of many individuals and groups. This will apply only in some circumstances and only to some people, so the state's claim to bind everyone will have to be appropriately qualified. But there is a deeper problem. Even if there are some things that only the state can do, it has not yet been shown that the state can do them only if its citizens have or recognize an obligation *to obey* it. The state can rely on a variety of techniques to secure compliance, including persuasion, exhortation, reward, and coercion. Why does it also need a general duty of obedience?

Not all traditional arguments for familial obligations were instrumental in these ways, so there may be more to say. Locke and Rousseau hold that, after children reach the age of reason, parental authority may continue with their consent or because it has become psychologically salient among reasonable authority structures.[15] Or childhood obligations may also persist as an appropriate expression of attitudes such as gratitude, trust, or honour. Why make an obligation of obedience an appropriate expression of an attitude?[16] Can we answer: it is a matter of custom? It is also an aspect of our moral customs to interpret 'appropriate' to mean a desirable or fitting expression and not just a common one. What Locke says about the biblical injunction to honour one's parents is instructive here:

> A Man may owe *honour* and respect to an ancient, or wise Man; defence to his Child or Friend; relief and support to the Distressed; and gratitude to a Benefactor, to such a degree, that all he has, all he can do, cannot sufficiently pay it: But all these give no Authority, no right to any one of making Laws over him from whom they are owing.[17]

---

[15] Locke writes: 'Thus twas easie, and almost natural for Children by a tacit, and scarce avoidable consent to make way for the *Fathers Authority and Government*. They had been accustomed in their Childhood to follow his Direction, and to refer their little differences to him, and when they were Men, who fitter to rule them?': *Two Treatises of Government* (P. Laslett ed., Cambridge University Press, 1963) II, s. 75, 360. Salience arguments, however, are relevant to the question of who should have authority, not to the question of whether any authority is justified. That is one of Locke's mistakes in s. 82 where he defends the authority of husbands over wives on the ground that men are 'abler and stronger'. Even if the factual claim were sound, the argument fails because it does not show why either of them must have authority over the other. Disagreements about common interests can be settled in many other ways.

[16] For a defence of obedience as an expression of identification with one's society, see Joseph Raz, 'Government by Consent', in J. Roland Pennock and John W. Chapman eds, *Authority Revisited: Nomos XXIX* (New York University Press, 1987). I examine Raz's position in Leslie Green, 'Law, Legitimacy and Consent' (1989) 62 *Southern California Law Review* 795.

[17] Locke, *Two Treatises of Government*, II, s. 70, 356.

Locke thus distinguishes obligations imposed by the legal system from the other kinds of duties we typically owe. Organic social relationships may bring very stringent obligations without any obligation of obedience. One thanks a benefactor, respects the wise, and defends a friend. But one need not obey them as an expression of those relationships. For Locke, obedience is out of place in all these contexts whereas it would be fitting in the relationship of Creator and created, or of parent and child. But that is because there are other, primary, grounds sufficient to validate authority in those contexts. We do not 'double-count' the expression of these primary grounds along with the primary grounds in an argument for obedience. The child gets the duty of obedience from the primary grounds; the separate duties of honour, respect, or gratitude arise as themselves fitting expressions of the filial relationship.

Dworkin offers an example. He asks us to suppose a community has a practice of arranged marriages according to which daughters have an obligation to defer to their father's choice of spouse for them while sons do not. We are to suppose further that this is a 'true' community; that its practices can sustain a good-faith interpretation as being grounded in respect and equality between the sexes. If that is the case, he argues, daughters owe their fathers a genuine associative obligation of obedience. The obligation is a prima facie one that may ultimately be overridden 'by appeal to freedom or some other ground of rights', but although defeasible it cannot be ignored:

> The difference is important: a daughter who marries against her father's wishes, in this version of the story, has something to regret. She owes him at least an accounting, and perhaps an apology, and should in other ways strive to continue her standing as a member of the community she otherwise has a duty to honour.[18]

This liberal-minded conclusion does not seem consistent with the story as related, however. What the community requires of daughters is obedience to their father's will, not respectful audience followed by free judgement and, if necessary, apology. So the apology should be understood as reparative: it is the moral residue of some other, unfulfilled obligation. But we cannot infer from the fact that an apology is now appropriate that the demand for obedience must have been justified, at least prima facie. If I cannot perform a contract, I may owe you damages—performance is infeasible, so you are entitled

---

[18] Dworkin, *Law's Empire*, 205.

to second best. If I need not perform a promise because of a conflicting superior obligation, I may again owe you an apology—another kind of second best. But in the hypothetical, the disobedient daughter of the domineering father can still obey and she is morally permitted, not obligated, to go her own way.

We cannot argue this way: 'Because there is now a residue or trace of duty shown by a valid obligation to apologize, it must be the residue of a prior valid obligation to defer.' Deference was indeed what her father demanded, but the duty to apologize does not show there was anything to his demand, morally speaking. In general, the presence of a residual, second-best obligation does not reveal what the primary obligation was. The fact that P claims that he and D had a contract of which D is in now breach, together with the fact that D *does* owe P compensation, does not entail that P was right all along in thinking they had a contract. D may now owe P compensation on some other ground, in tort for example. Likewise, the daughter of the paternalist father may owe him an accounting or an apology, not as a shadow of her prior duty to obey, but only out of respect for his age, or in gratitude for his earlier support.

We must not get distracted by the fact that associative obligations have prima facie force. The normative character of an obligation is not identified by whether it is prima facie or conclusive, but by the function it is meant to play in the practical reason of those whom it binds. A duty to defer requires that daughters act on their father's wishes rather than their own in cases where they conflict. The question is not whether, once the father's wishes are in the balance, they must win out. The question is how and in what form they got into the balance in the first place.

We have found no argument to show that associative obligations in politics are entitled to the force they (are said to) claim. At most, Dworkin shows that two objections have replies: the state is too large for intense social relations, and some associations treat their members iniquitously. The de-psychologized view of community meets the former point, and the normative conditions for true community rule out some kinds of iniquity. These may be among the necessary conditions for legitimacy. But they do not prove consent dispensable. They do not prove that there are no other necessary conditions on legitimate state authority. A community must not only be well ordered internally, it must also have appropriate relations with other communities. A caste system creates no obligations because it treats its members badly; but neither does the Ku Klux Klan, however it treats its own. We are a long way from a case for political obligation.

4. Integrity and Obedience

I have not yet mentioned the centrepiece of Dworkin's argument. He holds that 'the community has its own principles it can itself honour or dishonour, that it can act in good or bad faith, with integrity or hypocritically, just as people can'.[19] A community with integrity is a community of principle, and it satisfies the conditions of true community as well as can be expected in the real world. 'A community of principle . . . can claim the authority of a genuine associative community and can therefore claim moral legitimacy— that its collective decisions are matters of obligation and not bare power - in the name of fraternity.'[20]

Dworkin's theory of integrity is complex; I will only examine the relevance of the basic idea to the problem of legitimacy.[21] If integrity is important only because it shows that the conditions of true community are satisfied, then it adds nothing to the argument just considered and rejected, for true community is not sufficient for obligation. That leaves open the possibility that a state with integrity is both a true community and, on independent grounds, entitled to obedience. Integrity may be working in a less direct way.

Dworkinian integrity is a kind of consistency, but not just the bare formality of treating like cases alike; it is a principled coherence which also provides criteria for the likeness of cases. A community of principle is one whose directives can be interpreted as a coherent and defensible (though not necessarily ideal) scheme. Integrity explains why we would prefer either a regime prohibiting all abortions or one allowing free choice to one in which women born on even days are allowed abortions while those born on odd days are not. Such 'checkerboard' regimes incorporate arbitrary, unprincipled distinctions among people and cannot be interpreted as schemes of principle at all, not even when they give each citizen an equal say over the outcome and when that outcome minimizes injustice. So argues Dworkin.

How does a scheme satisfying integrity have a prima facie claim to the obedience of those under it? Dworkin's personification of the community gives it ideals with which it can keep or break faith. Perhaps we can learn

---

[19] Ibid., 168.
[20] Ibid., 214. Sometimes (e.g. 216) Dworkin only claims that a community with integrity has a *better* claim to legitimacy than other communities. This is too weak. Franco's Spain may have had a better claim to legitimacy than Hitler's Germany, but both fell far below any plausible threshold at which their citizens could owe a duty of obedience.
[21] For some other difficulties, see Denise Réaume, 'Is Integrity a Virtue? Dworkin's Theory of Legal Obligation' (1989) 39 *University of Toronto Law Journal* 380.

about the force of integrity by considering the way it operates in our evaluation of other agents. All but the crudest rigorists discriminate among judges whose politics they reject. On the other side of the barricades there are hacks, hypocrites, and bumblers; but there are also committed, sincere, and principled people. We admire the latter even though they are, from the perspective of justice, more dangerous precisely because they are immune from *ad hominem* attack. While rejecting their principles, and even fearing their influence, we can respect them nonetheless.

Our regard for a person with integrity is based on what unites us, not on what divides us. We are both people, whose aims, projects, and values are subject to the distortions of self-interest, backsliding, dissembling, and all the other ordinary vices of human life. Those who apply the values they hold in a steady and fair-minded fashion thus deserve respect for having mastered what anyone must master. But these are merits of the person, not of the principles. It may be true that to identify the aims as a scheme of principle at all we must first be able to see it under the aspect of some good, to conceive of it as connected, however remotely, to intelligible values. We could not, to adapt Philippa Foot's example,[22] regard someone as acting on principle who is devoted to regularly clasping and unclasping their hands, unless they also think that it is a kind of exercise, or prayer, or music, or something else whose general type we recognize as valuable. Canyons of incomprehension can still divide this plateau of understanding. (Consider, for example, the worldviews of pro-choice and right-to-life activists.) To establish a bridgehead of intelligibility with someone's principles does not show that they are admirable, only that they are capable of being admired.

This makes it doubtful whether integrity provides an independent ground for a duty to obey one who displays the virtue and claims obedience. The integrity of an agent does not even justify their right to issue directives, never mind the duty of others to take them as they are intended. Notice that this is not correctly described as saying that they have prima facie authority over us, which is then outweighed by the fact that the principles are wrong. Might it be said that to obey people of integrity would be a fitting display of trust in their judgement and good faith? We have already seen the error in that argument. A person of integrity may be entitled to admiration or respect (though it is forced to say that we have a *duty* to admire them); but they are not, just on that account, entitled to obedience as well. The sheer fact that someone is

---

[22] Philippa Foot, 'Moral Beliefs' (1959) 59 *Proceedings of the Aristotelian Society* 83.

INTEGRITY AND OBEDIENCE 319

trying in good faith to rule you according to some scheme of principle is no reason to obey.

None of this changes when integrity is an attribute of a community personified rather than an individual. We may impute personality to the community, says Dworkin, if it is morally desirable to do so. Why would that be desirable? Dworkin says that if we personify the community we can think of it as having integrity, and

> a political society that accepts integrity as a political virtue thereby becomes a special form of community, special in a way that promotes its moral authority to assume and deploy a monopoly of coercive force. This is not the only argument for integrity, or the only consequence of recognizing it that citizens might value.[23]

Now, why is talking about the community in a way that makes its coercive power liable to justification a 'consequence... that citizens might value'? Do they value their community being the kind that *has* justified coercive power, or the kind that, *if coercion should be justified*, has the capacity to coerce? We do not want to argue that since subjects are liable to coercion anyway, it is best that their coercer be justified, and therefore best that the subjects think about it in ways that promote that conclusion. All of this *is* desirable only if the state's coercive power *is* justified on some ground. If it is, we might have reason to hope that states have the effective capacity to coerce, at least under the conditions in which coercion would be legitimate. But it is odd to think of justification of the state's coercive power as itself being something that *citizens* value. Could Dworkin be confusing integrity's value to the citizens with a different one: its value *to a theorist* who is aiming to offer an apology for the (*presupposed*) legitimacy of the state? I return to this possibility in Section 6.

Consider now the other supposed advantages of integrity. Dworkin says that if we impute personality to the community and see it as capable of integrity, we will have the further instrumental benefits of a more open and efficient legal system, as well as the non-instrumental value of being self-legislators who set up a scheme of principle and are united in a continuing effort to keep faith with it. Imputing personality to the community is good because it makes possible the sense of integrity, which is good. This is indecisive. Personifying the community may make it possible to see it as having the

---

[23] Dworkin, *Law's Empire*, 188.

new virtues Dworkin mentions but it also makes it possible to see it as having a new set of *vices*, such as hypocrisy and bad faith. Like the hypothesis of free will, integrity opens some doors only by closing others. In any case, none of these virtues suggests a ground of obedience. Openness, efficiency, and moral autonomy do not require that citizens take the law as binding, nor do they imply reasons for doing so. A legal system may promote these ends if it enjoys sufficient conformity to work well; but that does not require universal conformity, nor does it require that those who conform take the existence of law as among their reasons for conforming. Perhaps these virtues contribute to the idea that our community is attractive, but not to the different and more ambitious thesis that it has legitimate authority over us.

Does Dworkinian integrity at least capture the social dimension of political life better than competing theories do? Dworkin holds that obligations may be controversial because it is a matter for interpretation what the law (really) requires. He says that all social obligations are to be interpreted in light of 'a protestant attitude that makes each citizen responsible for imagining what his society's public commitments to principle are, and what these commitments require in new circumstances'.[24] Interpreting the law, or any other social practice, is thus not a matter of trying to understand what it demands of us, it is a matter of imposing or projecting *our* purposes onto it: 'Each citizen, we might say, is trying to discover his own intention in maintaining and participating in that practice'; he is engaged in 'a conversation with himself'.[25]

This has profound consequences for a social theory of obligation. It turns principled civil disobedience into obedience to true law, since the disobedient are trying to keep faith with their own intentions in maintaining the practice of law.[26] Moreover, since not only the requirements of the community but even its boundaries are matters of interpretation, it turns my question of whether another person is a member of my community into a matter of trying to discover my own purposes in *regarding* them as a member. I ignore the issue of whether this is a plausible theory of interpretation.[27] But if

---

[24] Ibid., 413.
[25] Ibid., 58.
[26] Those who are civilly disobedient 'act to acquit rather than to challenge their duty as citizens': Ronald Dworkin, *A Matter of Principle* (Harvard University Press, 1985) 105. Note that they acquit their duty as citizens, not merely in the trivial sense of disobeying the law to obey other, more stringent, duties of citizenship, for example, to improve the law. Dworkin's claim entails that, properly understood, they are obeying what the law really requires, that is, what each does well to understand it as requiring.
[27] See Gerald J. Postema, 'Protestant Interpretation and Social Practices' (1987) 6 *Law and Philosophy* 283.

it is, the sort of admiration due personal integrity is without analogue here, not because the state is a collectivity rather than an individual, but because its *bona fides* and single mindedness are *our* contributions to it. They are part of our own attempts to see it in its best light. If we succeed at this, what deserves admiration—the law or our own ingenuity in interpretation? For Dworkin, there is little difference, because the law's requirements are, for each individual, their own best interpretation of what law requires. They are, in his favoured metaphor, the upshot of a 'protestant' attitude to interpretation, guided by an inner light rather than by any external fact. But in collapsing the distinction between a social practice and an individual's view of it we lose grip on the ideal of admiring an agent with whom we disagree. What was offered as a way of tempering the individualism of consent theory now returns, through the protestant character of interpretation, as individualism with a vengeance. The communal-sounding notion that an association of integrity must keep faith with its own principles turns out to mean that each must create a monadic view of its aims and see it as keeping faith with him. Who, now, is obeying whom? The sense in which this is an associative theory of political obligation is vestigial.

5. Individuality and Community

It is common to feel the urge for a social account of legitimacy, but important to yield to it in the right way. There are two options. Some, like Dworkin, attempt to make community part of the *normative* conditions for legitimacy, by which I mean the way duties are acquired. But one might instead incorporate community into the *evaluative* conditions that justify a particular mode of acquiring duties. One combination of these positions could hold that political obligation binds only through consent, while maintaining as an evaluative thesis that the case for requiring consent rests on social rather than individual considerations.

It is time to get clearer about social values. Although there is no agreement about what ethical individualism amounts to, three theses are commonly associated with it. The first is *egoism*, the view that everyone should act only to promote their own interests, such as increasing their own wealth, status, or power. The second is *instrumentalism* which holds that all social relations and institutions are of value only to the extent that they are efficient means to the ends, whatever those may be, of individual persons. Finally, there is the thesis that I will call *humanism*, according to which morality must have some connection (not necessarily instrumental) with the interests of persons.

A generation ago, political theorists used to imagine a 'liberal vs communitarian' debate that pits an individualist outlook against a sort of social outlook, and which underlies most disputes in political thought. It was rarely made clear which, if any, of the theses I mentioned were in issue. A surprising amount of ink was spilled criticizing egoism which, Hobbes and some neoclassical economists aside, no serious moralist defended as an ideal or a virtue. More interesting are the other theses. Humanism is accepted by most moralists except for Nietzscheans, divine command theorists, and certain animal right advocates.[28] Whatever its merits in general moral philosophy, I will assume that humanism is fundamental to any acceptable theory of political morality. There are other ends in life, but the political realm is concerned with the fates of people (and the fates of creatures whose fates are inextricably bound up with the fates of people). The live battle is over instrumentalism.[29]

Classical liberals did often justify consent by instrumental considerations arguing, for example, that it gives individuals the power to protect themselves from duties they do not want, or to enter beneficial arrangements with others. Some even thought it was needed to set up human society. The instrumental value to individuals of the power to consent is real, but it is not the only value the power has. Consider its role in marriage as it exists in our cultures. No one can get married except by their own consent, though marriage brings with it duties not all of which are results of consent. Some object to this. Should consent not structure the whole relation, such that each spousal duty is subject to a separate agreement to bear it? Some would find such contractualization of personal relationships appealing, others would no doubt find it appalling. It is clear, however, that to defend the institution of marriage as we have it, we need to show that there is value in a common social role which cannot be characterized as a sum of individually undertaken duties. A society that only has individual, ante-'nuptial' contracts is a society without marriage.

Role duties have a relative objectivity, by which I mean that they are beyond the control of their subjects. Roles are social and not individual creations. One can choose not to be a judge, but not to be a judge with no duty

---

[28] See Sue Donaldson and Will Kymlicka, *Zoopolis: A Political Theory of Animal Rights* (Oxford University Press, 2011).
[29] For a contemporary liberal view that has practically no patience for *any* instrumental argument in politics, see Alon Harel, *Why Law Matters* (Oxford University Press, 2014). I offer a qualified defence of instrumentalism in Chapter 2, this volume.

of impartiality. Not all roles impose valid duties. The traditional gender roles in our societies did not: they unjustly assigned to women the primary burden of domestic labour. When are role duties morally binding? No single explanation is applicable to all roles. But there is a constraint on all sound explanations: they must explain not only the value of people being subject to the relevant duties but being subject to them *as occupants* of the role they constitute.

That calls for a two-part explanation. First, one needs to justify the clustering of duties into a role at all. Why not instead have flexibility in these matters and allow people to construct their own roles as they go and according to their circumstances? Radical individualists might favour this as giving fullest expression to the sovereignty of will. They might concede some minor instrumental benefits to having standard patterns of social interaction, and they might permit roles as default options. Ideal human relations, however, they would see as polymorphous and contractual. Against such a view, considerations like those, which Joseph Raz elaborates with great power in his discussion of the social nature of value, seem to me persuasive.[30] Common roles may be valued because they are common and embody social relations which are valuable for their own sake and not merely as means to individual ends. They are valuable *to* individuals, so humanism is not denied, but they are valued *as* social relationships in a way that egoists and instrumentalists would reject. Beginning with the ancient world, part of the value of citizenship was recognized to lie in its character as a shared status purporting to transcend other divisions among people. An individualist ideal of a multiplicity of different social contracts would not capture that.

Nonetheless, to defend common social roles does not explain why they bind their incumbents. Thus, we come to the second problem. Why should socially constituted roles create valid duties? Again, there are various considerations. Some role duties bind non-voluntarily, most plausibly when others are non-voluntarily dependent[31] on their performance (such as infants on their parents) or when the duties benefit others but are modest in their demands (e.g. the duty of teachers to be punctual). Others bind only when assumed by agents with a degree of awareness about the duties the role brings. Is the role of citizenship one which can bind non-voluntarily? If it can, is that its best justification?

---

[30] Joseph Raz, *The Morality of Freedom* (Oxford University Press, 1986), chap. 12.
[31] For a defence of dependence as a ground of obligations, see Robert E. Goodin, *Protecting the Vulnerable* (University of Chicago Press, 1986).

It might seem initially plausible that other people are non-voluntarily dependent on our performing our duties as citizens. If one breaks the law, it will often harm others, or fail to promote our mutual interests, or impose unfair burdens on them. Often—but not always, and that is important to remember. Moreover, these are good reasons on their own for doing as the law requires. We are seeking a case that establishes that the fact that law requires something is *itself* a reason warranting moral consideration. Consider, then, a case where the law requires some action, but the above considerations are absent. Two things are evident: in this case the law still claims to obligate, but other citizens are not dependent on one's doing as it requires. They are not dependent on our being obedient subjects. At most, they are dependent on our complying with the law in cases in which it would be harmful or wrongful not to do so. No plausible argument establishes that every act of disobedience harms or wrongs someone. Nor can it be said that what citizenship requires of us is modest, for every state makes extensive claims to our allegiance. The state can demand that we kill, or be killed. The social role of citizenship is not therefore liable to the same justifications as most other sorts of non-voluntary roles.

Roles can, however, also come to bind with our consent. Because not every kind of consent will be valid, necessary background conditions must still be satisfied. Suppose that Dworkin correctly identified these in his account of true community and suppose that consent to obey such a community would be valid because it partly constitutes the valuable common status of citizenship. Consent therefore binds, not because it protects citizens or opens up valuable bargains, but because it is part of a valuable social relation. On this view, the obligations *of* members are defined socially, through the role as practised in their society, but no one has an obligation *to become* a member unless they undertake to do so. This barely scratches the surface of a role-based theory of consent, and before it could be developed several objections would have to be met. Dworkin has put the more important ones:

(1) Consent to the role of citizenship, even if given, would never be valid. Here, Dworkin joins Hume in maintaining that there can be no real choice about membership in the state. '[E]ven if the consent were genuine, the argument would fail as an argument for legitimacy, because a person leaves one sovereign only to join another; he has no choice to be free from sovereigns altogether.'[32] It is true that a free

---

[32] Dworkin, *Law's Empire*, 193.

choice depends not only on the mere existence of alternatives, but also on their quality. But the implied description of the available alternatives is wrong and perpetuates a fallacy. It supposes that one must either accept the authority of the state or emigrate. There are many other alternatives recognized and practised in our own political cultures. One may remain in the country, participate in its affairs, be attentive to the law, obeying when conscience counsels, yet reject the comprehensive moral authority of the state. Those who comply in a peaceful and principled fashion will, in a reasonably just state, support the government and avoid sanction, but the law itself creates no obligations for them. We might say they are *in* though not *of* the political community. Still, it would be wrong to think of them as deeply alienated. They may continue to identify with many of the traditions and values of the community, they are engaged citizens, but their allegiance does not extend to the state.

(2) Role duties are 'not formed in one act of deliberate contractual commitment, the way one joins a club'.[33] Consent theory does not require duties be assumed by one act, whatever that means. Nor are all consent-based duties contractual, in the sense that they define the terms of a bargain. (Joining a health club may be contractual, joining a church rarely is.) A role may be assumed by actions, by omissions, and by series of actions and omissions which collectively amount to the deliberate assumption of the role. (Consider the commitments involved in choosing to become a lawyer.)

(3) Role duties extend beyond explicit agreement to include the spirit or purposes of the relationship in question.[34] Again, consent theory is not committed to the impugned view. An ordinary act of consent may create duties both explicitly and implicitly. Consent to an end, for example, may imply consent to its necessary means. If Dworkin's general theory of interpretation were correct it would apply here too, and acts of consent would bind agents to many duties required by implication and coherence.

(4) Role duties are often not thought of as voluntary. '[W]e are rarely even aware that we are entering upon any special status as the story unfolds.'[35] '[P]eople in the bare community have the obligations of a true

---

[33] Ibid., 197.
[34] Ibid., 200, 210.
[35] Ibid., 197.

community whether or not they want them . . .'[36] This is the crux of the matter; but it begs the question. We must not confuse undertaking a role with wanting to do so, or wanting to have an obligation with wanting to perform it. I may assume an obligation that I do not want and hope never to have to fulfil, in order to get something else that I do want. And it is characteristic of all valid obligations, whatever their source, that they must be performed irrespective of the agent's wishes. Dworkin's observation that we become most conscious of our obligations at the point of performance is irrelevant. He is correct, however, to hold that choice is absent if a role or status was blundered into, or happened upon, without even an awareness that anything significant was happening. If political roles bind in such circumstances, then even a socialized version of consent theory is a failure. But do they? The arguments from true community and from integrity did not establish it.

I think we should accept that the political role is weakly voluntary, in the sense that one has no obligation to assume it and it can be terminated at will. A consent theorist holds that weak voluntarism is not enough in this context. What is true of a role like 'neighbour' need not hold of a role like 'citizen' or 'subject'. Why is a high degree of awareness and engagement necessary on the part of citizens to validate their duties to obey? Remember that in the political community the stakes are the highest: it claims authority to regulate all other communities, to support or to undermine all other roles. Drifting in or out of an association claiming that sort of authority, dimly aware of what is happening, is much more serious than in the normal ebb and flow of relationships like friendship. What is more, every state is liable to change. It is not enough to trust the present rulers, because political obligations are not held to bind only to a particular administration or government. These are powerful reasons for thinking that the political role (or roles) is a special one and that full membership—the sort that brings a general duty to obey—should be deliberately triggered.[37]

[36] Ibid., 201.
[37] There could be weaker forms of association that bring some political duties, but not political obligation or full membership. Locke's position is that 'an *express Consent*, of any Man, entring [sic] into any Society, makes him a perfect Member of that Society, a Subject of that Government' (*Two Treatises of Government*, II, s. 119). But Locke also acknowledges statuses short of a 'perfect Member'. See John Simmons, '"Denisons" and "Aliens": Locke's Problem of Political Consent' (1998) 24 *Social Theory and Practice* 161. For complications of membership in more fluid societies, see Ashwini Vasanthakumar, *The Ethics of Exile: A Political Theory of Diaspora* (Oxford University Press, 2021).

All this is intelligible, however, only if we can think of people as giving or withholding their consent. Some communitarians (but not Dworkin) used to hold that this is inconsistent with a sound view of personal identity. They said that people cannot be distanced from their social roles, for these *constitute* their identity; the idea of an essential, noumenal Self, capable of giving or withholding its consent is foolish and politically dangerous abstraction. That was the argument. It fails because it is sufficient for consent theory that people can distance themselves from their *political* role. Consent is intelligible provided only that fully constituted agents—with their genders, religions, values, and all the rest—can put, understand, and answer the question: Should I concede the authority of the state? Might someone deny even this much distance, and insist that citizenship itself must be constitutive of our personalities, so that the question cannot even be asked? Put that way, it is clear which view is the foolish and dangerous abstraction.

Consent theorists insist on the importance of a lively awareness of role duties and deliberateness in entering certain roles, but may, and should, reject instrumental or egoistic views which reduce consent to a bargain. Their political sociology may learn from Hegel, Burke, or Durkheim in as much as it places community and custom at centre stage in explanations of why people obey their rulers. But they will give them only bit parts, and certainly no speaking roles, in the theory of legitimacy.

6. The Universality of Obligation

Let us take stock. I rejected Dworkin's account of associative obligation and defended a version of the thesis that consent is necessary for a role-based obligation to obey the law. But I did not show that everyone consents to obey and, indeed, any theory purporting to show that would be suspect. It therefore follows that some people may have no obligation to obey, even when the state is reasonably just and the conditions of true community are satisfied. Is the scent of *reductio* in the air? Doesn't every theory of law *have to* explain how law morally obligates? Dworkin thinks so: 'A conception of law must explain how what it takes to be law provides a general justification for the exercise of coercive power by the state, a justification that holds except in special cases when some competing argument is specially powerful.'[38] I conclude with some doubts about that.

---

[38] Dworkin, *Law's Empire*, 190, cf. 110.

There is something backwards here. We would not begin a theory of criminal justice by first assuming that our practices of punishment are justified and then seeking the theory which best shows why they are. It may be the nature of punishments that they *purport to be* a form of justice rather than terror, but our theories must test the credentials of that claim. We therefore start tentatively, and ask *whether* punishment is ever justified, in what forms, and under what conditions. Why is this not also the right procedure for thinking about the claims of the state?

For Dworkin, law is a controversial and value-laden concept. Nonetheless, like H. L. A. Hart,[39] he thinks that we agree at an abstract level about the kind of thing that law is. He says that there is an uncontroversial[40] consensus that ties the concept of law to that of justified coercion. '[F]or us', he writes, 'legal argument takes place on a plateau of rough consensus that if law exists it provides a justification for the use of collective power against individual citizens or groups'.[41] This is a somewhat dark formulation. The existence of a legal system obviously does not justify every sort of collective power. Governments coerce people without relying on law (e.g. by using their market power) and are sometimes justified in doing so. Moreover, the rule of law is at most one necessary condition for justified coercion. Not only the forms of justice but also its substance must be in order.

In fact, however, Dworkin's view of law does incorporate a substantive theory of justice, as in this narrower restatement of it.

> Our discussions about law by and large assume, I suggest, that the most abstract and fundamental point of legal practice is to guide and constrain the power of government in the following way. Law insists that force not be used or withheld, no matter how useful that would be to ends in view, no matter how beneficial or noble these ends, except as licensed or required by individual rights and responsibilities flowing from past political decisions about when collective force is justified.[42]

Here, the plateau erodes to become the narrow ledge of Dworkin's own rights thesis. This is a much more substantial claim than his general one, but it is

---

[39] The only important difference between Dworkin's methodological claims for the plateau and Hart's account of the concept of law is that Dworkin explicitly limits the range of his theory to Anglo-American common-law legal systems.
[40] Dworkin, *Law's Empire*, 94.
[41] Ibid., 108–9.
[42] Ibid., 93.

miles from any uncontroversial plateau of agreement about what 'our' discussions about law assume. Dworkin's rights thesis is one of the most controversial claims of modern jurisprudence.

The plateau has two interesting features. First, it exhibits a Kelsenian vein that often works to the surface of Dworkin's thought. On his view, the point of law is not to govern interpersonal relations directly, by imposing duties or setting standards of behaviour, it is to govern them indirectly by instructing officials when to use and withhold force. Is this plausible or does it distort the point of, say tort or contract, to see them as primarily guiding and constraining governments in their use of force? Our discussions about these areas of law do not require that assumption. Second, Dworkin's plateau makes it a necessary condition of all justified forcing, and all refraining from forcing, that it be authorized by past political decisions. Can we not regard force as justified in some matters about which there have been no prior decisions at all? We can; but 'past political decisions' is for Dworkin just a metaphor for his coherence argument: a coercive act can be brought within its ambit if it is arguable that it is not inconsistent with past decisions and that it furthers whatever purposes it is morally desirable to impute to those decisions.

I think that both are mistaken as claims in legal theory, but here it suffices to see that this narrow view of law has no consequences for an argument about the moral obligation to obey. One person may be justified in coercing another without first needing, or consequently acquiring, a right to obedience, not even when the justification for coercion is the protection of rights. Dworkin resists this idea, however:

> These two issues—whether the state is morally legitimate, in the sense that it is justified in using force against its citizens, and whether the state's decisions impose genuine obligations on them—are not identical. No state should enforce all of a citizen's obligations. But though obligation is not a sufficient condition for coercion, it is close to a necessary one. A state may have good grounds in some special circumstances for coercing those who have no duty to obey. But no general policy of upholding the law with steel could be justified if the law were not, in general, a source of genuine obligations.[43]

---

[43] Ibid., 191.

It is true some obligations should not be enforced, but that is irrelevant to the question of whether the state can enforce some requirement only if there is a prior obligation *to obey*. The above passage confounds

(4) the state may only coerce people to make them perform actions which they have an antecedent obligation to perform,

with

(5) the state may only coerce people who have an obligation to obey it.

Now (4) is probably false: there are *mala prohibita* that the state is justified in coercively enforcing. But what matters more is the truth of (5), and (4) does nothing to establish that. One may have an antecedent obligation to do or refrain from some action even if there is no obligation to obey the state. An anarchist can believe that there is a moral obligation not to murder and also deny that the criminal law creates any moral obligations at all.

In most contexts the difference between justified coercive power and authority—the normative power to impose obligations on others—is clear enough.[44] I am justified in resisting unlawful arrest but have no authority over the offender. The Allies were justified in coercing the Nazis but gained no right to rule German citizens. In cases of self-defence and sometimes also in other defence one may be justified in coercing those over whom one has no authority at all. A reasonably just state may sometimes coerce outsiders, at least to protect its own citizens and probably for some other purposes too.

What remains of the claim that if law is to employ coercive sanctions as a general policy then it must in general be a source of moral obligation? I take the implied contrast to be between a general policy and special cases, or between a rule and its exceptions. One could acknowledge that, when fighting a just war or acting in self-defence, one is entitled to coerce others but see these as exceptions to the general policy that one may only coerce those over whom one has legitimate authority. But *are* these exceptions to a general policy? Why are these circumstances the special ones? If we had an independent argument to the effect that a government requires authority to be justified in resorting to coercion, then that would be a good start; but that is at issue. Moreover, the government's right to enforce its will need not rest

---

[44] Green, *The Authority of the State*, 71–5, 149–53, 242–3.

on any general policy but only on a cluster of different considerations which, taken together, generally justify its use of force. It may be justified in coercing those who murder to protect those at risk, in coercing those who break contracts to protect valued social practices, and in coercing those who negligently harm others to establish a public framework for reciprocity, and so on. Taken together, the set of such different reasons covers most legitimate enforcement. Coercion can be generally justified without a general justification for coercion.

Finally, even if there were, over and above the heterogeneous 'special' considerations a further general one, it would almost certainly be weaker than the special considerations themselves. Reflective opinion is divided on the theoretical question of whether, apart from the moral obligation not to assault people, there is also a further and separate obligation to obey a law prohibiting assaults. But it is united in thinking that if there is, the first is the weightier. The main moral reason for not assaulting people is that it wrongs them, not that the law prohibits it.

The existence of a general obligation to obey is not a necessary condition for the state to be justified in enforcing the law. It is not even a sufficient condition, for a just state has a duty to use the least harmful means effective in securing a reasonable degree of compliance. Other things being equal, direction, exhortation, and inducement are preferable to steel as means of upholding the law. There is, then, no warrant for the transcendental tone of Dworkin's question—how is it possible that there is a general obligation to obey the law?—and no threat to consent theory from that quarter. Universal political obligation is not a fixed point of moral consciousness, crying out for explanation. It is not even something that most people believe as a pre-theoretical matter.[45] It is a controversial and, I think, false political claim. Any residual unease with the notion of a reasonably just state, or a 'true community', which lacks authority over some of its members can be dispelled by considering that, on anyone's theory, every just state imposes no obligations on *some* people, namely, those living in other just states. If states with imperial ambitions should purport to create duties for people resident elsewhere, we would hardly add those to some list of political obligations that legal theory must 'explain'. We would explain them away. The

---

[45] Leslie Green, 'Who Believes in Political Obligation?', in John T. Sanders and Jan Narveson eds, *For and Against the State*, Rowman and Littlefield, 1996) 1–17.

question is whether anyone within a state's own territory is in the same position. Put that way, the denial of a general political obligation begins to look less strange and consent, as rare and special as it may be, begins to look more attractive as an account of a relationship that is a rather special one. That is a pleasing symmetry.[46]

---

[46] I thank Juhani Pietarinen and his colleagues at the University of Turku, Finland, where this chapter was first aired. Ronald Dworkin commented on a later version in *Dworkin and his Critics* (Justine Burley ed., Blackwell, 2004). This chapter attempts to clarify the points on which we still disagree.

13
The Forces of Law

1. Law and Things We Do Not Want To Do

'Law makes us do things we do not want to do. It has other functions as well, but perhaps the most visible aspect of law is its frequent insistence that we act in accordance with its wishes, our own personal interests or best judgment notwithstanding.'[1] So writes Frederick Schauer in his bold defence of the view that modern jurisprudence systemically neglects the coercive character of law.

There are two interesting claims in that opening. The first is that law *makes us* do things we would not otherwise want to do. The second claim is independent of the first, or so it seems to me. It is that law *insists that* we act in accordance with its wishes, irrespective of our own interests or judgement about the matter. Schauer treats those two claims as nearly interchangeable, or at any rate he interprets the second in light of the first. Characteristically if not necessarily, law makes us do things by forcing us, and forcing is how the law goes about insisting. The question then arises: if the law can insist without forcing why is force of special interest to jurisprudence?

One answer is that force is of moral interest. Forcing people to do things calls for justification of some sort, and resorting to coercive force bears a special burden of justification. A less obvious answer is defended by writers like Hobbes, Bentham, Austin, and Kelsen. They say that, even when it appears otherwise, law *is* a sort of coercive force—commands backed up by threats, or commands to deploy force under certain conditions. On this point, H. L. A. Hart parts company with his positivist forebears. Hart thinks coercive force is very important to law and, as we shall see, to jurisprudence. But he does not think we can identify law with force or with any organization of force: law is an organization of social rules and its resort to force, though humanly necessary, is not conceptually necessary. Schauer does not disagree with that, strictly speaking. But he thinks that we miss a lot of what is

---

[1] Frederick Schauer, *The Force of Law* (Harvard University Press, 2014) 1.

important about law if we insist on speaking strictly. Philosophers like Hart (and me) are said to make 'efforts to marginalize the place of raw force in explaining what makes law distinctive'.[2] Better we should give up the obsession with finding out what features, if any, are necessary to law and legal systems and think more about what is broadly typical of them. We need less analysis and more accounting. And that is the second fish in Schauer's frying pan: a methodology for jurisprudence, a philosophy of legal philosophy.

Jurisprudence is certainly overdue a re-examination of the place of coercion in law, and Schauer's challenge is a welcome opportunity to make a start on it. In doing so, I defend three claims:

(1) The force of law is not one thing but three: the imposition of *duties*, the use of *coercion*, and the exercise of *power*. Duties are norms and cannot be explained in terms of either coercion or power. People are coerced by law only when subject to a certain kind of threat. People are subject to power whenever the existence of law exerts significant causal influence over their action or interests.

(2) In modern jurisprudence, the role of coercion is more central than Schauer allows. He focuses too much on a few negative claims, and too little on a series of important positive claims that Hart and others defend about the role of coercion in law.

(3) If jurisprudence needs more attention to contingent, typical, truths about law, then it needs something else too. Before we can know what is typical, we need to count. Before we can count, we need to know *what counts as what*—especially, what counts as coercion. Counting-a*s* is a matter of identifying necessary and sufficient conditions.

2. The Force of Duty

All legal systems impose duties on people. That is the primary sense in which law 'insists' that we do certain things, whether we want to or not. A duty is a norm to which its subjects must conform, not one to which they may conform when it suits them, benefits them, or when they consider it right to do so.

---

[2] Ibid., 2.

You may wonder whether it is true that we cannot have law without duties. We all know that even a 'society of angels' would need rules, if only to help them coordinate their altruistic activities.[3] Angels need standing answers to question like this: 'Should Seraphim give way to Cherubim when their flight paths cross, or vice-versa?' They need to settle this, and not on a one-off basis. A regular priority needs to be assigned on some principle or other, whether hierarchy, direction of approach, or urgency of message. A rule to settle this, one might argue, is not itself a duty-imposing rule. The way settlement rules work, when they do, is by giving angels a way to get what they want: speed without danger. Angels need information, not motivation. If there is an effective rule the question whether they are to comply with it (whether they want to or not) does not arise. They *want* to comply; they need to know how to do it. If most did not want to comply with a settlement rule, that rule could not yield a settlement. So perhaps if human nature were angelic, a legal system could consist entirely of rules settling what conduct is appropriate, providing information but adding no motivation to what is already in place. Not only would it have no need for coercive sanctions, it seems it would also have no need to insist on anything. There could be law without duties.

Two considerations tell against that conclusion. First, as to the angelic subjects. The fairy tale assumes away recalcitrance and shows that even without it rules are needed. But it does not assume away rational conflicts. Angels may reasonably hold different views about what is appropriate in certain circumstances, and a reasonable view is one on which there is a reason, *pro tanto*, to act. When the circumstances only require coordination, then the fact that there is an effective rule will give a reason to follow it outweighing the reasons to do anything different. Conformity dominates. But what if they aren't? Urgency and hierarchy may conflict even if we cannot compare them on a common scale. In that case angels need to opt for one rule to the exclusion of the other or there will be no prospect for conformity. Having opted, the rule they pick becomes salient and conformity brings its own reward—even flawed humans would conform in those circumstances, without any need for sanctions. But to get there, the angels need to opt, and to do so in the spirit that the opted-for rule *is to be* operative, notwithstanding the reasons

---

[3] Augustine says in his *Exposition of the Psalms* (32) that the society of angels is a place 'where neither adversary there shall be in battle to be tossed nor sluggard from the earth to be stirred up'. Lon Fuller says it is a place without 'man's selfish, quarrelsome, and disputatious nature'. Lon Fuller, *The Morality of Law* (rev. edn, Yale University Press, 1969) 55. Both agree that rules will nonetheless be needed to guide angelic conduct. So, too, does Joseph Raz, *Practical Reason and Norms* (2nd edn, Oxford University Press, 1999) 157–61.

favouring any other rule. This duty is not created by an operative rule; the duty is to opt and thus *make* a rule salient (and therefore operative).[4] It is a duty to legislate.

There is also a second place duties always turn up in law. Even in a world that is not only angelic but without incommensurability, there will be disputes about the bearing of the rules on individual cases, if only because of the ineliminability of vagueness. Law need not resolve every such dispute, but it will need to resolve some of them. To do that, it will need to give someone the power and duty to make rulings about what is to be done. The legal rules themselves could be created informally and unintentionally through the emergence of custom—the most basic rules in every legal system must be created that way—but, however they are created, there must be someone with a duty to make binding determinations about what the rules require in cases of doubt. Without that, we could not have a legal system at all.

It follows that duties are one of the things no legal system fails to create. And duties have a further importance. Although law also has other sorts of rules, including rules that confer rights, grant permissions, create powers, and so forth, these can only be fully understood by their relation to duty-imposing rules. Rights have correlative duties; permissions cancel duties; powers give the capacity to create, waive, or modify duties (or rights, or permissions or powers, which in turn can only be understood in relation to duties). It is not that these can be *reduced* to (conditional) duties, or that the various normative terms can be dispensed with in favour of statements about duties. The point is that we do not fully understand them without reference to duties.

There is one last moral to be drawn from the fairy tale. Although duty-imposing rules are necessary even among a society of angels, coercive sanctions are not. Angels need no supplementary motivation to comply with their duties. Things are different among mortals. Our law needs a back-up plan that comes into effect when we fail to conform to the demands of duty. Plan A is that we should conform without further direction or motivation, whether we want to or not. Plan B is that we will be subjected to coercive sanctions or other incentives if we do not conform. When Plan B comes into effect, the law is past hoping that we will conform to our duties whether we want to or not. It now

---

[4] This differs from a typical convention (drive on the right or the left, measure in metres or in yards, etc.) where the problem is in predicting what most others will do, who are also predicting what most others predict *they* will do, and so on. For further discussion see Chapter 3, this volume.

deploys arrangements that make us want to do so, by making conformity the lesser evil or greater good. I say 'normally' because, here, the law must place fallible bets on human motivations. A threat of jail induces most people to comply with the law; but it may induce the homeless to break it. Sanctions are subject to the ordinary economy of threats: costs against benefits. Motivation by threat thus lacks the binding, categorical force that Plan A claims. And this shows that when coercive sanctions are present—as they generally are—they do not explain the normative character of legal duties.

Now, all this does not *quite* show that coercive sanctions are 'not a logical feature of our concept of law',[5] or that 'as long as there could possibly be a coercion free legal system, coercion would no longer be a conceptually necessary property of law'.[6] It shows that there are possible legal systems that do not *deploy* any coercion. That leaves open other possibilities. Here is an important one: because the authority of law is comprehensive, there are no legal systems that lack norms capable of imposing sanctions if necessary.[7] Even the angelic legal system contains all the powers necessary to get a coercive apparatus up and running in short order. It is unusual only in that it does not use its necessary powers in that way. It is a feature of our concept of law that it is *coercive if necessary*, though not necessarily coercive. This is not what Bentham, Austin, or Kelsen had in mind when they said that law is, of its nature, a coercive instrument. They meant that law not only necessarily has such powers, but that law necessarily uses them. It might be conceptually necessary to a kind of normative system that it include certain powers in order to be a system of that kind. But whether any power is used is a question of fact. If all legal systems use their coercion-creating powers to create coercive norms and institutions, the explanation for that must lie in whatever it is about the world that makes this so useful to them.

3. The Force of Coercion

Schauer does not deny the soundness of an argument like the one I have set out in Section 2. In fact, he accepts it.[8] But while he agrees that coercion is not

---

[5] Raz, *Practical Reason and Norms*, 158.
[6] Schauer, *The Force of Law*, 93.
[7] John Rawls, *A Theory of Justice* (Harvard University Press, 1971) 236; Raz, *Practical Reason and Norms*, 150–4; Leslie Green, *The Authority of the State* (Oxford University Press, 1990) 71–8; Grant Lamond, 'Coercion and the Nature of Law' (2001) 7 *Legal Theory* 35.
[8] Schauer, *The Force of Law*, 93–4.

a necessary feature of law, he denies the significance of that fact. Laws and legal systems may not be essentially coercive, but they are typically coercive, and the presence of coercion in various guises in all known legal systems is more salient than its absence in some purely theoretical, made-up, fairy-tale legal system. Schauer has an explanation for why so many legal philosophers get things backwards:

> Understanding law as typically coercive is hardly a revelation. But there are reasons why Hart and his followers have downplayed this seemingly obvious feature of law. In particular, it is often claimed that many people obey the law just because it is the law and not because of what the law can do to them if they disobey.[9]

Invoking a range of empirical and anecdotal evidence Schauer goes on to argue that this motivational claim is false. But I did not mention or rely on the belief that 'many people obey the law just because it is the law' anywhere in Section 2, and Schauer concedes that an argument of that sort is sound. Why then does he think that belief lies at the root of the alleged errors? I think it is because he misinterprets a remark of Hart's and then fails to notice the many ways Hart (and Hartians, and Dworkinians) give coercion a central role in jurisprudence.

I begin with the misinterpretation. At page 40 of *The Concept of Law*, Hart assesses Kelsen's argument that the content of every legal system could be represented as a set of orders, directed at judges, to apply sanctions under certain conditions. On this theory, law directly guides only the courts and other officials, by telling them when they ought to impose sanctions on people; law's ordinary subjects are guided indirectly. Offhand, that seems plain wrong. The formation rules of contract, for example, do not prescribe coercive sanctions for anyone. And the prohibition on homicide certainly seems addressed to ordinary subjects, not to judges alone. Ingeniously, Kelsen develops a reply to such objections. Rules that do not order sanctions can be represented as fragments of rules that do: as triggers for them, as restrictions on their scope, on their validity, and so on. As for the primary duty not to murder, we can regard it as normatively superfluous in a legal system whose courts already have a secondary duty to order sanctions against murderers, and whose constitutional ground rules that authorize judicial orders are presupposed to be

---

[9] Ibid., x.

binding. Every legal system contains normatively surplus material, from preambles to chapter numbers to declarations of value. The (apparent) duty not to murder is only a less obvious specimen.

Hart has various objections to this—but none of them show that Kelsen's programme of reconstruction is impossible to realize; they aim to show that it is distorting. Our theories of law, says Hart, ought to represent law as it is for any of those who use it, people outside courts as much as people in them. And 'conditional orders to judges' are not how most people see law, most of the time. He then asks whether Kelsen could reply to this criticism by relying on Holmes' edict that, 'If you want to know the law and nothing else, you must look at it as a bad man, who cares only for the material consequences which such knowledge enables him to predict . . .'[10] Now we arrive at the idea Schauer misinterprets. Hart continues:

> It is sometimes urged in favour of theories like the one under consideration that, by recasting the law in a form of a direction to apply sanctions, an advance in clarity is made, since this form makes plain all that the 'bad man' wants to know about the law. This may be true but it seems an inadequate defence for the theory. Why should not law be equally if not more concerned with the 'puzzled man' or 'ignorant man' who is willing to do what is required, if only he can be told what it is? Or with the 'man who wishes to arrange his affairs' if only he can be told how to do it.[11]

Now, bear in mind that this is part of Hart's reply *to Kelsen*. It is not Hart's reply to Oliver Wendell Holmes. Hart's (main) reply to Holmes is, in fact, the very same as Kelsen's reply to Holmes: statements of law are not predictions of coercion and not predictions of anything else either. They are norms.[12] Holmes has a (crude) theory of the springs of obedience in the bad man. But Kelsen has *no* theory of the springs of obedience in anyone, since whatever explains people's obedience to law is an empirical, psychological matter, and is therefore excluded from a jurisprudence developed under the constraints of his 'pure theory'. Hart's remark about the 'puzzled man' is thus no counterexample to Kelsen's theory of why people obey, for Kelsen advances no

---

[10] Oliver Wendell Holmes, Jr, 'The Path of the Law' (1897) 10 *Harvard Law Review* 457–78, 459.

[11] H. L. A. Hart, *The Concept of Law* (3rd edn, Penelope A. Bulloch and Joseph Raz eds; Leslie Green, intro, Oxford University Press, 2012) 40.

[12] Hans Kelsen, *General Theory of Law and the State* (Anders Wedberg trs, Harvard University Press, 1946) 166–7; Hart, *The Concept of Law*, 84.

such theory, and Hart's objection to Holmes' theory of law is not based on an objection to Holmes' theory of motivation. The 'puzzled man' example expresses or presupposes *no view* about why people generally conform to the law. Having no view, it cannot have a false view of the matter.

This makes trouble for Schauer's use of the example and the theory he builds on it. Schauer's argument, in essence, is this:

(1) The puzzled man is one who is disposed to comply with the law without the need for coercion 'just because it is the law'.[13]
(2) In actual legal systems, few people if any are disposed to comply with the law just because it is the law.[14]
(3) In actual legal systems, many laws would not enjoy the compliance they do but for the threat of coercion.
(4) So coercion is central to a theoretical understanding of law, and it is a mistake to 'denigrate', 'deny', or 'ignore' it: 'Relegating the coercive aspect of law to the sidelines of theoretical interest is perverse. And thus, adopting a conception of the philosophy of law that facilitates such relegation is even more so.'[15]

It will now be clear what I want to say about this. Let me take the steps in turn.

3.1 The Puzzled Man

As I argued, the 'puzzled man' example does not presuppose that most people comply with law 'just because it is the law'. The puzzled man is willing to do *what law requires*, provided he knows what that is. The basis for his willingness is left entirely open. He may be willing to conform because he thinks legal requirements are a reliable indicator of what morality requires, or because he wants to fit in with others. In either case he is still using legal norms to guide his conduct in a way that the bad man is not. Nor is the puzzled man one who typically 'internalizes' the norms he follows.[16] The puzzled man uses norms *as* norms, which means having the attitude towards those

---

[13] Schauer, *The Force of Law*, 42, 46.
[14] Ibid., 61.
[15] Ibid., 2, 44, 94, 167.
[16] *Pace* Ibid., 35–7, 41–2.

norms that Hart calls 'acceptance'. This is a term of art. To 'accept' a norm is to be disposed, *on whatever grounds*, to use it as a standard for the guidance and evaluation of conduct.[17] If one conforms to *what* a standard requires only because one is forced to perform the conforming behaviour, then one does not accept it. But if one uses the standard or applies it to others because one is forced to, then one does 'accept' it in the pertinent sense. Thus, judges who apply the law because they are afraid that if they do not they will be impeached, accept that law, provided they therefore use it as a standard to guide and evaluate conduct, demand conformity to that standard, criticize deviations from it, and use normative language in stating it—the typical marks of using something as a norm.

3.2 The Quantum of Obedience

Schauer's second proposition is correct: most people who conform to the law do not do so because of a general disposition to obey the law as such. Some probably have a piecemeal disposition to obey laws on certain subject matters, or laws created by certain governments, for example, those they voted for. Many more respond, in ways that Schauer illustrates, to law-provided incentives of various kinds. But quite a lot of conformity is not of either kind. No one can obey a law of which they are unaware. They can conform to *what* it requires, but the fact that the conduct *is* legally required cannot be normatively salient to them if they are unaware of it. Most people are unaware of most laws that apply to them. They conform because they have law-independent reasons for avoiding what are, coincidentally, delicts. Such people conform to law without obeying it. Luckily for them, the law does not generally punish failure to obey unless it is accompanied by failure to conform. The exceptions are the cases in which repudiation of the law's authority is itself an element of the offence (e.g. in contempt of court). The law claims obedience, but it mostly settles for conformity.

---

[17] Hart, *The Concept of Law*, 56. The motivation for taking the 'internal attitude' can include: 'calculations of long-term interest; disinterested interest in others; an unreflecting inherited or traditional attitude; or the mere wish to do as others do. There is indeed no reason why those who accept the authority of the system should not examine their conscience and decide that, morally, they ought not to accept it, yet for a variety of reasons continue to do so.' (Ibid., 203).

3.3 The Need for Coercion

The truth of proposition (3) depends on what we mean by coercion. In Section 4, below, I argue that Schauer's account is too broad, but here I will simply assume a narrower view as embraced by philosophers like Bentham, Austin, Kelsen, or Dworkin according to whom law coerces only when, by threat of physical force or serious deprivation of resources, it leaves its subjects without any option but to comply. Possibly this is too narrow. But we do not need anything broader to show that contemporary jurisprudents do not 'denigrate' coercion, think it 'irrelevant', or 'relegate it to the sidelines'. Even making allowances for polemical overstatement, none of these charges applies to Hart's account (nor to mine, Kelsen's, or even Dworkin's). For example, Hart unambiguously holds all of the following positive theses about the role of coercion in law:

(C1) All existing legal systems make extensive use of coercive sanctions.[18]

(C2) The emergence of law is partly explained by the greater efficiency of organized sanctions over diffuse social pressure in maintaining order.[19]

(C3) If a social order is dominated by coercive sanctions, that is prima facie reason for thinking that it is a (rudimentary) form of law.[20]

(C4) Sanctions are 'vital' in all legal systems, because only they give adequate assurance to those who would voluntarily comply that they will not be taken for suckers.[21]

(C5) Effective sanctions are the presupposed background of all true statements about any individual's legal obligations.[22]

Some of these theses may be doubtful, and some may actually *over*emphasize the role of coercion in law.[23] But it cannot be denied that someone who

---

[18] Ibid., 23–4, 197–200.

[19] Ibid., 94–5, 249–50.

[20] '[W]hen physical sanctions are prominent or usual among the forms of pressure, even though these are neither closely defined nor administered by officials but are left to the community at large, we shall be inclined to classify the rules as a primitive or rudimentary form of law.' (Ibid., 86)

[21] Ibid., 198

[22] '[U]nless in general sanctions were likely to be exacted from offenders, there would be little or no point in making particular statements about a person's obligations. In this sense, such statements may be said to presuppose belief in the continued normal operation of the system of sanctions.' (Ibid., 84–5).

[23] Are sanctions really the only way adequate assurance could be provided, as (C4) would have it? Why not rewards?

accepts all of them is alert to the typically, and importantly, coercive character of law. The same is true of Ronald Dworkin who holds that:

> the most abstract and fundamental point of legal practice is to guide and constrain the power of government in the following way. Law insists that force not be used or withheld, no matter how useful that would be to ends in view, no matter how beneficial or noble these ends, except as licensed or required by individual rights and responsibilities flowing from past political decisions about when collective force is justified.[24]

This, too, makes coercive force central to the concept of law, by making the deployment and regulation of coercion the defining function of law.

Perhaps Schauer's complaint lies not with such affirmative theses about coercion, but with three negative theses that Hart (among others) defends, two of which we have already encountered:

(C6) In every legal system there are some laws that are not enforced by any coercive sanction.

(C7) If human nature were different, it would be possible to have a legal system without any laws that prescribe coercive sanctions.

(C8) The normal function of sanctions in a legal system is ancillary; law's primary functions are those of guiding and evaluating conduct.

These theses, though compatible with (C1) to (C5), do entail that coercion, for all the importance Hart assigns it, cannot play the role it does in the theories of Bentham, Austin, or Kelsen. (C8) entails that coercion cannot even play the role it does in Dworkin's theory. But (C6) to (C8) do add up to a very important role for coercion in a theory of law.

Here, things get cloudy. Schauer actually *agrees* with (C6) and (C7). He affirms that 'non-coercive law both can and does exist'[25] and he acknowledges the soundness (though not the significance) of the argument I sketched in Section 2. Does the whole matter then turn on the single thesis (C8)? I am not sure what Schauer thinks about that one. Perhaps he assumes that to consider sanctions as ancillary to a primary norm is to regard them as unnecessary or unimportant. Not so. It means that we can 'subtract' the sanction and

---

[24] Ibid., 93.
[25] Schauer, *The Force of Law*, 15.

be left with an intelligible directive, and that the function of coercive back-up is to give support to that directive by making it more effective (support that is 'vital': (C4)). What is more, for Hart, an obligation-imposing norm is either partly constituted by, or normally concomitant with, 'serious social pressure' to conform: this is part of what marks it as an obligatory norm.[26]

Now, (C1) to (C5) add up to a significant place for coercion in our understanding of law, at any rate, to a place that cannot be said to deny, ignore, or relegate coercion to the sidelines of jurisprudence. It is true that (C6), (C7), and (C8) mean that the provision of coercion is not essential to law, and that there can be law without coercion. But, as I said, Schauer accepts that. Apart from the false dispute generated in his treatment of the 'puzzled man' example, then, the lines of substantive disagreement are becoming difficult to discern. (There does remain a clear methodological disagreement; I return to it in Section 5.)

4. The Force of Power

So far, I have been working with a view of coercion shared by writers as diverse as Bentham, Austin, Kelsen, and Dworkin. I argued that such coercion is more central to contemporary jurisprudence than Schauer allows. But it is a further feature of Schauer's view that legal coercion should be understood more broadly. Dialectically, this is unnecessary if we are only trying to establish the centrality of coercion to law: we have done that on the narrower view. But there is the independent question of whether a broader view is, for some other reason, superior. I now state some independent reservations about that.

Schauer does not give much attention to the concept of coercion as such; he mainly proceeds via a cornucopia of examples of what are said to be legal, or para-legal, coercion. Punishments and penalties, of course; but sometimes also rewards for compliance, some taxes, and even the nullification of transactions. The loss of reputation that comes with being a law-breaker can, he claims, be coercive. Also, locks on doors, since they prevent people from doing what they might otherwise want to do—and, for the same reason, speed bumps. At points, Schauer seems to assume that most law-induced changes in people's preferences are coercive. It is not surprising, then, that he thinks coercion looms large in law, and that he is convinced that many laws

---

[26] Hart, *The Concept of Law*, 86. I am here describing, not endorsing, Hart's view.

would not enjoy the level of compliance that they do but for coercive backup. Almost any significant incentive that produces compliance with law he counts as coercive.

Schauer is rightly interested in law's range of motivating incentives; he is enormously illuminating on the question why some incentives are chosen over others; and he brings us down to earth by reminding us what a fantasy it would be to imagine law without any kind of ancillary motivation for compliance. But is all ancillary motivation coercive? Not according to Kelsen.[27] Nor to Bentham, Austin, Hart, Dworkin, or me. Schauer maps the territory as follows:

> [I]f we were looking for a rough distinction among the various terms that have been used up to now in this book, we might say that sanctions are what law imposes in the event of noncompliance with legal mandates; that the application of force—meaning physical force—is among law's available sanctions; that law is coercive to the extent that its sanctions provide motivations for people, because of the law, to do something other than what they would have done absent the law; and that law can be said to exercise compulsion when its coercive force actually does induce the aforesaid shift in behavior.[28]

Then he adds disarmingly, 'All of these definitions are stipulative, of course...'[29]

For reasons I will give in Section 5, I find curious the pendant comment—'stipulative, of course'. But for the moment, consider the distinctions themselves. The fact that a law imposes S, and S motivates people to act in ways they would not have acted but for that law, shows no more than the fact that the law is, by dint of S, to some degree causally effective in motivation.[30] But not all causation, not even all law-determined causation, is coercive. The issue is both dialectical and theoretical.

---

[27] 'As a coercive order, the law is distinguished from other social orders. The decisive criterion is the element of force—that means that the act prescribed by the order as a consequence of socially detrimental facts ought to be executed even against the will of the individual and, if he resists, by physical force.' Hans Kelsen, *Pure Theory of Law* (Max Knight trs, University of California Press, 1967) 34.
[28] Schauer, *The Force of Law*, 129.
[29] Ibid.
[30] I say, 'to some degree' because the law-provided motivation may not succeed: if it does succeed Schauer counts it as 'compulsion'. And I assume, consistently with various passages in Schauer's book, that the 'imposition' of S by law need not *itself* be a coercive act.

The dialectical point is that when jurisprudents deny that law is necessarily coercive, we are not denying that the existence of law often provides motivation for people to do things they would not otherwise have done. I have never denied that, and it is hard to see how Hart could deny it while affirming (C1) to (C5).

The theoretical point is that although the ordinary semantic range of 'coercion' is broad enough to cover all sorts of things (including social embarrassment, brick walls, and tempting offers) its use in jurisprudence is shaped by two considerations. First, the normative character of law: law is a guide to action, and those who defend the coercion thesis take the view that law guides by coercive proposals, normally by threats.[31] Second, coercion is marked by the intention to direct someone's will in a particular way, by a proposal they would not normally welcome, and which will make them significantly worse off if they do not behave that way. We say figuratively that coercion leaves people with 'no choice' or, less figuratively, with 'no reasonable choice', but to comply. This explains why we have moral concerns about deploying coercion, and why we prefer non-coercive means of securing compliance to coercive means where both are equally effective. It also explains the connection between coercion and responsibility: those subject to coercive threats are less blameworthy for what they do than are those who choose freely.

It is only by washing out such distinctions that Schauer can treat so many law-provided incentives as forms of coercion. This unhelpfully merges coercion with the more general phenomenon of social power: the capacity to influence people's actions and interests. Now, power is a massively neglected topic in legal philosophy, much more neglected than coercion ever has been.[32] Attention to it raises a host of new questions: whether the power of law need be intentionally produced, whether structures as well as agents can have power, whether those with power are always responsible for whether and how they use it, and so on. But not all power is coercive.[33]

---

[31] And possibly by certain offers that share normative features of coercive threats: Virginia Held, 'Coercion and Coercive Offers' in J. Roland Pennock and John W. Chapman eds, *Nomos XIV: Coercion* (Aldine-Atherton, 1972); David Zimmerman, 'Coercive Wage Offers' (1981) 10 *Philosophy and Public Affairs* 121–45; Onora O'Neill, 'Which are the Offers *You* Can't Refuse?' in R. G. Frey and Christopher Morris eds, *Violence, Terrorism, and Justice* (Cambridge University Press, 1991) 170–95.

[32] So I suggest in Leslie Green, 'General Jurisprudence: a 25th Anniversary Essay' (2005) 25 *Oxford Journal of Legal Studies* 565–80, and in the 'Introduction' to Hart, *The Concept of Law*, 3rd edn, xxvii–xxxiii.

[33] Nor is all influence power. For a range of views on the question, see Michel Foucault, *Power/Knowledge: Selected Interviews and Other Writings 1972–77* (C. Gordon ed., Pantheon Books, 1980); Steven Lukes, *Power: A Radical View* (Blackwell, 1974); Peter Morris, *Power: A Philosophical Analysis* (Manchester University Press, 1987). I comment briefly on the issue in

There is no doubt that effective legal systems use and deploy many different techniques to influence their subjects. In addition to issuing coercive threats, they educate, propagandize, offer services, intervene in markets, and much more. Many activities of the military and administrative state, and what is left of the welfare state, are conducted through the instrumentalities of law. One reason Bentham focused so much on law's power to punish, and so little on the capacity to reward, is that the governments he knew had nothing like the capacity of the modern state to provide benefits.[34] This shows how the power of law takes new and possibly more insidious forms in our world, but it does not give us a reason to think that benefits are the new coercion. A *threat to withhold* benefits may be coercive, but that is because it is a kind of threat.

You can see, now, another reason why I am put down as one of the jurisprudential coercion-minimizers: not only do I endorse (C6) to (C8), but I also take the narrower view of coercion. Schauer writes:

> Leslie Green, for example, claims that a regime of 'stark imperatives' that simply 'bossed people around' or that employed a 'price system' to '[structure] their incentives while leaving them free to act as they pleased' would not even count as a 'system of law' at all. Such efforts to marginalize the place of raw force in explaining what makes law distinctive follow on Hart's seemingly sound observation that law often empowers rather than coerces.[35]

Neither stark imperatives nor steep prices exemplify 'raw force'. Nor is the existence of legal powers my reason for denying that there could be a legal system that resorted only to stark imperatives or market incentives. My point is rather that a regime consisting *solely* of stark imperatives—bare orders such as 'Shut up!' or 'Move over!'—makes no claim to authority: that is why they are 'stark'.[36] I hold that law necessarily makes such a claim: law's 'self-image', as I have called it, is that of a legitimate authority.[37] As for a price system, it does not work via directives of any sort: it leaves people free to

---

Leslie Green, 'Power' in E. Craig, ed., *The Routledge Encyclopedia of Philosophy* (Routledge, 1998), vol. 7, 610–13.

[34] As Schauer acutely observes: *The Force of Law*, 111–12.
[35] Ibid., 2.
[36] I take the term 'stark imperatives' from Matthew Kramer, *In Defense of Legal Positivism: Law Without Trimmings* (Oxford: Oxford University Press, 1999) 83–9. Kramer and I disagree about the role of such imperatives in law.
[37] Green, The Authority of the State, 63–88.

do whatever they can afford to do. ('Free' in the thin, non-moralized, and sometimes valueless sense of 'free'; the sense in which poor people are free to send their children to expensive private schools, and free not to.) I think Schauer actually needs to agree with me here, for, as the first sentence of his book proclaims: 'Law makes us do things that we do not want to do.' Neither stark imperatives nor steep prices do that. They do not *make* us do anything. But, like other systems of power, they are very influential in shaping human behaviour.

Law's power takes many forms and runs in many channels—Schauer traces interesting and often surprising ones. Still, it is the force of power, and not coercion, that we see operating in this sort of case:

> When law creates the very possibility of engaging in an activity, it often supplants a similar and law-independent one. And if the law-independent activity is part of people's normal behavior and background expectations, eliminating this possibility and compelling people to use law's alternative operates as a form of coercion.[38]

Admittedly, if the law really did *eliminate* options and then *compelled* people to use its alternative, they would be forced to do what the law wants. But the sort of examples Schauer gives—for instance, the law of contract 'crowding out' promises or a regime of wills displacing informal testamentary directions—do not fit that description. The law does not eliminate the possibility of making promises or disposing of one's estate by means of informal direction. Nor, in the usual course of events, does law compel people to make contracts or wills.

To focus the issue, consider marriage. It is a familiar worry that, when legal marriage arrives on the scene, informal unions come under competitive pressure, and marriage, being the attractive package deal it is, brings a flattening, homogenizing quality to people's intimate lives as they pile into it. The incentives to marry can be very powerful, and their structure and terms are rarely accidental. They are commonly the product of deliberate government policies to encourage certain forms of life and discourage others. This is the foundation for the radical critiques of marriage that we heard as sex-neutral marriage regimes became available. They were said to be a conservative push to get gay people to leave behind the creative existentialism of their lives and settle down to bland normality, just like everyone else. Nonetheless, it bears

---

[38] Schauer, *The Force of Law*, 28.

insisting, because it is simply true, that in the usual marriage regimes no one is forced (by law) to marry, that many of the rewards of marriage can be accessed in other ways, and that sex-neutral marriage has not in fact homogenized gay lives or made gay people invisible. Contrast all that with genuinely coercive marriage regimes, for example, those that support forced marriages in which unwilling girls are sold off for a price. Here, it is not only that the law causes people to do things they would not do apart from the law; the law forces girls to do things (or helps men force girls to do things) that they do not want to do at all, or do not want to be forced to do. The conceptual and moral differences between the two cases are of the first importance. Marriage law always is, and expresses, a system of social power, whether a benign one that recognizes and stabilizes valuable relationships, or a malignant one that makes bad relationships durable and undermines valuable ones. But we do not need, and should not use, the concept of coercion to explain how law does that, except where coercion is actually on the cards.

5. Concepts and Counting

I come, finally, to the methodological stance underpinning Schauer's case. Recall that he concedes that coercion is not a 'conceptually necessary' feature of legal systems: there are possible legal systems that contain no coercive norms at all, and it is possible for a legal system to be effective without such norms. His aim is not to reject these propositions, but to deny their importance to jurisprudence. They are products of an effort to understand the necessary and sufficient conditions for something being law or a legal system, an activity Schauer regards as a misguided, 'essentialist' obsession with *what must be* at the expense of a more productive interest in *what normally is*. Conceptual truths about law, if there are any, matter less than contingent, empirical truths about the law we have. In addition to trying to redress the balance in favour of a coercion thesis, Schauer therefore throws down 'a challenge to a prevalent mode of jurisprudential inquiry':

> For most contemporary practitioners of jurisprudence, the principal or even exclusive task of their enterprise is to identify the essential properties of law, the properties without which it would not be law, and the properties that define law in all possible legal systems in all possible worlds.[39]

---

[39] Ibid., x.

It is a monomaniacal devotion to that task that drives the view that, 'if coercion is not essential to the very idea or concept of law ... then coercion loses its philosophical or theoretical interest in explaining the nature of law...'[40]

I think this claim is unfair (which is not so important) but also that it is incorrect (which is important). It is unfair to say that an attempt to understand the necessary properties of law is the 'principal or even exclusive task' of 'most' contemporary legal philosophers. It is unfair even if one brackets off all 'special jurisprudence'—the theory of criminal law, tort, constitutional law, and so forth—and considers only general jurisprudence. Other tasks squarely at the centre of contemporary attention, tasks undertaken by most if not all of the writers he criticizes, include these:

- Determining whether there are any moral standards to which law, as law, should conform.
- Determining whether there is a moral obligation to obey or respect the law as such.
- Understanding the benefits and costs of regulating conduct by law.

If one has no idea what law is, one is likely to make a hash of these problems, and to that extent they depend on understanding the nature of law as a social and political institution. Apart from that, however, it is going too far to say that contemporary jurisprudence takes the definitional question as its principal, let alone exclusive, task. It is a minority interest. By far the greatest quantity of writing in jurisprudence is either applied moral philosophy—arguments about what our laws and legal institutions ought to be—or doctrinal advice of the 'What-the-Supreme-Court-Should-Have-Said' variety. (The latter is sometimes called 'interesting' or 'useful' jurisprudence: though to whom or for what purpose is unclear. The courts mostly ignore it.)

More significant than the unfair diagnosis of monomania is the following error. Schauer holds that if coercion is not part of the concept of law, then coercion loses its philosophical or theoretical interest in jurisprudence. I argued in Section 3 that this is incorrect. For one thing, if (C8) is true, then coercion plays a very important role in understanding legal obligations, the sort of role Kelsen is fumbling for when he says that 'a legal order as a whole, and a single legal norm, can no longer be regarded as valid when they cease to be effective.'[41] If (C8) identifies a presupposition of a key class of legal statements,

---

[40] Ibid., 3.
[41] Kelsen, *Pure Theory of Law*, 212.

then that is a matter of enormous interest. For another thing, even if coercion is not a conceptually necessary feature of law, the fact that it is pervasively used is *no accident*. There are non-trivial explanations for why coercive force is a feature of all historical and all existing legal systems. Schauer reminds us of the familiar ones and adds some more to the list. But I am not sure how this amounts to any challenge to the prevalent mode of jurisprudential inquiry. After all, even Hart insists that 'a place must be reserved, besides definitions and ordinary statements of fact, for a third category of statements: those the truth of which is contingent on human beings and the world they live in retaining the salient characteristics which they have'.[42]

Compared to the state of play in 1961, we now have more sophisticated ways of understanding the modalities 'necessary' and 'possible', and new views of the relationship between what is necessary and what is knowable *a priori*. But along the way jurisprudence has tended to lose sight of the 'third category' of statements. So we strain to assimilate them either to empirical generalizations—like the (sound) generalization that legal systems generate social hierarchies and disproportionately serve the interests of the powerful—or else to a matter of 'definition'. For many philosophical purposes a tightly disciplined understanding of necessity is critical, and one modelled on the behaviour of the ordinary quantifiers 'some' and 'all' has certain advantages. But in the human sciences, as soon as we start down the dark path of things that hold true in 'all possible worlds' we hear a lot of whistling to keep up courage, since we do not have a secure grasp of which worlds are possible. To the extent that Schauer is on Hart's side here, I am on Schauer's. What is 'humanly necessary' is as important to jurisprudence as what is 'strictly' (logically, conceptually, metaphysically, nomically...) necessary.

Sometimes, however, it seems that Schauer wants to go further. At points he seems sceptical of anyone's ability to work out any necessary and sufficient conditions for anything of interest in law. We see that scepticism in this comment: 'Rather than defining law in terms of the nature of its norms or the nature of its sources, we might instead think of law simply as the activity engaged in by courts, lawyers, and the sociologically defined array of institutions that surround them.'[43] Yes, we might: if something definite were picked out by the phrase 'the activity engaged in by courts etc.', or if there were some reason to tie the definition of law exclusively to the activity of those institutions. Unfortunately, among the familiar 'activities' engaged in by courts,

---

[42] Hart, *The Concept of Law*, 199–200.
[43] Schauer, *The Force of Law*, 121.

lawyers, etc. there is also regular and predictable law-*breaking*, and outside court a large amount of law-application and law-following. So defining law as 'whatever courts do' will not be a fruitful approach, as we learned from the failure of legal realism to produce any plausible way to identify the law of a given jurisdiction.

In addition to this recrudescence of legal realism, there may be a deeper source of scepticism here. We see it in this passage: 'the existence of live philosophical disputes . . . should caution against too quickly accepting the idea that looking for the nature of the phenomenon of law must be an exercise in searching, even in the central or standard cases, for law's essential properties.'[44] This thought obtrudes again when, in response to my snark that some legal theorists seem unable to grasp the difference between things being *like* law and things *counting as* law, Schauer writes: 'one of many more charitable readings would say that some theorists simply disagree with Green's view that law "properly so called", to use Austin's term, excludes special purpose norm systems such as those of clubs . . . .'[45]

I am not sure that it is in fact more charitable to my interlocutors to say that they 'simply disagree' with me. There is a difference between denying a proposition and refuting it. But, together with the comment about 'live philosophical disputes', this does suggest a known anxiety. Legal philosophers try to understand what is necessary and sufficient to some feature of law; they assemble examples and arguments; they strive for a deeper understanding of our concepts; they sharpen them in ways meant to be useful or illuminating. Then other philosophers disagree! I am unmoved. There are important areas of jurisprudential consensus, but no philosophical explanation of law (or anything else in the human studies) commands universal assent; live philosophical disputes are what to expect in a subject that is both difficult and disputatious.[46] There is no proposition whatever about law that has not been denied by some legal theorist or other: that there are legal rules, that they may conflict, that there are unsettled cases, that judges make law, that there is a difference between law and other social norms—whole careers have been built around denying, with energy and panache, such banal truths.

Schauer's worries about 'essentialism' and about finding necessary and sufficient conditions for things are, moreover, inconstant. Among the most

---

[44] Ibid., 40. I have elided the words, 'and somewhat of an empirical consensus'—a consensus about the springs of compliance.
[45] Ibid., 223, n. 25.
[46] See the Introduction to this volume.

CONCEPTS AND COUNTING 353

compelling parts of his argument is its demolition of incorrect accounts of 'obedience' casually passed around by social scientists as distinguished as Tom Tyler and Stanley Milgram.[47] Schauer shows why they are wrong to go from the fact that people's conformity to law is not wholly self-interested to the conclusion that people generally obey the law as such, or think it legitimate. That is indeed a mistake. We cannot assume that just because people do *what* an authority figure tells them, they must be doing it *because* they accept that figure's authority. I agree.[48] We will get nowhere with these problems until we can distinguish conforming *to* a directive and complying *with* that directive. Getting that right can be delicate, and to do so 'we must engage in careful analysis'.[49] What we need is a good account of 'the very idea of obeying the law *qua* law'.[50] Recall that Schauer charges Hart with a mistake on this score, by failing to 'clarify carefully exactly what it is to obey the law just because it is the law'.[51] Nor is Schauer willing to let Tyler, Milgram, or Hart displace a compelling analysis with something as flip as a mere *stipulation*, any more than he is willing to tolerate Austin's stipulation that rewards cannot count as sanctions: 'these issues cannot be determined by definitional edict'.[52]

Indeed, they cannot. But I have no idea what *'careful analysis'* or *'clarify[ing] exactly what it is* to obey', or *'the very idea'* of obedience, amount to if they are not attempts to state necessary and sufficient conditions for an action to count as obedience—maybe even the 'essence' of obedience—or at least the essence of its paradigm case. A bare stipulation gets us nowhere; a conceptual error sets us back. It is possible that obedience will turn out to be something that cannot be explained in terms of conditions necessary and sufficient for application of the relevant concepts. We will not know until we try. And even if we succeed, we can predict with confidence that at least one philosopher will disagree with the analysis, and they will see their disagreement as a live one. Moreover, they are unlikely, at least early in the game, to say they 'simply disagree'. There will be more arguments, fresh examples, counterexamples, and so on. If their 'line' is sufficiently startling, it may attract attention, and some may infer from its attention-grabbing allure that

---

[47] Tom R. Tyler, *Why People Obey the Law* (Yale University Press, 1990); Stanley Milgram, *Obedience to Authority: An Experimental View* (Harper and Row, New York, 1975).
[48] And so argued in Leslie Green 'Who Believes in Political Obligation?' in William Edmundson ed., *The Duty to Obey the Law* (Rowman and Littlefield, 1999) 301–17.
[49] Schauer, *The Force of Law*, 6.
[50] Ibid., 76.
[51] Ibid, 96.
[52] Ibid., 113.

there could be something in it. This is what philosophy can be like, including legal philosophy.

When Schauer is criticizing inept analyses of 'obedience', I am with him. His acuity on these points will come as no surprise to those who have profited from his own influential analyses of rules and other concepts central to jurisprudence.[53] The sudden downshift to naïve empiricism is therefore surprising. Unhappy with the idea that coercion proves not to be part of the concept of law, at least not by the exacting standards that he himself applies to the concept of obedience, Schauer begins to wonder if legal philosophers even know what a concept is. Maybe the concept of X is more like a stereotype of an X? He tells us: 'Cognitive scientists who study concept formation have almost universally concluded that people do not use concepts in the way that the "essential feature" view of concepts supposes.'[54] Have they? If so, the first thing we need to know is whether it is in fact the formation of concepts that these scientists were studying—just as we need to know whether it is in fact obedience that Tyler or Milgram were studying. This will call for 'careful analysis', 'clarifying exactly' what *a concept* amounts to, and so on. How else do these cognitive scientists and social psychologists know that they are studying concepts? Do they mount a second set of experiments or surveys to determine what most people think counts as 'concept formation'? Then a third set to figure out how they attribute thoughts to each other? Followed by a fourth? Or maybe it is all stipulation, all the way down? Concept-blind empiricism is going nowhere fast. Before anyone starts counting anything we need to know what counts as what. There is no *counting* without *counting-as*.

This is not a disciplinary point, as if the philosophers have it right and the social scientists have it wrong. The point is internal to social science: a measure of X needs to measure X, not something X-ish, let alone non-X or not-X. The best social science is sensitive to this. But we do not always see the best social science in many empirical 'tests' of propositions in general jurisprudence. Famous studies of why people 'obey' the law turn out to be studies of something quite different; influential investigations of correlates and consequences of the 'rule of law' establish little more than the fact that the investigators have a shaky grasp of the rule of law.[55] We need to do better.

---

[53] Frederick Schauer, *Playing by the Rules: A Philosophical Examination of Rule-Based Decision Making in Law and Life* (Oxford University Press, 1993).
[54] Schauer, *The Force of Law*, 37.
[55] For a good assessment of some bad analyses, see Tom Ginsburg, 'Pitfalls of Measuring the Rule of Law' (2011) 3 *Hague Journal on the Rule of Law* 269.

6. Conclusion

We should not neglect the force of law. The intricate and influential power of legal systems is one of the things that make law worth theoretical attention, as all systems of jurisprudence acknowledge. But the force of law is the sum of three different forces: the imposition of duties, the provision of coercion, and the exercise of power. Coercion is an important member of the trio, but it is what it is, and not one of the other two things. Coercion typifies social control through law, though just how typical and in what respects requires some discriminating and some counting. Let us count the ways the law coerces us; but let us first know what counts as coercion. Contemporary jurisprudence, even when it denies that coercion is a necessary feature of law as such, has shown that coercion is central to law in important ways. We can probably improve on that. The tools needed for the job are at hand. They have been for some time.[56]

---

[56] Thanks to Damiano Canale and Giovanni Tuzet for the workshop at Bocconi University where this chapter was first presented; to Andrew Simester and Grégoire Webber for sharp comments on a later version; but most especially to Fred Schauer for many years of instructive, and enjoyable, debate.

14
The Duty to Govern

1. Introduction

In a subtle discussion of the continuity of law after revolutions, John Finnis advises that it is 'usually reasonable to accept the new rules . . . proposed by successful revolutionaries who have made themselves masters of society and thus responsible for meeting the contingencies of the future'.[1] In *Natural Law and Natural Rights* he situates that idea in the context of a general justification for political authority: 'Authority (and thus the *responsibility* of governing) in a community is to be exercised by those who can in fact effectively settle co-ordination problems for that community.'[2] In his sympathetic treatment of Aquinas' legal philosophy, he comments that 'public authority is not merely a moral liberty but essentially a responsibility (a liberty coupled with, and ancillary to, a duty)'.[3] These thoughts mark a theme that I want to examine here: the idea that there is a primary duty to govern and that its ultimate justification lies in the rulers' effectiveness at a certain morally urgent task.

The problem of governance is the most neglected aspect of a theory of legal and political authority. Contemporary legal philosophers have mainly directed their energies to two other issues: the problem of *legitimacy* or the right to rule, and the problem of *obligation* or the duty to obey.[4] This cannot be explained by considerations of practical urgency. Based on the volume of writing on political obligation you would be forgiven for supposing that compliance in Western states is at risk, and that people need to be reminded of the virtues of obedience. The truth is pretty much the opposite. Even in the mature democracies there is no shortage of sheep-like subjects, too many of whom have already ended up in the slaughterhouse. Nor are we experiencing anything that could properly be called a crisis in legitimacy. While

---

[1] John Finnis, 'Revolutions and Continuity of Law', in A. W. B Simpson ed., *Oxford Essays in Jurisprudence 2nd Series* (Oxford University Press, 1973) 76.
[2] John Finnis, *Natural Law and Natural Rights* (2nd edn, Oxford University Press, 2011) 246.
[3] John Finnis, *Aquinas: Moral, Political, and Legal Theory* (Oxford University Press, 1998) 283.
[4] I am as guilty as anyone. I failed to recognize governance as a separate problem in *The Authority of the State* (Oxford University Press, 1990).

there are always particular complaints that this government or that is meddling where it has no business, serious doubts about the state's right to rule are confined to philosophers, political theorists, and (other) fringe groups on the margins of society. Were we to direct our energies in proportion to the urgency of the question, the problem of governance would be a better candidate. Fashionable theories display an instinctive bias against anything that could properly be called 'governing', that is, setting and supervising authoritative rules for the guidance of people in a society. Some theories do not even grasp that this is what governing involves; they refer to anarchic ordering (bargaining, lotteries, self-help, and so on) as so many forms of 'regulation' to be considered in our 'choice of governing instruments'. That is like thinking atheism is a form of heresy.

Then there is the much-discussed disengagement from public life. You may say that this is not surprising, for most people do not aspire to rule and they have more important priorities in their lives. No doubt. But the worry is not that ordinary subjects do not seek political engagement above all, or that they are unwilling to sacrifice personal interests to it. Even very modest burdens of citizenship are shirked. People vote less, seek more exemptions from jury duty, and massively neglect the basic knowledge and capacities they need to acquire if they are to have any part in governance. Nor are things much better among officials, including politicians who aggressively seek public office at spectacular expense. Absenteeism in legislatures is routine, and those who cannot go AWOL eagerly subcontract their work to private entities, from outsourcing policy development to publicity firms and think-tanks to contracting with private prisons and armies for law enforcement.[5] The idea that our political leaders might have a fundamental *duty* to govern, and to bear the responsibilities of doing so, seems quaint.

Legal philosophy is unlikely to influence these trends, which reflect cultural shifts in the relationship between the public and private realms. But our inherited theories of governance are not even much help in understanding the issues. They tend to lurch between high-minded views that make the duty to govern seem impractical and narrow-minded views that make it seem impossible. Many of the former descend from one interpretation of Aristotle's idea that the free person is one who rules and is ruled in turn. Sharing in governance is not, on this account, simply one of the liberties of citizenship; it is a fundamental duty constitutive of it.[6] In the modern era it was Rousseau who

---

[5] See Paul Verkuil, *Outsourcing Sovereignty: Why Privatization of Government Functions Threatens Democracy and What We Can Do about It* (Cambridge University Press, 2007).
[6] At any rate, citizenship in a democracy. Cf. Aristotle *Politics*, BK 3, 1274b33–1275a34.

carried this conception furthest, concluding that the general will is therefore incapable of representation, and that the duty to govern is a duty to govern directly. The attractions of civic republicanism never entirely faded, and there is much that remains admirable in that tradition. But Rousseau also identified its difficulties: it depends on social foundations (tiny states, social equality, and common experiences) that are remote from modern political life. Large, inegalitarian, multicultural, anonymous, and mobile societies are not environments in which direct and continuing engagement in politics thrives, and the attempt to achieve it in those circumstances can, as Rousseau warns, easily backfire.

Bentham, on the other hand, denies not only the practicality but the coherence of a duty to govern. Blackstone had held that not only does the supreme power have the right to make any law whatever, 'but farther, it is its duty likewise. For since the respective members are bound to conform to themselves to the will of the state, it is expedient that they receive directions from the state declaratory of that its will'. To fulfil this duty to legislate, the sovereign must at least promulgate general rules. Bentham balks. If the sovereign has a right to govern, 'Its duty then is to do—what? To do the same thing that it was before asserted to be its right to do, to make laws in all cases whatsoever . . .' Bentham is not hostile to the principles of legality that Blackstone derived from the duty to rule—he sometimes made a fetish of them. But Bentham cannot not see how a sovereign could both have a right to legislate as it pleases and also be subject to an obligation to legislate. Sovereigns are not subject to legal obligations (or else they are not sovereign), and they are constituted by the fact that they govern, so, concludes Bentham, they have neither a legal nor a moral duty to do that without which they do not exist.

There are replies, qualifications, and modifications available to both Rousseauan and Benthamite theories of governance. Finnis offers a direct defence of a contrasting view. He argues that some have a non-voluntary duty to govern, grounded in their effectiveness at a morally necessary task. It is a defence unencumbered by nostalgia for the town meeting or the unitary sovereign.

2. The Primary Duty to Govern

The problem is one of justifying a primary duty to govern. This is a duty not derived, directly or by delegation, from any positive right. In functioning legal systems, many people have derivative duties to govern (or, more commonly, to do their part in a system of governance). American presidents have a duty to execute their office and to preserve, protect, and defend their Constitution. Subjects of common-law systems have a duty to serve on juries if asked. Australian citizens have a duty to vote. Were there a general moral duty to obey the law, there would be a duty to obey these laws, and thus a derivative duty to govern in these ways. This does not reach our question. It may reasonably be doubted whether there is a prima facie duty to obey, or at any rate, one that applies to all of law's subjects and on all occasions on which their obedience is required. More important, the duties just enumerated depend on the contingent existence of laws that attempt to secure them. We are after a justification that covers also the primary duty to make and apply laws, possibly including laws such as these (or to provide a set-up through which laws can be made, when necessary). The duty in question is also a positive one: not merely a duty not to interfere with morally justified governance that is up and running, but a duty to get it going in the first place. Put another way, it is a duty that binds as much in 'the state of nature' as in any functioning legal system. Who, if anyone, might have such a primary, positive duty to govern, and on what grounds?

This problem is related to the two other main problems of political authority—legitimacy and obligation—but it is conceptually distinct. A theory of legitimacy may provide warrant for someone or other ruling—it may show they are at liberty to do so and even that they have good reason to do so—without going so far as to claim that they violate any moral duty by failing to do so. And a theory of political obligation presumes that someone is *already* ruling, and whatever justification it offers for obeying their directives need not suppose that they issue directives in fulfilment of some duty they have. Suppose, for example, that fairness requires complying with the law whenever you are assured that others will too, or even that it requires doing one's share in ruling subject to similar assurance. None of this proves it to be unfair if nobody rules at all, or if social order is maintained without resorting to authoritative governance. Though linked in various ways, the problems of legitimacy, obligation, and governance are different and involve questions of different sorts.

3. Effectiveness

Finnis says that: 'Authority (and thus the *responsibility* of governing) in a community is to be exercised by those who can in fact effectively settle co-ordination problems for that community.'[7] This is a normative thesis. Political authority, including legal authority, is in fact exercised on many other bases, including self-interest, charisma, superstition, etc. Those who make themselves 'masters of society' may do so in order to enrich themselves and their friends and may not even *try* to settle any sort of social problems. But in the realm of political authority and obligation there is a connection between the actual and the ideal: self-interest, charisma, etc. may stand in a causal relation to the *capacity* to settle problems effectively. The fact that someone is a charismatic leader, for example, Churchill during the Battle of Britain, may contribute to his effectiveness in settling problems of strategy by sustaining morale and inspiring obedience. An authority is not deficient *qua* authority if its effectiveness rests on such bases, and that applies even to superstitions about the divine rights of kings, the virtues of aristocrats, and so on. Authority should be exercised when there is a certain kind of problem that must be solved, and it should be exercised by someone who has the effective capacity to solve it. At this point, normative power depends on actual social power.

It is important to grasp how radical Finnis' version of this idea is. Many others have suggested that effectiveness is a *necessary* condition for justified political authority. If authority's role is to secure some valued end, be it justice or finality in social ordering, then it is bound to count against a putative authority that it lacks any capacity to do so. It may be that in 1745 the Young Pretender still had the best right to the British crown; but it is certain that after the disaster at Culloden the political claims of the Jacobites became a fantasy shrouded in tartan. Few legal philosophers (and fewer courts) would now doubt that. What is striking is that Finnis not only regards effectiveness as in such ways necessary for justified authority, but that he also regards it as defeasibly sufficient: 'the sheer fact of effectiveness is presumptively (not indefeasibly) *decisive*'.[8] A casual reader may be shocked by Finnis' repeated insistence that raw power plays a pivotal role in both the right to rule and the primary duty to govern. It sounds uncomfortably close to the claim that might makes right—and that is not the sort of thing we expect to hear from a natural lawyer.

We can tolerate this discomfort. Effectiveness (and, more generally, social power) is a feature of law of which analytic jurisprudence sometimes seems embarrassed. It is as if, having exfoliated reductivist theories that *identify* law

---

[7] Finnis, *Natural Law and Natural Rights*, 246.
[8] Ibid., emphasis added. And cf. 246.

EFFECTIVENESS   361

with a certain structure of power or with predictions about the deployment of power, we have become reluctant to explore other relations that may hold between social power and law as a normative system. We acknowledge that law is not a matter of what we are obliged to do but of what we are obligated to do; but it is also true that what we are obliged to do can affect what we are obligated to do. We say that law consists not only of duty-imposing rules but also of power-conferring rules; but normative power is not the only sort of power that those rules confer. We hold that a society of angels could still have need for law and thus that coercion is not of law's essence; but there is also a pervasive association of the ultimate capacity for coercion with the concept of law.[9]

Even Hans Kelsen, who asserts that legal systems are distinguished from other forms of social organization by their deployment of coercive force, dithers on the contribution effectiveness makes to law, ultimately offering the opaque suggestion that: 'Effectiveness is a condition for validity—but it is not validity. . . . right cannot exist without might and yet is not identical with might.'[10] Whatever a 'condition' for validity is supposed to be, it cannot here amount to a presumptive justification for it. Kelsen regards moral justification as an ideological matter to be excluded from his 'pure' theory of law. But neither can it contribute to a legal authorization for, as Kelsen also insisted, the reason for the validity of a norm can only be another valid norm. After hesitation, he eventually comes to see effectiveness as a requirement of the basic norm of international law that confers authority on de facto municipal authorities. This norm supposedly directs states to treat as binding the norms they customarily treat as binding, including the norm that those exercising persistent, effective control over a territory have lawful authority.

H. L. A. Hart avoids the reduplicative norm, 'Do what your norms tell you to do!' by acknowledging that customs *are* norms, and by arguing that effectiveness is neither a condition nor a pre-condition for the intelligibility of normative discourse in law; it is a *presupposition* of the normal contexts in which we use it.[11] We do not normally help ourselves to terms like 'validity', 'authority', or 'obligation' unless the legal system in question is a going concern, any more than we talk about champions of matches not actually played. This is not meant to solve the justificatory problem. But it is unclear

---

[9] Chapter 13, this volume.
[10] Hans Kelsen, *Pure Theory of Law* (M. Knight trs, University of California Press, 1967) 230–1. I have slightly amended the translation.
[11] H. L. A. Hart, *The Concept of Law* (3rd edn, Penelope A. Bulloch and Joseph Raz eds; Leslie Green, intro, Oxford University Press, 2012) 84–5.

how far it even solves Hart's own problem of explaining the use of normative language in law, where the 'normal' context is not the only context. We commonly talk about valid rules under extinct legal systems, or about what rights and powers a proposed constitution would confer, in each case free from any presuppositions about effectiveness. These are familiar, typical sorts of legal discourse, unless we fix the norm according to the interests of lawyers and their clients, whose typical focus is indeed on what is, rather than what was or what could be. That seems as arbitrary as fixing it according to the interests of Holmes' 'bad man' whose only concern is when to duck.

Finnis' argument is different. He considers that the nature of law is best seen in its 'focal' case, and that is the case in which legal obligations are also morally binding. His argument for treating them as such gives effectiveness a key role in the justification for authority, not in its logical preconditions or its background presuppositions. And the effectiveness he invokes is not Kelsen's or Hart's (namely the fact that the norms of the legal system are generally obeyed and applied). Finnis has in mind effectiveness at a certain *non-legal* task: that of settling coordination problems for a whole community. When that sort of effectiveness rests with certain people, they acquire not only a right to rule and a correlative duty to be obeyed but, importantly, a prior duty to rule. The task is for them not optional. Contrary to Kelsen and Hart, Finnis holds that, under certain conditions, might (of a certain kind) does indeed make right.

Before panic sets in, we had better say something about these conditions. First, they are limited to the broad task of 'coordinating' human activity for the common good. According to Finnis, this consists in maintaining certain framework relationships in our pursuit of a list of objective, mutually irreducible, self-evident values that include life, knowledge, play, aesthetic experience, friendship, practical reasonableness, and even religion. These values are themselves 'common *goods*' in that they are good for anyone and everyone but are not subject to scarcity or rivalness.[12] Their reasonable pursuit by individuals gives rise to a problem of securing *the* common good, by establishing a set of framework conditions within which individuals can follow life plans in pursuit of common *goods*. In securing this effectively, rulers must conform to a requirement of practical reason that no violence is to be done to any one of the common goods. So while might is indeed a presumptively sufficient condition for legal right, it is so only in a context in which it is actually

---

[12] Finnis, *Natural Law and Natural Rights*, 155, 255.

oriented towards the common good and in which all the fundamental goods are properly respected.[13]

It is central to this argument that while no unique set of framework conditions is required by reason, failure to secure *some* such framework is unreasonable because it will frustrate the pursuit of the basic goods, leading not only to gridlock but also to injustice. We need to settle with finality such issues as how children are to be educated, how natural resources are to be managed, and how claims of right are to be reconciled or adjudicated. Most of these can be fairly settled in more than one way, so to eliminate indeterminacy—to ensure that there is a *settlement*—we need to fix on one of the (satisfactory even if suboptimal) solutions, to the exclusion of all others.[14] This is the role of political authorities. It is on this structure of practical reason that the positivity of law rests, and it is a structure related to Aquinas' notion of *determinatio*. The dual contribution of the common good and the capacity to select and secure a satisfactory-if-not-necessary means to it explains the justified normativity of positive law, at least in its focal case.

I have previously raised doubts about this theory, especially its highly abstract idea of a common good and its claim that resolution of coordination problems depends on treating one alternative as authoritatively binding.[15] It is doubtful whether that is needed in the situations Finnis has in mind, and doubtful too whether a 'coordination problem' is a helpful model (as opposed to a permissible name) for those situations. There is also uncertainty about the idea of *overall* social coordination. (Even if every coordination problem needs a solution, it does not follow that there is a (common) sort of solution that every problem needs.) And the law notoriously sustains a fair amount not-meshing, pockets of anti-coordination, etc.—so the overall picture looks more modular than homogeneous. It may be possible to reformulate the core thesis to deflect some of these objections, so I simply bracket them here.[16]

Finnis thus rejects the idea that political authority is solely a matter of securing what I have been calling legitimacy: a liberty-right to set general rules and enforce them against their subjects.[17] He accepts instead the usual

---

[13] Compare his discussion of Aquinas' list of defeating conditions: Finnis, *Aquinas*, 272–4.
[14] Finnis, *Natural Law and Natural Rights*, 232.
[15] Ibid., 234. Leslie Green, 'Law Co-ordination, and the Common Good' (1983) 3 *Oxford Journal of Legal Studies* 299.
[16] For some amendments, or perhaps clarifications, see John Finnis, 'Law as Co-ordination' (1989) 2 *Ratio Juris* 97. For further doubts, see Chapter 3, this volume.
[17] For that view, see Robert Ladenson, 'In Defense of a Hobbesian Conception of Law' (1980) 9 *Philosophy and Public Affairs* 134 and William A. Edmundson, *Three Anarchical Fallacies: An Essay on Political Authority* (Cambridge University Press, 1998) 7–70.

view that it involves treating directives as claiming an obligation of obedience. In a sympathetic exposition of Aquinas' position, he writes:

> [T]o say that some person or body has authority to make laws is to say that, presumptively and defeasibly, laws made by that person or body will be morally binding on their subjects. This correlativity is based not on some linguistic 'given', but rather on the judgement that the same common good which calls for lawmakers with authority calls also, and essentially to the same extent, for the compliance of law's subjects with their legal obligations.[18]

Note that, in this formulation, the common good *calls for* lawmakers. This is a key move: in ordinary (modern) circumstances *there must be law* and the task of making it, or at least providing the means by which it might be made if necessary, inherently falls to those who are able to do so. It is true that if law *is* to serve the common good, lawmakers also need a right to rule and a correlative right to obedience commensurate with their task. Hence, as a heuristic or expository matter we might begin to explore these ideas at any point: at the grounds of legitimacy, or the right to be obeyed, or the duty to govern. But as a matter of the logic of justification, there is a priority relation among them. There is justificatory primacy to the duty to govern. The liberty-right to do so and the other normative powers necessary to accomplishing are ultimately explained by reference to grounds and limits of that duty.

4. Task-Efficacy

Finnis' theory of governance falls into a class that I call arguments from necessity.[19] Elizabeth Anscombe states the archetype: 'If something is necessary, if it is, for example, a necessary task in human life, then a right arises in those whose task it is, to have what belongs to the performance of the task.'[20] Anscombe's preoccupations being with the right to rule and the duty to obey, she does not say much about how we are to determine 'whose task it is'. Finnis offers an answer: the task falls to whoever can as a matter of fact effectively

---

[18] Finnis, *Aquinas*, 269.
[19] I discuss some other variants in 'Law and Obligations', 535–9.
[20] Elizabeth Anscombe, 'On the Source of the Authority of the State' (1978) 20 *Ratio* 17.

settle problems of coordination for the common good. I am going to call this a *task-efficacy* justification for the duty to govern.

There are cases in which task-efficacy has this force. Suppose A arrives at a crossroads and finds a serious automobile accident dangerously obstructing traffic. A could drive on but is in no rush and can without danger to themselves pull off the road and wave oncoming traffic around the collision. They phone for an ambulance and direct traffic until it arrives. Here, A's right to direct traffic depends on their capacity to do so which, in the circumstances, gives others a reason to comply with their directives.[21] Moreover, in view of the nature of the benefit to others and the small inconvenience to themselves they also have a moral duty to do so, as a specification of the duty of beneficence (whether in general, or towards those with whom they share a territory, or even just the road). The hard-hearted might deny this, but to assert that A has in these circumstances no moral duty to direct traffic would probably also force the conclusion that they do not even have a duty to phone for an ambulance, which seems more than a bit severe. (We are not yet worrying about whether anyone ought to have an enforceable *remedy* against A in case of their breach of their duty; we are just worrying about what they are bound to do.) We could therefore say that, owing to the universality of these duties and the general importance to everyone of being able to count at least on an easy rescue, the duties have adequate foundation in the requisites for the common good in Finnis' sense (a good which is not a common destination, but a common framework for any destination.) There is a task that needs to be done, and here A finds themselves the only one in an easy position to perform it.

Does this suggest that task-efficacy generates duties *only* in such cases of very 'easy rescue'? The case of belligerent occupation suggests otherwise. Suppose that in the course of war B invades C and occupies part of its territory. The citizens of C are entitled to go on as far as possible with their ordinary lives, but to do so they need someone to organize the supply of food, water, and medicine and to suppress looting and violence. Their own government has been completely disabled by the occupying forces. In these circumstances B is plausibly bound by morality, and plainly bound by law,[22] to rule C, at least to maintain law and order. The occupant's duty to govern derives

---

[21] I bypass the question whether this reason amounts to a duty, and whether they would have any collateral rights to enforce their directives.
[22] See Eyal Benvenisti, *The International Law of Occupation* (Princeton University Press, 1993).

from its the duty to preserve the rule of law (if there are any remnants) or to establish it—even if they were the ones who destroyed it in combat. This derives from the natural duty to support institutions necessary to prevent the situational harms of anarchy or the harms of governance radically deficient in the rule of law. Common moral thought (in unison with international law) holds that this duty applies whether the invasion itself was just or unjust, and it binds even in the face of serious costs to B. To occupy a country and then to permit mayhem because keeping order is now hazardous or expensive to the occupant may even be morally worse than waging an illegal war in the first place. B may thus be expected to bear substantial costs, not as some kind of punishment for occupation, but because now B and only B is in any position to re-establish the order on which ordinary life in the occupied territory depends, and because securing this is of the greatest importance.

Note how task-efficacy figures in the traffic and occupation examples. If A cannot direct traffic, or if it is unlikely that anyone will obey her, she had better just get out of the way. If B cannot actually keep order (e.g. because B's forces and agents are incompetent or corrupt, or because B's rule provokes massive resistance) then B should withdraw from the territory and let someone else try to rule. Whether task-efficacy is here sufficient depends on the force of the underlying duties of beneficence and the duty to support just institutions, together with the absence of any defeating conditions. It does not depend on any voluntary undertaking by A or B (though in these two cases it falls to them as a consequence of their voluntary acts—the act of driving to that very crossroads, the act of occupying that very territory).

Waiving doubts about the stringency or scope of the duty of beneficence, there are still three other problems this account faces. First, it will often be difficult to judge whether anyone has the capacity for the task, and that judgement may have to be made before the task is even attempted. In many cases it may involve a leap in the dark, the only safety net being the fact that one may sometimes *get* the capacity to perform the task *ex post*. The mere act of getting out of the car and moving one's hands as if directing traffic may make A someone capable of providing a solution to this problem, or at least alerting others to the fact that a problem lies ahead. Here, nothing will succeed like success.

The second worry has to do with an artificial feature of these examples. In my sparse descriptions, things were fixed so that there was but one person or group in a ready position to govern (the first driver to arrive, the only army in occupation.) When there are multiples ones, we have not only the problem of working out what (set of) people have the requisite capacity, but also the problem of selecting amongst them. At this stage we will need to think about allocation procedures (such as elections or lotteries) and therefore about the existence of higher-order coordination problems. (How do we select amongst possible rulers, or amongst possible decision-rules to select rulers?)

The final worry runs deeper. As Anscombe notes, the concept of a 'task' already imports some degree of necessity—a task is something that *must* be done, *needs* to be done, or for some reason *ought* to be done. In already describing the situation in this way, perhaps we have stolen a conclusion that needs to be purchased by argument. What turns a possible governing function—to use a neutral term—into a necessary task, one capable of defeating the familiar reasons we have for being let alone to tend our gardens? Most answers turn on the importance of the function. Anscombe has in mind tasks that serve 'general human needs',[23] Finnis, those that serve 'the common good', and George Klosko ones that provide 'presumptively beneficial public goods'—goods that anyone would want but which require cooperation and mutual restraint to produce.[24] Without going so far as to suggest that theories amount to much the same thing, there are commonalties among them, and even a family resemblance to Hart's idea that anything we would be prepared to count as a full-blooded legal system must aim to secure a 'minimum content' of protection for the most urgent interests of at least some of its subjects.

To choose among these variants would require an argument that cannot be pursued here. But notice a feature they all share: however we understand 'necessary tasks' they are likely to carve out a duty to govern that is much narrower than the claims of modern states or the scope of legitimate governance. Yet the fact that a certain activity is not strictly necessary does not entail that it is impermissible. While one needs a right to do whatever one has a duty to do, one may have no duty to do things that one has every right to do. A legitimate government may establish national holidays and official languages, protect historic buildings, and support the arts, and declare the trillium to be the provincial flower of Ontario. If we say that the right to rule must be ancillary to and strictly commensurate with the necessity of the task, we will be driven to conclude *either* that the task of governance is a lot narrower than most people think (and much narrower than what most states claim) or that

---

[23] Anscombe, 'On the Source of the Authority of the State' 172.
[24] George Klosko, *The Principle of Fairness and Political Obligation* (Rowman and Littlefield, 1992).

these seemingly non-necessary, permissible activities actually do fall under some suitably abstract conception of a necessary good. (Play?)

This points to an asymmetry between the adequacy criteria for a solution to the problem of governance and the adequacy criteria for a solution to the problem of obligation, and this in turn gives an additional justification for distinguishing them. It always counts against a theory of political obligation that it cannot justify the duty to obey actual and permissible directives of a reasonably just state. The directives set the standard for success: the duty to obey the law is a duty to do what the law requires. But it may well be that the duty to govern is narrower than the right to govern, and that a satisfactory theory of governance is not hostage to the spectacular failures of scope that plague most justifications for the duty to obey. This is one of the more interesting conceptual payoffs in isolating the problem of governance. A consideration that cannot hope to justify a general obligation to obey the law as it claims to be obeyed may nonetheless succeed in justifying the existence of a primary duty to govern. We may discover that some failed theories of political obligation turn out to be adequate theories of governance.

5. What is the Task?

Let us look closer at the putative task. According to Finnis, the authorities' typical job is to 'adopt' one of the sets of reasonable solutions to the framework problem of serving the common good. If the thought is that they need to select, mark, or make salient one of the options, then we need to ask whether this is a correct characterization of a task that requires authoritative regulation. Many familiar coordination problems (which language to speak, what currency to accept, which keyboard layout to use) are solved without authority of any kind, and so it must be at the foundations of law, since the ultimate sources of legal authority cannot themselves rest on any authoritative legal act. But perhaps this misconstrues what I have been calling the 'task'. Along with others, Finnis writes as if the problem is how to *select* one solution from an acknowledged list of satisfactory ones, that is, how to effect a determination. This may get things backwards. Raz argues the subjective conditions that characterize coordination problems—the fact that people acknowledge at least two alternatives either of which could further the fundamental aim but neither of which can do so without general conformity— these conditions are often part of the *solution*, not part of the problem. '[T]he problem is to get people to *realize* that they are confronting a coordination problem....'[25] That accomplished, the solutions may take care of themselves (as many coordination problems do). On this view, duty to govern (and the derivative right to rule) rests not on the capacity authoritatively to *solve* problems, as in the case of directing traffic or belligerent occupation, but on the capacity authoritatively to *identify* problems that require solution. Practical authority will then be only one of the tools to which wise rulers need resort. Their primary duty to govern rests on their wisdom (and perhaps on their theoretical authority) in getting people to see coordination problems that need solutions. This will apply, however, only in certain types of problems. In the case of prisoner's-dilemma situations, full information about the nature and structure of the problem may even make cooperation less likely (for people will see very plainly the advantages in defection). But in some circumstances, it will help meet the objection that many acknowledged coordination problems, even socially important ones, need no authoritative intervention whatever. Common knowledge of our circumstances cannot always be assumed. One of the hardest tasks in law and politics is to get people to understand the need for cooperation, especially when it is very complex or involves people unlike or remote from themselves. Two sorts of error are common. First, there may be a need for cooperation that is not adequately felt. Managing climate change poses a coordination problem in Finnis' sense if anything does, and maintaining the planet as a viable habitat for *homo sapiens* is as clear an example of a humanly necessary task as we have. Any nation or group that could come close to providing an effective solution, or even steps towards an effective procedure *leading* to a solution, would have a powerful obligation to do so. But some people, owing to ignorance, wilful blindness, or self-deception, do not see that this is a task calling for cooperation of an unprecedented kind. The second type of error involves deeply felt coordinative 'needs' that are illusory. In some societies there is a felt need to organize the ritual cutting or amputation of parts of children's genitals, without anything that counts as their consent or is a morally adequate substitute for it. It would be much better if that 'need' were not felt and that no one undertook to organize it (which is not to say that others are thereby authorized to eliminate it).

Does the possible role of theoretical authority in reducing such errors sound alarms about Platonic guardians? Jeremy Waldron seems to think so. He says that a theory of authority ought to orient itself to 'questions

---

[25] Joseph Raz, 'Introduction', *The Authority of Law* (Oxford University Press, 1979) 9, emphasis added.

of common concern' wherever there is a need for a settlement, but also that: 'Which questions actually *are* questions of common concern in this sense is not something which a theory of authority ought to settle.'[26] This depends, I think, on what one takes a theory of authority to comprise. If it includes, as Finnis and I accept, a theory of legitimacy, then it is hard to see how it can avoid taking a view about what sort of things governments can and should undertake, and thus a view of what the questions of common concern properly are. Is the worry that we don't want authoritative *settlements* of those questions? Do we fear that, as the supremely salient coordinator, the ruler is always in a favoured position to discover 'tasks' that only it is well-positioned to fulfil—a sort of moral Keynesianism? The short answer is that one who does that makes moral errors, and if they are frequent enough they lose theoretical as well as practical authority.

In these cases, a duty to govern rests not on the capacity authoritatively to decide what needs settlement, but from a reliable capacity to know what needs settlement, how to assist in achieving it, and when to apply authoritative guidance to do so. Of course, people may disagree about all of this, and even when there is a right answer to the question, they may have no reliable method of ascertaining it. Once we get beyond examples like traffic direction or belligerent occupation, things get murky. (Some might even query Finnis' assertion that 'someone must decide' how children are to be educated[27]: if that means that someone must settle the substance of a common educational policy then J. S. Mill doubted it.) Should we therefore say that, in the face of such disagreements, we need to retreat to some procedure—for example, majority rule or bargaining—and allow the question of a duty to govern arise only when that procedure delivers the decision about the appropriate scope of governance? If only that could work. Part and parcel of the disagreement about the scope of governance is disagreement about what sort of procedures are a reasonable response *to* such disagreement. And then we need to know when to invoke any such procedure, and that is in turn liable to disagreement, which cannot itself be settled by bargaining or voting. As Montesquieu says, not everything can be decided by a vote, including the question of when we should decide things by a vote.

---

[26] Jeremy Waldron, 'Authority for Officials', in L. Meyer, S. Paulson, and T. Pogge eds, *Rights, Culture, and the Law: Themes from the Philosophy of Joseph Raz* (Oxford University Press, 2003) 50. For discussion of Waldron's view, see Leslie Green, 'Three Themes from Raz' (2005) 25 *Oxford Journal of Legal Studies* 509.

[27] Finnis, *Natural Law and Natural Rights*, 232.

6. The Question of Priority

What then are the relations among the duty to govern, the right to rule, and the duty to obey? For Finnis, governance comes first. (He is not alone in thinking this.[28]) I do not mean that the issue has methodological priority in jurisprudence: as I said, we can begin thinking about political authority at whatever point is convenient. Nor do I mean that we can fully understand the concept of governance without reference to what it implies for related notions. The question is not one of heuristics or conceptual correlates, it is about justificatory reasons. On a task-efficacy account, the justification for a duty to rule also influences its proper scope, and that in turn affects the permissible responses of its subjects.

In his various formulations of the theory, the first normative relation Finnis derives is the *responsibility* of governing, whether that falls to the revolutionary who is now among the 'masters of society' and therefore needs to think about the ground rules that will henceforth regulate the legal order, or to the practically reasonable person who has the capacity to select or notice solutions to society's coordination problems. This is reflected in Finnis' insistence that 'public authority is not merely a moral liberty but essentially a responsibility (a liberty coupled with, *and ancillary to*, a duty)'.[29] Now, if A is *ancillary* to B, then A is not merely a logical correlate or conceptual reflex of B; they are not just two sides of a coin. A is ancillary to B only if A is in some way *auxiliary* or *subordinate* to B. This is no minor point. To say that the right to rule is ancillary to the duty to govern is to take sides against that strand of the liberal tradition that puts legitimacy first. The emergence of this distinction (and of the related idea that there are moral rights that are not simply the logical the reflex of duties) was pivotal in the intellectual revolution of seventeenth-century political theory.[30] It set in motion the

---

[28] Locke thought this was true of parental authority, see below. The nineteenth-century Presbyterian theologian, C. G. Finney thought it held more generally: 'The mere fact, that one being is dependent on another, does not confer on one the right to govern, and impose upon the other obligation to obey, unless the dependent one needs to be governed, and consequently, that the one upon whom the other is dependent, cannot fulfil to him the duties of benevolence, without governing or controlling him. The right to govern implies the duty to govern. Obligation, *and consequently, the right to govern*, implies that government is a condition of fulfilling to the dependent party the duties of benevolence.' C. G. Finney, *Lectures on Systematic Theology, Embracing Lectures on Moral Government Etc.* (Saxton & Miles, 1846) Lecture 2, emphasis added.
[29] Finnis, *Aquinas*, 283, emphasis added.
[30] For a helpful account, see Knut Haakonsen, *Natural Law and Moral Philosophy: From Grotius to the Scottish Enlightenment* (Cambridge University Press, 1996).

debate about whether human rights fall out of an independently intelligible theology of divine command or teleology of the common good, or whether they have some kind of moral primacy that is susceptible to an independent explanation.

The passage just cited represents, I think, Finnis' considered position. But at other points he seems influenced by the idea that there *are* efficacy-independent foundations of political legitimacy. For example, he also says that 'the goods which define the range of lawmakers' and other rulers' responsibility—say, the goods of peace and justice—can be called the common good of, or specific to, the political community or state'.[31] That suggests the duty to govern, to which the right to rule is ancillary, is not an open-ended duty responsive only to the mandates of the common good. There are things that are Caesar's, and there are things that are not. So while governance must serve the common good, it may not serve just any and every aspect of the common good, but only those roughly demarcated as the provision of 'peace and justice'. Why should that be?

One explanation holds that to transgress such limits is to trench on the legitimate interests of individuals, interests which should remain under their control, even if they *are* interests in common goods (such as religion or friendship) and even if retaining such control means that they will achieve these goods less well than they otherwise would. This explanation flows not from limits on effective governance, but from the independent force of a doctrine of legitimacy that prizes something in the neighbourhood of individual (or group) autonomy. That suggests a different understanding of the priority relation: we need to explain the *kind* of goods that fall within in the legitimate sphere of governmental authority, and only then and only subject to that constraint can we work out who has any duties to provide them and what sort of attitudes their subjects should take to their efforts at provision.

How much tension this idea creates within a task-efficacy argument depends on how we explain the boundaries of the rulers' special responsibility. I am not confident of Finnis' position on this point. He asserts the ancillary character of the right to rule. He also endorses the principle of 'subsidiarity': the state should not try to rule where smaller, intermediate institutions (or individuals) can adequately govern. At the same time, the fact that 'particular individuals and groups have as their *prior* concern (as they should) their respective interests' is part of his reason for thinking that overall

---

[31] Finnis, *Aquinas*, 236.

coordination requires authority.[32] How then should we interpret the idea that individuals have their particular interests as their proper *prior* concern? Might this hint at efficacy-independent constraints on legitimacy?

There is one historically influential line of argument that makes legitimacy subordinate to the duty to govern. Its paradigm is parental authority, and for some time it cast a long shadow over theories of governance and legitimacy. The most plausible source of parents' rights to instruct and discipline their children flows from their prior duty to attend to the well-being of their children, together with certain facts about the intimacy of the parent–child relationship that make the duty especially theirs. As long as rulers felt safe that there was likely to be no earthly enforcement of such duties, they were quick to exploit the analogy. James VI of Scotland wrote that:

> By the Law of Nature the King becomes a natural Father to all his Lieges at his Coronation: And as the Father of his fatherly duty is bound to care for the nourishing, education, and virtuous government of his children; even so is the King bound to care for all his subjects. . . . As to the other branch of this mutual and reciprocal bond, is the duty and allegiance that the Lieges owe to their King.[33]

The duty to govern may be part of a 'mutual and reciprocal bond', but James considers that his end of the deal derives solely from his divine duty as *pater patriae*, not from any contract with his earthly subjects. In Locke's view such an analysis of *parental* authority is fair; but it does not carry over to the case of political authority, which has to apply to adults who confront each other as moral equals:

> The want of distinguishing these two powers; viz. that which the Father hath in the right of *Tuition*, during Minority, and the right of *Honour* all his Life, may perhaps have caused a great part of the mistakes about this matter. For to speak properly of them, the first of these is rather the Priviledge of Children, and the Duty of Parents, than any Prerogative of Paternal Power.[34]

---

[32] Finnis, *Natural Law and Natural Rights*, 230.
[33] King James VI and I, 'The Trew Law of Free Monarchies', in J. P. Somerville ed., *Political Writings* (Cambridge University Press, 1995 [1598]) 65. I have modernized the spelling.
[34] John Locke, *Two Treatises of Government* (P. Laslett ed., Cambridge University Press, 1963) II, s. 67.

The limited parental right to rule over children is thus wholly ancillary to the duty to govern. In fact, it does not amount to much more than that duty as seen from the parents' point of view. Though it is for the benefit of their children, parents are accountable to God for their performance of this duty. That coincides with the classical view of how natural law can generate subjective rights. But for Locke this *distinguishes* parental from political authority. He maintains that the latter can be established only by actual (though perhaps tacit) consent of the governed and is therefore subject to all the validity conditions for such consent (including, famously, the condition than no one may consent to any sort of rule that puts their life at the whim of their ruler). It is this rather than any functional appeal to the things that are somehow Caesar's that explains the differences between parental and political authority.

In emphasizing the difference between these two traditions of argument, I am not trying to hint that Finnis' theory is latently absolutist or even especially paternalist. It is a theory of limited government in which the limits are traceable upstream to the common good, and which have downstream effects on both the right to rule and the duty to obey. My suggestion is that there are further limits that flow *directly* from constraints imposed by the interests of individuals, independent of the inefficacy of authority at certain tasks, including the task of securing the interests of individuals as participants in the common good. It is a fine point, but on it turns the question of which of the relations constituting authority is primary.

7. The Alienability of the Duty to Govern

This discussion has been mostly exploratory, examining the ways a task-efficacy account of governance is illuminating and distinctive, and flagging some issues needing further inquiry. I conclude with a few remarks about its capacity to handle the worry I raised at the outset: the widening delegation of powers of governance to private entities. The matter is complex, and I will only scratch its surface here.

As we have seen, a task-efficacy theory of authority must explain how the need for governance becomes the duty of a *particular* person, your duty for example. Sometimes, there may be only one feasible candidate; more often choosing among several will be resolved by chance, custom, or convention; occasionally it will fall to an explicit decision procedure. Suppose that in some way or other, we do determine that the duty falls to A (who may, of course, be a person corporate). Does this mean that *A must govern*, or is it enough if *A sees to it that* someone governs?

I assume that any plausible theory will allow for some division of labour in governance and, *contra* Rousseau, that there is no general objection to limited and controlled delegation of some legislative authority. There are also cases in which private arrangements are more efficient or transparent than public ones, and cases where wisdom therefore dictates that we should not be governing at all. But there may come a point where the core responsibilities of necessary governance are delegated to a degree or in a direction that gives rise to the worries I mentioned at the outset. We should have reservations about any broad delegation of the primary duty to govern. Even if Dicey was right in thinking that the UK Parliament could lawfully commit suicide by transferring all its powers to the Manchester Corporation, it can scarcely be denied that this would be an improper alienation of its duty to govern.[35] Or, if a municipal government seems a tolerable recipient of sovereign powers, imagine instead that Parliament transferred them to the Disney Corporation. Actually, we begin to have serious worries well short of such fantasy cases of total and permanent alienation. A significant delegation of the US government's primary duty to legislate to the Brookings Institution, or its primary duty to adjudicate to the American Arbitration Association— to say nothing of its primary duty of enforcement to Blackwater USA—would be deplorable apart from any doubts about their constitutionality. This suggests that there may after all be a non-delegable core to the duty to govern, and that Rousseau may have been right in part.

This presents a difficult hurdle for any task-efficacy theory. In general, there is nothing wrong with delegating a task, even a necessary one, to someone who can do it at least as effectively as you can. Finnis' case for the presumptive sufficiency of the effectiveness criterion suggests as much. Here, the best a task-efficacy account can do is to say that one may not delegate governance in a way that would substantially interfere with effectiveness, for instance by reducing oversight, distorting incentives, or making people uncertain as to where authority really rests. Does this adequately explain what would be wrong with radical delegations of primary authority? I doubt it.

Locke maintains that parental governance may properly be delegated, as it often was, to nursemaids, governesses, and teachers.[36] But that is because he thinks the parents' duty to govern their children is really a duty to *see to it* that

---

[35] A. V. Dicey, *The Law of the Constitution* (10th edn, 1959) 68 n.
[36] Locke, *Two Treatises of Government*, II, s. 69.

this task is accomplished. Our own moral attitudes towards the family are somewhat different: we expect a certain amount of hands-on, first-personal, care of children, even from parents who could easily afford to farm their children out. In any case, Locke also recognizes *non*-delegable familial obligations: children are perpetually and indispensably obliged to honour their parents, and in the nature of the attitude required, that cannot be delegated at all. An adult child may hire someone to care for their aged parents, but they cannot hire someone to honour or love them. Perhaps the fundamental duty to govern shares some characteristics with the duty to honour a parent, to the extent that it too is anchored in a special relationship. Locke writes:

> The power of the *Legislative* being derived from the People by a positive voluntary Grant and Institution, can be no other than what that positive Grant conveyed, which being only the power to make *Laws*, and not to make *Legislators*, the *Legislative*, can have no power to transfer their Authority to making Laws, and place it in other hands.[37]

This is an attractive idea that takes a more radical form in Rousseau's hands.

Along with most contemporary legal philosophers, Finnis refuses consent any foundational role in a theory of authority. That fact that someone enjoys the consent of the people may contribute to his effectiveness as a ruler; it may make it more likely that his rule will be accepted; it may mark him as a source of salience in solving coordination problems. But these are just about the only roles consent can have in such a theory, and they all flow from its attitudinal rather than performative nature: they flow from consent as contentment rather than commitment.

The common philosophical view that consent theory is bankrupt contrasts with its popularity among subjects of modern states. (Those who resist consent theory on the ground that they think its consequences out of line with popular opinion about the *scope* of the duty to obey might want to be cautious before embracing that view.) Three main arguments are commonly held to undermine a consent theory of obligation: there has been no social contract; more people believe they have a duty to obey than have actually promised to do so; and consent is valueless unless it is valid, and when we give a full account of its validity conditions, we see that they do not require

[37] Ibid., s.141, 363.

any transmittal of authority. If consent *would have been* valid if given, then that is enough; if it would not, then actual consent cannot help.

I think these objections can be met, and I have addressed some of them in Chapters 11 and 12 of this volume.[38] But put that aside. Once we distinguish the duty to govern from the duty to obey, the route is open to a consent-based theory of governance, even if we reject a consent-based theory of obligation.

Even it is false that every subject has promised to obey, it may yet be true that many become rulers because *they* have promised (or otherwise committed themselves) to undertake the task of governance. Surely one reason we think fundamental delegations of the duty to govern are wrong is that we have nominated, elected, and appointed people with the intention that *they* should govern, and that we have done so because they deliberately put themselves in the way of being nominated, elected, and appointed to govern, knowing what that will involve. Whatever we decide about native-born subjects and naturalized immigrants, our rulers are generally volunteers, not conscripts. Through a variety of procedures, we have placed our trust in *particular* people, or *particular* political parties, not just in anyone who turns out to have a capacity to solve problems for the common good or identify problems that need solving. Of course, the fact that we have done so itself contributes to their effectiveness in solving the problems, but now the order of explanation is running the other way round. Some such special relationship between ruler and ruled—whether we think of it as flowing from consent, trust, or perhaps honour—is commonly thought central to governance, and it resists both delegation and explanation in terms of task-efficacy.

The duty to govern may, of course, be supported by more than one type of consideration. Even if my worries about delegation make us wonder whether task-efficacy is the whole story, it is probably part of the story. In any case, by calling our attention to the existence and importance of the duty to govern, Finnis re-opens important questions about power, authority, and law—questions that have too long been neglected in our obsession with legitimacy and obligation.[39]

---

[38] Some leads: Why should consent be a *contract*? Why assume that everyone *does* have an obligation to obey? Why do we *not* think that people are bound to do what it would have been reasonable for them to promise, even if they did not actually promise to do it?

[39] I thank Julian Culp, Bill Edmundson, Alon Harel, and, especially, John Finnis for discussion and criticism.

Name Index

For the benefit of digital users, indexed terms that span two pages (e.g., 52-53) may, on occasion, appear on only one of those pages.

Adams, T. 4n.3, 32-33n.2
Anscombe, E. 364-65, 367
Aquinas, T. 3-4, 26-27, 49, 60-61, 65, 73, 75, 173, 185, 203, 218-20, 226-27, 356, 363-64
Aristotle 3-4, 168, 173, 195-96, 203, 226-27, 255-56, 308-9, 357-58
Augustine 335n.3
Austin, J. 2, 3-4, 16, 38, 41, 44, 96-97, 105, 112-13, 127n.4, 179-80, 200n.6, 206, 333-34, 337, 342, 343, 344, 345, 352

Baier, A. 295
Barry, B. 166-67
Bentham, J. 2, 3-4, 14, 26-27, 38, 41, 60, 65, 78, 96-97, 100-1, 105, 193, 200n.6, 206, 226-27, 333-34, 337, 342, 343, 344, 345, 347, 358
Berlin, I. 154
Blackstone, W. 14, 119, 132, 147-48, 358
Bodin, J. 154
Bradley, F.H. 234, 305
Bressan, P. 66-67
Brownlee, K. 220n.63
Buddha 255-56
Bulloch, P. 32-33n.2
Burke, E. 327
Butler, J. 135-36

Carnap, R. 123
Child, R. 220n.63
Cicero 34
Cohen, F. 110-11, 113, 114, 115, 122-23
Cohen, H. 36n.8
Coleman, J. 105, 177, 179
Conaghan, J. 129-30, 131-34, 135-36, 137, 138, 139, 141, 142, 143-44, 145, 146, 147-49

Darley, J.M. 265-66, 267, 270-71, 277-78

Devlin, P. 166-67, 207, 250, 254, 261-62, 264-65, 268-70, 272, 273
Dicey, A.V. 25-26, 216-17, 259, 375
Dickson, J. 105, 129n.9, 143
Dilthey, W. 52-53
Durkheim, E. 327
Dworkin, A. 139
Dworkin, R. 3-4, 5n.5, 10-11, 14, 16, 22-23, 32-33n.2, 41-42, 44, 49n.31, 51n.33, 53, 73, 96-97, 98, 106n.3, 110-11, 127n.3, 130, 143, 157, 173-74, 250, 305, 307, 310, 311-12, 313, 315, 316-18, 319-21, 324-26, 327, 328-29, 331-32, 342-43, 344, 345

Erskine, J. 119, 120

Feinberg, J. 163n.28
Finney, C.G. 371n.28
Finnis, J. 5n.5, 24, 130, 143, 179, 211-12, 356, 358, 359-60, 362-65, 367, 368-73, 374, 375, 376, 377
Foot, P. 318
Fuller, L. 11, 58, 59, 61, 70-72, 73-75, 76, 77, 78-79, 154, 166, 176, 177-78, 184-85, 189, 190, 195, 196-97, 239, 335n.3

Gallie, W.B. 18-19
Gardner, J. 20n.18, 105, 155-56, 161, 166, 177
Gauthier, D. 297-98n.40
George, R.P. 147n.62
Gilmore, G. 190
Guest, S. 191

Habermas, J. 130
Hägerström, A. 121
Hale, Sir M. 37n.12
Hamilton, A. 236-37
Harrison, J. 287-88

Hart, H.L.A. 2–4, 5n.5, 9, 10–11, 14, 16, 24, 31–56, 58–59, 60, 61, 70–71, 72, 73, 74, 78–79, 81n.2, 82, 97–99, 105, 107, 109–11, 112–13, 114, 115–17, 118–19, 120–21, 124–25, 129–30, 143, 148, 149, 154–55, 156–58, 160, 164, 166–67, 175–76, 177, 178–80, 181–82, 183–84, 185–87, 188, 191, 193–94, 195, 196–97, 198, 199, 201, 203, 205–6, 207, 208–9, 210–12, 214–15, 217, 218, 221, 238–40, 250, 253–56, 257–58, 262–63, 273, 328, 333–34, 338–41, 342, 343–44, 345, 346, 350–51, 352–53, 361–62, 367
Haslanger, S. 138–39
Hegel, G.W.F. 327
Henry VIII 88
Heraclitus 153
Hobbes, T. 38, 96–97, 145–46, 154, 158–59, 173, 185, 210–11, 213–14, 215, 218, 293–94, 299, 322, 333–34
Holmes Jr., O.W. 47, 68, 113, 114, 116–17, 339–40, 362
Honoré, T. 52n.37, 189, 190n.45
Hume, D. 2, 7, 9, 10–11, 69n.31, 84–85, 86, 161–62, 171–72, 184–85, 203, 206–7n.26, 209n.34, 210, 218, 255–56, 283–304, 307, 313–14, 324–25

James VI of Scotland 373
Justinian 132

Kahan, D. 277–78
Kant, I. 65, 158–59, 173, 185, 246
Kelsen, H. 2–4, 9, 35–36, 41–42, 46–47, 50, 57–59, 61–62, 65–66, 69, 70, 78, 91, 96–97, 105, 108, 109–10, 111, 113, 114, 116, 122–24, 130–26, 148, 149, 154–55, 158, 164–67, 184, 186, 199n.2, 200n.6, 203–5, 210, 226–27, 333–34, 337, 338–40, 342, 343, 344, 345, 350–51, 361
Klosko, G. 367
Kramer, M. 105, 154–55, 157, 158, 163–64, 188n.41
Kropotkin, P.A. 72

Lacey, N. 129n.9
Langton, R. 276–77
Leiter, B. 5n.5, 7, 42n.21, 105, 107, 112–15, 117, 122–23, 124–25, 221–23

Llewellyn, K.N. 113, 115–16, 120, 122, 201–2
Locke, J. 173, 185, 203, 286, 293–94, 296–97, 298, 304, 313, 314–15, 326n.37, 371n.28, 373, 374, 375–76
Lukasiewicz, J. 84n.8
Lyons, D. 155–56, 195n.59

MacCormick, N. 210, 263n.24
MacKinnon, C. 139
McTaggart, J. 66
Madison, J. 267–68
Marmor, A. 81, 105
Marx, K. 60, 196, 268n.36
Milgram, S. 352–53, 354
Miller, D. 159, 285, 286, 288, 291, 292–93, 303
Mill, J.S. 12, 173, 247–48, 250, 253–54, 274–75, 370
Montesquieu 370
Moore, M. 5n.5, 225–27, 231–32, 236, 237–38, 241–42, 243, 244, 245, 246, 247, 248
Murphy, L. 5n.5

Nozick, R. 161

Oliphant, H. 117

Pashukanis, E. 131–32
Perry, S. 178n.18
Planck, M. 7
Plato 145–46, 155–57, 158, 185
Popper, K. 223
Postema, G.J. 100–1

Quine, W.V.O. 122–23
Quinton, A. 169

Radbruch, G. 54, 55–56
Radin, M. 117
Rawls, J. 18, 88, 161, 166–67, 171–72, 202–3, 292, 294–95, 308
Raz, J. 2, 3–4, 32–33n.2, 40–41, 52, 60, 75–76, 99, 105, 130, 177, 179–80, 202–3, 229, 231–32, 250, 323, 368–69
Réaume, D. 129n.9
Robinson, P. 264–66, 267, 270–71, 277–78
Rosati, C. 129n.9
Rosenberg, G.N. 267–68
Ross, A. 121

NAME INDEX 381

Rousseau, J.-J. 158–59, 173, 182, 309–10, 312–14, 357–58, 375, 376

Schauer, F. 3, 5n.5, 7, 105, 333–34, 337–38, 339, 340, 341–42, 343–45, 346, 347–48, 349, 350–53, 354
Searle, J. 81
Sherwin, E. 129
Shiffrin, S. 129n.9
Sidney, A. 302n.56
Soper, P. 240–41
Stair, J.D. 119, 120
Stephen, J.F. 250, 254
Stevenson, R.L. 212–13
Strawson, P.F. 34

Tamanaha, B. 58–59
Thompson, E.P. 191, 217–18

Tocqueville, A. de 20, 196
Toh, K. 42n.21
Tyler, T. 352–53, 354

Vaihinger, H. 36n.8
Vico, G. 52–53, 221
Voltaire 264–65
von Ihering, R. 60, 78

Waldron, J. 5n.5, 18, 162, 369–70
Wallace, D.F. 25–26
Waluchow, W. 105
Warnock, G. 208n.31, 255–56
Weber, M. 50, 52–53, 60, 63–64, 196
Weitzman, L. 135n.26
Wilmot-Smith, F. 166–67
Wittgenstein, L. 67

Subject Index

For the benefit of digital users, indexed terms that span two pages (e.g., 52–53) may, on occasion, appear on only one of those pages.

Act of Settlement 259–60
adequacy criteria 368
adjudication 173–74, 194, 243
administrability 209
'against the law' *in sensu composito/in sensu diviso* ('against the law') 242, 243
agency 38
alienability 374–77
allegiance *see* Hume on allegiance
American legal realism 7, 107, 112–13, 116–17
analytic philosophy 145
anti-discrimination law 267
anti-essentialism and constructivism 37
anti-positivism 158–59
appreciation 13–14
arbitration 172–73, 238–39
artefacts 61, 62, 106, 221–24
artificiality thesis 299
assault 159
see also sexual assault
associative obligations and the state 305–32
bare community 311–12, 325–26
citizenship 323, 324–25
coercion 328, 329, 330
coercive power 319
community, personification of 317–18, 319–20
community of principle 317
consent 305–10, 320–21, 322, 324–25, 326–27
egoism 321–22, 323
humanism 321–22, 323
individuality and community 321–27
instrumentalism 321–22, 323
integrity and obedience 317–21
legitimacy 305–10, 317, 319, 321, 324–25

role duties 322–23, 324, 325–26
true community 310–16, 317, 324, 325–26, 331–32
universality of obligation 327–32
authority
parental 373–74, 375–76
regulative 202–3
see also under Hume on allegiance

'bad man' 47, 114, 361–62
balancing tests 100
Bayesianism 123
beneficence, duty of 365, 366
bias 238
see also partiality
'black letter' law 23
British Social Attitudes survey 260

Canada 311n.8
Charter of Rights and Freedoms 230–31
Québec Civil Code 69
'capacity to think' and jurisprudence 25–26
case-law method 220
categorical requirement 43
causal efficacy 63
choices 5–9
citizenship 323, 324–25, 357–58
civil law 237
Code of Canon Law 1983 80–81
coercion 37, 46–48, 65
associative obligations and the state 319, 328, 329, 330
-based theories 41
duty to govern 360–61
force *see* coercive sanctions

coercion (cont.)
  forces of law 333-34, 337-45, 346, 349, 350-51, 354, 355
  justified 328
  law 8, 32
  morality in law 214-15
  and responsibility connection 346
coercive sanctions 65-66, 96-97, 330-31
  forces of law 336-37, 342, 343-44, 345
  morality in law 203-4, 205
cognitive capacities 274-75
common good 362-63, 364-65, 367, 368-69, 371-72, 374
common law 23, 69
  gender in jurisprudence 142, 144-45, 146, 148
  judges 237, 242
  morality in law 222
  social morality 259, 276
communication, authoritative and non-authoritative 220
community
  bare 311-12, 325-26
  and individuality 321-27
  personification of 317-18, 319-20
  of principle 317
  true 310-16, 317, 324, 325-26, 331-32
compliance, voluntary 2-3, 214-18
conflict and disagreement 44, 102-4
conflicts-of-law rules 202-3
conformity 111, 153, 341
connections
  contingent 181-82, 183-84
  necessary 178-79, 181, 182-83
consensus 87, 88, 98-99, 101-3
consent
  absence of 286
  as agreement 273-74
  associative obligations and the state 305-10, 320-21, 322, 324-25, 326-27
  and capacity 274
  duty to govern 376-77
  as given by publicly understood means 274
  Hume on 286-87, 292-93, 295-96, 298, 299, 301, 302
  in marriage 300
  performative 274-75, 276-77
  tacit consent theory 290-91
  to sex 265-66, 273-79

voluntariness 274-76
constancy 153-55, 157, 158, 163-64, 169-70, 185-86
constitutional law 350
constitutional originalism 90
constitutions 20, 35-36, 212
  informal 20
  see also under United Kingdom; United States
constitutive aims of law 49-50
constructivism 37, 51
consummation of marriage 142, 144-45, 146, 148
content-independent reasons 32
contract law 202-3
conventions 10-11, 42-43, 82, 83-89, 91, 99-100, 101-4
  social 10, 82, 87-88, 91-92
  see also custom and convention
convergence 18-19
coordination problems 363, 364-65, 366-67, 368-69, 371-72, 376
copyright infringement 263-64
core offences 278
core and penumbra 32
criminalization 263-64, 265-66, 267, 270-71, 276, 350
custom 10-11, 31, 35-36, 45-46, 106, 118-19
  see also custom and convention
custom and convention 80-104
  conflict in jurisprudence 102-4
  conventional rules 103
  conventionalism 82, 85-89, 91, 102-3
  conventions 83-85, 99-100, 101-2, 103-4
  customary law 86-87
  customary norms 80-81, 84
  customary obligations 96-97, 102
  customary rules 101-2, 103-4
  customs 80, 83-84, 101-2
  foundations of law 80-83
  informal conventions 81
  law, rule of 80
  non-arbitrariness 89-91
  non-normativity 91-95
  non-obligatory aspect 95-102
  enforced norms 96-97
  peremptory norms (structure) 96, 99-102
  weighty norms 96, 97-99

normativity 92, 93–95, 101–2
norms 82, 83–84, 85, 86–87, 91–95, 101–2
  obligatory 99, 100, 101–2
  recognition rules 81, 82, 86–88, 90–91, 95, 96–99
  rules 80–81, 86
  social convention 82, 87–88, 91–92
customary law 61, 86–87, 222
customary practices 38

damages, law of 228
date-rape and 'token refusal' 275–76
decisions 118–19
decriminalization of homosexuality 267
demarcation problem 221–22, 223–24
deontic logics 23
determinatio 363
directives 220
discretion 238
discrimination
  sex 131–32, 135–36, 137, 148, 175, 278–79
  sexual orientation 143–44
distributive constraints (in punishment) 78
divine law 80–81
division of labour 44–46, 217
divorce, no fault 135
domestic law 37
domination
  elite 31
  male 147–48
Donoghue v Stevenson 118
due consideration 238–39
duty 3, 175, 334–37, 355
  of beneficence 365, 366
  familial 262, 311–12, 313
  -imposing rules 47–48, 360–61
  natural 235–36, 307–8
  non-voluntary 291, 358
  primary 358–59, 360
  -related norms 3
  role 322–23, 324, 325–26
  to obey *see* obligation or duty to obey
  to support just institutions 366
  see also duty to govern
duty to govern 356–77
  alienability of 374–75
  citizenship 357–58
  common good 362–63, 364–65, 367, 368–69, 371–72, 374

coordination problems 363, 364–65, 366–67, 368–69, 371–72, 376
duty of beneficence 365, 366
effectiveness 359–64, 375
legitimacy or right to rule 356–57, 359, 360, 363–65, 367–69, 371–73, 374
necessary tasks 367–68
non-voluntary duty 358
obligation or duty to obey 356–57, 359, 364–65, 368, 371, 374, 376–77
primary duty 358–59, 360
priority 371–74
responsibility 371–72
task-efficacy 364–71, 372–73, 374–75, 377

egoism 321–22, 323
eliminativism 121
empiricism 3, 7
evidence 3, 7
enactment 118–19
ends in themselves 65
enforcement and social morality 250–52, 253–55, 258
English law 135–37, 143–44, 212, 228
equality 160, 166–67, 169, 175, 230–31
equity 100
essentially contested concepts 18
evaluation
  instrumental 77–79
  see also internal criteria of evaluation
evaluative cluster-concepts 18–19
evaluative disagreements 18

fact and value distinction 31–32
fairness 78, 194
fallibility 193–97
falsifiability criterion 223
family law 267, 272
felicity conditions 276–77
feme covert doctrine 126
feminist legal theory 13, 126–27, 128–37
fidelity to law
  Fuller on 73, 176–77
  Hume on 296–300
forced marriage 348–49
forces of law 333–55
  coercion 333–34, 337–45, 346, 349, 350–51, 354, 355
  coercive sanctions 336–37, 342, 343–44, 345

386 SUBJECT INDEX

forces of law (*cont.*)
  concepts and counting 349–54
  duty 334–37, 355
  obedience 341, 352–54
  power 334, 344–49, 355
  'puzzled man' 339–41, 344
form and substance distinction 163–64
formalism 109, 169
foundationalism 123
free speech 25–26

gender and jurisprudence 126–49
  analysis and evidence 145–48
  analytical jurisprudence 129, 132–33, 141–44, 145, 148, 149
  concepts 133–34, 135
  conceptual jurisprudence 127–28
  consummation of marriage 142, 144–45, 146, 148
  description and evaluation in jurisprudence 142–45
  descriptive jurisprudence 127–28
  feminism 126–27, 128–37
  gender discrimination 141
  gender norms 134
  general jurisprudence 127–28, 145–46, 148
  law and jurisprudence 126–28
  marriage 132, 133, 136–37, 141, 142, 143–44, 146–48
  normative jurisprudence 148
  same-sex marriage 132, 135, 144–45, 146–47
  sex and gender distinction 135–42, 146–47
  sexual activity 146–47
  special jurisprudence 127–28, 132–37, 145–46, 148
gender and sex distinction 38, 55–56, 135–42, 146–47
general equilibrium theory 16–17
general opinions 283–84
generic end for law 73–75
germ of justice 153–74
  constancy 153–55, 157, 158, 163–64, 169–70
  domain of justice 159–63
  form of justice and formal justice 163–70
  measure and means of justice 170–74
  Plato 155–57

positive law and ideal justice 157–59
separability thesis 194
thesis 155–60, 170, 185–86
governing *see* duty to govern
Grundnorm (basic norm) 35–36, 38

habits, internalized 102
Hart and *The Concept of Law* 31–56
  coercion and power 46–48
  division of labour 44–46
  morality 48–52
  social construction, law as 31, 33–43, 50
    anti-essentialism 37
    constructivism 33–34, 35, 36–37
    legal positivism 31–32, 35
    normativity 34–35
    norms 34–37
    rules, constructions of 38–43
    'true law' 34–35
homicide law 262, 338–39
homosexual conduct and relations 260–61, 264, 265–67, 273
humanism 21–22, 321–22, 323
humanities 26–27
Hume on allegiance 283–304
  artificial virtue 298–99, 301
  artificiality thesis 299
  common opinion as justification for authority 289–95
    negative argument 289–91
    positive argument 289, 291–95
  consensual obligation 291
  consent 286–87, 292–93, 295–96, 298, 299, 301, 302
    absence of 286
    marriage 300
  consent theory, failure of 284
  fact and superstition in politics 301–3
  facts and principles in politics 283–84
  fidelity, foundations for 295–300
    incompleteness 296–97
    redundancy 297–300
  obedience 297–98
  obligation to obey 289
  political authority, allocation of 285–89
    consent and salience 288–89
    transference of property by consent and authority 287–88
  political morality 283
  promises 290–91, 295, 296, 297–300

SUBJECT INDEX 387

promissory obligation 290, 300
  tacit consent theory 290–91
  transference of property by consent 286
  voluntary obligation 290–91

identity politics 15
ideology 35–36, 131–32, 207–8, 216, 217–18
immorality 7, 11, 225–26, 240, 245
impartiality 166–69, 229, 238–39
  failures of 164
imperativalists 112–13
in sensu composito ('against the law') 242
in sensu diviso ('against the law') 242, 243
inclusive positivism 51n.33
India: Penal Code 264
individuality and community 321–27
inequality 160
inference 23
injustice 153–54
  formal 164, 169
  substantive 162–63, 169
inner morality of law 61, 71
institutional support thesis 218–21
institutionalization 45–46
instrumental values 63, 64, 66, 67–68, 69, 70–73
instrumentalism 60–61, 251–52, 321–22, 323
  Marxist 217–18
  teleological 61
instrumentalism/fallacies about 65–79
  generic end for law 73–75
  instrumental evaluation 77–79
  instrumental value 66, 67–68, 69, 70–73
  neutrality of law 75–77
  non-instrumental value 66–69, 78
instrumentalist thesis 57–59, 62–63
integrity, Dworkinian 157, 317–21
internal criteria of evaluation 77–78
  moral criticism 77
  moral significance 77
internal point of view 32, 55, 113, 257–58
international law 37
invalidity 70
irrationality 160–61
'is' and 'ought' gap 283

judges 225–49
  bias 238
  consistency 229
  discretion 238
  on immorality 225–26, 240, 245
  impartiality 229, 238–39
  judging and law 225–27
  judicial creativity 241–44
  judicial role 236–41
  judicial virtues 238
  jurisprudence and conceptual choices 245–49
  law-applying obligations 240
  law-improving obligations 240–42
  law-protecting obligations 240–42
  moral considerations 233–34
  moral obligations 226, 227, 231–32
  moral principles 229–30, 245
  moral values 244
  morality 229, 230, 231–32, 240–41, 244, 247–48
  neutrality 238
  obligations 236
  partiality 238
  roles and obligations 231–36
  simple view 227–31
  special obligations 232–33
judicial creativity 241–44
judicial reasoning 106
jurisprudence 2, 3–4, 5–6, 10
  'canon' 14–16
  and 'the capacity to think' 25–26
  and conceptual choices 245–49
  descriptive 160
  displacement 122–24
  external 227
  general 5, 7, 176–77, 178, 237–38, 248–49
  internal 226–27
  and law 21–23
  methodology 4–5
  and moral thought 24–25
  naturalized 112
  problems, understanding in 20–21
  sociological 7, 110–11
  special 350
  see also gender and jurisprudence; progress in jurisprudence
justice 31–32
  administrative 166
  commutative 161
  comparative 163n.28
  corrective 166
  distributive 166
  domain of 159–63

justice (cont.)
  formal 154, 155–56, 157, 158, 163–70, 185–86
  forms of 163–70
  general 244
  ideal and positive law 157–59
  measure and means of 170–74
  natural 166
  non-comparative 163n.28
  procedural 154–55, 160, 163–64, 166
  procedural, *see also* justice, formal
  retributive 161, 166
  substantive 154, 158, 160, 169, 172–73
justice-aptitude of law 188–90
justification
  accepted, endorsed or proclaimed 23
  moral 23

kingship 195–96

law
  broad concept of 53–54
  content of 76
  effectiveness of 359–64, 375
  foundations of 80–83
  merit-dependence of 193–94
  narrow concept of 54
  see also forces of law
law as a means 2–3, 57–79
  instrumentalist thesis 57–59, 62–63, 79
  instrumentalist view 60–61
  means-ends relationship and instrumental reasoning 61–65
  see also instrumentalism/fallacies about
law and morality 2–3, 5, 11, 22–23, 32–33, 48–52
  see also separability thesis
law, rule of 9, 31–32
  associative obligations and the state 328
  constancy 153–54, 156
  custom and convention 80
  duty to govern 365–66
  forces of law 354
  instrumentalism 72, 75–76
  judges and 227, 236, 239–41, 243, 248
  legal realism and positivism 112–13
  morality in law 209
  separability thesis 191, 195, 196–97
  social morality 268, 269–70
law vs jurisprudence 21–23

legal philosophy 32–33, 130, 145, 246
  analytical 148, 149
  judges and 246
  separability thesis 176–77, 188, 189
  see also philosophy of legal philosophy
legal positivism 2, 10–12, 44, 54, 55–56
  custom and convention 91–92, 94–95
  Hart and *The Concept of Law* 31–32, 35
  ideal justice 157–59
  inclusive and exclusive 51–52, 106n.4
  instrumentalist view 60, 61, 70–71, 74, 78–79
  judges 227, 245
  law as a means 62
  legal realism and sources of law 105–7, 109–10, 111, 112–17, 118, 120–21, 124–25
  separability thesis 175–77, 179–80, 184, 193, 194–95
  soft 51n.33
  upshots 107–9
legal realism 13, 183, 352
  American 7, 107, 112–13, 116–17
  and legal positivism conflict 12–13
  Scandinavian 112–13
  see also legal realism and sources of law
legal realism and sources of law 105–25
  indeterminacy and realism 109–12
  jurisprudence, displacement of 122–24
  legal positivism 105–7, 109–10, 111, 112–17, 118, 120–21, 124–25
  legal positivism, upshots of 107–9
  legal realism 106–7, 108, 109
  permissive sources of law 117–22
legal sociology 13
legalism 196
legitimacy
  associative obligations and the state 305–10, 317, 319, 321, 324–25
  evaluative conditions 321
  normative conditions 321
  or right to rule 356–57, 359, 360, 363–65, 367–69, 371–73, 374
lex injusta non est lex 225–26
lex posterior 237
liberty 32
litigation 22–23

managerialism 78–79
marital rape 144–45

SUBJECT INDEX 389

marriage 322, 348–49
   consummation 142, 144–45, 146, 148
   gender 132, 133, 136–37, 141, 142, 143–44, 146–48
   same-sex 132, 135, 144–45, 146–47
   sex-restricted laws 143–44
Marxism 131–32, 191
Marylebone Cricket Club (MCC) cricket rules 201–2, 205–6, 213–14
means-ends relationship and instrumental reasoning 61–65
mediation 238–39
minimum content thesis 174, 185–87, 367
   morality 211–12, 214–15, 217–20
   social morality 262, 278
modus ponens and law 23
moral claims of its subjects, law making 187–88
moral credibility 270–71, 272
moral decision-making 53–54
moral disputes 18
moral judgement 24
moral minimum 205–10
moral philosophy 23
moral principles 229–30, 245
moral reasoning 178–79
moral requirements 230–31
moral riskiness of law 190–93
moral thought and jurisprudence 24–25
moral vices 11
morality 10, 32, 52–53
   critical 32, 48–49, 253
   customary 48–49, 181, 277–78
   ideal 48–49, 180–81, 189, 206, 253, 254–55, 258, 259–60
   ideal justice 158–59
   inner or internal 70–71, 189, 195
   judicial 229, 230, 231–32, 240–41, 244, 247–48
   law as regulator of objects of 186–87
   legal improvement 273
   legal realism 105
   liberal 251–52
   measure and means of justice 170–71
   political 176–77
   popular 259–60
   popular, *see also* morality, customary
   positive 180–81, 206, 253, 254, 269–70
   public 259
   separability thesis 179–80, 181, 183–84, 185, 186, 189, 190, 192–93, 194, 196–97
   sexual 207, 273–79
   traditional 251–52
   valid 180–81
   see also morality in law; law and morality; social morality
morality in law 48–52, 198–224
   aim of law 49–50
   artefact, nature of 221–24
   content 200–203
   ideal morality 206
   inner 61, 71
   institutional support thesis 218–21
   legal validity and moral principles 50–52
   minimum content thesis 211–12, 214–15, 217–20
   moral minimum 205–10
   positive morality 206
   sexual morality 207
   social morality 206, 207
   structure 200–4
   theories, choice of 52–56
   viability thesis 210–14, 215, 218
   voluntary compliance 214–18
multiculturalism 250–51
murder, prohibition of 204–5, 338–39
   see also homicide law

natural law 74–75, 186, 209, 226–27, 245, 374
natural sciences 7
naturalism 6–7, 122–23
   in jurisprudence 112
necessary connection 178–79, 181, 182–83
necessary tasks 367–68
necessary truths 182, 183–84
necessity 221, 222
   conceptual 181–82
   natural 181–82
negligence, law of 95–96
neutrality of law 75–77, 238
   methodological 178–79
no fault divorce 135
no guarantees thesis 158
non-allocative prohibition 162–63
non-arbitrariness 89–91
non-coercive laws 48
non-cognitivism 164–65

390 SUBJECT INDEX

non-neutrality of law 75
non-normativity 91–95
normative debates 187
normative guidance 93
normative systems, limited-purpose 202–3
normative theory 129
normativity 34–35, 92, 93–95, 101–2
norms 45–46, 70, 73, 106–7
  acceptance of 257–58, 340–41
  allocation 161–62, 166, 170–71
  assurance 102
  basic (*Grundnorm*) 35–36, 38
  child-rearing 210
  coercive 3, 203–4
  conduct-regulating 201
  conformity to 165–66
  constraint 102
  conventional 103
  customary 38, 80–81, 84, 118–19, 257, 259, 262–63
  customary and conventional 82, 83–84, 85, 86–87, 91–95, 101–2
  duty-related 3
  dynamically derived 210
  enforced 96–97
  gender 38
  general 83–84
  Hart and *The Concept of Law* 34–37
  indeterminacy and realism 111
  individual 83–84
  judges 225–26
  jus cogens 171
  legal 46–48, 62, 183, 247
  legislated 84
  mandatory 200–1, 209
  see also duties; obligations
  moral 183, 255–56
  morality 258
  morality in law 200–1, 203, 209, 258
  obligation-imposing 187, 343–44
  obligatory 99, 100, 343–44
  peremptory 96, 99–102
  permissive 20
  positive 101–2
  power-conferring 46–47
  putative 93
  recognition *see* recognition rules
  social 44–45, 201, 247
  special-purpose 202
  static derivation of 210
  weighty 96, 97–99
nulla poena sine lege principle 153
nullity 46–48

obedience 297–98, 341, 352–54, 356–57
  and integrity 317–21
obligations in child-rearing 313–14
obligations 20, 42, 96–97, 101–2
  consensual 291, 308
  customary 96–97, 102, 119
  dependence between 299
  or duty to obey 356–57, 359, 364–65, 368, 371, 374, 376–77
  familial 262, 311–12
  fraternal or sororal 313
  judges 236
  law-applying 240
  law-improving 240–42
  law-protecting 240–42
  legal 41
  moral 10–11, 41, 184–85, 226, 227, 231–32, 306–7
  non-consensual 291, 308
  other-things-being equal and all-things considered distinction 24
  political 305, 306–7
  promissory 290, 300
  rule-dependence of 41
  separability thesis and 186
  social 320
  social morality 258
  special 232–33, 311–12
  to obey 289
  universality of 327–32
  voluntary 290–91
  see also associative obligations and the state
obscenity law 250–51, 265–66, 276–77
operationalization 8

parental authority over children 373–74, 375–76
parliamentary statutes 42–43
partiality 168–69, 238
payoffs to jurisprudence, value of 21–26
  jurisprudence and 'the capacity to think' 25–26
  jurisprudence and law 21–23
  jurisprudence and moral thought 24–25
penalties 84, 220
permissive sources of law 117–22

SUBJECT INDEX 391

personal injury cases 228
personification of the community 317–18, 319
persuasive sources/permissive sources distinction 190n.45
philosophy of legal philosophy 1–27
  choices in 5–9
  progress 16–21
  theories vs theses 10–16
  value of 21–26
plain meaning rule 228–29
political authority *see* duty to govern
political disputes 18
polycentric issues 76
pornography 276–77, 278–79
positive law 2–3, 10, 83, 156
  and ideal justice 157–59
  indeterminacy in 111
  judges and 230–31, 248
  permissive sources of law 118
  separability thesis 185, 186
  see also legal positivism
positivism 23
  inclusive vs exclusive 13, 51n.33
  normative 53, 54
  'soft' 193–94
  see also legal positivism
post-colonial theory 15
power 20, 46–48
  -conferring rules 47–48, 360–61
  forces of law 334, 344–49, 355
  individual 48
  normative 360–61
  social 3, 47–48, 346, 360–61
  voluntary 46–47, 48
practice theory 39–40
precise laws 189
predictivism 116
primary rules 31, 32, 38–39, 45–46
  measure and means of justice 170–71
  morality in law 201, 220–21
  separability thesis 192–93
principles 20, 73
  moral 229–30, 245
  regulatory 195n.59
priority 371–74
prisoner's-dilemma situations 368–69
procedural justice 154–55, 160, 163–64, 166
progress in jurisprudence 16–21
  convergence as mark of 18–19
  shrinkage as mark of 17

understanding as mark of 20–21
promise-not-to-compete cases 117
promises 184–85, 232–33, 253, 300
  associative obligations and the state 307–8
  Hume on allegiance 290–91, 295, 296, 297–300
property
  and authority 287–88
  protection 72
  rights 10–11, 262
  transference by consent 286
prospectivity requirement 189, 243
prostitution 265–66, 273
pseudo-law 223–24
publicity requirement 274–75
punishment 162
'puzzled man' 339–41, 344

queer theory 15

radicalism, philosophical 105
rape 159–60, 273, 275–77, 278–79
  marital 144–45
  reform law 276–77
  shield laws 276
realism
  moral 22–23, 248
  see also legal realism
reasonableness 194
reasoning
  instrumental 63
  moral 178–79
reciprocity 78
recognition rules 32, 38–39, 41, 42–43, 44, 50, 51–52
  custom and convention 81, 82, 86–88, 90–91, 95, 96–99
  judges 243
  morality in law 223–24
  social morality 269–70
  ultimate 81n.2, 97, 98, 118
reductivist theories 112–13, 121
relativism 164–65
religion 204–5, 207–8, 211–12
  and abortion 265–66
responsibility 47–48, 371–72
Reverse Polish Notation (RPN) 84n.8
right to rule 356–57, 359, 360, 363–65, 367–69, 371–73, 374
  see also legitimacy

rights thesis (Dworkin) 328–29
Roman law 21–22
rule-utilitarianism 40–41
rules 32–33, 36–37, 73, 74, 106–7
  application of 58, 168
  concurrent practice 41–42
  conflict-resolving 109
  constitutive 90
  constructions of 38–43
  contract 338–39
  conventional practice 41–42
  creation of 58
  custom and convention 80–81, 86
  customary 44–45, 101–2, 103–4, 118, 258
  duty-imposing 47–48, 360–61
  as exclusionary reasons 40–41
  -following 121–22, 157
  from external point of view 39
  general 70–71, 157–58, 185–86, 239
  individual 40
  internal aspect of 257–58
  interpretation 48
  legal realism and positivism 113
  obligation-imposing 41, 43, 95, 258
  obligatory moral 257–58
  power-conferring 47–48, 360–61
  as reasons 40–41
  sanction-bearing 46–47
  scepticism 113, 116–17, 118
    conceptual 112–13
    empirical 112–13
  secondary 31, 32, 38–39, 45, 170–71, 192–93, 201, 220–21
  settlement 335
  social 36–37, 39–40, 43–44, 87, 106–7, 116, 121–22, 201–2
  survival-promoting 186–87
  see also norms; primary rules; recognition rules
ruling 106

same-sex marriage 132, 135, 144–45, 146–47
sanctions 46–48, 62, 84, 97–98, 101–2
  see also coercive sanctions; penalties
scarcity 161–63
Scotland 10–11, 69, 119
self-defence 330–31
separability thesis 175–97
  connection 181–82
  fallibility 193–97

legal philosophy 176–77, 188, 189
legal positivism 175–77, 179–80, 184, 193, 194–95
methodological neutrality 178–79
necessary connection 178–79, 181, 182–83
refutation 183–93
  derivative connections 184–86
  justice-aptness of law 188–90
  law making moral claims of subjects 187–88
  law regulating objects of morality 186–87
  moral riskiness of law 190–93
  non-derivative connections 186–93
social thesis 179, 180n.25, 194
sources thesis 179–80, 193–94
understanding of 180–83
see also morality
separate-interests/separate-obligations thesis 299
serious social pressure condition 97–98
sex discrimination 131–32, 135–36, 137, 148, 175, 278–79
sex and gender distinction 38, 55–56, 135–42, 146–47
sex and social morality 251–52
sex-restricted marriage laws 143–44
sexual activity 146–47
sexual assault 273, 276, 278
sexual offences 265–66
Sexual Offences Act (UK) 278n.55
sexual orientation discrimination 143–44
sexual victimization 275
social construction, law as 83, 206
  see also under Hart and The Concept of Law
social contract theory see consent theory
social control 31, 44, 47–48, 49, 58
social convention 10, 82, 87–88, 91–92
social law 8
social morality 7, 167, 206, 207, 250–79
  changes in and changing the law 258–68
  consent to sex 265–66, 273–79
  constitutive view 261–62
  criminal law 265–66, 267, 270–71
  criminalization of 263–64, 265, 267, 276
  enforcement of 250–52, 253–55, 258
  Hart and The Concept of Law 32, 45–46, 48–49, 254–55

homosexual conduct and relations 260–61, 264, 265–67, 273
and ideal morality distinction 254–55
law-induced moral change 268–72
moral credibility 270–71, 272
obscenity law 250–51, 265–66, 276–77
pornography 276–77, 278–79
prostitution 265–66, 273
rape 273, 275–77, 278–79
sexual assault 273, 276, 278
sexual morality 273–79
sexual offences 265–66
sexual victimization 275
social morality, existence of in society 256–58
social thesis 129, 179, 180n.25, 194, 206
sociological jurisprudence 7, 110–11
'soft' positivism 193–94
see also inclusive positivism
sources of law
  permissive 117–22
  see also legal realism and sources of law
sources thesis 2, 179–80, 193–94
sovereignty 25–26, 38, 358
state *see* associative obligations and the state
statute and constitutional law 222
strict liability 208
subjection, female 147–48
subordination 139, 149, 216
subsidiarity 372–73
substance and form distinction 163–64
'suicide club' 212–13
support thesis, instrumental 220–21
survival, individual 210–12, 213–14

tacit consent theory 290–91
task-efficacy of authorities 364–68, 371, 372–73, 374–75, 377
tax codes 272
theories and theses 10–16
  appreciation 13–14
  'canon' 14–16
  complexity 10–12
  perceptions 12–13
tolerance 258
torture 159–60, 171
transcendental logical presupposition 35–36
transference of property by consent 286
treating like cases alike 157–58, 160–61, 163n.28, 166

see also formal justice
'true law' 34–35
truths, contingent 182, 183–84

Uganda: Anti-Homosexuality Bill 264
United Kingdom 10–11, 42–43, 119
  associative obligations and the state 311n.8
  common law 69
  Constitution 108, 243
  duty to govern 375
  English law 135–37, 143–44, 212, 228
  Gender Recognition Act 2014 137
  Laws in Wales Act 1535 88
  marriage law 147–48
  Parliamentary law 82, 98–99
  social morality 259, 260–61, 266–67
  sovereignty 25–26
  see also Scotland
United States 41–42
  appeals courts 120–21
  associative obligations and the state 311n.8
  Code 46n.26
  Constitution 20, 23, 42–43, 69, 80–81, 82, 90–91, 98, 115–16
  duty to govern 375
  Fewer School Boards Act (Ontario) 57, 62
  First Amendment 25–26
  free speech 25–26
  Jim Crow laws 168–69
  legal system 58–59
  marriage law 147–48
  promise-not-to-compete cases 117
  social morality 263–64, 267–68, 270–71
unjust laws 11–12

validity 45, 70, 106
  continuing 111
  hypothetical-relative 70
values
  dependent and free-standing distinction 64
  and facts distinction 31–32
  formal 167
  instrumental 63, 64, 66, 67–68, 69, 70–73, 77–79
  intrinsic 64–65, 66–67, 68, 69
  material 167
  moral 48–49, 53–54, 70–71, 178, 244

values (*cont.*)
  non-instrumental 66–69, 78
  non-relative 70–71
  relative 63–64, 70
  social 321–22
  see also instrumental values
viability thesis 210–14, 215, 218
virtues 159, 164
  artificial 298–99, 301
  intellectual 25
  judicial 238
  of justice 161–62
  moral 159–60
  personal 166
  practical 25
voluntariness
  compliance 2–3, 214–18
  of consent 274–76
  obligation 290–91
  powers 46–47, 48

wishes and choices, facilities for
  realization of 58
Wolfenden Report (1957) (UK) 273

The manufacturer's authorised representative in the EU for product safety is
Oxford University Press España S.A. of el Parque Empresarial San Fernando de
Henares, Avenida de Castilla, 2 – 28830 Madrid (www.oup.es/en or product.
safety@oup.com). OUP España S.A. also acts as importer into Spain of products
made by the manufacturer.

www.ingramcontent.com/pod-product-compliance
Lightning Source LLC
Chambersburg PA
CBHW061917120525
26572CB00004B/23